The Walled Garden

The Walled Garden

Law and Privacy in Modern Society

Lawrence M. Friedman
Joanna L. Grossman

ROWMAN & LITTLEFIELD
Lanham • Boulder • New York • London

Published by Rowman & Littlefield
An imprint of The Rowman & Littlefield Publishing Group, Inc.
4501 Forbes Boulevard, Suite 200, Lanham, Maryland 20706
www.rowman.com
86-90 Paul Street, London EC2A 4NE, United Kingdom

British Library Cataloguing in Publication Information Available

Library of Congress Cataloging-in-Publication Data
Names: Friedman, Lawrence M. (Lawrence Meir), 1930– author. | Grossman, Joanna L., author.
Title: The walled garden : law and privacy in modern society / Lawrence M. Friedman, Joanna L. Grossman.
Description: Lanham : Rowman & Littlefield, [2022] | Includes bibliographical references and index. | Summary: "This book examines our basic understandings of privacy as they are challenged by modern technology, changing social mores, and evolving legal understandings that both reflect and reinforce underlying changes in society"— Provided by publisher.
Identifiers: LCCN 2021036200 (print) | LCCN 2021036201 (ebook) | ISBN 9781538162293 (cloth) | ISBN 9781538162309 (epub)
Subjects: LCSH: Privacy, Right of—United States. | Privacy—United States.
Classification: LCC KF1262 .F759 2022 (print) | LCC KF1262 (ebook) | DDC 342.7308/58—dc23
LC record available at https://lccn.loc.gov/2021036200
LC ebook record available at https://lccn.loc.gov/2021036201

To Leah, Jane, Amy, Sarah, David, Lucy and Irene
—L.M.F.

For my sister, Alison Grossman, with apologies for the many ways I violated her privacy during our childhoods.
—J.L.G.

Contents

Acknowledgments

This project is the second book to arise from our many decades of friendship, intellectual collaboration, and lively games of Boggle. In the first, *Inside the Castle: Law and the Family in 20th Century America* (Princeton Univ. Press, 2011), we explored the law and social norms surrounding the family. We joked about the need to move our focus "outside the castle," and that was the provenance of this book. Little did we know where those musings would take us. We had great fun exploring the law and social norms that dictate the relationships individuals have with the outside world—relationships that are made increasingly complicated by technology and rapidly changing social norms.

The cover image, Édouard Manet's *Le Déjeuner sur l'herbe* (1863), depicts an ordinary situation—two men and two women sharing a picnic—with one shocking detail: one of the women is completely nude. Until that time, female nudes in paintings had always represented allegorical or mythological figures. This stark rejection of tradition, further emphasized by the woman's direct gaze at the viewer, made the painting a key departure point for modern art. It also raises questions about privacy, social norms, and individual choice, which are explored in this book.

We are grateful to a long line of research assistants who provided help along the way, including, from SMU Dedman School of Law, Stephen Chance, Alexandra Jeffus, Joanna (Firth) Pearce, and Kaitlyn Thorson; and from Stanford, Lauren Gorodetsky, William Havemann, and Jacqueline Smith.

Introduction

The *Oxford English Dictionary* traces the word "privacy" back to the fifteenth century. Still, it's fair to say that the range of meaning, and probably the use of the term itself, has expanded greatly in the last century, or perhaps century and a half. As a rough measure, of the 80,000 times the phrase "right of privacy" appeared in the *New York Times* between 1851 and 2010, the decade of the 1870s accounted for only 118. Between 1960 and 1969, on the other hand, the figure reached some sort of climax: 17,205 uses. Since then, it has somewhat mysteriously declined (4,800 appearances between 2000 and 2009); but this still means that the phrase appeared in the newspaper on average once a day or more. In any event, privacy, the right of privacy, and the problems of privacy, are high on the policy agenda today. The literature on privacy, as a legal and as a social issue, could reach up to the moon.

But it is tricky and elusive to come up with a definition of "privacy," or the "right of privacy." These are quicksilver terms, with many meanings and nuances. It would be hard to arrange them into a single, all-inclusive definition. We might isolate one core meaning, at least for the phrase "right of privacy": some sort of right to be left alone. There is also the famous constitutional right to privacy, which the Supreme Court of the United States more or less discovered or revealed (or invented) in the 1960s. This right is connected by the thinnest of threads to the actual words of the constitution, and modern cases would have left the founding fathers scratching their collective heads. This right was the legal basis of the famous abortion case *Roe v. Wade*: the idea of some sort of right to make fundamental choices about sex and reproduction. This notion ultimately doomed not only legal bans on abortion but also laws against sodomy and same-sex marriage. Needless to say, the political struggles over these issues have never gone away. Indeed, the Supreme Court is poised to get rid of the right to abortion, even though it's been protected under the Constitution for almost 50 years. In this book, we will not totally ignore this line of cases, and the ideas that underlie them, but in the main, this book will deal with other social and legal meanings of privacy, and the so-called right of privacy.

What are these meanings? Imagine a young couple, Caleb and Lucinda. They live together in an apartment in Boston, Massachusetts. They don't have children yet. They have jobs; he's a construction worker, she's a receptionist. When the workday is over, they come home, by bus or by car. They enter their apartment (or condo or house), and shut the door. At this point, they have entered what they (and everybody else) would consider a zone of privacy. Most evenings, they're alone at home. If it's a hot night, and the apartment is stuffy, they might sit around and watch TV in their underwear. Later on, if they're in the mood, they might have sex. They would surely be shocked—and outraged—if a peeping Tom looked in on them, or installed a video camera in their bedroom, bathroom, or shower. What they do indoors is part of their "private life." They feel entitled to keep this life private, keep it to themselves, keep it secret, at least if they are so inclined.

Where did this feeling come from, this concept of a zone of privacy? Caleb and Lucinda's privacy is not something that has been part of human experience since the days of early man. The caveman surely shared his cave with others. Peasants in the middle ages lived in huts with their children, not to mention perhaps an old grandma, along with the chickens and pigs. Even the rich and the high-born had less privacy than the middle class enjoys in our day. Courtiers and nobles customarily watched Louis XIV get dressed. Queens gave birth before a crowd of people. These were practices we would consider grotesquely inappropriate today. The idea of a private sphere, an individual sphere, an exclusive sphere, is, for the most part, distinctly modern; it belongs to the age of the industrial revolution, the technological and scientific revolution, and, in fact, the sexual revolution. Caleb and Lucinda have a sensibility, a consciousness of rights, a consciousness of privacy, very different from that of their ancestors.

Closely related to the idea of privacy is what we might call the right to *anonymity*. When we walk down the street, go to a movie house, go shopping, or eat in a restaurant, we are "in public." But we don't expect to be watched; a friend might come over and say hello, but if a stranger started dogging our footsteps, we would feel distinctly uneasy. An outdoor crowd is, or was, a kind of mass anonymity. During the daytime, Caleb and Lucinda are often out of doors in public spaces. She might be eating lunch in a restaurant; he might be sitting on a bench, having a sandwich. On weekends, they might go to a movie or visit a park. People can and do see them in all of these places. There is no absolute, iron-clad boundary between the public and the private. You can be private and alone in the midst of a crowd. If one of Lucinda's co-workers persistently stared at her at work or followed her on the street, she might find this intolerable—an invasion, as it were, of her privacy. If somebody started obsessively photographing Caleb as he worked on his construction job, this would violate some norm, though he might not be clear exactly what norm, or how to enforce it. The home is a zone of privacy, but there are other zones, invisible zones, that surround us wherever we go. We resent people who "violate our space." There is a norm of anonymity, a zone of anonymity, which photographers would invade, if they filmed us without permission—even on a public street.

In short, we don't expect to be noticed in a crowd; we certainly don't expect snapshots or video recordings of our actions, even in public. At any rate, this *was* the expectation. Anonymity, today, is not what it used to be. This is in large part because of fear of crime or terrorism. In some cities, surveillance cameras are everywhere on the streets and people tend to accept, with a shrug of the shoulders or with downright approval, cameras that record us cashing money at an ATM or entering a courthouse. It is the price we pay (we think) for personal safety.

In addition, there is also something we might call the *right to evanescence*—the right to make the past disappear. At one time, if we got a letter, we could keep it if we wished, or throw it away. When the letter was gone, it was truly gone, unless someone had made a copy, which rarely happened. The right to evanescence is under severe pressure these days from technology. We can press a key on our computer and "delete" an email. But it turns out that the message is never really gone. People with the right skills can find it—somewhere. In the computer age, nothing gets deleted; everything, it seems, is recorded. If young people say foolish things on social networks or send a foolish picture, they sometimes find that their folly comes back to haunt them.

In general, it is modern technology that threatens older, and conventional, ideas of privacy, anonymity, and evanescence. One hundred years ago, a shopper who walked into a grocery store outside of his neighborhood and bought a loaf of bread for cash enjoyed all three. The customer who pays for the bread with a credit card today has actually or potentially *lost* all three. Technology, of course, is a tool. The machines that are robbing us of privacy are not rogue robots; they are manned by human beings, acting because of decisions made by human beings, and for purposes that human beings consider important.

Caleb and Lucinda's private life, their private sphere, their home life, represents one important part of the privacy equation—the rights half. People's homes are supposed to be their castles. The outside world cannot, in general, intrude. Or should not. This kind of privacy—the privacy of the home, the privacy of private life—includes an element of choice: you can close the door or leave it open, you can stay in or go out, you can pull the blinds or not. Privacy rights, in one important sense, are, essentially *elective*.

There is also the *duty* half, the other side of privacy—that which *must* be kept private. Suppose Caleb and Lucinda are strolling through the park at noon on Sunday. It is high summer, and the sun is beating down on them. They might feel like taking off their clothes. Or the warm sun might arouse an urge to have sex. They would be well advised to go home or forget these urges. Nudity or sexual behavior in public might be (and perhaps is) against the law; it would certainly shock some people and would violate all sorts of social norms and customs. The *duty* to maintain some aspects of privacy is as important as the right to *be* private; law (and custom) prescribe rules about things that must stay hidden—private, in a word. A lawyer who blurts out what his client has told him in private or a priest who betrays the confessional—these would be violations of a duty to keep certain matters private. These privileges can be waived but there are rules about who can waive them, and how.

Privacy, obviously, is a *social* concept; different societies define it in different ways. We are concerned here with the modern concept as it has evolved and as it continues to evolve. Probably each society defines privacy its own way; each society has its own norms and customs. And of course there are always ambiguities—unanswered questions and gray areas. Privacy rights are controversial, at least at the margins. Where do they begin and end? Some "privacy" norms are social customs, rules of etiquette, widely observed, but unenforceable. Others have hardened into law. This is true with regard to both rights and duties.

Not everybody has the same right of privacy. In this regard, privacy is different from, say, the right to practice a religion (or not). That is a right that everybody enjoys, from the president on down. But as the rules of privacy have evolved, some people have more privacy rights than others. Caleb and Lucinda have more right to the sanctity of their private lives than people who are considered "celebrities" or "public figures."

This book is an exploration of some of the aspects of modern privacy, as a legal and social phenomenon. It deals with both rights and duties. The literature on *rights* of privacy far outweighs the literature on *duties*. But both are important. Both say something significant about law and society; both have changed in crucial ways over the years.

WHAT MUST BE HIDDEN

In the biblical story of Adam and Eve, the primal couple starts out naked in the Garden of Eden. They disobey orders, enticed by the snake, and eat fruit from the tree of knowledge. Suddenly, they realize that they are naked; they become embarrassed and cover their organs with fig leaves. They understand now that nakedness is wrong. According to the Bible, then, the awareness of nakedness—and its shamefulness—is a kind of primal, original instinct.

Babies are naked, too; but this is no shame. As we grow up, we learn that some parts of the body—the "private" parts—are not meant to be seen by outsiders. What is acceptable in an infant is taboo for an adult—for those who are sexually mature

Taboos against nakedness lie far back in history—older even than the Bible. The taboo was particularly powerful in the nineteenth century. Not all societies, of course, have shared these taboos. And what would be considered indecent in Saudi Arabia is normal on a beach in Greece, in a public bath in Japan, or perhaps among some tribe in the Amazon jungle. And what is acceptable today on the streets of San Francisco might get you arrested in Kansas.

In modern times, old body taboos have weakened. This is part of a larger story: the sexual revolution. Probably every society has rules about sexual behavior. In the Western tradition, these rules were perhaps unusually stringent. Behind them is the idea that sex, which the human race cannot do without, is both powerful and dangerous. It is like a caged tiger. Society would be in danger if we let it out of its cage. Sex cannot be left to the marketplace of emotions and drives.

There are many sexual rules and taboos; each society has its own home-grown cluster. The idea that "private parts" have to be kept private is one of the most common of these rules, in some form or another. There is no taboo against the naked arm or nose or shoulder; the taboo relates specifically to sex organs, somewhat less so to the human posterior, or to women's breasts. (In some very conservative societies, women's hair can be added to the list of taboos). The taboo also extends to *pictures* of the naked body, especially sexualized pictures. Works of art, however, have enjoyed a certain degree of latitude.

The taboo also applies to words, to language, to texts. Sexual *language*, especially in the nineteenth century, was strongly proscribed—at least in public. Newspapers and books in the Victorian period, and well into the twentieth century, almost never discussed sex openly and avoided talking about what people did in their bedrooms. Where babies come from, and how married (and unmarried) people produce these babies, was almost always veiled and implicit in Jane Austen, Charles Dickens, or Herman Melville. Using foul language in public was against the law in many places. Even the august *Oxford Dictionary*, the most massive dictionary of the English language, which claimed to be both scientific and complete, simply could not bring itself to mention two very common English words.

But the most powerful enforcers of taboos, verbal or pictorial, were always social rather than legal. Law reinforced these norms, to be sure—for example, by making pornography a crime and through the use of censorship laws. In the United States, states quite generally pass laws against filthy speech and writing: the so-called Comstock law (1873) supplemented and nationalized these laws against pornography; the law made it an offense to send obscene material by mail. The Comstock law also banned mailing any material about abortion or contraception.

Until the 1930s or so, extreme prudery in speech and writing was the social norm. Like nudity, it was somehow thought important to control sexual expression in books, plays, and other written forms. Underlying these norms were ideas associated with traditional religious codes but also, most likely, vague and half-formed ideas about what the moral health of society required—some notion that free discussion and depiction of sex endangered the very structure of society, that this too was a tiger that had to be confined to its cage.

The Victorian period was a period of outright censorship in the United States and England, and in other countries as well. Plays were subject to censorship; some local authorities also undertook to censor books (Boston was famous for this practice). In the early twentieth century, when a new medium, the movies, became wildly popular, some cities and states censored movies as well. There was a distinctly elitist flavor to movie censorship. As elites saw it, the movies appealed to the masses in a way that plays could never do. Hence movies were, or could be, much more of a threat to the morals of young people. The courts, on the whole, upheld censorship laws against legal attack.

In the last half of the twentieth century, the situation changed dramatically. Censorship ended in the age of the sexual revolution. Restraints on pornography were loosened almost to the vanishing point. The criminal codes were amended to get rid of laws against adultery and fornication (for the most part). And even the laws against nudity weakened. Law—and custom—started to distinguish between "simple" nudity and nudity that was threatening or pathological. After all, nudist camps and colonies were not illegal and their propaganda insisted (less so today) that these were harmless, family-oriented colonies of ordinary people, that there was something healthy and nonsexual about taking off your clothes. Nudity in the wrong place—on a public street—remains controversial. And "flashers" grossly violate the norms of proper behavior.

At one time, too, pregnant women tended to isolate themselves. Their swollen bellies were embarrassing in an age of enforced prudery. It was as if these women wore a big neon sign telling the world they were sexually active. Today, pregnant women no longer hide in the shadows or lock themselves up at home. And breastfeeding in public, once also subject to a kind of taboo, is now explicitly allowed by law; only a shrinking minority still finds this practice offensive.

If a young woman, in the old days, became pregnant but had no husband, this was a scandal, a matter of shame, something to be hidden and disavowed.

Many of these women gave up their babies for adoption. The mother's sin, and the baby's origin, were kept secret, a private matter not to be known to the outside world. Here, too, there has been dramatic social change. The stigma of illegitimacy is vanishing. Adopted children demand to know their "true" origins. Doors that were once tightly shut, with locks enforced by the state, can be and increasingly are unlocked.

ILLEGAL AND ILLICIT PRIVACY: DOUBLE LIVES

The nude body is an example of something we are *required* to keep private (on the whole). Are there other aspects of life that are in the opposite category: they must *not* be kept private? Are there areas where keeping certain matters private is socially condemned or downright illegal? All of us, in a sense, lead double or triple or quadruple lives; we have an inner life and an outer life, a life that people see and a hidden or invisible life, one life in one context another in another. This is something we have a perfect right to do. But some exaggerated forms of double life are felt to violate legal or social norms. Pretending to lead one way of life and practicing another can be a crime in certain instances. The second life stays deeply underground precisely because it is illegal, illicit, or socially disfavored.

One clear case of this type of illegality is espionage. The spy works for one country and secretly betrays another country. The con man also leads a double (and illegal) life: he adopts a fake identity to squeeze money out of his "mark." The bigamist, too, hides a new wife from an old wife; in this way, he commits fraud against wife number two (the vast majority of bigamists are men). The con man and the bigamist commit crimes that depend on social mobility. They would be difficult or impossible to carry out in a traditional village where everybody knows everybody else, but in the fluid, rootless modern world, a world in which people wander and migrate from place to place, these crimes find fertile soil.

Spies can be executed; bigamists and con men can go to jail. The gay closet, until very recently, hid a sexual orientation that, if acted upon, *would* be a crime. It remains a crime in many societies; in Western societies, this is no longer true, but for many people, same-sex behavior comes with religious and sometimes social stigma. In developed countries, a preference for a ban on same-sex behavior has become a minority view. The criminal laws against same-sex behavior have been abolished and even gay marriage has been validated in a number of countries. In 2015, the Supreme Court imposed this rule on the United States.

There are many other examples of hidden, private identities. For much of our history, white society visited crushing disabilities on those who were legally and socially defined as "black." Escape from this situation was important to those who could carry it off. Light-skinned men and women, with some African blood in their background, sometimes "passed" for white, and thus transitioned into white society. There are, of course, no real figures on the numbers of people who "passed," but surely there were many; some have become famous.

There are many other historic examples of double lives: Jews who hid their religious origins, ex-convicts hiding their past, even women who pretended to be men. The need to "pass" for many of these groups is much diminished today. Mixed blood is less of a stigma. Gays and lesbians have come out of the closet in substantial numbers. "Illegitimate" children, as we mentioned, no longer hide their origin. Yet there still are people who want or need to keep some corner of their lives walled off from the rest of the world. The scarlet letter is ancient history but sex offenders may face something even worse: laws that follow them for life, forcing them to make themselves known to their neighbors and the world at large.

PRIVILEGES AND ANTI-PRIVILEGES

The law also makes some kinds of information "privileged." This means that you can chose to keep this information secret; in some cases, you *must* preserve secrecy. What you say to your lawyer is strictly confidential; she would be violating her oath if she let the world know what you said. The same is true to a degree for what you say to your doctor, what a good Catholic confesses to his priest, or what husbands and wives say to each other. A network of rules protects these privileges. These privileges are particularly important in litigation: there is also a constitutional privilege against self-incrimination (you cannot be forced to testify against yourself, or to testify to anything that might get you into legal trouble) and you can also prevent others from testifying as to matters that are equally privileged.

The point of these privileges in most cases is pretty obvious: people would be less likely to speak to doctors, lawyers, or priests if they thought they could not rely on confidentiality. There are also what we might call anti-privileges, and they too have an obvious point. Parents, let us say, bring their child to a pediatrician. The doctor sees injuries that she suspects must come from child abuse. The doctor has a duty to report this to authorities. In modern law, there are many rules about who must report what and under what circumstances—situations, in short, where the right of privacy is trumped.

Privileges and anti-privileges can of course collide with each other. In the famous *Tarasoff* case in California, a patient told a psychiatrist who was on the staff of the University of California that he, the patient, had thoughts about killing his girlfriend. Later he did exactly that. The family sued the University: why did nobody warn us? The California Supreme Court, in a surprising decision, overrode the privilege of confidentiality. The doctor had to do something: warn the authorities or take some other step. Psychiatrists disliked the decision; it interfered, they argued, with their therapeutic mission. But the decision was more or less consonant with a growing legal trend: abuse and threats must be reported.

Traditionally, a person's home—the home of Caleb and Lucinda, for example—was a kind of sacred zone of privacy; it was, as one author put it, a "haven in a heartless world." But the haven, or sanctuary, can hide its own brand of heartlessness. Feminists have argued, rather strongly, that the "privacy" of the home could mean, and often did mean, immunity for men who beat or abused their wives or girlfriends. In fact, historically, the law was not quite so callous: wife-beaters could be, at times, severely punished. Nonetheless, for thousands of women (and some men), the home was a hell of tyranny and physical abuse and the sanctuary, if there was one, was not the home at all, but a shelter for battered women. The proverbial castle, protected against the state, could sometimes be more like Dracula's castle than a peaceful oasis. The modern law of domestic violence is something of an assault against this kind of Dracula's castle.

ELECTIVE PRIVACY

Much of the vast literature on privacy is about what we could call *elective* privacy: the right of people to decide for themselves how much to keep private, and when, and how to do this—the right of Caleb and Lucinda to shut their doors and pull down the blinds.

The law formally recognizes a right to privacy. The usual story about this right begins with a famous law review article, "The Right of Privacy," published in 1890, and written by two elite lawyers, Warren and Brandeis. These men of distinction argued for a common-law right to be left alone. In the background were the mass-market newspapers, the so-called yellow press, noisy, vulgar, gossipy, and intrusive. Warren and Brandeis also took notice of a new technology: the candid camera, which could capture motion; this had not been possible before. For the first time, a photographer could take pictures of people who did not want to be photographed or who did not even know their picture was being taken.

Warren and Brandeis were worried about protection for elite, respectable people, people like themselves. Some courts took up their argument but the right to privacy made at first slow progress in the courts. Paradoxically, doctrine ultimately came to give the *least* protection to the very people Warren and Brandeis had in mind: the people on top of society. The law still protects *some* aspects of privacy. It defines zones of privacy—the home, for example. You cannot intrude, either physically or with some device that can listen or peek into these zones. If you record or film what goes on in somebody's bedroom, you can be made to answer for your sin.

Here, too, many of the norms and laws about privacy revolve around issues of sex and sexual behavior. Peeping Toms are not interested in gawking at people eating supper in the dining room. Intrusions are intrusions on "intimacy," intrusions on a person's "private parts." The modern peeping Tom has newfangled weapons: these enable, for example, the obnoxious practice of "upskirting," that is, taking secret pictures of women underneath their outer clothes.

Paparazzi are photographers who make a living taking pictures that, very often, invade the privacy of their subjects. Most people are safe from this breed. It is the fate, or curse, of the rich and famous to be pursued by these noxious photographers. We live in a celebrity culture. Celebrities, as we will argue, are not merely famous people: they are famous and *familiar* people because of the media, especially television. Only a handful of people in Great Britain have ever actually met the Queen of England but everybody has seen her on TV, heard her voice, and learned something about her family, her habits, her way of life. She is a celebrity, unlike her great-great-grandmother Victoria. Celebrity culture pervades the mass media and celebrities are an endless source of public fascination. That fascination gives rise to a widespread feeling that the public has the *right* to know whatever there is to know about celebrities, including intimate details if possible.

Celebrities are also, legally speaking, "public figures." Modern law makes a sharp distinction between ordinary people and "public figures"; celebrities are public figures. In fact, all public figures are or become celebrities to a certain degree. Public figures have much less privacy protection than ordinary people; the public's right to know takes precedence. Of course, this makes a lot of sense when the public figure is the president of the United States (though the public may not be entitled to know whether he or she likes dogs and cats or eats cottage cheese). It is less obvious when the public figure is a movie star or an athlete, but the law does not usually make this distinction. For example, the right of a movie star to privacy, or at least the right to exercise control over publicity, conflicts with the hunger of the public to know about romances and sexual adventures, even what kind of clothes the star may wear. American law allows the media to feed this hunger if it can.

On this point, American and European law seem to have diverged somewhat. American law comes close to adopting a fairly extreme right to know. The public is entitled to learn about anything that interests them—anything at all—about a public figure. Or, to put it another way, any information that interests the public is therefore in the public interest. European courts are more circumspect, more respectful of privacy, even for public figures. Can you snap pictures of the princess of Monaco—innocent pictures, as it turned out—and sell them to the mass media? Does the princess have any privacy rights? In Europe, perhaps yes. In the United States, probably no. To European courts, the public's interest (or curiosity) does not automatically trump the right of privacy. Just because the public might be curious about some news does not mean that the news is in the public interest.

Nowadays, gossip magazines and websites are everywhere. Juicy tidbits about celebrities are their bread and butter. The mass media were once more cautious. The media kept silent about some matters—illnesses of American presidents, for example, or the love affairs of the British royal family. President Grover Cleveland had a serious jaw operation (the problem was cancer). The public knew nothing about it. Scores of reporters must have known about President Kennedy's rather obsessive sex life; not a word appeared in the mainstream press. When, in the 1930s, King Edward VIII proposed marrying an American divorcée, the British press maintained an eerie silence. Yet Kennedy's love life may have included women involved with gangsters or spies. And the king's marriage plans provoked at least a minor constitutional crisis.

That was then. This is now. All restraint has been swept away. The development of celebrity culture is surely one factor. And modern media, including social networks, the internet, and ubiquitous cellphone cameras, are both cause and effect of the change.

PRIVACY BE DAMNED

Elective privacy is that level of privacy that people can and do choose for themselves. Most of us are eager to weave a kind of cocoon around ourselves. We want to be the sole guardian of information about how much money we make, what diseases we suffer from, what we look like in the shower. Such information is for a few intimate relatives and friends. Or not even them.

Strikingly, some people—a minority, certainly—choose the opposite route. They drop their privacy with glee; they undress, as it were, in public. They flock to reality TV, for example. They bring their little problems to Judge Judy. They volunteer for quiz programs. They wash their dirty linen in public. They are eager to take part in TV shows about men looking for women or women looking for men or families looking for a house or fat people trying to lose weight. They may be willing to eat tarantulas in competition with people who are doing the same—and they might be willing to do it while "naked and afraid." For them, that this all takes place before an audience of millions is not a minus but a plus.

What motivates these people? That's not an easy question to answer. But, clearly, celebrity status is both alluring and infectious. We can't be the queen of England or the president or the pope or a movie star or a billionaire or a basketball hero. But through the wonders of reality TV, we can become an instant celebrity, at least for a while. We can have that proverbial "fifteen minutes of fame," which may be in fact a bit more than fifteen minutes. And for some people—not most of us, of course—this lure outweighs our normal instinct for privacy.

PRIVACY AND NATIONAL SECURITY

Privacy is a right we enjoy against each other and very definitely against the government. Indeed, rights against government are historically among the oldest explicit privacy rights. Under the Fourth Amendment (part of the Bill of Rights, added to the Constitution in the late eighteenth century), the people are to be protected from "unreasonable searches and seizures." A judge can issue a search warrant, but only on "probable cause." The founders were worried about an oppressive central government. This is still a major issue; and growing more major all the time. The technology of the search has, however, mushroomed. After all, what constitutes a search? Wire-tapping? Thermal imaging? Today, ways to spy on people and burrow into their lives and habits have become more sophisticated. Personal privacy is in danger. This is the age of the surveillance camera, for example, of the eye that never sleeps.

Fourth Amendment cases used to come mostly out of the war against crime or, to put it another way, the issue was how to balance rights of individuals against the rights of society (and the rights of the police). Today the war on terror hangs like a dark cloud over the issue of searches and seizures—legally, politically, and psychologically. The attack on the World Trade Center in 2001 was a profound shock to the system in the United States. Dramatic shocks occurred in other countries: explosions in the London Underground, on a train in Madrid, on the beachfront in Nice. There were, of course, dramatic assassinations in the nineteenth century: Abraham Lincoln and Alexander II, the czar of Russia, for example. Attempts were made on the life of Queen Victoria. Today, the killing seems random, indiscriminate; the victims are ordinary people. At the airport, passengers go through security procedures. Machines look inside their bodies. Metal detectors guard courthouses. At one time, people would have protested. Now they submit. Invasions of privacy in the name of the war on terror are accepted almost without question, at least in some regards.

Governments also hoover up vast amounts of personal information, covering millions and millions of citizens. Laws, to be sure, set limits on data-gathering. But are these laws effective? Government agencies, one suspects, routinely violate them in the name of national security or personal security. Cameras sweep over city streets. They peer down at the entrances of buildings. They hide inside cash machines. People hardly notice, and if they do, they approve.

This is another way in which life has turned Warren and Brandeis upside down. Those jurists were afraid of mass media, not the government. Encroachments today come from government and from big institutions. Government can perhaps commandeer the powers of private companies like Google or Apple, so that a kind of unholy partnership develops. Businesses, of course, use data-gathering for their own purposes. They are not looking for jihadists. They are monitoring their workforce. They are also looking for clues to people's likes and dislikes: what they want to buy, what they've bought in the past, what they're likely to buy in the future. They want to be able to flash you a message that might pry open your wallet. Some people find these messages helpful but others find them intrusive: they resent a kind of commercial peeping Tom. People do not want companies (and charities) to sell their lists to other organizations. Every organization has a "privacy policy," usually posted on their website in small print. Whether anybody reads these, and whether the companies follow them, is another question.

Privacy, in short, is a quicksilver term, as we said; it has many meanings, many aspects. In the chapters of this book, we will explore some of those meanings, as these pages have suggested. In particular, we will try to show how and why notions of privacy have evolved over the years, and how the law has both shaped and been shaped by evolving norms.

Here are a few preliminary points.

1. Privacy is, on the whole, a modern invention and a modern idea; people probably always had some awareness of privacy, some sense of a private zone, some aspect of life that belonged to them and them only. The modern concept is different. It is, among other things, the product of modern individualism. The notion is that the self, like a plant, needs to be watered, needs privacy, needs room to grow, needs personal space. Modern privacy norms also owe a lot to affluence—to middle-class life, for example, to the idea that kids need and should get a room of their own.
2. Human beings are social animals. Group life and family life have always been enormously important, indispensable, in fact. This is not likely to change fundamentally. *Privacy* defines, in many ways, where

the individual begins and ends, how much of life is the social part, how much is each person's secret garden.

3. Ideas about privacy depend on modern technology but technology is also at the same time the greatest threat to privacy. A kind of arms race is going on. Society develops legal and social tools to control invasions of privacy. At the same time, technology has developed tools—wire-tapping was an early example—whose sole point is the invasion of personal privacy; cameras morph into surveillance gadgets and modern ways of talking and communicating with people leave traces behind. Nothing is ever gone with the wind.
4. In our times, emphasis has shifted from *duties* of privacy—taboos against nudity, censorship of books, plays, and movies—to rights of open and free expression. Censorship has almost vanished. So has much self-censorship. In a celebrity society, too, news and gossip about public figures flood the media. The right to know has developed into a powerful enemy of privacy.
5. Privacy norms, when they are not matters of personal or national security, are closely tied to norms of sexuality. The most jealously guarded zone of privacy is the zone of human sexuality. Much has been changing, however, in the age of the so-called sexual revolution—an age of extreme permissiveness. A surprising number of the older taboos and prohibitions have been abolished, both by law and society. The older traditions survive, to be sure; in fact, they give rise to controversy and fierce debate.

More than anything else, the message is that *privacy* is a cultural concept; that the cultural concept gives birth to its legal definition; and that, like all cultural (and legal) concepts, it evolves over time and in response to social pressures. The following chapters on privacy as a duty and a right illustrate this central theme. The final chapter explores how modern technology challenges long-standing beliefs about privacy, as well as how the pandemic, which upended the world as we know it, upended privacy norms as well.

PART I

Mandatory Privacy

Chapter 1

The Tiger's Cage

INTRODUCTION

Like millions of US travelers, John Brennan was fed up with the indignity and hassle of airport security screening procedures. After being patted down, the security officer referred him for further screening; the officer detected nitrates on Brennan's clothes. Something inside Brennan snapped and he stripped off every stitch of clothing to prove he was harboring no explosives. As he stood naked in the Portland airport, police arrived and hauled him off in handcuffs. Brennan, a veteran of an annual naked bike ride, insisted he had done nothing wrong. Nudity was an act of protest, he claimed, protected by the First Amendment. Why should the government be offended by his nudity when using technology that produced a near-naked image of every traveler's body?[1] After a brief trial in July 2012, a judge agreed with Brennan and dismissed the charge of public indecency.[2] There was precedent for his argument about nudity as a form of protest and, in any event, although a local law prohibited public indecency, exposure of genitalia was illegal only if done "with the intent of arousing the sexual desire of the person or another person."[3] Arousing TSA agents was surely far from Brennan's mind. "Sir Godiva," as one of his friends called him, walked out of court a (fully dressed) free man.

Probably other people in the security line had been shocked or amused or just plain surprised to see Brennan's naked body at the airport. At most, they might have expected to see bare feet and perhaps a wisp of underwear poking out of a man's trousers. Most people assume that public nudity is illegal. But even in Portland, people who strip off their clothes to make a political point would be well advised to make sure the point is crystal clear. Brennan did escape the charge of indecent exposure but TSA slapped a civil fine of $500 on him as a penalty for obstructing their work. The Ninth Circuit upheld the fine.[4] And he lost his job as a result of the arrest and publicity. But wasn't Brennan's nakedness "expressive conduct" protected by the First Amendment's guarantee of freedom of speech? No, said the court, because he failed to "carry his burden of showing that a viewer would have understood his stripping naked to be communicative."[5] He needed to do more to make clear that his actions were in protest rather than simply the product of his frustration. So much for nakedness as political protest.

But that was then. In 2020, a woman the press calls "Naked Athena," a "light-skinned woman of color and outspoken feminist," who probably knew nothing of John Brennan and his legal struggles, "strolled into a recent Portland protest" naked except for a "mask . . . and skullcap."[6] Protests against racism and police brutality were going on at the time. In the midst of all this, "Athena" proceeded to sit down "with her legs wide" and did some "yoga poses."

Brennan and "Athena" are perhaps extreme examples of public nudity displays. But the law can be confusing and easily misunderstood, even in more ordinary circumstances. The police themselves are apt to confuse social norms and social customs about nudity, with the actual law on the subject. The New York City police department recently agreed to pay $15,000 to settle a wrongful arrest suit by a woman they had arrested for public nudity. She was completely naked in public, top to bottom, but she was demonstrating the art of body painting, and state law exempts nudity undertaken in the course of a performance, play, or exhibition.[7] So nothing she had done gave the police authority to drag her away in handcuffs, to be naked and ogled in the police station for fifteen minutes before they allowed her to dress.[8]

In fact, the law of public nudity is more nuanced and generally less strict than most people imagine. Nor do most people, including lawyers, think nudity has anything to do with the important and much discussed issue of personal privacy. In fact, it does. The literature on privacy—what it is, how we can protect it, what it means in today's world—is enormous. There is endless discussion about the definition of privacy: what the word means and doesn't mean. No wonder. The word is used in a great many senses. It is so hard to pull all these senses together that some scholars simply throw up their hands and dismiss the whole question as hopeless.

As we mentioned in the introductory chapter, we have no intention of adding our two cents to this literature. We suspect that the doubters are right: it is not really possible—or worthwhile—to try to frame some definition that would include a woman's right to an abortion, the right to pull down your shades at night, the right to keep your health problems to yourself, and the right to keep the FBI from reading through your mail. From 1965 on, the U.S. Supreme Court has decided that there is a constitutional right of privacy, which includes the right to make certain fundamental personal decisions: for example, whom to marry, whether to have children or not, and whether to have sex or not and with whom.[9] This is a very important line of cases, and oceans of ink have been spilled about it. We will for the most part leave these issues alone. Instead, we want to talk about a mundane and common-sense notion of privacy: the right to be left alone, the right to keep some things secret, and the right to retreat into a private world.

Today, we live in a world of surveillance cameras and Google Earth. It is a world where, every time we buy a can of peas at the supermarket or a detective novel on Amazon, this act gets recorded somewhere and that information is liable to be used later on for advertisements and for who knows what other purposes. It is a world in which government has the *technical* power to eavesdrop on people's conversations, tap their phones, and, for all we know, peek inside peoples' bedrooms.

In general, the literature on privacy stresses, quite naturally, our right to keep things private, or to make our own decisions. The individual, the citizen, is the center of gravity. There is a great deal of material on the limits of privacy, on threats to privacy, and the like. In this chapter, we begin the discussion of what one might call *mandatory* privacy: those aspects of life that we are required to keep secret, hidden, or private—the things you cannot shout (or display) from the rooftop. These are the things that we *must* keep private, whether we want to or not. This is a subject that has been mostly, although not entirely, ignored in the privacy literature.[10]

One of the most obvious examples of things that must be private is the naked human body—at least in some circumstances. The taboo against nakedness has a long history in Western societies. Many ancient societies shared this taboo, along with some (but not all) preliterate societies. The taboo did not apply to the ancient Greeks, however, as anybody who has looked at Greek sculpture knows. Whenever a (male) Greek statue seems to have lost its penis, the reason is not prudery but rather the ravages of time. Moreover, while nude bathing may be a modern thing in St. Tropez, it is an old habit in Japan.

The taboo against nudity is, in modern times, a taboo against exposing sex organs, at least in the Western countries. Or, to be more exact, the sex organs of grown-up men and women, and of boys and girls once past a certain age. Nobody seems to object to nudity in little tiny babies (although distributing pictures of naked children may constitute a crime). In some traditional societies, the taboo goes much further than in Western societies. In conservative Muslim countries, in addition to the usual strictures (which apply to men and women alike), there are special and very stringent rules for and about women. It is considered indecent or immodest for women to show their hair, legs, or even faces (in some countries), outside of the home.

In Western society, the taboo went much further in the past than it does today. Photographs of people at bathing beaches in the nineteenth century make this point clear. Much more of the body was covered up. Today it is neither a crime nor an offense to wear sexy clothes or skimpy bathing suits and the like, although people would definitely raise their eyebrows if you sauntered into a grocery store or an insurance office wearing nothing but a bikini or short shorts. In general, sexy clothing has definitely emerged from the closet. The most popular issue of *Sports Illustrated* is the swimwear issue. It probably attracts thousands of men who have little or no interest in swimming, diving, or perhaps, for that matter, any sport that takes place outside of the bedroom. Millions of men smack their lips over what used to be called "pin-ups" or "glam shots"—pictures of women in skimpy and sexy clothing, or nothing at all; "beefcake" was the term for the male equivalent, for women and gay men to wallow in. Still, respectable journals and magazines recognize an invisible line and they are careful not to cross it. *The Sun*, an English tabloid, specialized in the breasts of nubile women (always on page three). It also once featured on the front page, under the headline "Heir It Is," a picture of Prince Harry, the Queen's grandson, fully exposed with only his hands to cover his genitals.[11] After receiving criticism, the tabloid excused itself, claiming that it decided to publish the photos (despite palace pressure) only after they were widely available on internet sites. But even in that tabloid, and this instance, full frontal nudity was avoided.

The rules of the game are complicated, but it is fair to say that, in our times, and in developed countries, the taboo against exposing the body has shriveled to the point where basically it is restricted to sex organs. The taboo against exposing a woman's breasts or an adult's posterior is not dead, but it is considerably weaker. And the taboo against nudity in general seems to be losing steam. What is left of it, and why, and why and how it has changed, is a subject we will briefly deal with.

In our society, we can see two quite distinct trends. The more general taboo, against what one might call simple nudity, is no longer in full force. Society has simply become more permissive. In many places in the Western world, public nudity may not be illegal at all. But there is quite a sharp distinction between *lewd* nudity and just plain nudity. If anything, the distinction is sharper than ever. The taboo on public nudity that can be considered "lewd" remains quite strong.

THE TIGER'S CAGE

We might begin with a few basic questions: Why are there taboos against nudity at all? What is wrong with nudity? Is there something shameful about the human body?

The taboos, obviously, are taboos about sexual behavior, and sex taboos, rules about sex, strictures about sex, and the like, are probably present in every society. In some countries, rules about nudity, particularly rules about female "modesty," seem to rest on beliefs or assumptions about the overheated sexual drives of men. It is as if just seeing a woman's hair or legs, or her naked body, would drive men to wild, impulsive, and dangerous acts. Or perhaps it would suggest that the woman is herself immoral, that she lacks "modesty" and is openly inviting brazen sex.

The naked male body in public poses a different sort of danger: it suggests a man who is also without modesty, who flaunts his sexuality, and is, in a way, like a tiger on the loose. This man is a threat to all of the women in his path. Of course, we will happily provide the tiger with a mate to keep him company in the cage. Otherwise, tigers would die out altogether. But only a mate, nothing more.

Norms about bodily privacy seem to assume that society, the family structure, and just about everything else depend on keeping the tiger in its cage. The male sex drive is both extremely powerful and extremely addictive. There are also, to be sure, beliefs about the wild, uncontrolled sex drives of certain evil and seductive women. However, these, we think, play less of a role in most societies. But the male drive has to be controlled. The taboos about nudity are part, then, of a large and complex structure of laws and customs that deal with sexual behavior and misbehavior. Feminists will be quick to point out that men make up the rules about sexual behavior, and make them up, on the whole, for their own benefit. But the rules, insofar as they are enforced, are also meant to restrict the behavior of men—if not for the benefit of women, then at least for the benefit of society in general.

The Western Judeo-Christian tradition has had a fairly suspicious attitude toward sex in general. Celibacy was considered a worthy ideal. Holy people—monks, nuns, priests—were celibate. The Shakers, an American sect, also believed in celibacy. Celibate monks can be found in Eastern religions as well—notably in Buddhism. But of course, celibacy cannot be the choice for everyone; we would quickly go extinct. Celibacy is simply an extreme form of sexual control or self-control. But sex in general is supposed to follow definite rules and recognize definite limitations. Rigid enforcement of sexual privacy is part of that system of rules and limitations.

Throughout most of our history, and the history of most societies, a powerful social norm has dictated that sexual behavior not only may be, but must be, kept private. Taboos against nudity support this. The Old Testament tells us that Noah had three sons. The old man drank wine, became drunk, and lay naked inside his tent. Ham, one of his sons, saw him naked. The other sons walked in and covered their father's body, turning their faces so that they would not see him naked. When Noah awoke, he pronounced a curse on Ham.[12] This Biblical passage expresses a powerful norm about bodily privacy, a norm that has by no means gone extinct. The limits on the norm, and the contours of the norm, do, however, change from time to time and place to place.

We have drawn a distinction between what we called *simple nudity* and *lewd* or *sexually threatening nudity*. The two extremes are fairly easy to see, but there is a puzzling middle ground.

SIMPLE NUDITY

Even in the high and palmy days of Victorian prudery, there was no absolute bar against displaying the naked human body. Museums contained classical statues of naked bodies, models posed naked for artists, and boys swam naked in the rivers and waterholes. "Art" has always been something of an excuse for the naked body. Of course, there is always the question: what makes something "art," as opposed to, well, pornography. In 1936, the vice chairman of the Richmond Academy of Arts, in Richmond, Virginia, was arrested on a warrant sworn out by one F. M. Terrell, who took offense at certain murals with "nude and semi-nude figures."[13] John Ashcroft, attorney general under George W. Bush, refused to be photographed in front of two partially nude statues standing in the Great Hall of the Department of Justice. Drapes, costing $8,000, were ordered to block the statues—a female, representing the "Spirit of Justice," with one breast exposed, and a male representing the "Majesty of Law" with a mere cloth over his pelvis. Apparently photographing Ashcroft, a notorious prude, in front of the statues had "been something of a sport for photographers."[14] Edwin Meese, the attorney general under President Ronald Reagan, had been similarly manipulated when photographers "dived to the floor" to get an ironic photograph of him raising a report on pornography "in the air, with the partially nude female statue behind him."[15]

Nudity reached beyond art, however. From the late nineteenth century on, there was in fact a nudist movement. This was particularly strong in Germany. To be nude was to be free, natural, close to nature, and healthy.[16] The nudist movement is by no means dead. It seems to appeal to a fair number of people. The American Association for Nude Recreations claims to have more than 260 affiliates—"family nudist" resorts—in North America.[17] Nude beaches are certainly not evenly spread across the country. Alaska has none, perhaps because public nudity is illegal as a matter of state law; in any event, the weather makes nudism extremely unappealing for most of the year. California, on the other hand, is littered with nude and clothing-optional beaches, hot springs, and resorts.

The nudist movement, historically, tried earnestly to divorce nudity from sex and to make nudity seem as benign as possible. To nudists, sensuality had no role in the matter. Indeed, nudity was an antidote to unhealthy and excessive interest in sex. The movement insisted that there was nothing lewd or obscene about walking around naked, playing volleyball, chatting, and doing normal life activities without any clothes on. Their literature tended to show whole families, children and all, taking part in the wholesome activities of the nudist colony, without embarrassment and, more importantly, without sexual overtones.

The rest of us may find this a bit unrealistic or somewhat eccentric and cult-like. Indeed, nudists themselves have been aware of this problem. A study of nudist colonies, published in 1965, documented how careful the camps were to maintain an air of "modesty."[18] The ideology of the camps was that "nudism and sexuality are unrelated." Some camps did not allow single men to join, or restricted their numbers or charged them higher rates for membership. Staring and ogling was frowned on. As one observer put it, "They all look up to the heavens and never look below." Members avoided telling "dirty" jokes. Body contact was taboo and nude dancing was forbidden. In a way, of course, all of this merely reinforced the common notion that nudism and sexuality *were* in fact related, whatever the nudist movement might have thought.

At all points, moreover, moralists opposed nudism and the nudist movement. Germany was in a way the mother church of the nudist movement, but when the Nazis came to power in 1933, they tried to stamp the practice out. Goering declared nudism a "cultural aberration." In women, it deadened the sense of shame and in men it destroyed "respect for womanhood."[19] Nudist colonies faced legal troubles in the United States as well. In 1936, one Stephen P. Holish made films at a nudist camp near Roselawn, Indiana. The Eastman Kodak company refused to develop them. Holish went to court. Holish's attorney argued that the pictures were "as good and clean as movies of any Sunday school pictures." They lacked the "leer of the sensual." But Judge Samuel H. Trude, after watching the films, decided they were "indecent" and gave Eastman power to destroy them.[20]

This kind of legal action is much less likely to happen today, unless the photos show naked children, which might raise suspicions of child pornography. (A young Utah couple suffered the wrath of child protective services and immigration officials after a Walgreens' technician called the police over some naked bath-time photos.[21]) Sedate, organized nudism does not lend itself to any sense of outrage. The movement even boasts an American Nudist Research Library, founded in 1979. It is on the grounds of Cypress Cove Nudist Resort, in Kissimmee, Florida, "next to the tropically landscaped pool area." This romantic setting "provides the visitor a vivid memory of our identity with sunlight, fresh air, relaxation and a oneness with nature." The library itself is a "clothing optional facility," although, in order to maintain the "integrity of our aging documentation," the facility is "air conditioned to a temperature in the mid to lower 70's F." Donations to the library are "tax-deductible."[22]

In any event, cozy and bourgeois nudist camps clearly stand at one end of a continuum. A bit further down (or up) the scale, are nude beaches. They are common today around the world. For example, there are at least four in Lithuania, and a great many in such countries as Spain and France. There are none, of course, in Saudi Arabia.

It would not be quite honest to say that these nude beaches, like the "family nudist" resorts, sharply separate sensuality from nudity. Indeed, they carry with them at least a mild tang of sexual liberation. There is certainly a good deal of ogling and gawking, which would be definitely frowned on in the most rigorous and ideological of the nudist colonies. Indeed, a website on "Nude Beach Etiquette" specifically condemns "gawking" as "impolite." The website suggests, that if this is your first time at a nude beach, "look for the regulars": they're the ones who "don't have any tan lines" and they tend to be a "friendly bunch of people" who will "answer your questions and loan you a bottle opener if you need it." Also, although it "happens less often than you might think," if "you start getting physically excited, the best advice . . . is to roll over on your stomach and wait until it subsides" (clearly this is advice for men).[23]

These rules of etiquette are clearly meant to apply to open, public beaches that are "clothing-optional." But there are also other kinds of nude spas and resorts, which lack the nonchalance of nude beaches, and which also lack the prudish air of the classic colonies, with their pictures of volleyball courts and children playing games. On public nude beaches, sex is definitely taboo, but this is not the case at some of the spas and resorts. For example, one premier spa hotel is for adults only; the facilities are described as "luxurious" and "romantic" and it labels itself a "sensual boutique hotel, a private nude resort paradise, a safe environment," with "less stress, less clothes." German enthusiasts for nudity would surely have disapproved; and perhaps the patrons of the American Nudist Research Library would do so also.

If the question is whether or not simple nudity is illegal today, the answer depends on when and where. Clearly it's not illegal in one's own home. Taking a shower unclothed is not a crime. It is also probably not illegal in discreet nudist colonies that are carefully fenced in from prying eyes. (There was one strange recent case in which a woman was arrested for lewdness after her teenage stepchildren saw her topless in the garage, under a statute that bans exposure of the female breast even in a private place "under circumstances which the person should know will likely cause affront or alarm to, on, or in the presence of another who is 14 years of age or older."[24] The American Civil Liberties Union challenged the constitutionality of the law, arguing that a woman should be able to bare her breasts if a man is allowed to bare his chest. A judge dismissed the challenge, however, and permitted the criminal case to proceed.[25]) Nudity is not illegal, either, in carefully marked nudist beaches. Many of these are officially authorized as nude beaches; in others, the nudity is a matter of custom and official tolerance. Their legal status could be questioned if anybody bothered to ask the question, but apparently nobody has. And what about nudity elsewhere—in other more-or-less public places that are not nude beaches or nudist colonies? Sometimes there is formal law on the subject; more often, it is the living law of prosecutors and the police that matters. The short answer is, nudity can be illegal, but this is usually when it amounts to something called "indecent exposure."

INDECENT EXPOSURE

"Indecent exposure," or something equivalent, is quite generally against the law in the American states. The language varies from place to place.[26] "Indecent exposure" is starkly different from simple nudity. It is overtly sexual, and is thought of as perverse, threatening, or pathological. The crime is committed almost exclusively by men.

Every state has some sort of law about indecent exposure. The texts vary from state to state, but the message is essentially the same everywhere. In Alabama, the crime of public lewdness is committed when a person "exposes his anus or genitals in a public place and is reckless about whether another may be present who will be offended or alarmed by his act."[27] The definition of "lewdness" in Utah is fairly elaborate. A number of acts are lewd if they are done "in a public place," or "under circumstances which the person should know will likely cause affront or alarm," or if the act is done "in the presence of another who is 14 years of age or older." The "lewd" acts include "sexual intercourse or sodomy," masturbation, or exposure of "the female breast below the top of the areola," or of "the buttocks, the anus, or the pubic area," or exposure of genitalia.[28] In Connecticut, a person is guilty of "public indecency" if he performs certain acts in a "public place": sexual intercourse, a "lewd exposure of the body with intent to arouse or to satisfy the sexual desire of the person," or "a lewd fondling or caress of the body of another person."[29]

The key term in these statutes is *indecent* (sometimes the word used is *lewd*). Exposure, in most states, is not a crime unless it is "indecent." Indecency comes not only from what is exposed, but where, when, and with what purpose in mind. What parts must people keep hidden? Obviously bare feet, even dirty feet, aren't indecent. The statutes are about exposing *private parts* (the very term is significant). Some state statutes use the phrase *private parts* without any further elaboration, or simply forbid the "indecent exposure of his or her person."[30] The California Penal Code makes it a crime for a person to expose his or her "private parts . . . in any public place, or in any place where there are present other persons to be offended or annoyed" if this is done "willfully and lewdly." It is particularly bad to do this "after having entered, without consent, an inhabited dwelling house, or trailer coach . . . or the inhabited portion of any . . . building."[31] The Indiana statute goes further than most. It includes in the definition of indecent exposure male genitals even when they are "covered," if they are "in a discernibly turgid state."[32]

These statutes—at least nowadays—do not seem to criminalize what we have called simple nudity. At least not obviously. Certainly, in California, for example, exposing "private parts" is a crime only if there are people around who might be "offended or annoyed" and if the act is done "lewdly." Many statutes are particularly fussy about exposing children to the sight of "private parts."[33] Going to a nudist colony would not be a crime under this statute; nor would taking a sunbath at a nude beach or acting in one of the plays these days that call for actors to be naked on the stage. The same is true under the statutes of many other states.

In a California case from 1972, *In re Smith*, the defendant took off his clothes at a public beach where there were only a few other users. He was lying on his back on a towel and he fell asleep. The police came and arrested him. Defendant was completely naked, but at no time did he have an erection and he did not engage "in any activity directing attention to his genitals."[34]

Smith was convicted of indecent exposure and had to pay a fine ($100); he was also given a three-year suspended sentence. This was not particularly severe and he might have swallowed it. But he learned that he would also have to register as a sex offender and that would be no small matter. So he appealed, arguing that his nudity was not "lewd." The California appeals court agreed. Sleeping naked on the beach, without sexual overtones, was not a violation of the statute; it was not in any way "lewd." The conviction was reversed. Cases after *Smith* seemed to adopt an unspoken distinction between harmless pranks and aggressively sexual behavior. Lewdness requires a sexual motivation. An appellate court reversed a finding of juvenile delinquency for a minor who mooned oncoming traffic, but another court upheld the conviction of a driver who exposed himself while uttering a vulgar sexual phrase during a road rage incident.[35]

Public nudity, then, may not be "indecent exposure," at least in some states. Simply being nude is not a crime per se. As we said, nobody would claim that taking a shower or getting undressed in your own bedroom are crimes. Even outside the home, as we have seen, attitudes have relaxed greatly. In the 1880s, an unfortunate man in New Jersey urinated in the yard of a house and was apparently seen by people who lived in the house. He was convicted of "indecent exposure."[36] We doubt very much that he would be convicted today in California or in many other states, perhaps most states.

There is no question that true "indecent exposure" is or can be a social problem or at any rate a psychiatric problem. The cases that uphold convictions involve overt sexual acts. According to a study published in the 1970s, one-third of all sex offenses reported to the police were the acts of men who committed the crime of indecent exposure. Ten percent of the sex offenders in the New Jersey state prison in 1950 were exhibitionists.[37] Attitudes toward sex may have changed but "indecent exposure" is still very much a crime. A study in California in the late 1970s reported that in 1976 there were 115 felony arrests for indecent exposure, in 1977 there were 109, and in 1978 there were 72.[38] The courts have struggled, to be sure, with problems of definition and boundaries. The exposure has to be "public,"[39] but exactly what does this mean? Not necessarily outdoors, for one thing. Some courts have allowed convictions even when the exposure took place in a private home. In a 2007 case in Maryland, Gerald Eugene Wisneski, a guest in the home of Bridgette Penfield, exposed himself to another guest and the guest's fifteen-year-old sister. Wisneski asked her if she was "on her period," took out his penis and testicles, and started shaking them. Wisneski was convicted of indecent exposure (and other offenses). Wisneski appealed; his argument, essentially, was that indecent exposure had to be "public," and not inside a private home. The court, however, affirmed his conviction. Because Wisneski deliberately exposed himself to "actual observation by two . . . people," Wisneski had in fact "publicly" exposed himself.[40] There are a number of fairly similar cases; they do not all agree. Much hinges on how the particular court interprets the word "public." But in cases like Wisneski's, what the defendant did was fairly shocking; prosecution is also more likely when the victims are young children.

In contemporary society, then, something more than just displaying the body, something more than simple nudity, is required to constitute "indecent exposure," as a general rule. There has to be something overtly sexual: an erection, masturbation, sexual intercourse, or the like. Yet there are many people, and many jurisdictions, that find public nudity offensive even without these features, and feel that offenders should be punished. Even in California, the penal code gives localities the right to pass ordinances that regulate the "exposure of the genitals or buttocks of any person, or the breasts of any female person, who acts as a waiter, waitress, or entertainer."[41] Another section of the Code gives local governments power to regulate "live acts, demonstrations, or exhibitions occurring within adult or sexually oriented business [that] involve the exposure of the genitals or buttocks of any participant or the breasts of any female participant."[42]

These provisions were put in the code in 1969 to allow cities and towns to regulate nudity in restaurants and "adult" establishments. The California Supreme Court had held, in an earlier case, that the state preempted the whole field of control of sexual activity in public places; the provisions were meant to give back to cities and towns authority to regulate live performances and such people as topless waitresses.[43] These ordinances and statutes thus have aims very different from the usual norms about indecent exposure; they are tools in a battle against sex clubs and strip joints. Clearly, the people who flock to "adult" establishments are hardly victims, are definitely not small children, and are paying good money precisely because they want to see as much "indecent exposure" as possible.

Nonetheless, in 1993, the notoriously liberal city of Berkeley enacted an ordinance banning all public nudity. Under this ordinance, it is a misdemeanor for "any person to appear nude in any place open to the public or any place visible from a place open to the public."[44] In the background was the case of a certain Andrew Martinez, nicknamed the "Naked Guy," a student at the University of California. Martinez stood up for what he considered were his rights, by going everywhere naked—including classes, where he appeared dressed (if that is the word) in sandals and a backpack. The university adopted a no-nudity policy for public areas of campus. Martinez was expelled for showing up naked at his disciplinary hearing. He was arrested in the city but won his case on the grounds that it was not illegal to walk around naked in Berkeley. That prompted the city to adopt its no-nudity ordinance.[45]

Another famously liberal city, San Francisco, had its own ordinance on public nudity.[46] It took the hint from the penal code; its ordinance originally applied just to waiters, waitresses, and entertainers. People in those jobs must keep their genitals, buttocks, and female breasts concealed. The original ordinance, however, allowed the customers to be naked while dining. And the general public could be nude out in the open, as long as their nudity was not "lewd"—interpreted in the *Smith* case to mean intending "to direct public attention to his genitals for purposes of sexual arousal, gratification, or affront."[47] In 2011, a city supervisor, Scott Wiener, proposed controls over public nudity. He noticed an uptick in the number of public nudists in Castro, the city's gay district. Under the aptly named "Wiener's Law," naked people could no longer enter restaurants.[48] And while naked people could continue to visit parks and beaches and ride city buses, they would be required to place a towel or other barrier under their genitals or buttocks when sitting "on any public bench, public steps, or other public seating area."

The good citizens of the Castro district did not take kindly to Wiener's Law. In response, they organized a public "nude-in" to add to the Folsom Street Festival (an enormous gathering of fetish paraphernalia and leather).[49] This was a far cry from classical nudism, of the nudist colony type, which is discreet, likes privacy, and insists on conventional morality. The nude-in, rather, is a form of rebellion. It is an expression of contempt for bourgeois morality, a finger stuck in the eye of respectability. Why the organizers were so exercised by Wiener's law is unclear. It was already standard etiquette for nudists to put a towel under their tailbones.[50] If Wiener thought his ordinance would have some tendency to curb nudism in San Francisco, he was badly mistaken. According to one prominent local nudist (a man of sixty-five), nudity is one of San Francisco's tourist attractions, along with cable cars and the Golden Gate Bridge. Tourists, he said, love to have their picture taken with naked people; the only ones who object are "religious nutcases."[51] The San Francisco nudists seem to be mostly men; moreover, they are men who are frankly, as one account put it, hardly "supermodel types."[52] Why is it, one woman asked a reporter, that "it's always the people who should not be naked who get naked."[53] Another said that the participants looked as if they had been "put through the wrong cycle in the wash-and-dry machine and then not ironed properly" and that they have "pathetic, ugly unkempt bodies."[54] They would not do, in short, as poster people for the American Association for Nude Recreations. It is certainly true, alas, that most people look a lot better with their clothes on. In any event, the "nude-in" came and went.

The Board of Supervisors eventually voted six to five to enact an even broader ban on public nudity than the one Wiener initially proposed. The ordinance cites concerns that public nudity interferes with people's ability to enjoy public space without unwilling or unexpected exposure to other people's naked bodies, distracts people in a way that can be a public safety hazard, and discourages outsiders from visiting or moving to San Francisco.[55] The ordinance prohibits exposure of one's "genitals, perineum, or anal region on any public street, sidewalk, street median, parklet, plaza, or public right-of-way . . . or in any transit vehicle, stations, platform, or stop of any government operated transit system in the City and County of San Francisco." The ordinance does not seem to apply to beaches, and it expressly exempts permitted events like parades and festivals, as long as the event organizers do not object to the nudity. The penalty for violating the ordinance starts with a $100 fine and increases with subsequent violations. Two "body freedom advocates" sued the city, arguing that the anti-nudity ordinance violated their First Amendment right to expression. The law, however, was upheld as a content-neutral regulation of expressive conduct (which is less protected than expressive speech).[56]

Before the nudity ban, San Francisco was, in many ways, an outlier. Most states and cities have a lower level of tolerance for public nudity, even simple nudity. Naked people may have wandered about the Castro district but it is hard to imagine such people in downtown Wichita or even downtown Philadelphia. Any such behavior would lead to an immediate arrest based on whatever charge seemed handy and whether or not the police could make the arrest stick in court.

In short, both socially and legally, there are problems with what we might call the middling sort of nudity—nudity that neither takes place in, say, a fenced-in colony, on the one hand, or that is plainly offensive and sexually threatening, on the other. People who roam the streets naked, in most places, would strike observers as, well, somewhat strange, and their mental condition would be suspect. There is also what one might call recreational public nudity: nudity done to have fun, by shocking or amusing onlookers or bystanders; this is usually the work of young people and is done in groups. The men in the nude-in fall into this category and it explains the various nude affairs at colleges and universities, such as the "naked donut run" at Brown University, which traditionally took place just before exams. Streakers (about which more later) are also just having fun, for the most part, or relieving the stress and strains of young life.

There are, however, difficult and ambiguous cases, like fifty-four-year-old Dean Maginnis, who went fishing in Medical Lake, Washington, in August 2011, without bothering to put on clothes. One wonders what he had in mind. The Spokane County authorities, after complaints about the "eyeball-scarring" view of Maginnis, arrested him and charged him with indecent exposure. In fact, Maginnis had a criminal record: a prior charge of indecent exposure and a warrant for stalking.[57] These facts no doubt influenced the police to do something more than tell him to kindly put his clothes back on.

Apparently, most people, even police, are not sure what the law allows and what it prohibits. The so-called Topless Woman of Union Square sauntered around New York City baring her breasts. Moira Johnston did this to "raise awareness that it's legal for [a] woman to be topless anywhere a guy can be without a shirt."[58] When asked to define her personal style, she described it as "kind of artsy" with "roots in social activism." She got "mixed reactions" from onlookers, to be sure, who were not used to seeing a woman who is otherwise respectable-looking walking the streets topless. The police were surprised as well and arrested her repeatedly, only to learn later that she had broken no law. The NYPD held a special training session to make sure officers were aware of the law on toplessness.[59] A woman in Brooklyn was arrested for sitting topless on a park bench; she informed the officers that it was legal for her to be topless but was instructed to "stop mouthing off" and then arrested. The charges were dropped, but she sued.[60]

NUDITY IS FUN

The United States is, perhaps, rather puritanical—if that's the word—compared to many other Western countries. Or perhaps we should say: *parts* of the United States and some segments of the population are rather puritanical.

Others are decidedly not; some have embraced modern permissiveness with enormous gusto.

In many places, we find periodic outbursts of nakedness, either to make a political point or simply to poke the eye of the bourgeoisie. People take off their clothes to ride bicycles, to indulge in "performance art," or simply to show that one can (and should?) do all sorts of "normal" things without the benefit of clothing.[61] An English television channel tried out a nude television show, *Naked Jungle*, in 2000: it "featured nude contestants pitting themselves against an assault course"; the presenter was also naked. It did not last very long, even though it had two million viewers and very high ratings. It was denounced in the House of Commons, but the public was, in general, "amused rather than outraged."[62] But the reality show *Naked and Afraid* is on its thirteenth season in the United States. Contestants work in pairs, outfitted with only a cross-body satchel that contains a camera and one survival item of each party's choosing, and they try to survive for twenty-one days.[63] The commercial possibilities of nudity have not escaped the greedy eye of business. In 2003, a clothing store in Lisbon offered "two free items of clothing to anyone who shopped in the nude"; they had plenty of "eager customers" who wanted to take them up on the offer. A record store in Melbourne, Australia, used to hold "annual nude shopping days," while a department store in Vienna, in 2000, offered a voucher for 5,000 Austrian schillings to "the first people to enter the store naked."[64]

In 2012, the Museum of Contemporary Art Australia, in Sydney, began offering nude art tours, where the patrons, not the images, were in the buff.[65] Attendees were led on a tour of a show by an artist, Stuart Ringholt, also naked, who explained that "[w]e are sexualized with our clothes on—with them off, we are not." Tour participants were divided as to whether it enhanced the experience to look at the art while naked. For those who want a more extended and varied experience, there are "Bare Necessity Cruises" on luxury liners, which include visits to nude beaches. (Clothes, however, have to be worn "in the main dining room" and at the "Captain's reception").[66] There is an American Association for Nude Recreation, a "naturist" organization, founded in 1931 as the American Sunbathing Association. It sponsors, among other things, "clothing-optional" races; runners "compete in age and gender categories." McDade, Texas, for some reason, specializes in such runs: there is a "Chilly Cheeks" run in October of each year and the "Bare Buns 5K" run was scheduled for April 10, 2021 (registration was $35 for adults, $15 for children).

For a while, too, there was a positive epidemic of "streaking," that is, running naked (usually quite quickly) in a public place. This was eagerly pursued on some college campuses. There was a mass streaking event at the University of Maryland in 1973. A celebrated incident took place during the broadcast of the Academy Awards in 1974, although it may have been something less than spontaneous. That year, 1974, seemed to be some sort of high point of the streaking movement, or craze, or fashion. But there have been sporadic incidents ever since at universities and colleges, and very notably at sports events. Here, too, the audience is generally amused, rather than shocked. And the streakers—this is part of the rules of the game—usually run by so quickly that nobody has much of a chance to dwell on their nakedness. College streakers, of course, have no particular commitment to nudity. A few individuals do. Mark Roberts, who is British, has been called the world's greatest streaker; he began this dubious career in 1993 and by 2018, he had some 565 streaks to his credit (if that is the word) in many countries. He has done his thing at a Miss World contest, in a great number of sports events (his specialty), at the running of the bulls in Pamplona, and at the 2008 World Snooker championship. He has been arrested a number of times for such offenses as trespassing. No doubt many people (including the management of sports teams) consider him a nuisance but he is hardly a menace.[67]

EROTIC NUDITY

The naked body—mostly female—pops up in another context. In between simple and playful nudity, on the one hand, and indecent exposure on the other, is a shadowy domain we might call *erotic nudity*. Here the nudity is frankly and openly sexual. But it is not by any means forced on innocent victims. To the contrary: as we noted earlier, people pay good money for the privilege of seeing other people, usually women, in the nude in various establishments. Or, as in the classic burlesque show, the performers may be almost nude (the so-called strip tease), or, as in certain "adult" establishments, more than nude: women gyrating and dancing, or going even further. (In this age of creeping gender equality, women can also go to see male strippers in action.)

How far can the state go in regulating and controlling such bawdy shows? The question reached the august halls of the U.S. Supreme Court in *Barnes v. Glen Theatre, Inc.*[68] In two clubs in South Bend, Indiana, the Kitty Kat Lounge and the Glen Theatre, customers could watch women, so-called exotic dancers, who were completely nude. Indiana had a law that outlawed nudity; the women were supposed to wear pasties and G-strings. The Seventh Circuit struck down the statute; Judge Richard Posner's opinion in fact poked fun at it. Posner called censorship of erotica "ridiculous" and wondered what kind of person would make a career of "checking to see whether the covering of a woman's nipples is fully opaque?" But the Supreme Court was not amused; it reversed the Seventh Circuit. The law was valid, in that it promoted order, morality, and decency. Four justices dissented.

The general issue came back to haunt the Supreme Court nine years later in *City of Erie v. Pap's A.M.*, in 2000.[69] Here the city had an ordinance that made it illegal to appear in public in a "state of nudity." The defendant ran a club called Kandyland, where customers could see completely nude "exotic" dancing. Like Indiana, Pennsylvania wanted the women to wear pasties and G-strings. The highest court of Pennsylvania thought the ordinance was unconstitutional. The Supreme Court disagreed. The lawyers for the clubs had invoked such noble ideals as freedom of speech and expression. But the Supreme Court refused to take the bait. The court quoted the preamble to the ordinance: "nude live entertainment" has a deleterious impact on "public health, safety and welfare"; it creates "an atmosphere conducive to violence, sexual harassment, public intoxication, prostitution, [and] the spread of sexually transmitted diseases."

In a way, these cases might well remind us of the old tale about King Canute, who tried to command the waves. In the early twenty-first century, the United States—and other Western countries—are flooded with pornography: hard-core movies, videos, magazines, books, and pictures. That a place like Kandyland could even *claim* constitutional protections would have shocked and horrified people in the nineteenth century (and much of the twentieth century as well). That the Supreme Court *almost* struck down regulation of "exotic dancing" would have been equally shocking. Even more shocking was what the Court plainly *would* allow: women who swiveled and gyrated (and worse) in front of men, with nothing on but a G-string, along with tiny covers on their nipples. Judges (mostly middle-aged or elderly men, who—in Posner's opinion—tended to be "snooty" about popular culture) still fumble and mumble about the issue. But sex sells, and millions seem willing to buy, In our era, "prurient" issues are powerful and more and more they seem to prevail.

SEX IN PUBLIC

The internet is full of sex; people talk about sex, magazines feature articles about sex: sex is, in a way, everywhere. To some extent, the tiger is out of its cage. Some people, to be sure, are still squeamish about sex talk. They cover it with fig leaves. *Thought Catalog* lists four hundred euphemisms for sex.[70] *Bustle* offers twenty-six "amazing historical euphemisms for sex."[71] Other sites offer compilations of the "funniest sex euphemisms," "Downton Abbey euphemisms for sex," and even the best euphemisms for sex from the 1800s. So, while to some extent sex talk has come out of the closet—indeed, it seems inescapable—there are still limits and taboos, and sex itself remains a quintessentially private activity.

Earlier in this chapter, we discussed at length the laws and norms governing public nudity, which are driven in large part by fear of what might happen if no restraints were put on sexual behavior and behavior that has sexual overtones. Would naked women provoke sexual assaults? Are naked men sexually threatening to women? Nudity in public spaces may or may not be illegal, depending. Sexual activity itself—perhaps the most private of acts—most certainly *is* illegal in public. The regulation of sexual behavior is legally and socially a can of worms. Hundreds of civil and criminal laws deal with sex, regulating the who, what, when, where, and how of sexual behavior. We focus here only on those that have privacy implications. Must sexual behavior be kept private, away from the eyes of third parties? Can one's sex life be kept a secret? If so, from whom? From the government? An employer? A minor's parents? An angry ex-boyfriend?

"GET A ROOM"

This is a familiar retort when people see a couple engaging in public displays of affection—those that go beyond a certain limit (hand-holding and genteel kissing is okay). There is no law against "necking." But there is a point of no return. Going further is to act in a way that has to be confined to private places. This subject is regulated by indecency laws. Almost universally, these laws prohibit "lewd" or "indecent" exposure of sex organs. Actually *using* these sex organs in public would be even more "lewd" or "indecent." Sometimes the statutes say so explicitly. In Arizona, for example, a person commits the misdemeanor of "public sexual indecency" by engaging in any sex act (graphically listed in the statute) "if another person is present, and the [offender] is reckless about whether [the witness], as a reasonable person, would be offended or alarmed by the act."[72] And if the offender is reckless about the possible presence of someone under age fifteen, the same act becomes a felony. Colorado criminalizes any "act of sexual intercourse" in a "public place or where the conduct may reasonably be expected to be viewed by members of the public."[73]

New York's highest court was called on in *People v. McNamara* (1991) to decide whether a car parked on a public street was a "public place" within the meaning of the state's indecent exposure law. The law prohibited lewd exposure of private parts and banned "any other lewd act" in a "public place.[74] The case arose from three separate incidents of sex in cars—two on the same street at the same time. The defendants admitted they had had sex and did not argue that sex in this sense was not a "lewd act," but they argued that their cars were not public places. The law's purpose, the court wrote, was to protect "the public—in essence, 'unsuspecting, unwilling, nonconsenting, innocent, surprised or likely-to-be offended or corrupted types of viewers'—from the sight of offensive activities and materials."[75] The meaning of "public" does not depend on whether the alleged offenders had a reasonable expectation of privacy, nor on whether they intended to cause harm; it depends, rather, on whether passersby are likely to have seen them *in flagrante delicto.* Thus, cars are neither always public nor always private; "the interior of a vehicle parked on the side of a desolate road is not a 'public place' in the same sense that the interior of a car parked at a busy downtown shopping area might be."[76] The government needed to show that sex in the parked car could have been seen, and likely would have been seen "by the casual passerby, whose sensibilities the statute seeks to protect." This was good news for the defendants, since the charges against them had failed to allege that these sexual acts were "capable of observation." One judge dissented, pointing out that the defendants were "in fact, observed performing their sex acts in public"—the police, after all, had seen enough to describe their actions fully. This judge felt that it "defies the natural, plain, and commonly understood meaning and purpose" of the law to hold that "sexual activity performed in vehicles parked on residential streets is not committed in a 'public place'"[77] Other courts have had to decide whether sex is "public" in places as varied as a massage parlor, the communal shower room at a fitness center, and the drunk tank at a city jail.[78] Sex, after all, can be and often is anywhere. The idea that sexual behavior should be kept private extends beyond conduct in public spaces. Society may impose consequences on those who fail to keep their sex life under wraps—especially if their private behavior flouts social norms. Employers have discriminated against workers who are open about their membership in the LGBT community. Until very recently, employers could do this with impunity.

In 2014, Flint Dollar learned a lesson the hard way when he lost his job as a music teacher at a Catholic school in Georgia. Dollar, who had been a popular teacher at the school for four years, was fired for announcing on Facebook that he planned to marry his same-sex partner. Dollar sued the school, and the parties ultimately reached a confidential settlement.[79] Gay and lesbian teachers face job loss in religious schools if details of their personal relationships come out.[80] But the problem was not just at religious schools. In 2009, Jason Koren, a gay newlywed working for a telephone company, was unexpectedly terminated when a supervisor learned that he married a man and took his husband's last name. When he worked under his "maiden name" at Ohio Bell, Koren was treated with respect. But as soon as information about his marriage was revealed, he was subjected to a great deal of hostility, and then he was terminated, supposedly for taking time off to attend his father's funeral.[81] After the district court denied Ohio Bell's motion for summary judgment, the case was settled.[82]

But in 2020, things turned out differently for Gerald Bostock. Bostock, a child welfare advocate in Clayton County, Georgia, was fired after he joined a gay recreational baseball league. His case rose to the level of the US Supreme Court, along with two companion cases involving a lesbian employee and a transgender employee, respectively. The Court decided, six to three, that terminating Bostock for no reason other than his sexual orientation was a violation of the Civil Rights Act of 1964 (which prohibits discrimination on the basis of "sex"). The Court also held that the law protected transgender employees.[83] The very nature of LGBT discrimination involves punishing people for failing to conform to expectations based on their biological sex—whether it be how they dress or present themselves or to whom they are attracted. Public opinion—and now the law—had shifted rapidly on this issue. Yet for many gay and transgender people, it is still probably risky to assert rights too openly. And of course *where* rights are asserted makes a difference. Bostock worked in Clayton County, Georgia, not San Francisco County, California.

Cases like *Bostock* represent a massive legal and social change. For most of American history, states tried to keep a tight leash on sexual activity. Sex was supposed to be for married people only; moreover, only married people were supposed to have children. Of course, the government never really had the kind of tight control formal law implied. Far from it. But the formal criminal law, working in tandem with social norms, was supposed to confine sex to its proper place—and proper people. Those laws prohibited fornication (sex by unmarried persons); adultery (sex between people who were married, but not to each other); sodomy (sexual contact between people of the same gender or oral-genital contact between people of different genders); bestiality; incest; and, at least in some states (at one time), the use of contraception.[84] These laws were often tinkered with—some periods were stricter than others—but, in essence, they survived throughout the nineteenth and into the twentieth century; they were part and parcel of a system that was meant as a tool to enforce a strict moral code.

The development of a constitutional right of privacy was a blow to the inherited tradition. This reduced the power of government to interfere with key decisions about private life. In some ways, this constitutional right is not about "privacy" in the usual sense at all; but it has an impact on legal and social culture. This right of privacy was dimly foreshadowed in *Skinner v. Oklahoma* (1942). An Oklahoma statute authorized the state to sterilize habitual criminals and the "feeble-minded."[85] This law, and sterilization laws in other states, came out of the eugenics movement. The laws were influenced by the idea that crime, immorality, and mental defects were hereditary.[86] Restrictive marriage laws were a primary control point, since marriage was the normal gateway to reproduction. Sterilization prevented unsuitable people from passing on their bad seed through the generations.

Skinner was up against a tough obstacle: a prior Supreme Court decision. In 1927, the U.S. Supreme Court had held, in *Buck v. Bell*, that the state of Virginia could forcibly sterilize Carrie Buck, the "feeble minded" child of a "feeble-minded mother," who had also given birth to "an illegitimate feeble-minded child."[87] Oliver Wendell Holmes Jr. declared, in a famous (and unjustified) statement: "[t]hree generations of imbeciles are enough." The Court upheld the Virginia sterilization law.[88] But the world changed dramatically between *Buck* and *Skinner*. The Nazis had eagerly embraced eugenics and its racist corollaries; Nazi thinkers in fact cited American precedents for their own brand of eugenics. Nazi "eugenics," of course, went much further than the American version, including simply murdering handicapped and feeble-minded people.[89] Meanwhile, scientists were arguing, persuasively, that eugenics was based on junk science. In *Skinner*, which was decided during the war against the Nazi regime, the Court struck down the Oklahoma statute on sterilization. Skinner faced a vasectomy for stealing chickens; if he had been an embezzler, he could have kept his right to reproduce. This, in the Court's view, violated the Equal Protection Clause of the Constitution. The right to have children, the Court said in passing, was a fundamental right.[90]

While *Skinner* removed a brick, the house came tumbling down two decades later in *Griswold v. Connecticut* (1965).[91] Connecticut made it a crime for any person to use "any drug, medicinal article or instrument for the purpose of preventing conception" or for any person to assist or abet another person's use of contraception. To challenge the law, a doctor and an executive at Planned Parenthood opened a clinic in New Haven; in it, they gave "information, instruction, and medical advice to *married persons* as to the means of preventing conception."[92] They then "examined the wife and prescribed the best contraceptive device or material for her use." The doctor and clinic director were arrested and convicted under local law. The question for the Supreme Court, then, was whether the state of Connecticut could criminalize use of contraceptives by married couples. In a blissfully short majority opinion (at least by today's long-winded judicial standards), Justice William O. Douglas cited many provisions of the Constitution that he felt supported the idea of what he called a general right to privacy—the right against unreasonable search and seizure, the right to freely associate, and the right to raise children without interference from the government, for example. The Connecticut statute, Justice Douglas wrote, "concerns a relationship lying within the zone of privacy created by several fundamental constitutional guarantees."[93] And in criminalizing not only the sale of contraceptives, but their *use*, Connecticut sought to achieve its goals—restricting sex to reproductive purposes—with "a maximum destructive impact upon that relationship."[94] Would Connecticut have the police "search the sacred precincts of marital bedrooms for telltale signs of the use of contraceptives?" Surely, he concluded, the "very idea is repulsive to the notions of privacy surrounding the marriage relationship." And "a right of privacy older than the Bill of Rights" had the function of keeping the police out of those "sacred precincts."

In 1972, the Court extended this right to single people, expanding this right of "privacy." A Massachusetts law, challenged in *Eisenstadt v. Baird,* allowed distribution of contraceptives only to married couples. Anything else was a criminal offense.[95] But the Supreme Court, in an opinion by Justice William J. Brennan, held that the right of privacy was a right of individuals, married or not. The decision whether to have a baby had to remain free of "unwarranted governmental intrusion."[96] Then came the decision, in 1973, on the decision to terminate a pregnancy, at least in the earlier months of gestation.[97] This was the famous—or perhaps notorious—case of *Roe v. Wade*. Controversies over this case, and over abortion rights in general, have had a life of their own; abortion remains a bitter and controversial issue. In recent years, conservative states have passed law after law infringing on abortion rights, nibbling away at core and periphery; the religious right has never given up hope of overruling *Roe v. Wade*.[98] Its fate hinges on a closely divided Supreme Court—it is widely believed that a majority of the Court would vote to overrule; it is poised perhaps to do so in 2022.

Abortion is still wildly controversial but the right to *use* contraception established in *Griswold* is essentially sacrosanct. There are questions—for example, over coverage of contraception under the Affordable Care Act—but few people, regardless of their place on the political spectrum, feel that the government should be able to block access to contraception (which most married and unmarried couples freely use). Judge Robert Bork's open opposition to *Griswold* helped cost him a seat on the Supreme Court in 1987.[99]

It was never entirely clear how far the Court was and is willing to go in expanding the "right of privacy"; even the underlying principle seems murky, to say the least. Sex was, of course, an issue in these cases—celibate people have no need for contraception or abortion—but the Court has shied away from any frank discussion of sexual behavior. The decisions were couched primarily in terms of decision-making, specifically the zone of privacy that surrounded *decisions* about intimate and family life rather than the conduct itself. The early rulings probably reflected the Court's endorsement of rational family planning; they were not a license to have sex and more sex.[100] *Griswold* meant contraception would be freely available and, gradually, condoms emerged from their hiding place in the drugstore into plain view. And, after *Roe v. Wade*, abortion was more available as a legal backstop to unwanted pregnancy. Condoms, abortions, and sexual paraphernalia, in other words, were no longer hidden, private, or secretive; like the naked body, they emerged into the public sphere.

And this meant that the core of this privacy right was no longer rational family planning but sexual rights plain and simple. In 1986, in *Bowers v. Hardwick*, two men challenged a law that criminalized same-sex sexual behavior in Georgia.[101] The Court upheld the law—but narrowly. The right to same-sex behavior was not "fundamental," not "implicit in the concept of ordered liberty." But this decision turned out to be nothing but a detour on the road to sexual permissiveness. Seventeen years later, the Supreme Court reversed itself in *Lawrence v. Texas*.[102] This case struck down a Texas law that made sodomy a crime. The Texas penal code prohibited "deviate sexual intercourse with another person of the same sex."[103] Police had arrested two men caught in the act. The statute, said the Court, violated the Due Process Clause of the Fourteenth Amendment. A shift in the makeup of the Court surely played a role, but the more important change was in social attitudes about homosexuality and gay rights.

Even in *Lawrence*, the Supreme Court talked about sex in cautious and guarded tones. Adults were entitled to conduct consensual personal relationships "in the confines of their homes and their own private lives."[104] People were entitled to decide on "intimacies of their physical relationship, even when not intended to produce offspring."[105]

Lawrence put an end to sodomy laws, which were already gone in all but some thirteen states. The case did seem to have a broader meaning. Some states at the time still had laws against adultery, but after *Lawrence*, the District of Columbia got rid of this "outdated" crime.[106] In *Reliable Consultants, Inc. v. Earle*,[107] a Texas law banned the sale and promotion of sex toys. No good, said the Fifth Circuit: an "individual who wants to legally use a safe sexual device during private intimate moments alone or with another" should be able, constitutionally, to buy such a device in Texas.[108] And in 2015, in *Obergefell v. Hodges*, the Supreme Court held (by a bare majority) that states could not forbid same-sex marriage.[109] Same-sex relations were definitively made legitimate, and on a national scale. Forbidden private sex and love and commitment were now able to step forward proudly and officially. Gay marriages announce themselves in the *New York Times*. In 2019, a married gay man was a serious candidate for the Democratic nomination for president.[110] That same married gay man, Pete Buttigieg, is now, in 2021, a member of President Biden's cabinet.

Sex, even when protected by the mighty Constitution, can still scandalize; it can jeopardize or end a career. Eliot Spitzer, caught using a high-priced call girl service, lost his job as governor of New York. Sexual predation cost James Levine, the country's most famous conductor of opera, his career. There is more, not less, sensitivity to sexual predation, and abuse of sexual power. Still, behavior that would have shocked and appalled the Victorians often barely registers on the screen of modern life. The political career of Donald J. Trump is strong proof of that fact. The sexual revolution may not have overthrown the old regime absolutely but, as we have seen, it has turned inside out a tradition that once dominated the American legal order. And it dramatically changed the rules about modes of conduct and styles of life that were once relegated exclusively to the private sphere.

THE MEANING OF IT ALL

Throughout all the ups and downs of the law—and the ups and downs of norms—a few things remain constant. Every society insists that some kinds of sexual activity *must* be kept private. There are usually rules about exposure of parts of the body. What parts of the body must be concealed and how to conceal them is itself socially determined. There is enormous cultural and historical variation. We live in an age of extraordinary permissiveness. It is an age of "triple x" movies, sex clubs, pornography on the internet, and even live sex shows. But there are limits. Sexual intercourse in the public square would probably lead to arrests, everywhere in the Western world.

Why must sex—and sex organs—stay private, hidden, masked, and disguised? It will not do to simply claim religious reasons or reasons of morality. Our hypothetical couple, making out in the public square, is offending, even if they are married, that is, even if they are people who are permitted—and, indeed, encouraged—to have sex. Married or not, privacy would be an absolute requirement. Part of the reason is surely the idea, common to so many societies, that sex is a vital and yet somehow dangerous activity; it is mighty and disruptive, and it must be carefully limited and controlled. If unchecked, it could destroy what people have considered civilization. Moreover, sex is both infectious and addictive. Yet, unlike alcohol or heroin, people cannot give it up completely; not only would that be too much to ask of people, but it would also be the end of the human race. Infectious seems more like it. Infections can be cabined and quarantined. The same may be true of sex.

This notion was widely accepted, at least implicitly, in the nineteenth century. Sex between married people was okay in limited amounts. Anything else was forbidden. It was a period of enormous prudery, on the surface at least. There was a vigorous Victorian underground, a massive world of hidden sexuality. But public life, public literature, and public discussion were riddled with taboos. Victorians justified some of their prudery by quoting the Bible and religious norms. But the Victorian attitude toward sex clearly went beyond religion. It was grounded on a theory of society: a theory of what society needed, what society must have, to keep on an even keel.

This theory of society led to a rigorous insistence on bodily privacy. The naked truth of the body had to be kept private, out of view. Nudity was bad. It was also uncommon. Ordinary people did not bathe, or did so pretty rarely. The modern shower is a late development. In crowded houses, where, as we said, there was little privacy, there was also little nudity. Indeed, many married people took off as little clothing as possible, even during the sex act. In the famous Kinsey Report, published in 1953, on the sexual behavior of women, a third of the women born before 1900 said they were generally "clothed" during intercourse. Sex was private; and the act was done as surreptitiously as possible. Krafft-Ebbing thought that only "savage races" had sex in the open, like animals.[111] Dr. Frank Lydston, who wrote books about sex hygiene in the early twentieth century, called for a "less intimate association of husband and wife." He made this recommendation for the sake of "health and morals." The less man and wife knew about each other's bodies, the better: privacy was "an individual right, in or out of matrimony." The couple should not, he thought, sleep in the same bed. Sharing a bed made "personal privacy" impossible and could lead to sexual "excess."[112] One wonders who, if anybody, actually followed Lydston's advice, but the fact that he gave this kind of advice tells us something about social attitudes, at least among certain elites.

CONCLUSION

Privacy norms surrounding sex remain strong, but, as we have seen, there is no longer an ironclad rule that the body, or at least its "private parts," have to remain that way: private. Exposing the body has become more a matter of choice or context. You can, if you wish, join a nudist colony or visit a nude beach. Similarly, you can go to San Francisco and join a "nude-in" or go with the flow of naked bike-riders. *Forced* bodily privacy has declined; now it is essentially a matter for each person to decide. In *Lake v. Wal-Mart Stores*, a Minnesota case from 1998,[113] Elli Lake and Melissa Weber—nineteen and twenty years old, respectively—went on vacation in Mexico, in 1995, along with Weber's sister. The sister photographed Lake and Weber naked in the shower together. After their Mexican adventure, Lake and Weber gave five rolls of film to Wal-Mart in Dilworth, Minnesota, but Wal-Mart refused to print the offending pictures "because of their nature." Apparently, though, one employee did print out the photographs and copies "were circulating in the community." The two brought an action against Wal-Mart for invasion of privacy. The Minnesota court was sympathetic: "One's naked body is a very private part of one's person and generally known to others only by choice."[114] The key word is "choice."

Not that the old taboos are completely dead. The law on nudity is complex and the corpus of social norms—customs, rules of etiquette, common understandings—is even more complex. And that corpus of norms is not necessarily consistent with the letter of the law. Most people know, by instinct, and by life in society, what social "rules" govern nudity and partial nudity. A bikini is fine at the beach. It would be scandalous in church and weird in a department store. Region also makes a different. Some parts of the United States (and the world) are far less tolerant than, say, San Francisco. When, in August 2012, it was revealed that a congressman from Kansas had gone skinny-dipping in the Sea of Galilee during a political junket to Israel—he was in the water for all of ten seconds—it made headlines; he earned for himself a harsh scolding from the House majority leader.[115]

Behavior that seems threatening or abusive or pathological is still mostly forbidden. Otherwise, stripping is in many ways (although not entirely) a matter of free choice. In 1998, when the *Wal-Mart* case was decided, film still had to be developed. This put Lake and Weber at the mercy of Wal-Mart. Lake and Weber chose nudity, and chose to record it; they were "public" in the sense that Weber's sister took the photographs and perhaps they wanted to share these beautiful moments with other people. Because of the technology of film at the time, they lost control of their choice. Today, they would have more control—in a way. They could take photographs on their smart phone, and mail these photos to other people, without the mediation of a third party. The ordinary camera, too, is now supplemented by more powerful and intrusive surveillance devices—a whole armory of ways to invade people's privacy, without their permission and without their knowledge. This makes the problem of bodily privacy, as we will see in later chapters, much more complicated.

Our brief jaunt through the law of bodily privacy has shown us how much the old rules, the Victorian rules, have been eroded. But the nudist utopia of a world where clothing is optional is still a long way off (and we may never get there). The rules have simply been refined and redefined. There are well-understood norms and customs that practically everyone follows. The underlying *theory* of bodily privacy has also changed drastically. Still, it is far from gone. The average person might not be able to articulate a really good reason why sex in broad daylight in the park, or even on a nude beach, should be illegal. But that average person is sure that the behavior would be wrong. And illegal to boot. Mandatory privacy, as discussed in this chapter, has changed its form, but is still very much alive.

NOTES

1. On the privacy implications of this type of airport screening technology, see Jeffrey Rosen, *The Naked Crowd: Reclaiming Security and Freedom in an Anxious Age* (New York: Random House, 2004), 3–7, 93–95.

2. Aimee Green, "Northeast Portland Man Who Stripped Naked at Airport Is Acquitted of Indecent Exposure Charge," *Oregonian*, July 18, 2012; Kate Mather, "Naked Man Arrested at Portland International Airport after Disrobing at Security Checkpoint," *Oregonian*, Apr. 17, 2012; Sara Roth, "After Ninth Circuit Loss, Naked Airport Protester John Brennan Says 'I Would Do It Again,'" *KGW8.com*, May 17, 2017.

3. Or. Rev. Stat. § 163.465(1)(c) (2020).

4. *Brennan v. U.S. Dep't of Homeland Security*, 691 Fed. Appx. 332 (9th Cir. 2017).

5. *Id.* at 332.

6. Mitchell S. Jackson, "Who Gets to Be a 'Naked Athena'?," *New York Times*, July 25, 2020.

7. N.Y. Penal Law § 245.01 (McKinney 2020).

8. Bruce Golding, "Naked Gal Gets Deal on a Suit: 15G for Times Sq. Bust," *New York Post*, Sept. 4, 2012.

9. *See Roe v. Wade*, 410 U.S. 113, 165–66 (1973), the famous abortion case, resting on a line of cases that goes back to *Griswold v. Connecticut*, 381 U.S. 479, 485–86 (1965), in which the Court recognized a constitutional right of privacy that included the right of married couples to buy and use contraception.

10. *But see* Anita L. Allen, *Unpopular Privacy: What Must We Hide?* (Oxford, UK: Oxford University Press, 2011).

11. *See* "Heir It Is! Pics of Naked Harry You've Already Seen on the Internet," *Sun*, Aug. 24, 2012, at 1.

12. Genesis 9:24–26; *see also* Leviticus 18:5–30, which lists a series of sexual taboos against "uncovering" the "nakedness" of relatives. What this seems to mean, however, is that sexual intercourse with these relatives (by blood or marriage) is forbidden, rather than a ban on exposing their bodies.

13. "Art Leader Jailed as Virginians Battle over Murals and Morals," *Atlanta Constitution*, Feb. 29, 1936, at 17.

14. "Justice Department Covers Partially Nude Statues," *USA Today*, Jan. 29, 2002.

15. *Id.*

17. Martin S. Weinberg, "Sexual Modesty and the Nudist Camp," *Social Problems* 12, no. 3 (1965): 311, 312–16. *See* Maren Möehring, *Marmorleiber: Koerperbildung in der deutschen Nacktkultur (1890–1930)* (Göttingen, Germany: Bohlau Verlag, 2004); Chad Ross, *Naked Germany: Health, Race, and the Nation* (New York: Berg Publishers, 2005), 1.

19. "Germany Suppresses Nudist Movement as Menace to Morality," *Chicago Tribune*, Mar. 8, 1933, at 7.

20. "Judge Glimpses Nudist Movies; Says: Indecent," *Chicago Daily Tribune*, Sept. 18, 1936, at 3.

21. *See, e.g.*, Sarah Netter, "Family Pics May Lead to Deportation," *ABC News*, Mar. 30, 2010.

22. American Nudist Research Library, http://www.anrl.org.

23. Betsy Malloy, "Nudist Beach Etiquette: Guide to Nude Beach Behavior," *Tripsavvy*, Dec. 31, 2018.

24. Utah Code Ann. § 76–9–702(1) (West 2020).

25. *See* Laurel Wamsley, "Utah Woman Charged with Lewdness after Being Topless in Her Own Home," *NPR*, Nov. 21, 2019; Maria Cramer, "Utah Judge Rules against Woman Who Was Topless in Her Own Garage," *New York Times*, Jan. 22, 2020.

26. For a state-by-state rundown, *see* Richard A. Posner and Katharine B. Silbaugh, *A Guide to America's Sex Laws* (Chicago: University of Chicago Press, 1996), 83–97.

27. Ala. Code § 13A-12–130 (2020). This code section also has a more general provision, against any "lewd act in a public place," which is likely to be "observed by others who would be affronted or alarmed." *Id.*

28. Utah Code § 76–9–702 (2020). Here, too, there is a general clause that covers "any other act of lewdness."

29. Conn. Gen. Stat. § 53a-186 (West 2020). "Public place" is defined as "any place where the conduct may reasonably be expected to be viewed by others." *Id.*

30. Cal. Penal Code § 314 (West 2020); Mich. Comp. Laws Ann. § 750.335a.

31. Cal. Penal Code § 314 (West 2020). It is also a crime to help or advise anybody to commit the crime, or to "take part in any model artist exhibition, or to make any other exhibition of himself to public view," if this is "offensive to decency, or is adapted to excite to vicious or lewd thoughts or acts." The California Code also specifically allows counties and cities to have ordinances that regulate the "exposure of the genitals or buttocks . . . or the breasts" of waiters and waitresses. Cal. Penal Code § 318.5 (2012).

32. 28 Ind. Code sec. 35-45-4-1 (West 2020)

33. *See, e.g.*, 18 Pa. Cons. Stat. § 3127, which bumps up indecent exposure to a more serious misdemeanor if it is committed in the presence of a person who is under sixteen; *Gabbard v. State*, 285 S.W.2d 515, at 515 (Ark. 1956), arose under a statute that made it a crime to "knowingly and intentionally expose . . . private parts" to anyone under the age of sixteen, if done "with lascivious intent."

34. 497 P.2d 807, 808 (Cal. 1972).

35. *Compare In re Dallas W.*, 85 Cal. App. 4th 937 (2000) *with People v. Archer*, 98 Cal. App. 4th 402 (2002).

36. *Van Houten v. State*, 46 N.J.L. 16 (1884).

37. John M. Macdonald, *Indecent Exposure* (Springfield, IL: Charles C. Thomas Publisher, 1973), 3, 10.

38. These figures were dwarfed by the number of arrests for "lewd and lascivious behavior," which were on the order of a thousand a year. California State Assembly, Assembly Office of Research, "A Statistical Description of Arrests and Disposition of Arrests for Twelve Sex Crimes in California," (1979); *see also* Stuart P. Green, "To See and Be Seen: Reconstructing the Law of Voyeurism and Exhibitionism," *American Criminal Law Review* 55 (2018): 203; Home Office & Office for National

Statistics, Ministry of Justice, "An Overview of Sexual Offending in England and Wales," 6 (2013).

39. However, in the past, "public" exposure was not always necessary if the victim was a child. *See, e.g.*, *Gabbard v. State*, 285 S.W.2d 515, at 515 (Ark. 1956). The case construed an Arkansas statute that read: "It shall be unlawful for any person with lascivious intent to knowingly and intentionally expose his or her private parts or genital organs to any other person, male or female, under the age of sixteen (16) years."

40. *Wisneski v. State*, 921 A.2d. 273, 275 (Md. 2007).

41. Cal. Penal Code § 318.5(a) (West 2020).

42. *Id.* § 318.6.

43. *Crownover v. Musick*, 9 Cal. 3d 405, 425 (1973), overruled by *Morris v. Mun. Court*, 32 Cal. 3d 553 (1982).

44. "Nude" was defined to include male and female genitalia, and female breasts "below the areola."

45. Martinez was arrested under the ordinance, pleaded guilty, and was put on probation. In the following years, he showed more and more signs of mental illness. In 2006, he was arrested after a fight in a halfway house. He committed suicide in his cell.

46. S.F. Police Code art. 15.3, § 1071.1 (2011).

47. *In re Smith*, 497 P.2d 807, 810 (Cal. 1972).

48. S.F. Ordinance 110967, introduced Sept. 6, 2011.

49. "Proposed San Francisco Law Provokes Naked Ambitions," *Pioneer Press*, September 24, 2011.

50. *Id.*

51. Joanna Grossman and Lawrence Friedman, "Towels Under Tailbones? Naked San Franciscans Protest Proposed Restrictions on Public Nudity," *Justia: Verdict*, Oct. 4, 2011.

52. Denis Binder, "Public Nudity and the Arousal Police in San Francisco," *Binder's Blog*, October 1, 2011.

53. *Id.*

54. Grossman and Friedman, *supra* note 51.

55. S.F., Cal., Police Code art. 2, § 154 (2020).

56. *Taub v. City & County of San Francisco,* 696 Fed. Appx. 181 (9th Cir. 2017).

57. Chad Love, "Washington Man Spotted Fishing Nude," *Field & Stream*, August 16, 2011.

58. "A Brief Conversation with a Topless New Yorker about Her Outfit," *Racked.com*, May 18, 2012.

59. J. David Goodman, "See Topless Woman? Just Move On, Police Are Told," *New York Times*, May 13, 2013, at A21.

60. Lauren Evans, "Woman Sues NYC After Arrest for Going Topless in Brooklyn Park," *Gothamist.com*, Oct. 8, 2013.

61. For a rich documentation of all of this, *see* Philip Carr-Gomm, *A Brief History of Nakedness* (London: Reaktion Books, 2010).

62. *Id.* at 144–45.

63. *See Naked and Afraid*, Discovery.com.

64. *Id.* at 233–34.

65. Mark Whittaker, "New Tour at Museum Reveals All," *New York Times*, May 2, 2012, at C1.

66. Dailymail.com, April 4, 2018; for more on Bare Necessities Cruises, *see* their website, https://cruisebare.com.

67. Mark Roberts, The Streaker, http://www.thestreaker.org.uk/main.htm.

68. 501 U. S. 560. 562–63 (1991). On this and the following case, and the case law in Canada as well, *see* Allen, *supra* note 10, at 78–91.

69. *See* 529 U.S. 277, 282–83 (2000).

70. *See* Jim Goad, "400 Euphemisms for Sexual Intercourse," *Thought Catalog*, Dec. 31, 2014.

71. *See* J. R. Thorpe, "26 Amazing Historical Euphemisms for Sex, Because You Could Stand to Have Your Corn Ground," *Bustle*, Mar. 13, 2015.

72. Ariz. Rev. Stat. § 13–1403 (West 2020).

73. Colo. Rev. Stat. § 18–7–301 (West 2020).

74. *People v. McNamara*, 585 N.E.2d 788, 789 (N.Y. 1991).

75. *Id.* at 791–92.

76. *Id.* at 793.

77. *Id.* at 794–95 (Bellacose, J., dissenting).

78. *See People v. Brown*, 564 N.W.2d 919, 921 (Mich. Ct. App. 1997), which held, in a case where a man was invited into the back room of a massage parlor where he observed two women engaged in a sexual act, that the "key issue in determining whether an act of oral sexual conduct was performed in a 'public place' is not so much the exact location of the act, but whether there is the possibility that the unsuspecting public could be exposed to or view the act"; *State v. Black*, 545 S.W.2d 617, 619 (Ark. 1977) held that the city jail's drunk tank was a "public place" for purposes of the law against lewd acts, because it is "not uncommon for groups of persons to tour a jail and these tourists would "have no difficulty in seeing acts committed." Moreover, the court noted, "families and friends frequently visit inmates and . . . persons coming into the jail customarily pass the 'drunk tank'"; *Del Pilar v. State*, No. 13–11–00191-CR, 2011 WL 6318035 (Tex. Ct. App. 2011), treated, without discussion, a shower room as a public place for sexual indecency purposes.

79. *See* Adam Ragusea, "Gay Teacher Files Sex Discrimination Claim against Georgia School," *NPR*, July 9, 2014. *See also* Amy Leigh Womack, "Mount de Sales, Fired Gay Band Director Settle Discrimination Lawsuit," *The Telegraph*, Aug. 11, 2015.

80. *See, e.g.*, Kate Abbey-Lambertz, "Supporters Rally for Lesbian Teacher Who Was Fired after Getting Pregnant," *HuffPost: Queer Voices*, Sept. 8, 2014; Meredith Bennett-Smith, Carla Hale, "Gay Teacher, Fired from Catholic High School after Being 'Outed' by Mother's Obituary," *HuffPost: Queer Voices*, Apr. 18, 2013.

81. *Koren v. Ohio Bell Tel. Co.*, 894 F. Supp. 2d 1032, 1033–35 (N.D. Ohio 2012).

82. *Id.*; Chris MacColl, *Case Profile: Koren v. Ohio Bell Tel. Co.*, C. R. Litig. Clearinghouse (March 22, 2014).

83. *Bostock v. Clayton County*, 140 S. Ct. 1731 (2020).

84. On this history, see generally Sara Sun Beale, "From Morals and Mattress Tags to Overfederalization," *American University Law Review* 54 (2005): 747, 752–53; Maura Strassberg, "The Crime of Polygamy," *Temple Political & Civil Rights Law Review* 12 (2003): 353; Melissa Murray, "Strange Bedfellows: Criminal Law, Family Law, and the Legal Construction of Intimate Life," *Iowa Law Review* 94 (2009): 1253; Jennifer M. Collins, Ethan J. Lieb, and Dan Markel, "Punishing Family Status," *Boston University Law Review* 88 (2008): 1327, 1345; Martin J. Siegel, "For Better or for Worse: Adultery, Crime & the Constitution," *Journal of Family Law* 30 (1991): 45.

85. *Skinner v. Oklahoma*, 316 U.S. 535 (1942). *See also* Victoria F. Nourse, *In Reckless Hands:* Skinner v. Oklahoma *and the Near Triumph of American Eugenics* (New York: W. W. Norton & Company, 2008).

86. For similar statutes, see 1907 Ind. Acts, ch. 215; 1909 Cal. Stat., ch. 720. *See generally* Mark H. Haller, *Eugenics: Hereditarian Attitudes in American Thought* (New Brunswick, NJ: Rutgers University Press, 1963).

87. *Buck v. Bell*, 274 U.S. 200, 205 (1927).

88. Apparently, the decision was not only callous, but based on wrong facts; none of the women involved were in fact "feeble-minded." *See* Paul A. Lombardo, "Three Generations, No Imbeciles: New Light on *Buck v. Bell*," *New York University Law Review* 60 (1985): 30.

89. *See* James Q. Whitman, *Hitler's American Model: The United States and the Making of Nazi Race Law* (Princeton, NJ: Princeton University Press, 2017); Edwin Black, "Hitler's Debt to America," *The Guardian*, Feb. 5, 2004.

90. Today, involuntary sterilizations of the mentally disabled are allowed, if at all, only in narrow circumstances designed to protect the patient's health or well-being—and not to protect the gene pool. For a modern statute regulating involuntary sterilization, see, for example, Cal. Prob. Code § 1950 *et seq.* (2020).

91. 381 U.S. 479 (1965). *See* John W. Johnson, Griswold v. Connecticut: *Birth Control and the Constitutional Right of Privacy* (Lawrence: University Press of Kansas, 2005); *see also* Joanna L. Grossman, "The Seeds of Early Childhood," *Florida Law Review Forum* 71 (2019): 117; Deborah L. Brake and Joanna L. Grossman, "Reproducing Inequality Under Title IX," *Harvard Journal of Law & Gender* 43 (2020): 171.

92. *Griswold*, 381 U.S. at 480.

93. *Id.* at 485.

94. *Id.*

95. *Eisenstadt v. Baird*, 405 U.S. 438 (1972).

96. *Id.* at 453.

97. *Roe v. Wade*, 410 U.S. 113 (1973). There is, of course, a huge body of literature on this case. *See, e.g.*, David J. Garrow, *Liberty and Sexuality: The Right to Privacy and the Making of* Roe v. Wade (Berkeley: University of California Press, 1998).

98. *See Planned Parenthood v. Casey*, 505 U.S. 833 (1992), holding that abortion restrictions are only invalid if they pose an "undue burden" on a woman's fundamental right to choose; *Gonzales v. Carhart*, 550 U.S. 124 (2007) upheld a federal law banning a particular method of abortion, deemed "partial-birth abortion" by opponents. On these current controversies, *see* Joanna L. Grossman, "What's the

Matter with North Dakota and Arkansas? Two States Pass Highly Restrictive and Unconstitutional Abortion Laws," *Justia: Verdict*, Apr. 2, 2013.

99. *See* Tamar Lewin, "The Bork Hearings: Bork Is Assailed over Remarks on Contraceptive Ruling," *New York Times*, Sept. 19, 1987.

100. *See generally* Thomas C. Grey, "Eros, Civilization and the Burger Court," *Law & Contemporary Problems* 43 (1980): 83.

101. *Bowers v. Hardwick*, 478 U.S. 186 (1986).

102. 539 U.S. 558 (2003).

103. Tex. Penal Code Ann. § 21.06(a) (West 2003).

104. *Lawrence*, 539 U.S. at 567.

105. The Court did set limits: the case did not involve minors, or coercion, or "public conduct or prostitution." *Id.* at 578; *see* Dale Carpenter, *Flagrant Conduct: The Story of* Lawrence v. Texas (New York: W. W. Norton & Company, 2013). Much has been written on the meaning of *Lawrence*. *See, e.g.*, David D. Meyer, "Domesticating Lawrence," *University of Chicago Legal Forum* (2004): 453, 454, arguing that *Lawrence* "is best understood as expanding the boundaries of the fundamental right of privacy, and that the linchpin of this expansion is a broadening conception of *family*." *See also* Cass R. Sunstein, "What Did *Lawrence* Hold? Of Autonomy, Desuetude, Sexuality, and Marriage," *Supreme Court Review* 55 (2003): 27; Ariela R. Dubler, "From *McLaughlin v. Florida* to *Lawrence v. Texas*: Sexual Freedom and the Road to Marriage," *Columbia Law Review* 106 (2006): 1165; William N. Eskridge, Jr., "*Lawrence v. Texas* and the Constitution of Disgust and Contagion," *Florida Law Review* 57 (2005): 1011; Katherine M. Franke, "The Domestic Liberty of *Lawrence v. Texas*," *Columbia Law Review* 104 (2004): 1399.

106. *See* Elimination of Outdated Crimes Amendment Act of 2003, D.C. Law 15–154 (effective Apr. 29, 2004). This law repealed, among other provisions, D.C. Law 22–201 § 3(B), which criminalized adultery.

107. 517 F.3d 738 (5th Cir. 2008).

108. *Id.* at 744. But the Alabama Supreme Court upheld a law aimed at sex toys. *1568 Montgomery Highway Inc., v. City of Hoover*, 45 So. 3d 319 (2010). The company sold books about sex toys (including *The Little Bit Naughty Book of Sex Toys*, along with the toys themselves. For a discussion of these cases, see Curtis Waldo, "Toys Are Us: Sex Toys, Substantive Due Process, and the American Way," *Columbia Journal of Gender & Law* 18 (2009): 807; Manuel Possolo, "Morals Legislation after Lawrence: Can States Criminalize the Sale of Sexual Devices," *Stanford Law Review* 65 (2013): 565.

109. *Obergefell v. Hodges*, 135 S. Ct. 2584, 2607–08 (2015); Karthik Subramanian, "It's a Dildo in 49 States, but It's a Dildon't in Alabama: Alabama's Anti-Obscenity Enforcement Act and the Assault on Civil Liberty and Personal Freedom," *Alabama Civil Rights & Civil Liberties Law Review* 1 (2011): 111.

110. Ella Nilsen, "The Pete Buttigieg Surge, Explained," *Vox*, Nov. 21, 2019.

111. Alfred C. Kinsey et al., *Sexual Behavior in the Human Female* (Bloomington: Indiana University Press, 1948); Krafft-Ebing, *Psychopathia Sexualis* (Philadelphia: F. A. Davis Company, 1894), 2. Obviously, animals have sex without benefit of clothing. Krafft-Ebing saw nudity in sex as primitive, animalistic. Kinsey saw the matter

quite differently: for him, nudity in sex was more natural than unnatural. The human being, after all, was just another animal.

112. G. Frank Lydston, *Sex Hygiene for the Male* (Chicago: The Riverton Press, 1912), 133.

113. 582 N.W.2d 231, 332 (Minn. 1998).

114. Neil M. Richards, "The Limits of Tort Privacy," *Journal on Telecommunications & High Technology Law* 9 (2011): 357, 364–65. Apparently, this was the first case to recognize the tort of invasion of privacy in Minnesota. *See id.*

115. Jennifer Steinhauer, "House Member Is Rebuked after Nude Swim in Israel," *New York Times*, Aug. 21, 2012, at A12.

Chapter 2

Aesthetics and the Body

In chapter 1, we examined the laws and social norms surrounding the naked body, which are rooted, for the most part, in sex-linked taboos. But sex is not the whole story. The law (and custom) sometimes force people to conceal their bodies—or at least bodily functions—in order to protect public "sensibilities" or some sort of aesthetic sense or some sense of what is right and proper. These rules are not, strictly speaking, reflections of sexual taboos, but they are not unrelated.

PUBLIC URINATION AND DEFECATION

Ashley Warden, an Oklahoma mother, was fined $2,500 in 2012 for allowing her three-year-old son, who was undergoing potty training, to pee in the front yard of their house.[1] A police officer spotted the boy before he could finish peeing and issued the ticket. Laws that outlaw urinating and defecating in public reflect a strong social taboo. As the Supreme Court wrote in a case about the privacy implications of a law requiring urine testing for railroad employees: "There are few activities in our society more personal or private than the passing of urine. Most people describe it by euphemisms if they talk about it at all. It is a function traditionally performed without public observation; indeed, its performance in public is generally prohibited by law as well as social custom."[2]

These prohibitions reflect current notions of decency (and disgust).[3] A New Hampshire statute provides that a "person is guilty of a violation if he or she urinates or defecates in a public place, other than a public restroom, under circumstances where the person knew or should have known [it] would likely cause affront or alarm to another."[4] Other state and local laws also use the language of "affront or alarm" to distinguish between criminal and noncriminal public urination.[5]

Urinating and defecating in public have also been prosecuted under laws against public nuisance, littering, or disorderly conduct. The Nebraska Supreme Court upheld a conviction for disorderly conduct on grounds that public urination would be "embraced within the general term 'indecent behavior' and could, by shocking the public sense of morality, be a disorderly act which in our society might tend to disturb the peace and quiet of the city."[6] In New York, the penalties for public urination or defecation depend on whether the citation is written up as a health code violation (a misdemeanor) or as a city littering ticket ($150).[7] Records from 2011 show that New York City issued over fourteen thousand summonses under the health code for public urination and over eleven thousand under the littering provision.[8] A new law enacted in 2017 gives police officers the option of issuing a civil rather than a criminal summons for public urination, as part of a set of reforms designed to "reduce unnecessary interactions with the criminal justice system, especially for minorities."[9] Criminal summonses for public urination were already dropping but the new law resulted in a significant additional reduction. Officers wrote only 387 criminal summonses for public urination in 2017, along with 1,900 civil summonses. Overall, the trend is toward less stringent enforcement of the rule against public urination.

California's public nuisance law allows for punishment of "[a]nything which is injurious to health, or is indecent, or offensive to the senses or an obstruction to the free use of privacy" and which interferes with the "comfortable enjoyment of life or property by an entire community or neighborhood, or by any considerable number of persons."[10] A California appellate court interpreted the word "indecent" to include conduct that is "grossly unseemly or offensive to manners and morals"; this justified upholding the conviction of David McDonald for urinating in a restaurant parking lot.[11] McDonald argued that public urination was not a crime in California; hence the search incident to his arrest—which uncovered his stash of cocaine—was also illegal. (Not surprisingly, much of the litigation over the crime of public urination is really about something more serious.)[12] The prosecutor had argued that even without a statute on urination, McDonald's conduct could be cited as a form of "littering"; his urine constituted a type of "waste matter" that he was forbidden to deposit on the ground. On this point, the appellate court disagreed: urine was not something "ordinarily carried on or about the person," nor something appropriately deposited in trash cans.[13] Nor was it illegal under a statute that targeted intentional dissemination of foul substances (think stink bombs) in public places.[14] In fact, no California law makes public urination explicitly illegal, except in a bus or train.[15] But urinating in public, even in an empty parking lot, was considered a public nuisance in the McDonald case. According to the court, public urination was "injurious to health," "indecent," *and* "offensive to the senses"; any one of these labels would be enough to make this act a public nuisance. The very fact that urination is traditionally performed in private makes its performance in public "indecent." And, given that the "sight and smell of urine are vile and offensive, and those who use the public streets and sidewalks cannot be freely subjected to such unpleasantness," urination near a busy street clearly interfered with the comfortable enjoyment of life and property.[16]

Where McDonald did his deed was crucial. What he did was offensive to the public; hence discreet urination or defecation is less of a concern. The appellate court conceded that "there might well be circumstances in which a single, discreet act of public urination" would not be illegal, such as a "hiker responding to an irrepressible call of nature in an isolated area in the backwoods."[17] A federal court in Michigan had held that a sheriff had no business stopping a man seen urinating along a dirt road at night in the wilderness. Although "public urination in an urban setting would fall within the scope of Michigan's disorderly person statute . . . urinating in the wilderness presents an entirely different matter."[18] Indeed, the court seemed to take judicial notice of local custom, observing that "the act of relieving one's bladder in the woods is not uncommon in northern Michigan"; the officer herself stopped on the way to the police station to allow the man to urinate in the woods a second time. Courts are not blind to the physical realities of the human body; a person accused of public urination or defecation can often claim urgency or necessity.[19]

A New York case observed that a disorderly conduct conviction required more than proof that a person merely urinated in a public place. "A persuasive defense of urgency, necessity or incontinence," the court wrote, "at least when coupled with the unavailability of nearby restroom facilities and with reasonable efforts by the defendant to conceal his act, would negative some or all of the elements required for conviction under [the disorderly conduct law.]"[20] An appellate court in a prior New York case had dismissed charges of public urination against someone who urinated in a classroom where he had been taking an exam on the grounds that the defendant's conduct might have "resulted from a momentary and unanticipatable lack of physical control."[21] But Jeffrey Churchwell inexcusably violated local custom when he had the practice of defecating near a building in a public park and did this for two years.[22] A high school English teacher, Churchwell was caught after police received a complaint and observed that his car was frequently at the scene in the presence of brand-new fecal matter. He was fined $375 for disorderly conduct and had to pay $5,705 in restitution for the past clean-up jobs by the public works department. Churchwell was clearly not driven by necessity—or an "irrepressible call of nature." He had access to toilets at home and work. He told the investigators that he did the dirty deed in the public park "to be disrespectful, but also because it was convenient." But he realized after getting caught that he was "being an idiot."

Although public urination is not a new problem, the homelessness issue has made it more salient. This issue has led many cities to adopt express bans on public urination, if they did not have one on the books already. This is of course a controversial move.[23] Most cities do not have enough public restrooms to handle the needs of the homeless; piling up public urination fines against this poor and downtrodden population only leads to a cycle of imprisonment.[24] Some cities have deliberately kept the number of public restrooms small and used public urination laws as a dragnet; others have tried to address the problem with more public toilets.[25] And some cities have gone for more creative solutions to the problem of public urination. Officials in Hamburg, Germany, painted walls outside of bars and nightclubs with "hydrophobic" paint that makes the walls pee back—urine bounces off the wall and onto the ankles of the offender.[26] San Francisco began to experiment with this paint after conceding defeat in the battle to enforce a public urination ordinance the city adopted in 2002. The "constant acrid stench all over the city" suggests that citations and fines do not deter people who "prefer to answer the law of nature over the law of the city."[27] In 2014, the city started its "Pit Stop" program to install public toilets in neighborhoods with high homeless populations; in 2016, the city installed its first open-air urinal designed to combat the city's public urination problem.[28]

But for the homeless, it seems cruel and ironic to talk about what they "prefer." They often have no choice in the matter. Privacy is not the issue; the very existence of an army of the homeless poor irritates and disturbs the comfortable classes. People would like somehow to get rid of the sad figures dressed in rags, pushing shopping carts, and mucking up the urban landscape. Panhandlers, beggars, and tramps have never been popular. And when they foul the streets in front of, say, a restaurant, they are bad for business, as well as offensive to eyes and noses. Public toilets in many cities and parks, if they are truly public, quickly become filthy, smelly, and sinister. Hence the proliferation of pay toilets in many cities—clean, sanitary, and beyond the pocketbooks of the homeless. In society, there is a kind of perpetual battle between classes, between the poor and the nonpoor. The poor almost always lose these battles. A well-dressed member of the middle class walking about in downtown Chicago or Philadelphia who suddenly feels the call of nature can simply walk into the lobby of a hotel and search for a restroom; no one will notice or care. The homeless man with a shopping cart has no such privilege.

This distinction in habits and privileges is obvious. Is there any solution to the problem? Many cities have tried harsh measures. Others have gone the other way and tried to help the homeless. In November 2019, San Francisco elected a new district attorney, Chesa Boudin. Boudin, the most liberal candidate in a liberal city, announced that he would no longer enforce rules against public urination.[29]

The controversies about public urination reflect the tension between meeting the basic human needs for some residents and protecting the sensibilities of other residents who want to use the streets and parks without stumbling over human waste. Installation and maintenance of public toilets would ease this tension but the homeless issue led to the opposite situation: a decline rather than an increase in public facilities. Homeless people are not the only ones who suffer from the lack of public toilets. Taxi drivers have no obvious place to go to the bathroom while working, and neither do people working on power and phone lines.[30] But, as Taunya Lovell Banks argues, American society resists the provision of public toilets because "American societal norms treated bodily excretions with a sense of disgust and disdain."[31] The potential exposure of genitals during urination adds an additional wrinkle; as Banks pointed out in 2020, "thirteen states require persons convicted of public urination to register as sex offenders!"[32]

People in the developed world, for the most part, do not worry about privacy in urinating or defecating. For them, technology, indoor plumbing, and middle-class norms and rights have made this a nonissue. In poor countries, millions of people do not have this luxury. Bangladesh is one such country. Authorities in Bangladesh put up signs in Arabic reading "Do not urinate here!" The point was to induce the Muslim population not to relieve themselves in public; Arabic is the language of the Koran, and the theory was that using Arabic might dissuade the population from peeing in public.[33] One wonders if this tactic could have much success. Public urination and defection are huge problems in India, where tens of millions have no alternative. This is seen—obviously—as a public health issue, if nothing else. The Indian government is trying to solve this problem by providing toilet facilities for those who lack access to ways to satisfy this basic human need.[34]

UGLY LAWS

Few people in the United States would be surprised to learn that their city or state prohibited public urination or defecation; the laws reflect a pretty universal sentiment that these bodily functions should be tended to in a hygienic manner and in private. But local governments have not always limited their privacy mandates to these common affronts. A Chicago ordinance, adopted around 1881, was addressed to "Any person who is diseased, maimed, mutilated or in any way deformed as to be an unsightly or disgusting object or improper person to be allowed in or on the public ways or other public places in this city." Such a person was not to "expose himself to public view, under a penalty of not less than one dollar for each offense."[35] The law further provided that the fine could be suspended "if it shall seem proper and just," and if the convicted person could be "well cared for" at the police station until "he can be committed to the county poor house." This last portion makes clear the law's goal: not to punish but to remove the "unsightly" person from public sight. Indeed, according to one researcher, there was only one newspaper report about the Chicago ordinance when it was first passed, and it declared in all capital letters that it "WILL BE A PUBLIC BENEFIT" to move "crippled beggars" to the poorhouse because they can impose a "shock to the ordinary nerves."[36]

Laws making it a crime for people with certain disfigurements to appear in public had in fact appeared earlier—as early as 1867 in the case of San Francisco, according to Susan Schweik.[37] Schweik documents the rise, use, and fall of these "unsightly beggar" laws—laws which the disability rights movement later called "ugly laws."[38] The Chicago ordinance was adopted in part because an alderman wanted to rid the city of "street obstructions," especially an injured mother who incessantly played "Mollie Darling" on a street organ.[39] Other cities had already adopted "unsightly beggar" laws, to prevent the truly disfigured—and those faking it for sympathy—from offending people or, worse, relying on guilt to elicit a handout. Although disfigurement was explicitly a requirement under each of these laws, their real focus was begging rather than simple exposure of a maimed body.[40] The Chicago ordinance makes no reference to beggars, however; any person with an offending body who appeared in public could be guilty of violating it.[41] Although the text of the law and the language used to describe it suggest a general dehumanizing of disabled people, the reality seems somewhat more complex. It was the combination of disability and economic need that triggered the harsh law. "It was understood," one scholar noted, "that the ugly law was not intended as a blanket indictment of all physically disabled people but would only affect those disabled people who were unable to support themselves through their wages or pensions."[42] The "ugly" were permitted to work for wages, as far as historians can tell.[43]

The laws were repealed at various points during the twentieth century, but enforced, at least in one reported case in Nebraska, as late as 1974.[44] The Chicago ordinance was still on the books in 1973, when two aldermen successfully called for repeal of the "barbaric" law they deemed a "throwback to the dark ages."[45] The passage of the Americans with Disabilities Act—and changes in the culture—probably means that no such law or ordinance could survive a challenge today; in any event, this kind of discrimination solely on the basis of looks would be struck down on any number of grounds.

No one these days would be so crass as to come out in favor of laws against the ugly. But more subtle forms have persisted. And here, too, sex, the tiger in the cage, is at the bottom of these rules—rules that insist on keeping the body private. In parts of Nepal, menstruating women are banished from society; they live apart from the rest of the community, in sheds and huts, until their period is over.[46] And although laws in the United States do not go this far, there are many ways in which they reflect the common narrative that people who menstruate are "dirty, impure, and even dangerous."[47] In the next sections, we discuss rules about breastfeeding in public and rules that discriminate, in one way or another, against women who are obviously pregnant.

THE FEMALE BREAST

As we discussed in chapter 1, laws about public nudity focus chiefly on the genitals. The female breast is a more complicated case. For the most part, indecent exposure laws do not include the female breast in the definition of indecency. The Model Penal Code, for example, mentions only exposure of genitals (and only if done "for the purpose of arousing or gratifying sexual desire").[48] Many state laws refer to "private parts" or some other vague category, without specifying whether breasts are included. In at least some of those states, courts have ruled that exposing the female breast is not "indecent," and thus is not banned by the statute.[49]

A handful of states clearly and intentionally define "private part" to include the female breast "below the areola." But even those laws, in most cases, require "lewdness" in addition to simple exposure. In a 1972 New York case, *People v. Gilbert*, the court held that a woman sunbathing nude at a public beach was not guilty of indecent exposure, even though the law expressly applied to the female breast; she was not behaving "lewdly," which the statute required.[50]

Female toplessness is not part of American culture, at least outside of theaters and other places that feature "adult" entertainment and there are definitely social restrictions on bare breasts. They do not always go unchallenged. Sometimes feminists protest over the unequal treatment of the female versus the male breast. Sometimes the focus is on the occasional nude sunbather. More often the issue is public breastfeeding, which we will deal with later.

In the 1980s, four women went bare-chested in a public park in Rochester, New York, to protest a ban on toplessness that applied to women but not men. After the *Gilbert* decision, in favor of the nude sunbather, the legislature had amended its indecency law to prohibit all nudity, lewd or not. The women, part of a group known as the "Topfree Seven"—they deliberately avoided "topless" in favor of "topfree" to avoid association with strip clubs—apparently did this every year, and got arrested every year, but the district attorney always dismissed the charges.[51] But not in 1986. The women were prosecuted for indecent exposure and convicted. They appealed on constitutional grounds. The state's highest court, in *People v. Santorelli*, reversed the convictions. The court did not reach the constitutional issue.[52] It held, instead, that the statute, despite its blanket prohibition of the exposure of the female breast, was "'aimed at discouraging 'topless' waitresses and their promoters'" and did not apply to bare breasts in situations that were neither commercial nor lewd.[53]

A concurring judge in *Santorelli* wrote separately, arguing that the judges were misreading the statute. It was not limited, he thought, to bare breasts that were either exposed as an incidence of a business that thrived on bare breasts or were just plain lewd. The majority, he felt, had merely indulged in "artful means of avoiding a confrontation with an important constitutional problem."[54] In his view, the statute did apply to the Rochester women, but was invalid because it violated the equal protection guarantee of the New York and federal constitutions. The state did not, in his opinion, have a good enough reason for singling out women and making them wear shirts. The statute "betray[ed] an underlying legislative assumption that the sight of a female's uncovered breast in a public place is offensive to the average person in a way that the sight of a male's uncovered breast is not."[55] But "protecting public sensibilities" is not enough to outweigh the harm to women of differential treatment. The judge relied on evidence from the Kinsey report and other sources on human sexuality, to the effect that the "female breast is no more or less a sexual organ than is the male equivalent."[56] This of course is debatable, if not downright wrong. But the good judge did have a point. The very fact, he felt, that the female breast might arouse men more than the converse is "itself a suspect cultural artifact rooted in centuries of prejudice and bias toward women."[57] Therefore, according to the judge, the state could not justify a "law that discriminates against women by prohibiting them from removing their tops and exposing their bare chests in public as men are routinely permitted to do."[58]

It follows that Moira Johnston—the topless woman of Union Square we mentioned in chapter 1—was right when she claimed the right to go topless on the streets of New York City. Perhaps, too, the New Hampshire woman who voted topless in a primary election of 2020 was also within her rights. She had been wearing an anti-Trump T-shirt. Told that she could not vote while wearing a shirt with a political candidate featured on it, she whipped it off and voted. After voting, she put it back on.[59]

The movement in support of public female toplessness grew stronger in the 1990s. The "Free the Nipple" movement began in 2012 but was inspired by the Topfree Seven, who litigated the *Santorelli* case two decades earlier.[60] Advocacy groups like this one have brought several lawsuits to challenge public nudity laws that ban exposure of the female breast. Their advocacy has also led to the repeal of several public nudity laws. Although many of these challenges have been unsuccessful, a federal appellate court held in 2019 that an ordinance in Fort Collins, Colorado, that banned the exposure of women's but not men's chests violated the Equal Protection Clause of the Fourteenth Amendment. In that case, *Free the Nipple—Fort Collins v. City of Fort Collins*, the court viewed the ordinance much as the court had in *Santorelli*. The government's only interest in banning female toplessness was rooted in impermissible stereotypes about female breasts.[61] The court in the Fort Collins case was simply not convinced that female breasts were different in a way that could justify the discriminatory rule. Other federal appellate courts had ruled to the contrary—holding, respectively, in three cases that banning female toplessness was necessary to protect "traditional norms and public order"; to protect "the order, morality, health, safety, and well-being of the populace"; and to "protect . . . moral sensibilities."[62] At the root of these cases is a fear of what might happen if the "erogenous" breast is unveiled. Major League Baseball issued a lifetime ban on two women who exposed their breasts during a World Series game; they are forever barred from all games and stadiums.[63]

PUBLIC BREASTFEEDING

New York law, like the law in many states, expressly deals with one common form of toplessness: breastfeeding. In New York, women are exempt from any criminal prosecution for any exposure of the breast that may result from breastfeeding.[64]

Many other states make it clear, by law, that breastfeeding, in public as well as in private, is not an offense. The law in Washington State, for example, specifically states that neither breastfeeding nor expressing breast milk constitutes "indecent exposure."[65] In Illinois, breastfeeding an infant "is not an act of public indecency."[66] Louisiana makes clear that breastfeeding is not "obscene."[67] Montana adds that breastfeeding is neither "sexual conduct," "indecent exposure," obscene, nor a "nuisance."[68] Rhode Island says it is neither "indecent exposure" nor "disorderly conduct."[69]

Clearly, under these statutes, a woman can breastfeed in any public space—outdoors, in parks, on beaches, and the like. But nursing moms want to be able to breastfeed wherever they happen to be—in Walmart, a doctor's office, or on a crowded airplane. There have been incidents where women have been thrown out of private establishments or asked to cover up. What rights, if any, do women have to breastfeed in these places?

As a general matter, proprietors of private businesses have the right to set their own rules for customer behavior, as well as the right to exclude customers for noncompliance. Civil rights laws do prevent businesses from using their rights in a discriminatory way. Federal law (the Civil Rights Act) addresses race and sex discrimination; it prevents restaurants, for example, from keeping out African Americans or from segregating customers by race.[70] In many states, public accommodations laws are broader than the federal law: they ban, for instance, discrimination on the basis of sex or sexual orientation; Courts are unlikely to interpret the law in such a way as to force restaurants to admit naked customers or even topless women, but it might apply to breastfeeding in restaurants.[71]

This might not even be necessary. Women's groups have long agitated for broader breastfeeding rights. Most states now explicitly provide, in their public accommodations laws, that women may breastfeed in public or private places.[72] Most of these provisions were adopted in the last twenty years. The public breastfeeding laws have minor variations. Some are tied explicitly to the public accommodations law, and thus would depend on what is defined as a "public accommodation." Others are stand-alone provisions that apply only to breastfeeding. California's law, for example, protects a woman's right to breastfeed in any location other than someone else's house.[73] Illinois provides an unfettered right to breastfeed in public unless the mother is in a "place of worship," where she is expected to "follow the appropriate norms within that place of worship."[74] Virginia only protects breastfeeding on property owned or leased by the state.[75]

Most breastfeeding statutes, however, grant a mother the right to breastfeed in any location in which she is otherwise authorized to be. A few states allow breastfeeding anywhere, but require that it be done discreetly, which seems to mean that a woman should use something to cover the baby and the breast. Mothers in Missouri must exercise "as much discretion as possible," when nursing in public or private locations. The Minnesota provision, in contrast, states that a mother may breastfeed in a place of public accommodation "irrespective of whether the nipple of the mother's breast is uncovered during or incidental to breastfeeding."

Although the federal civil rights law does not cover sex discrimination in public accommodations (probably nobody thought it was necessary), Congress later directly addressed the issue of public breastfeeding. A 1999 amendment to a postal appropriations bill provided that "a woman may breastfeed her child at any location in a federal building or on federal property, if the woman and her child are otherwise authorized to be present at the location."[76] This makes courthouses, government buildings, and national parks and forests all safe places for public breastfeeding.

In states without broad protection for breastfeeding, nursing mothers may still be subject to the whims of private business owners. In one case, *DeRungs v. Wal-Mart* (2004), a federal appellate court held that Ohio's public accommodations law does not prohibit pregnancy discrimination and therefore does not prohibit lactation discrimination; discrimination against breastfeeding women, the court held, is not a form of unlawful sex discrimination.[77] The woman, while shopping at Walmart, attempted to nurse her son while sitting on a bench outside a dressing room. An employee told her to feed him inside the bathroom, or leave the store. Other plaintiffs in the case described similar experiences at Walmart stores. But Walmart won the right to exclude—at least temporarily. The Ohio legislature amended its code the following year to provide that "a mother is entitled to breast-feed her baby in any location of a place of public accommodation wherein the mother is otherwise permitted."[78]

As we saw, the police sometimes arrest topless women on the theory that they are breaking the law—even when they are not. Similarly, breastfeeding mothers are sometimes thrown out of public and private places even when the law clearly protects them. Emily Gillette was forced off a Delta Air Lines plane (still at the gate, fortunately) in 2006 for refusing to cover her baby's head with a blanket while she was breastfeeding. She and her husband and daughter occupied an entire row, near the rear of the plane. The nursing infant's head was facing the aisle, leaving little or none of the mother's breast exposed to passersby. But a flight attendant who claimed to be offended gave Gillette a blanket and insisted that she use it to cover the baby's head. She pleaded for the pilot to intervene, but he claimed that the flight attendant was in control of the cabin. Gillette and her family were escorted off the plane and told to take some other flight from Burlington, Vermont, to their final destination.

Yet Vermont very clearly protects a woman's right to breastfeed in public. Vermont's public accommodations law provides: "Notwithstanding any other provision of law, a mother may breastfeed her child in any place of public accommodation in which the mother and child would otherwise have a legal right to be."[79] The legislature added this provision in 2001, based on its finding that "breastfeeding a child is an important, basic and natural act of nurture that should be encouraged in the interest of enhancing maternal, child and family health." Another case before the Vermont Human Rights Commission made clear that this provision does not require that breastfeeding mothers cover themselves or their babies when nursing in a place of public accommodation. Yet Gillette—like the naked protester at Portland airport security discussed in chapter 1—had no way to insist on her rights at that moment.

After the incident, Gillette filed a complaint with the Vermont Human Rights Commission, the state agency charged with implementing the state's civil rights laws.[80] She went on to file a lawsuit against two smaller carriers who handled that particular flight for Delta. Each claim was settled for

$20,000.[81] But confrontations over public breastfeeding continue to occur. In 2012, a Michigan mother was loudly chided for discreetly nursing her five-month-old baby in the back of a courtroom; she was waiting to appear in court regarding a ticket.[82] The baby was sick and, after waiting for quite some time in the courtroom, also quite hungry. The baby had not escaped the watchful eye of the bailiff, who slipped the judge a note saying that "there is a woman breastfeeding in court." The judge then called the mother up to the front of the courtroom and asked her if she thought it was "appropriate" to breastfeed in court. Her response, according to her blog post about the incident, was, "Considering the fact that my son is hungry, and he's sick, and the fact that it's not illegal, I don't find it inappropriate." The judge, however, was of a different mind. The mother recalls that he said "something to the effect of 'It's my court, it's my decision, and I do find it inappropriate.'"[83] Michigan exempts public breastfeeding from the criminal law on public nudity but was one of the few states that did not protect breastfeeding in any other way.[84]

This courtroom exchange became a national news story. So did stories about women who were asked, in stores and government offices, to do their breastfeeding in restrooms rather than in more comfortable and sanitary places where, however, they could be seen by other customers or patrons.[85] These incidents provoked controversy and, from nursing mothers and their supporters, a good deal of outrage. In recent decades, breastfeeding has become more popular; it is considered both healthier and more natural. A kind of grassroots movement has grown up to protect and encourage the right to breastfeed. The La Leche League International is devoted to the promotion of breastfeeding.[86] According to its website, in 1950 or so, only about one mother out of five breastfed. Then the movement really got going. There are branches in dozens of countries and one can read promotional literature in all major languages, not to mention Icelandic and Basque.

The breastfeeding movement has had enormous success; it has convinced more and more mothers to breastfeed, and it has also been a factor in the adoption of some forty or more public breastfeeding laws in just over a decade. Still, many people seem to be unaware of the law and some institutions routinely violate it. Incidents like the Delta Air Lines dispute presumably raise awareness of the law, and they may help change attitudes. And companies, afraid of fines and bad publicity, might be induced to adopt more respectful policies.

Emily Gillette's incident with Delta Air Lines, for example, provoked not only litigation in federal court, but also, and perhaps more powerfully, a national "nurse-in"—a form of protest that is now a common response by activists when women are ejected from public places for breastfeeding. In a "nurse-in," breastfeeding mothers converge en masse at a particular business or location to protest the lack of support for public breastfeeding. The social media, Facebook, Twitter, and the rest, act (as usual) as tools of this small revolution. They can turn an incident into a national scandal in minutes. The nurse-in that followed Gillette's exclusion was staged at Delta ticket counters at thirty airports across the country.[87] Similar nurse-ins have been staged at Starbucks (the site of more than one breastfeeding incident), at Walmart, at Facebook headquarters (after the company was accused of removing photos that showed breastfeeding), and at Whole Foods. A 2011 nurse-in was held at 250 Target stores to protest an incident in which a woman who was nursing her baby while sitting on the floor of the women's clothing department was asked repeatedly to move to a fitting room.[88] Target issued a statement that female guests are welcome to "breastfeed in public areas," as well as to breastfeed in a fitting room "even if others are waiting to use the fitting rooms."[89] So-called lactation activists also stage marches and meetings to raise awareness about public breastfeeding rights. One held in August 2012 on the National Mall in Washington, D.C., was alternately referred to as the "Great Nurse-In" or the "Million Boob March."[90]

These events are attempts to give notice to businesses—and the public—about the right to nurse in public. Laws are already in place to protect the right to do this. The issue is how to make these laws respected and enforced. Obviously, the message has not gotten through to everybody—or to every company. In 2015, a "mom" was "humiliated," after she was told to nurse in a bathroom stall at Marshalls, a chain store in Oregon.[91] The company apologized and claimed that this action was against company policy. But in January 2016, Alyssa Milano organized a "virtual 'nurse-in'" in response to an incident on a television program, the *Wendy Williams Show*, where the host "referred to breasts as 'sexual things' and 'fun bags,' and said she didn't want to see women breastfeed. Milano objected to the "sexualization of women's breasts. . . . Biologically they're not made for sexual things. . . . That's what we've done to them."[92] In 2018, a Kentucky mother, Sadie Durbin, sued the Texas Roadhouse restaurant in Louisville after an incident in which she was asked to "cover up"; the manager claimed they'd been getting "a lot of complaints" and he tried to put a napkin over the offending breast. The incident, she said, caused "extreme emotional distress."[93] Clearly, whatever the law says, there are still people (both men and women) who feel "uncomfortable" about public breastfeeding. A study published in 2019 of Australian attitudes toward the practice found a good deal of ambivalence. At the root of the problem, they authors felt (no doubt correctly), was the "clash between the breast as a sexual object and as a functional organ."[94]

Controversies about exposed breasts arise in other contexts, too. Janet Jackson suffered an alleged "wardrobe malfunction" while performing with Justin Timberlake during the Super Bowl halftime show before a television audience of millions and millions; this fleetingly exposed her breast and set off a storm of controversy.[95] The fact is that Milano is, in one sense, clearly wrong: in American culture, and many other cultures, the female breast in fact *has* been sexualized.[96] The comparison with the male breast is misleading. To be sure, "shirtless" pictures of handsome men have some erotic resonance, but nothing like the erotic meaning of a woman's breasts.

Public breastfeeding, like the nudist movement, aims at damping down or ignoring the erotic meaning of women's breasts. Or, more accurately, compartmentalizing it. After all, even people in nudist colonies have sexual intercourse, although never on the volleyball court or in the dining hall. Nudist couples certainly find the naked body erotic; they have not, after all, taken a vow of celibacy. Their message seems to be: yes, the naked body can be erotic, but only under the right conditions.

Indeed, the battle over breastfeeding is all but over. Even the federal government has chimed in: the Fairness for Breastfeeding Mothers Act, which became law in 2019, provides generally for "lactation spaces" in federal facilities for federal employees and for tourists, visitors, and anybody else on the site.

THE PREGNANT BODY

To be sure, many conservative and traditional people still find public breastfeeding offensive, regardless of how acceptance of it has grown; they also, of course, find nudity offensive as well. They have trouble separating the erotic from the nonerotic in this and other contexts. In the past, at one time, pregnant women rarely showed themselves in public. It was shameful to let the world see a woman's pregnant body. Pregnancy, or at least the appearance of pregnancy, was another bodily aspect that had to be kept private. No law required this but it was a powerful social norm. Why should this be the case? Perhaps because a pregnant woman—an obviously pregnant woman—was a woman who, in a sense, wore a large bodily sign that said: look, I've had sexual intercourse, and this is the result. It was not that there was anything *shameful* about pregnancy, just as there is nothing shameful about sex between married couples, but it was shameful to talk about it openly, and consequently, it was shameful even to show it. Women "were expected to hide their pregnancy. Pregnancy, an indicator that sex has taken place, was simply considered too risqué for polite company."[97] When *Vanity Fair*, a magazine, posted a picture of a nude and pregnant movie star, Demi Moore, on its cover, it set off a "media firestorm," but thousands of extra sales of the magazine resulted from this "firestorm."[98] "Pregnancy," Lynne Henderson argues, "signals sexuality."[99] Sex was supposed to be a purely private affair. The same norm, more or less, helps explain why some school districts at one time prevented legally married students from taking part in extracurricular activities.[100] These were students who were regularly having sex—completely legitimately—but this was supposedly a bad model, or perhaps an infectious one, thus endangering the morals of other students.

Of course, rules of this sort were a particular source of disadvantage for women. In *Cleveland v. LaFleur*, the US Supreme Court struck down a Cleveland rule that forced pregnant teachers to leave their jobs.[101] Health considerations were the excuse. But perhaps it was because pregnant teachers, like married students, too openly advertised sexuality. As Justice Powell observed in his concurring opinion, the school district was clearly motivated by a desire "to keep visibly pregnant teachers out of the sight of schoolchildren."[102] Sexuality had to be kept in the private sphere. These attitudes, of course, have changed dramatically. Pregnant women no longer hide in the shadows. Poor women, of course, never had this option; they had to work, at home or outside it, pregnant or not. For middle-class women, the development of maternity clothes not only made life better, but it also helped end their isolation. Commercial sales of maternity clothes became common around 1900.[103]

Both in obvious and less obvious ways, then, taboos and norms about women's breasts and pregnancy do in fact reflect much broader sexual norms and taboos. That the woman's breast, in modern culture, is strongly sexualized is an obvious fact. As we said, the naked female breast has sexual connotations that the male naked breast almost entirely lacks. On the other hand, there is increasing emphasis on the health and other benefits of breastfeeding. At one time, only lower-class women breastfed; middle-class women tended to use "formula" instead. The situation has now in large measure reversed itself. Most middle-class and upper-class women breastfeed; they believe (on good evidence) that babies do best on the food nature designed for them. Poorer women breastfeed, too, but sometimes their jobs make this difficult. Still, on the whole, the women's movement and a permissive society have brought pregnancy and breastfeeding out of the closet. Sexualized or not, the breast in its historic biological function has won almost total legitimacy.

NOTES

1. *See* Meredith Bennett-Smith, "Ashley Warden, Oklahoma Mom, Gets $2,500 Public Urination Ticket after Toddler Pees in Yard," *HuffPost,* Nov. 6, 2012.

2. *Skinner v. Ry. Labor Executives' Ass'n*, 489 U.S. 602, 617 (1989) (quoting *National Treasury Employees Union v. Von Raab*, 816 F.2d 170, 175 [5th Cir. 1987]).

3. On the historical shift from public washrooms to toilets in private homes and other developments in the law and treatment of human waste, see Irus Braverman,

"Loo Law: The Public Washroom as a Hyper-Regulated Place," *Hastings Women's Law Journal* 20 (2020): 45, 50–53. *See also* Taunya Lovell Banks, "The Disappearing Public Toilet," *Seton Hall Law Review* 50 (2020): 1061.

4. N.H. Rev. Stat. § 645:1-a (2020).

5. "A person is guilty of public urination if the person urinates or defecates: (a) in a public place, other than a public rest room; and (b) under circumstances which the person should know will likely cause affront or alarm to another. Public urination is a class C misdemeanor." Utah Code § 76–9–702.3 (West 2020).

6. *State v. Cherry*, 173 N.W.2d 887, 888 (Neb. 1970).

7. The law, now repealed, prohibited "[t]hrowing or dropping offensive matter into streets, public places, rivers and other places prohibited." New York City, N.Y., Health Code § 153.09 (2020).

8. "Summonses Often Issued, Mostly Tossed," *New York Times*, June 16, 2012.

9. J. David Goodman, "Fewer Criminal Tickets for Petty Crimes, Like Public Urination," *New York Times*, Oct. 20, 2017; *see also* New York City, N.Y., Code § 16–118(6) (2020): "No swill, brine, offensive animal matter, noxious liquid, or other filthy matter of any kind, shall be allowed by any person to fall upon or run into any street, or public place, or be taken to or put therein."

10. Cal. Penal Code § 370 (West 2020) (enacted in 1872).

11. *People v. McDonald*, 137 Cal. App. 4th at 521 (2006).

12. *See, e.g.*, *State v. Villarreal*, 984 P.2d 1064 (Wash. Ct. App. 1999), another case in which the defendant claimed a search (it turned up cocaine) was illegal, because the defendant had been stopped and accused of public urination. The defendant claimed the urination was no crime but he lost the case.

13. *McDonald*, 137 Cal. App. 4th at 530–32.

14. *Id.* at 532–33.

15. Cal. Penal Code § 640 (a) (8) (2020).

16. *McDonald*, 137 Cal. App. 4th at 533–39.

17. *Id.* at 538–39.

18. *U.S. v. Whitmore*, 314 F. Supp. 2d 690, 698 (E.D. Mich. 2004).

19. *See, e.g., People v. Cooke*, 152 Misc. 2d 311, 315–16 (N.Y. Just. Ct. 1991); *Cleveland v. Pugh*, 674 N.E.2d 759 (Ohio Ct. App. 1996).

20. *People v. Cooke*, 578 N.Y.S.2d 76, 77 (Justice Ct., Rockland Cty., 1991), in which the court upheld the disorderly conviction of a man who urinated only moments after leaving a tavern with a working restroom, "in public view under a street lamp on a main thoroughfare without even making an effort to return to the tavern or to conceal himself."

21. *People v. Carter*, 13 A.D.2d 652 (N.Y. Ct. App. 1961). The defense is not always effective. The New York City Department of Sanitation fined William Giacobbe $100 for releasing "noxious chemicals onto the street" at LaGuardia airport. The administrative court upheld the citation despite Giacobbe's claim that he had a medical condition that limited his bladder control. *See NYC v. William L. Giacobbe*, ECB Appeal No. 1200568 (NYC Aug. 30, 2012).

22. Joseph Wilkinson, "A Wisconsin Teacher Was Pooping in a Public Park for 2 Years. Now He's Retiring from Both Teaching and Public Defecation," *New York Daily News*, Jan. 4, 2020.

23. *See generally* Maya Nordberg, "Jails Not Homes: Quality of Life on the Streets of San Francisco," *Hastings Women's L. J.* 13 (2002): 261.

24. "I had to pee, so I went down an alley behind a dumpster, and I pulled down my pants, but the police came by and arrested me for that and took me to jail." David M. Smith, "A Theoretical and Legal Challenge to Homeless Criminalization as Public Policy," *Yale L. & Pol'y Rev.* 12 (1994): 487, 492. The lack of public restrooms can affect the non-homeless population as well. On New York's lack of sufficient public toilets, *see* "It Ain't Easy Peeing Clean: Why Is It So Hard to Find a Bathroom in NYC," *Gothamist*, Apr. 18, 2013.

25. The Hawaii State Legislature considered a bill (which failed to pass) that would have provided more public toilets and thus cut down on public urination. The proposal specifically targeted areas frequented by the homeless population in downtown Honolulu. The push behind this bill was due to concerns over tourism. H. Res. 169, 27th Leg. (Haw. 2013).

26. Rick Noack, "When Peeing in Public in This Germany City, Beware Walls that Pee Back," *Washington Post*, Mar. 12, 2015.

27. Vivian Ho, "Streets of San Francisco Drenched in Urine," *SFG*ate, July 10, 2013; Jareen Imam, "San Francisco Starts Using 'Pee-Proof' Paint to Stop Public Urination," *CNN*, July 25, 2015.

28. Janie Har, "San Francisco Public Toilets Help Homeless, Cost $200,000," *abcnews.com*, Aug. 2, 2019; "Open-air Urinal Opens at San Francisco Park to Combat Public Urination," *L. A. Times*, Jan. 28, 2016.

29. *See* James Walker, "San Francisco's New DA Will Not Prosecute Prostitution, Public Urination Cases," *Newsweek*, Nov. 13, 2019.

30. *See* Laura Norén, "Only Dogs Are Free to Pee," in *Toilet: Public Restrooms and the Politics of Sharing*, eds. Harvey Molotch and Laura Norén (New York: New York University Press, 2010), 93, 94.

31. Banks, *supra* note 3, at 1068.

32. *Id.* at 1073–74.

33. "Bangladesh Uses 'Sacred Arabic' to Stop Peeing in Public," *Business Insider*, May 6, 2015.

34. *See* Jeffery Gettlemman, "For India, Toilets Are a (Mostly) Serious Issue," *New York Times*, Sept. 3, 2017.

35. Chicago, Ill., Mun. Code § 36–24 (repealed 1974). The fine was raised to $5–$50 in 1905.

36. Adrienne Phelps Coco, "Diseased, Maimed, Mutilated: Categorizations of Disability and an Ugly Law in Late Nineteenth-Century Chicago," *J. Soc. Hist.* 44 (2010): 23, 25–26 (citing "Annoying Nuisances," *Chicago Tribune*, July 13, 1881, at 8).

37. Susan M. Schweik, *The Ugly Laws: Disability in Public* (New York: New York University Press, 2009), 24.

38. Marcia Pearce Burgdorf and Robert Burgdorf, Jr., *A History of Unequal Treatment: The Qualifications of Handicapped Persons as a 'Suspect Class' under the Equal Protection Clause*, 15 Santa Clara Law. 856, 863 (1975), which described one "collection of strange provisions which discriminate against physically handicapped persons . . . best described as 'ugly laws.'"

39. Schweik, *supra* note 37, at 1.

40. *See* Susan Schweik, "Kicked to the Curb: Ugly Law Then and Now," *Harv. C.R.-C.L. L. Rev.* 46 (2011): 1, 2, which observed that whether explicit or not, all ugly laws "were at their core panhandling law." The status offense of "unsightliness" was "illegal only for people without means."

41. *See* Coco, *supra* note 36, at 24.

42. Coco, *supra* note 36, at 27.

43. *See generally* John Fabian Witt, *The Accidental Republic: Crippled Workingmen, Destitute Widows, and the Remaking of American Law* (Cambridge, MA: Harvard University Press, 2004); John Williams-Searle, "Charity: Manhood, Brotherhood, and the Transformation of Disability, 1870–1900," in *New Disability History*, eds. Paul K. Longmore and Lauri Umanski (New York: New York University Press, 2001).

44. Burgdorf and Burgdorf, *supra* note 38, at 864 n. 59, citing a 1974 newspaper article from Omaha, Nebraska, with title "Begging Law Punishes Only the Ugly."

45. Despite the broad sweep of the ordinance, "multiple sources indicate that the public expected many groups of disabled people to occupy public space," making it very unlikely that they were "the intended objects of the ugly law." Coco, *supra* note 36, at 23.

46. Jessie Yeung, "Girls in Nepal Sleep in 'Menstruation Huts' Despite Ban, Study Finds," *CNN,* Dec. 10, 2019. Some religious rules also impose isolation requirements on menstruating women. *See generally* Ilana S. Cristofar, "Blood, Water and the Impure Woman: Can Jewish Women Reconcile between Ancient Law and Modern Feminism?," *S. Cal. L. & Women's Stud.* 10 (2001): 451.

47. Margaret E. Johnson, "Menstrual Justice," *U.C. Davis L. Rev.* 53 (2019): 1, 22.

48. *See* Model Penal Code § 213.5 (1980) ("A person commits a misdemeanor if, for the purpose of arousing or gratifying sexual desire of himself or of any person other than his spouse, he exposes his genitals under circumstances in which he knows his conduct is likely to cause affront or alarm.")

49. *See, e.g.*, *State v. Crenshaw*, 597 P.2d 13, 14 (Haw. 1979); *State v. Jones*, 171 S.E.2d 468, 470 (N.C. Ct. App. 1970); *State v. Parenteau*, 55 Ohio Misc. 2d 10, 11 (Hamilton Cnty. Mun. Ct. 1990); *State v. Moore*, 241 P.2d 455, 459 (Or. 1952).

50. *People v. Gilbert*, 338 N.Y.S.2d 457, 459–61 (Crim. Ct. 1972).

51. Libby S. Adler, "A Short Essay on the Baring of Breasts," *Harvard Women's Law Journal* 23 (2000): 219, 220–21 & n.12.

52. *People v. Santorelli*, 600 N.E.2d 232, 233 (N.Y. 1992).

53. *Id.* at 233–34 (quoting *People v. Price*, 33 N.Y.2d 831, 832 (1973)).

54. *Id.* at 235 (Titone, J., concurring).

55. *Id.* at 236 (Titone, J., concurring).

56. *Id.* (Titone, J., concurring).

57. *Id.* at 237 (Titone, J., concurring).

58. *Id.*

59. Alex LaCasse, "New Hampshire Woman Votes Topless after Anti-Trump Shirt Disallowed," *Portsmouth Herald,* Sept. 9, 2020.

60. *See* Lina Esco, "'Free the Nipple' Is Not about Seeing Breasts," *Time*, Sept. 11, 2015. On the various lawsuits, see Maria Massimo, "Free the Nipple—Fort Collins and the Enduring Fight for Gender Equality," *B.C. Law Rev. E-Supp.* 61 (2020).

61. 916 F.3d 792 (10th Cir. 2019).

62. *See Tagami v. City of Chicago*, 875 F.3d 375 (7th Cir. 2017); *Ways v. City of Lincoln*, 331 F.3d 596 (8th Cir. 2003); *United States v. Biocic*, 928 F.2d 112 (4th Cir. 1991).

63. *See* Georgia Boulding, "Women Issued Lifelong Bans for Exposing Breasts at Baseball's World Series," *Yahoo! Sports*, Oct. 29, 2019.

64. N.Y. Penal Law § 245.01 (McKinney 2020).

65. Rev. Code Wash. § 9A.988.010 (2020).

66. 720 Ill. Comp. Stat. 5/11–30(2) (Supp. 2020).

67. La. Rev. Stat. § 51:2271.1E (2020); La. Rev. Stat. § 14:106 (2020).

68. Mont. Code Ann. § 50–19–501 (2020).

69. R.I. Gen. Laws § 11–45–2(e) (2020).

70. Civil Rights Act of 1964, Pub. L. 88–352, 78 Stat. 241, (1964). Forty-five states have public accommodations laws today, and all of them include sex as a protected characteristic. See also Nat'l Conf. State Legislatures, *State Public Accommodation Laws* (Apr. 8, 2019). research/civil-and-criminal-justice/state-public-accommodation-laws.aspx; see Joseph William Singer, "No Right to Exclude: Public Accommodations and Private Property," *Nw. U. L. Rev.* 90 (1996): 1283, 1478–95.

71. *E.g.*, Cal. Civ. Code § 51 (West 2020); N.Y. Civ. Rights Law § 40-c (McKinney 2020); Conn. Gen. Stat. § 46a-64, 81d (West 2020).

72. *See* Karen M. Kedrowski and Michael E. Lipscomb, *Breastfeeding Rights in the United States,* ed. Judith Baer (2008), 91–95; *see also Breastfeeding Laws*, Nat'l Conference of State Legislatures (May 24, 2011).

73. Cal. Civ. Code § 43.3 (West 2007).

74. 740 Ill. Comp. Stat. Ann. 137/10 (West 2010).

75. Va. Code §2.2–1147.1 (2020).

76. Treasury and General Government Appropriations Act, Pub. L. No. 106–58, § 647, 113 Stat. 478 (1999).

77. *Derungs v. Wal-Mart Stores, Inc.*, 374 F.3d 428, 437 (6th Cir. 2003).

78. Ohio Rev. Code § 3781.55 (2020).

79. 9 V.S.A. § 4502j (2020).

80. *See* Complaint and Demand for Jury Trial, *Gillette v. Freedom Airlines, Inc.*, No. 765–10–09 (Vt. Super. Ct. Nov. 24, 2009); *Gillette v. Delta Airlines*, Vermont Human Rights Commission, Investigative Report PA07–0007 (Mar. 27, 2008).

81. Liz Szabo, "Airline Settlement Fuels the National Breast-feeding Fight," *USA Today*, Mar. 14, 2012.

82. She had allegedly operated a boat without taking a water safety course.

83. Martha Neil, "Public Breastfeeding May Be Legal in Mich., But It's Not OK in My Court, Judge Told Mom," *ABA J.*, Nov. 11, 2011.

84. Mich. Comp. Laws § 41.181 (2020).

85. *See, e.g.*, Juhie Bhatia, "Moms Fight to Breastfeed in Public," *We News,* Nov. 22, 2004 (breastfeeding controversy at Starbucks); Ryan Jaslow, "Breastfeeding Moms Stage 'Nurse-in' Protests at Target Stores," *CBS News*; Martha Neil, "Mom Sues, Says Deputy Broke the Law OKing Public Breast-Feeding by Sending Her to Courthouse Bathroom," *ABA J.,* May 31, 2012; "Amy Strand, Mom, Told She Couldn't Carry Breast Pump on Plane," *HuffPost,* Mar. 2, 2012 (TSA agents told woman she could only pump milk in the bathroom); "Pastor Calls Breastfeeding Mom a Stripper," *SFGate,* Oct. 18, 2012.

86. The official website of La Leche League International is www.laleche.org.

87. See Cecilia Kang, "Mothers Rally to Back Breast-Feeding Rights," *Washington Post*, Nov. 22, 2006, at D1.

88. Michael Winter, "Mothers Stage 'Nurse-in' Protest at Target Stores," *USA Today*, Dec. 28, 2011.

89. *Id.*

90. Janice D'Arcy, "'The Great Nurse-In' to Take Place at the National Mall This Summer," *Washington Post*, Jan. 11, 2012; Martha Neil, "Moms Plan Nurse-In on National Mall in Washington, D.C.," *ABA J.,* Jan. 11, 2012.

91. Caroline Bologna, "Breastfeeding Mom Is 'Humiliated' after Being Told to Nurse in Marshalls Bathroom Stall," *HuffPost, Parenting*, Sept. 14, 2015.

92. Taylor Pittman, "Breastfeeding Moms Take a Stand with First Ever Virtual 'Nurse-In,'" *HuffPost, Parenting*, Jan. 15, 2016.

93. Scott Stump, "Mom Suing Texas Roadhouse over Public Breastfeeding Incident," *Today,* Nov. 30, 2018.

94. Athena Sheehan et al., "It's Okay to Breastfeed in Public But . . . ," *International Breastfeeding Journal* 14 (2019): 24.

95. The Federal Communications Commission fined CBS $550,000 for violating the policy against nudity and expletives during prime time (when children are likely to be watching). *See F.C.C. v. CBS Corp.*, 663 F.3d 122, 125, 128 (3d Cir. 2011). The Third Circuit vacated the fine, however, on grounds that it was an arbitrary departure from the agency's longstanding policy of ignoring "fleeting" indecency. *Id.* The Supreme Court declined to review the appellate ruling, but Justice Roberts dissented from that decision, questioning whether the "fleeting" exception had ever been applied to images, rather than expletives. *FCC v. CBS Corp.*, 567 U.S. 953 (2012) (Roberts, J., concurring).

96. In cultures where toplessness is common or the norm—as in some tribal societies—presumably the meaning would be different. See Florence Williams, *Breasts: A Natural and Unnatural History* (New York: W. W. Norton & Company, 2012), for a fascinating account of breasts from scientific, anthropologic, and sociological perspectives.

97. Renee Ann Cramer, *Pregnant with the Stars* (Stanford, CA: Stanford Law Books, 2015), 25.

98. *Id.* at 23.

99. Lynne Henderson, "Law's Patriarchy," *Law & Society Review* 25 (1991): 411, 428.

100. *See, e.g., Cochrane v. Mesick Bd. Educ.*, 103 N.W.2d 569 (Mich. 1960), which invalidated a policy prohibiting married high school students from participating in extracurricular activities on grounds that it was arbitrary and unreasonable.

101. 414 U.S. 632 (1974).

102. *Id.* at 653 (Burger, J., concurring).

103. *See generally* Kay Goldman, *Dressing Modern Maternity: The Frankfurt Sisters of Dallas and the Page Boy Label* (Lubbock: Texas Tech University Press, 2013).

Chapter 3

Speak No Evil, See No Evil: Forbidden Words and Speech

We have been exploring situations in which privacy is not a right but a duty: where law (and society) insist that you cover up. The rules relating to nudity are an obvious example. Legally and socially you are expected, and required, to hide certain parts of your body in public. We see a strong trend in the developed world toward weakening the ban on what we called simple nudity. Some nudity, of course, is far from simple. In the second chapter, we continued the theme, with particular emphasis on such matters as breastfeeding in public.

In this chapter, we expand on this general theme. Not only has nudity been taboo, but to a degree even talking about nudity has been taboo, and showing nude and salacious pictures was even more so. This chapter deals with the rise and fall of taboos against "dirty" words and pictures. As before, the root cause of the rise and fall of these taboos lies in social norms about sex and sexuality.

DIRTY WORDS AND PICTURES

Historically, law and society have demanded a cover-up for certain words and pictures as well as for parts of the body. Indeed, this has been a very active area of regulation. In the past, censorship of words and pictures has been the rule; modern ideas about freedom of speech and expression—insofar as they relate to sexual speech and expression—have been very much the exception. The literature on censorship is vast. Here we will do little more than sketch some aspects of censorship—those that are most closely related to our theme of privacy.

The connection between privacy and censorship may seem a bit remote but the two domains are clearly related. The point of censorship is to keep certain topics out of sight and out of hearing, to keep them away from the public sphere. These topics, in short, have to be kept private, like the naked body.

Married people, after all, are *supposed* to have sex; and they can talk about it to each other as graphically as they'd like, before, during, and after. But this discussion, like the sex act itself, had to be kept strictly private (at least in the past), and a whole range of subjects that (of course) could be discussed in private were completely taboo in public and in the media as well.

Political speech has, of course, always been widely censored; if there is anything that dictatorships and authoritarian governments have in common, it is that they cannot tolerate speech and writing that criticizes the rulers or expresses opposition to the rulers and the ruling group. A person published at his peril a book or pamphlet that denounced the regime of Elizabeth I, Peter the Great, Louis XIV, or any Chinese or Japanese emperor. Open dissent could be a fatal move in Stalin's Soviet Union or Hitler's Third Reich. Winning freedom of political speech was a hard-fought battle in society after society, and the battle is not over—perhaps anywhere—although it is obviously more of a problem in Putin's Russia and mainland China than in Finland or Australia.[1]

Political censorship is not hard to understand. No government wants to be subverted. No regime likes strong criticism. A country like China under President Xi keeps a tight lid on political dissent for pretty obvious reasons. Indeed, it is harder to understand the opposite: the wide latitude that democracies give to people who not only criticize the government but may even shout out that the whole thing is rotten and ought to be brought down. On the other hand, why censor books and pictures that deal explicitly with sex? If you ask people, they might say because these things are dirty and disgusting, but sex itself is neither dirty nor disgusting. The human species could hardly go on if people really found sex dirty and disgusting. A second (inadequate) explanation is religion. Millions of people believe that God has laid down definite rules about sex; people who violate those rules are committing grave or even mortal sins. Society can and maybe should protect against such sins. This explains some of the rules—the traditional ban on homosexual behavior, for example, which has a strong basis in the teachings of most major religions. But this hardly explains why it would be immoral to publish a picture of married people having sexual intercourse. The behavior itself is not immoral in the slightest; it is, in fact, as we have said, something close to a duty.

Social controls over sex vary, to be sure, from period to period, and from society to society. This book deals with a slice of modern times: roughly, the nineteenth and twentieth centuries and the beginning of the twenty-first century. And it concerns mostly the United States, with a glance at England and other countries from time to time. For this period, and these societies, there were rigid norms and rules about sexual privacy. Sexuality *had* to be strictly private. Most people thought this was a matter of morality and religion. But it was in fact more than this. The utter privacy of sex was part of a system of control; a system that kept sexual behavior within certain limits. If permitted to go beyond those limits, the very structure of society would be damaged. Sex, in other words, had to be carefully cabined and contained. What was banned—what had to be kept private—was anything that was "obscene," anything that appealed to "prurient interests." This means anything that aroused sexual desire. Of course, sexual desire could not be considered a bad thing in itself. But it was acceptable only within limits, just as people who drive cars (another good thing) must obey the speed limit and avoid reckless driving. "Prurient interests," although absolutely necessary for the human race, need their speed limits too. At least this has been the theory that undergirds regulation of sexual behavior.

The traditional system of control appeared gender-neutral, at least on the surface. That is, rules against obscene literature (for example) have always applied equally to men and women. But this neutrality was only apparent. Women, it was assumed, needed a system of prudery because they were (on the whole) weak, innocent, naïve, easily victimized and seduced; they were also supposed to be, by nature, less interested in sex than men. In some ways, the rules bore down more heavily on men: sexual speech and expression were not something respectable women indulged in anyway. But it was, after all, men who were in charge; they made up and enforced the rules.

That rules of privacy are gendered is blatantly obvious in countries like Saudi Arabia, where women dare not show their hair in public and have to cover themselves up on the streets; men, on the other hand, are free to dress more or less as they please (within limits, of course).[2] On the streets, in London or other cities with neighborhoods of traditional Muslims and Muslim tourists and visitors, the stark differences between the sexes are blindingly obvious: when one sees, say, a young couple strolling down the street, the man may be wearing blue jeans and T-shirt; his wife is all wrapped up from head to toe. Privacy rules in Western countries were always subtler and less extreme than this. But the rules, nonetheless, were part of a system of male domination. Words like "domination" are of course loaded words. Nineteenth-century men did not talk in terms of "domination," "hegemony," or "patriarchy"; they simply thought it was God's will, or at least part of the natural order, for men and women to play different roles in society (with men running the show, of course). The gendered division of labor was the way the world worked, and the way it was supposed to work. Most women probably agreed.

Not that Victorian prudery let men off the hook completely. Moralists—and doctors—believed that men too, with their raging sexual desires, had to be carefully monitored and controlled. Too much access to "prurient" material could bring about absolute mental and physical collapse. Unmarried people were not supposed to have sex at all; and the practice of masturbation was a nineteenth-century *bête noire*. "Self-abuse" was considered an extremely harmful practice. Women could also masturbate, of course, but for men and boys, the danger was greater, since their bad habits were particularly common. Anthony Comstock, the famous blue-nose, quoted an "eminent professor in a Southern College" who felt that from 75 to 95 percent of young men were "victims of self-abuse."[3] Dr. J. Richardson Parke, a former "Acting Assistant Surgeon" of the United States Army, condemned the practice as "a deadly evil" in his 1909 textbook; it was a practice that "destroys the very foundations of manhood and womanhood." "A child who indulges in this sin becomes pale or leaden in countenance . . . the eyes are sunken and dull . . . the general health begins to suffer. The appetite fails, the tongue becomes coated, [and] there is emaciation"; the end result is "hopeless neurasthenia, or even imbecility or lunacy."[4] Indeed, a 1916 handbook written for older boys warned not only about self-abuse but also against too much sexual excitement in general. The author talked about a "football player on one of the big university teams" whose game was suffering for some mysterious reason. The coach was puzzled and decided to investigate; he found that the player "had a suggestive picture hanging in his bedroom." The coach tore it down, and the football player's game quickly went on the upswing.[5]

The ban on sexual speech is closely allied with the ban on nudity. "Speech" here is a broader concept than talk; it includes books, pamphlets, pictures, movies, and the like. There is a vast body of scholarship on censorship and the struggle against pornography. In this section, we will confine ourselves to a few salient points—a few landmarks along the way. The central concept here is *obscenity*, a term frequently used in statutes and case law. "Obscenity" is a broad term that is hard to define, although many of the statutes and cases try to do so. Another common term, *pornography* refers to books and pictures that are obscene in content.

The central problem of obscenity is, as we said, its appeal to the "prurient interest"; it leads to unlawful use, or misuse, or overuse of the sexual organs. It contributes to masturbation and even worse sins. If sexual immorality—sexual gluttony—could ruin a football player's game, think of what it could do to society as a whole if the beast was allowed out of its cage.

Most people—and most jurisdictions—in the past simply took it for granted that the state had a right to ban obscene literature, and never bothered to ask why. If pressed for an answer, people might refer to obscenity and pornography as disgusting, immoral, and, implicitly, infectious; the harm could be spread from the corrupted to the uncorrupted. Dirty books and pictures endangered the immortal soul, not to mention a good, clean life on earth. But more than that, they were dangerous to society. Society depended on strict adherence to traditional morality. Traditional morality was, somehow, not only right but *necessary*; civilizations that gave way to debauchery were doomed to ultimate decay. A lot of people have had some sort of vague idea that vice and the like led to the fall of the Roman Empire.

Respectable society in the nineteenth century was positively obsessed with notions of control, self-discipline, and moderation in all things. A person should never get drunk; it was probably best not to drink at all. Married people of course could and should have sex, but please, not too often. As Lawrence Stone pointed out, "the extraordinary emphasis on prudery and sexual repression" was tied up with "the bourgeois values of frugality."[6] This emphasis on self-control and discipline was, arguably, functional in an industrial society; no factory owner wanted workers who were drunk, high on drugs, or sexually predatory, or who showed up only when they felt like it. The emphasis on self-control was perhaps also relevant to democracy, that is, the experiment (novel in modern times) of letting the public run the government as much as possible.

Democracy, however, depends on a corps of reliable, virtuous voters. It depends, in short, on self-control. An aristocratic society does not need underlings who can make intelligent decisions about governance. In a democracy, ordinary people control society (at least in theory). Whatever the reason, in the nineteenth and early twentieth century, what we might call Victorian sensibilities—extreme prudery and a huge emphasis on self-control and moderation in all things—reached its highest point.

Of course, not everybody found obscenity repulsive. Many people found it tempting and alluring, like other works of the devil. Others were simply weak-willed and vulnerable. People probably also knew that it was next to impossible to stamp out vice. Vice could be controlled but not eliminated. And if the law came down too hard on vice and pornography, they would be driven underground, into the sewers and basements of society. So long as vice and pornography were strictly *private*, they posed less danger to society. Private sin, private vice: of course these were bad, but open flaunting of the rules was worse; worst of all, and most corrupting, was to attack the rules quite openly, or make fun of them.

In the remainder of this chapter, we will take a look at this form of enforced privacy—rules about dirty books and pictures and related matters—then examine how and why the rules decayed in the latter part of the twentieth century, and then, finally, what remains of the rules (mostly concerning children) and why they survived.

THE NINETEENTH-CENTURY TRANSFORMATION

This chapter, as we said, deals with the period from about 1800 on. Of course, as everybody knows, rules about sexual behavior and misbehavior go as far back in history as we can go. Every society, perhaps, has had some sort of rules or customs about sexual behavior. The Old Testament had a lot to say about the subject. Thou shalt not commit adultery was one of the Ten Commandments.[7] In the American colonies, adultery was a crime as well as a deadly sin. Fornication, too, was a crime in the colonies. Under the Laws and Liberties of Massachusetts (1648), it was provided that if "any man shall commit Fornication with any single woman," he, and she, were liable to be punished, "either by enjoyning [*sic*] to Marriage, or Fine, or corporall [*sic*] punishment."[8] "Corporal punishment" meant whipping. The fornication rules were hardly dead letters; the pages of colonial records are full of examples of men and women punished for committing this offense. No crime, perhaps, was more frequently punished.

Rules about sexual behavior in all major religions claim to be based on eternal and divine principles. Adultery was a major sin, and the law in, say, Puritan Massachusetts Bay made little distinction between sin and crime; the fact that adultery or fornication might be consensual was irrelevant.[9] In the nineteenth century, the laws against adultery changed in an interesting and significant way. Many states no longer treated adultery per se as a criminal act. Rather, the statutes criminalized "open and notorious" adultery.[10] Not that these societies approved of hidden, sporadic adultery, but hidden, sporadic adultery was not a threat to the social order. Only those whose behavior was an open scandal were dangerous to society; only those people were actually *modeling* immoral behavior and it was these people who were singled out for punishment in the criminal code. So long as sexual speech and behavior were strictly private, they were less of a danger to society and could be tolerated.

Some of the statutes on fornication made a similar distinction. In Florida, for example, under a law of 1868, ordinary fornicators could get three months in jail, but if the couple "lewdly and lasciviously associate[d] and cohabit[ated] together," they could get up to two years in state prison.[11] In *Long v. State*, the sheriff broke down the door of Mary Long's house in the hopes of catching her in bed with Henry, to whom she was not married.[12] He found them there, in night clothes; Mary and Henry were convicted of "lewd and lascivious cohabitation" and sentenced to eighteen months in prison. But on appeal, the Florida Supreme Court vacated the convictions. While the evidence showed "one act of secret lewdness," it did not show that the parties were "cohabiting together, as though the marriage relation existed between the parties." The purpose of the statute was "to prohibit the public scandal and disgrace of such living together by persons of opposite sexes, and unmarried to each other" in order "to prevent such evil and indecent examples, with their tendency to corrupt public morals." Mary and Henry's private "sin" was a problem only when it became public. The secular authorities did not punish sin as such. The problem was open and notorious sin. Keeping sin in the closet—keeping it private—was beneficial in two ways. First, it prevented the situation from getting out of hand. And second, it announced, legitimated, and reinforced a code of discipline, moderation, and self-control, which was vital for preservation and protection of the social fabric.

By the early twenty-first century, the situation had altered drastically. Most states had taken adultery and fornication out of the penal codes. A few states still had laws against adultery on their books[13]—typically of the open and notorious variety—but enforcement was weak and sporadic. The landmark Supreme Court decision in *Lawrence v. Texas*, which struck down all laws against "sodomy," suggested that state interference with the sexual activity of consenting adults was likely to be considered unconstitutional. This, arguably, would include both adultery and fornication. Hence, as far as the Supreme Court is concerned, the legal status of the surviving laws on this subject is dubious at best.[14]

FORBIDDEN BOOKS

Censorship of books also has a long history. Before the rise of modern democracy, regimes quite generally suppressed political dissent. The Catholic Church, too, maintained a list of prohibited books, which loyal members of the flock were not supposed to read; these were books that the church considered evil and corrupting. Moreover, whatever contradicted church doctrine was liable to fall under the ban. Dissent and heresy were evils in themselves, to be suppressed if possible. The Church adhered to this position for centuries. The *Index Librorum Prohibitorum* was not abolished until 1966.

Victorians certainly knew people had sex lives—that people had sexual desires and acted on them. Nobody was about to stamp out "prurient" desires but stamping out obscenity was another matter. American states passed laws against obscenity and pornography in the nineteenth century. "Dirty" books and pictures were outlawed. This did not, of course, put an end to a flourishing underground trade in pornography. Suppressing this trade completely was probably always impossible. But legal harassment could keep it, perhaps, under control. Pornographers in New York, faced with crackdowns, moved their operations out of state, and began to send books and pamphlets through the mails, in the proverbial plain brown wrappers.[15] This made state control of obscenity more difficult, if not impossible. National legislation was needed.

The federal government controlled imports and interstate commerce; it also ran the mail system. A law of 1842 made it unlawful to import "indecent and obscene" pictures.[16] A law of 1865 made it a crime to "knowingly" mail obscene books and pictures.[17] In 1873, Congress followed up with a major piece of legislation, the so-called Comstock Law, named after Anthony Comstock, the famous blue-nose and anti-vice crusader. The Comstock Law expanded the list of things that could not be sent through the mails. The list included not only pornography but also devices "intended . . . for any indecent or immoral use" or "for the prevention of conception or procuring of abortion."[18]

At the time, strictly speaking, neither birth control nor abortion were flatly and plainly illegal. But they were pretty much taboo, as far as public discussion was concerned. It violated rules of propriety to advertise or spread information about these subjects and to sell "devices" that could be used for these purposes. These issues belonged to the private sphere, to the realm of locked doors and shade-drawn windows. In fact, contraceptive devices were widely used and even advertised (though discreetly).[19] But, like vice in general, contraception and abortion were not supposed to be openly discussed except as medical issues; taboos made them subject to a quiet and discreet form of control. Polite society aimed to keep these matters locked in the cage of propriety as much as possible.

Comstock himself expended prodigious energy hunting out obscenity and bringing it to justice. He was not alone. The New England Watch and Ward Society, centered in Boston, was an avid crusader against whatever it considered improper.[20] This organization began its life as the New England Society for the Suppression of Vice. It became famous, or infamous, for policing the written word and demanding that objectionable books be censored or suppressed. This was a private organization but it had a powerful influence on publishers, booksellers, and even on the Boston Public Library. Along with books that were, frankly, trash, the Society fought in court to ban even such classics as Rabelais's *Gargantua* and *Pantagruel.* Ironically, but not surprisingly, books that were "banned in Boston" often had enormous sales outside the city; "banned in Boston" gave these books a priceless (and costless) form of advertising.

This points to an obvious but important fact: pornography was and is genuinely popular with a large segment of the population (mostly, one supposes, men). Sex sells; forbidden depictions of sex sell even better. By the 1920s, the power of the Watch and Ward Society had begun to fade. By the end of the century, it had basically disappeared; its funds were transferred to other organizations. Book censorship had lost its luster by then. It was a victim of a more permissive society, and the so-called sexual revolution.

Censorship did not go quietly, though, or quickly. There were periodic purity campaigns, even without the help of *official* censorship. Kathleen Winsor's somewhat racy novel, *Forever Amber* (1944), was banned in fourteen states, starting with Massachusetts. Needless to say, it sold millions of copies. Lillian Smith's novel, *Strange Fruit*, published in the same year, also ran into difficulties. It was condemned as obscene, but probably the sticking point was something else: the novel dealt with sex and love between a white man and a black woman.[21] Irate parents have frequently demanded purges of offensive books in school libraries. The most frequent object of these campaigns, oddly enough, has been *The Catcher in the Rye*, J. D. Salinger's sensationally successful novel of 1951.[22] But these outbursts were basically aftershocks—except, of course, insofar as they related to kids. The later years of the twentieth century, as we shall see, were in fact quite dismal days for censorship, and for those who thought society should monitor the morality of books, plays, movies, and television shows. Except, as we said, for kids.

THE PLAY'S THE THING

Direct censorship of the theater was not common in the United States. For the most part, self-censorship did the job. But there were sporadic incidents of suppression for plays that dealt with taboo subjects, or which seemed otherwise immoral. The problem became more acute, perhaps, precisely because playwrights began pushing the envelope. In 1900, in New York City, the actress Olga Nethersole, along with her leading man, her manager, and a theater lessee, were arrested for putting on and acting in a played called *Sapho*, by the American playwright Clyde Fitch. According to the indictment, the defendants, "being persons of wicked and depraved mind and disposition," and "intending . . . to corrupt the morals of divers persons and to raise and create in their minds inordinate and lustful desires," staged a play that included "lewd, indecent, obscene, filthy, scandalous, lascivious and disgusting motions and . . . indecent postures . . . and indecent, obscene and disgusting words."[23] The play was based on a French novel by Alphonse Daudet; the actress's tights, and the fact that one could see too much female leg, probably scandalized enough people to set off this wave of arrests. The fuss no doubt helped the play at the box office. To their credit, the jury in the case did not see the play as morally dangerous. After deliberating all of a quarter of an hour, the jury acquitted everybody concerned.[24]

The city of Boston took a prominent role in censoring plays as well as books. Boston had an active censor. Lillian Hellman's play *The Children's Hour* (1934), with its treatment of same-sex love, naturally came under the ban.[25] But censorship, as was so often the case, simply added to the fame of whatever was censored. Forbidden fruit seems always to taste better. Charles Burnham, president of the Association of Theatre Managers in 1909, was aware of this regrettable fact: blame for "immoral plays," he said, had to be placed squarely on the public, on the audience. The theater, Burnham felt, was no longer only for the rich; it was for everybody, and if the word was out that the play was "indelicate," the "town runs wild."[26]

In England, censorship of plays was "formalized": under a Parliamentary statute, the Lord Chamberlain had the job of licensing plays.[27] Plays had to be submitted to his office fourteen days before they were going before the public. The main motive here was probably political; he sought suppression of "political caricatures and satires." But policing morality quickly became the focus of the censor's activity.[28] As was true of book censorship, serious plays did not escape the eagle eye of the censors. A famous instance was George Bernard Shaw's play *Mrs. Warren's Profession*. Mrs. Warren's "profession," of course, was brothel keeper. The discussion of prostitution and the presentation of a character like Mrs. Warren was, in the eyes of the censor, "not fitted for casual audiences of various ages."[29] Shaw himself, quite naturally, felt this was absurd. As he wrote in 1899, it reflected the idea that "only by a strenuous maintenance of restrictive laws and customs" could "society be withheld from casting all moral considerations to the winds and committing suicide in a general Saturnalia of reckless debauchery." Shaw called for the abolition of censorship, "root and branch."[30]

Needless to say, Shaw's advice was not taken. Censorship continued, although circumvented in part by "private" showings of such plays as Ibsen's *Ghosts*. But serious plays were still in trouble as far as the mainline theaters were concerned. In 1918, for example, a play, *Maternity*, by French playwright Eugene Brieux, ran afoul of the censor. Sir Douglas Dawson, an official in the Lord Chamberlain's office, recommended against allowing it to be shown on the London stage. There are subjects, he wrote, "on which we literally turn the key. In a civilized world we do not discuss openly the *details* of sexual intercourse, of visits to the W.C. and . . . such subjects as venereal diseases and procuring abortion." These subjects were only suitable "for discussion in privacy with the priest or the doctor."[31] In the last half of the twentieth century, unsurprisingly, in an age of permissiveness, censorship of plays came to seem anomalous. The practice came under more and more vigorous attack and the Theatre Act of 1968 finally got rid of it.[32]

GOING TO THE MOVIES

At the very beginning of the twentieth century, a new entertainment medium swept the western world: the movies. Movies were cheap, and in a short time they became exceedingly popular. Within a few years, movie houses (nickelodeons) sprang up like mushrooms all over the United States and elsewhere as well.

To many respectable elites, religious leaders, and other self-appointed guardians of morality, the very popularity of movies constituted a threat to national morality. People of all ages and classes went to the movies, including children. That was part of the problem. Movie theaters were dark, seductive places, and the content of movies, if left unchecked, could be wildly immoral and corrupting. There were loud calls for action to monitor the movies, to make sure they purveyed only wholesome material. Chicago adopted a censorship ordinance in 1907. The ordinance was challenged in court, but the Illinois Supreme Court upheld the ordinance. People who went to the movies, according to the court, needed "protection against the evil influence of obscene and immoral representations."[33] Other states and cities joined in the censorship parade. In Ohio, the Board of Censors was supposed to approve only movies that were "moral, educational or amusing and harmless."[34] In 1915, a challenge to the Ohio law came before the United States Supreme Court. The Court sustained the Ohio statute. Movies, the justices said, could be dangerous and corrupting; they could be a "force for evil." Freedom of speech? Not an issue. The First Amendment did not apply to mere entertainment—certainly not to the "shows which are advertised on the bill-boards of our cities and towns."[35] The Supreme Court was not alone in this attitude. Quite generally, the courts in that period affirmed, and approved of, laws and ordinances censoring the movies.

Censorship of the movies went much further than sex. The censors were worried about anything that struck them as dangerous to traditional morality. Race relations were a particularly thorny subject. Yet the first film screened in the White House was *Birth of a Nation.* This famous silent movie was blatantly racist; it glorified the Ku Klux Klan and portrayed blacks as ignorant, lustful creatures.[36] The NAACP protested, but the movie was a commercial success at the box office. In 1912, Congress passed the Sims Act, which restricted the interstate sale of boxing movies. The "more advanced" states had outlawed this "brutal and brutalizing sport," and the purpose of the law was to protect these states from exposure to fight films, which were "only a little less harmful than the degrading sport which they describe." The main impetus for this law, promoted by Congressman Thetus Sims from Tennessee, was probably racial: southern politicians did not want audiences in their states to see films showing the black boxer Jack Johnson defeating white boxers in the ring.[37]

Throughout the 1920s, many movies were condemned as raunchy and offensive, which was often quite true. The industry felt forced to take notice. Censorship was widespread but it was never truly national; some states and cities had censorship boards whereas others did not. The studios were haunted by fears that censorship might spread, that audiences might boycott films, or, worst of all, that some kind of federal regulation might emerge. In a state of panic, the industry set up a trade organization in 1922, the Motion Picture Producers and Distributors of America. The basic idea was to ward off censorship through rigorous self-policing. This might act as a kind of vaccination against government control. The trade group came out with a Production Code in 1930. The preamble to the Code drew a line between two kinds of entertainment: one kind "tends to improve the race," or at least tends to "rebuild human beings exhausted with the realities of life"; the other kind "tends to degrade."[38] The "moral importance" of entertainment was "universally recognized." Motion pictures had "special moral obligations." They reached "places unpenetrated by other forms of art," and they were much more vivid than books or newspapers. Images are more powerful than mere words. Films were also different from plays: they had a "larger audience" and this lowered the "moral mass resistance to suggestion."[39]

The Code, heavily influenced by the Catholic Church, was a severe and puritanical document. Under the Code, adultery was "never a fit subject for comedy," and should never be presented as "justified" or as "attractive or alluring." Movies were not allowed to show "lustful and prolonged kissing" or "lustful embraces." The "sacred intimacies of private life" were unfit for the movies, and although "pure love" was a "rightful subject of plots," the "passion arising from this love [was] not the subject for plots." Obscenity, forbidden by "divine and human law," would not be allowed on the screen. "Sex perversion," or any reference to it, was utterly taboo; so was "white slavery." "Miscegenation" was not to be shown on the screen. "Sex hygiene and venereal diseases" were not appropriate subjects for motion pictures.[40]

There were strictures against violence as well; and rules about crime and punishment. Movies must never glorify crime and criminals. Religion had to be treated with respect, and the "name of Jesus Christ should never be used except in reverence." The flag, too, had to be shown with respect. Despite all this, the heart of the Code was its attitude toward anything relating to sex. The Code recognized that in "normal human beings" there are "emotions" that "react naturally and spontaneously" when confronted with scenes of sex and passion. Nothing was to be shown that was "deliberately meant to excite these manifestations," that is, nothing that might make people sexually excited (if we can use blunter language than the code). And why? Because these "manifestations" are "subversive to the interest of society, and a peril to the human race." So: no scenes of undressing, no nudity (of course), dancing costumes were not to be indecent, and dances of the "type known as 'Kooch' or 'Can-Can,' since they violate decency . . . are wrong." Indeed, the discussion of nudity sounds the theme that runs throughout the Code. Nudity or seminudity, according to the Code, has an effect on the "normal man or woman, and much more upon the young person." Therefore, the "fact that the nude or semi-nude body may be beautiful does not make its use in the films moral."[41] A beautiful body—perhaps especially a beautiful body—would result in "manifestations" that had to be avoided at all costs.

In general, as H. L. Mencken put it, the work of the Code, censorship boards, and private, self-appointed guardians of morality led to a situation in which movies were "cribbed, cabined, and confined by regulations that would . . . seem oppressive in a Baptist female seminary."[42] This might be a shade overstated, but not by much. The Code was strict; and it was strictly followed—at first, at any rate. Amendments, however, were frequent. The Code was thoroughly recast in 1956. The 1956 version was much shorter than the original version, but it kept the same essential thrust.[43] By this time, however, the Code's reign of terror was fading rapidly; in the 1950s, it entered a period of twilight. Already, some distributors and theater owners were defying the Code, as we will see. The Code limped on until the 1960s, but by then it was a total anachronism.

WATCH YOUR LANGUAGE

Social norms have in the past made a sharp distinction between language that could be used in private (especially between men), and that which was fit for public use. Many states had statutes against obscene and vulgar speech.[44] In Alabama, for example, it was an offense to use "abusive, insulting or obscene language" in the "presence or hearing of any girl or woman."[45] Statutes of this type lasted into the twentieth century. An Arizona law similar to the Alabama law also prohibited "any obscene picture, writing or marking" on the walls of lavatories in Arizona mines.[46] A Mississippi law, still in effect, made it an offense to "profanely swear or curse, or use vulgar and indecent language" in a public place, "in the presence of two (2) or more persons."[47] In the heyday of Victorian prudery, fastidious people avoided even words like "belly" because they seemed vulgar and common. "Cock" was replaced by "rooster," for obvious reasons. The Motion Picture Production Code, naturally, did not allow vulgar language or obscenity.[48]

Quite apart from actual censorship, the media practiced a great deal of self-censorship, and not only in the movies. Newspapers, for the most part, were extremely prudish. Periodicals like the *National Police Gazette*, considered raunchy in its day, seem exceedingly tame by modern standards. Victorian literature, in general, is amazingly sexless. Sometimes there is a kind of sexual subtext, but you have to read between the lines. Sex is almost never explicit. Four-letter words never appeared in (respectable) print.

Indeed, the great *Oxford English Dictionary*, perhaps the world's most scholarly and comprehensive dictionary, which listed what the editors believed to be every word in the English language—including all sorts of rare, obsolete, technical, and regional words—deliberately left out two extremely common words, known no doubt to almost every adult in the English-speaking world (and probably most teenagers as well). These words were "fuck" and "cunt"—hardly rare and esoteric words.[49] But they were so taboo that the editors simply could not bring themselves to include them in the dictionary. Science here had to give way to propriety.[50]

Magazines and newspapers, well into the twentieth century, could be barred from the mails if the Postmaster General (who, in Mencken's phrase, headed "a bureau of snoopers and smut-snufflers") found something objectionable. For example, in 1943 and 1944 *Esquire* magazine ran afoul of the Postmaster by virtue of the "use of such perfectly harmless words as *backside*, *behind* and *bawdy-house*."[51]

The "four-letter words" do, indeed, relate, historically, to sex or excrement. But English-speaking people probably utter the word "fuck" millions of times a day, without any reference at all to sex. Sex or no sex, the word was considered totally "offensive," and could not be used in polite society or in print. To pronounce the word would violate rules of public etiquette about how people were supposed to act in public. Whether a word is considered polite, impolite, or vulgar is a matter of custom and fashion that defies easy explanation; for example, "belly" is a bit vulgar, while "stomach" is not. Words that were obscene, excessively vulgar, or forbidden were not to be used in the presence of nice women or young children, as previously mentioned. Needless to say, these strictures have now, for the most part, vanished from the law codes.[52]

Today, most people (but not all, of course) are on Mencken's side, and Victorian prudery tends to strike us as ridiculous. We have already mentioned what might have been the implicit social theory behind it. This theory was not and is not totally wrong. We all know the saying "Sticks and stones will break my bones, but words will never hurt me." We also know that this is just not true. Words can be terribly hurtful. Most hurtful, of course, are insults, but there are other forms of speech that can inflict grave wounds, or that, in the aggregate, can even pose some sort of social danger. Speech can amount to sexual harassment.[53] The Supreme Court, in a well-known case, allowed the states to proscribe "fighting words."[54] The case in question, decided in 1942, arose under a New Hampshire statute that made it an offense to "address any offensive, derisive or annoying word" to someone in any public place, or to "call him by any offensive or derisive name," with the intent to annoy or offend.[55] The defendant, Chaplinsky, a Jehovah's Witness, had called a police officer a "God damned racketeer" and a "fascist."

The Chaplinsky case, today, seems a bit overblown. But there are contemporary issues: universities and other institutions wrestle with the problem of hate speech. "Four letter words" are now common, but the "n-word" is totally taboo; using it in public, in a classroom, or even quoting from a book that uses it can set off feelings of outrage and hurt. When a white student at Rutgers Law School did this in May 2021—said the forbidden word by quoting from an actual judicial opinion—a storm erupted at the school.[56] This and other offensive words may not break bones but they can lead to serious consequences, and sometimes even violence. Cyberbullying, too, can be extraordinarily hurtful, and make a person's life almost unbearable. The Victorians had no such concepts as hate speech or sexual harassment. But they did have ideas about which forms of speech were deeply offensive, if not actually harmful, to the ears (and minds) of respectable people, particularly women and children. Vulgarity and obscenity were the worst offenders. And these notions cannot simply be dismissed as absurd—at least not within the Victorian social context. The rules are obsolete; and seem, in many ways, ridiculous. But at the time they were thought to protect the very structure of society.

ON THE AIR

Censorship of radio and TV is, of course, purely a product of the twentieth century. It was, on the whole, just as pervasive as censorship of books and plays, and has been longer lasting. There was, to begin with, a good deal of self-censorship. In 1934, Thomas Parran, the health commissioner of New York State, was told by CBS that he could not mention syphilis in a proposed speech on "Public Health Needs."[57] This finicky attitude was not confined to matters of sex. Radio and TV, like the movies, reached a national audience; and the networks were keen not to offend anybody—at least not anybody they considered important or influential. This included the racial feelings of white southerners. As late as 1954, the year *Brown v. Board of Education* was decided, CBS broadcast a version of Mark Twain's *Adventures of Huckleberry Finn* that totally eliminated the black slave Jim, a vital character in the book; CBS was anxious to avoid trouble below the Mason-Dixon line.[58] Apparently, CBS was not concerned with the feelings of African Americans.

There has also been genuine hard-law censorship. It still exists. Under current rules, broadcasters may not utter any "obscene, indecent, or profane language."[59] The Federal Communications Commission (FCC) can issue regulations on the subject and has the power to enforce this provision of the law.[60] The FCC created a list of "seven dirty words," which were absolutely banned on radio or television." The comedian George Carlin developed a monologue about this famous list, and his monologue was broadcast on the air. When the FCC took action, the case ended up in the United States Supreme Court. The Court, in *FCC v. Pacifica Foundation*,[61] narrowly upheld the FCC in a five-to-four decision. The majority felt that the First Amendment had least sway with regard to broadcasting, which penetrates into the privacy of the home.

Radio and television, like the movies, were genuinely popular. By the 1930s, just about every family had a radio; this meant that the audience for radio shows would certainly include great numbers of women and children. The same reasoning that supported movie censorship supported censorship of radio and TV: fear that some material was dangerous to the moral health of the nation. Of course, radio was considerably less vivid than the movies—and was less vivid than television, which burst on the scene in the 1950s, and was as bad as the movies, or even worse, because its images became pervasive in American homes. It did not take long for television to be an almost universal presence in households, and soon in vibrant color as well. Even in our permissive era, an age in which the moral panic over obscenity has abated, censorship survives for radio and TV. Much of this is due to the ever-present fear that children might listen to, hear, or see the wrong stuff. Movies could be controlled, more or less, by a rating system but that would not work for radio and TV. Hence radio and TV had to remain, in the words of Justice Scalia, a "safe haven for children."[62]

The FCC has stuck to its guns and insisted on verbal purity. *FCC v. Fox Television Stations, Inc.* dealt with the issue of "fleeting expletives."[63] There, the villain, once more, was that fine old English word "fuck," but used as an "expletive," without any reference to actual sex, and in a "fleeting" way—that is, casually, and not repeatedly. The FCC had a censorship policy, which it enforced by slapping fines on stations and programs that dared to utter offensive words. The tone of the majority in the *Fox* case seemed to suggest that the Justices, overall, were willing to let the FCC keep its policy of censorship.[64] But the case was decided on narrow procedural grounds and the First Amendment issue (free speech) was deliberately avoided.

Television, of course, is more than words—it is pictures, images, and film. If naughty words are forbidden, naughty images are all the more so. The Consumer Guide of the FCC tells listeners and viewers that obscenity is not under the sheltering wing of the First Amendment. It is prohibited by law "at all times of the day." But "indecent and profane" material is only forbidden between 6:00 a.m. and 10:00 p.m., when children might be watching. Indecent material is "sexual or excretory" material that "does not rise to the level of obscenity." This material is protected by the First Amendment but it can be banned at times when the kids are likely to be watching. The material is indecent if it is "patently offensive as measured by community standards." The FCC considers material "patently offensive" if it "appears to pander or is used to titillate or shock."[65] The spread of cable and satellite TV has made a difference; these are "subscription services," and the rules for indecency and profanity do not apply to them.[66]

Citizens can complain to the FCC about "obscenity, indecency or profanity," and they do. For the year 2005, the FCC received 233,531 complaints, covering 488 radio programs, 707 TV programs, and 355 cable programs;[67] in the first six months of 2006, 327,198 complaints were received against 389 radio programs, 312 TV programs, and 290 shows on cable. The FCC has imposed fines in a number of well-publicized cases. The citizens who complain may be trying to command the waves in an increasingly permissive society. But they do not give up. The FCC continues to receive complaints, though apparently at a rate much lower than was reported for 2005 and 2006. For 2014, for example, the FCC reported about one thousand complaints of "indecency and obscenity"; in 2019, they received around two thousand complaints and inquiries along these lines with regard to television, and just over five hundred for radio. A Texas disc jockey who used the phrase "blow job" in a morning program cost his employer a fine of $37,500 three years later, in 2014. In 2015, the FCC imposed a "forfeiture" of $325,000 on Station WDBJ, in Roanoke, Virginia, because of a news story, broadcast at 6:00 p.m., in which "to the right of the screen in a small window box" the viewer might see "an erect penis being stroked" by a "former porn star." This image was shown for all of three seconds, so the cost to the station was more than $100,000 per second for this lapse of taste.[68]

THE TRIUMPH OF VICE

In the second half of the twentieth century, dramatic legal and social changes in society spelled doom for the regime of censorship. The Victorian and post-Victorian systems eventually collapsed under the weight of social change. It was society, of course (or most of it), which "repealed" the rules of censorship, before the law ever did so.

We have already mentioned the decline of book censorship. As early as the 1930s, there were cracks in the armor. The Postmaster had the job of fighting smut, and he did not lightly give up the battle. In one interesting case in 1949, in the federal Second Circuit, the Postmaster had banned three books from the mails. One of them, *Waggish Tales from the Czechs*, was labeled obscene. The other two, oddly enough, were excluded on the grounds of fraud: they *claimed* to be seriously dirty ("salacious") books, while in fact they were not. Had the Postmaster abused his discretion? The appellate court rather reluctantly upheld his decision.[69] Jerome Frank, who wrote a concurring opinion, confessed to a certain reluctance; he had yielded, he said, only to the "more experienced judgment" of his fellow judges, but with "much puzzlement," and he hoped the Supreme Court would weigh in on the case (which never happened). He doubted the underlying premise of the war on smut. "[N]o sane man," said Frank, thinks it is "socially dangerous" to arouse "normal sexual desires." If "reading obscene books has merely that consequence," he went on to say, Congress had no more right to suppress these books than to "prevent the mailing of many other objects, such as perfumes, for example, which notoriously produce that result."[70]

In one sense, Frank was clearly wrong: perfectly sane men in Congress and state legislatures had in fact voted for laws against obscenity, laws that, at their very core, assumed that peddling material that aroused sexual desire—material that appealed, as they put it, to "prurient interests"—was wrongful and dangerous. But times and cultures were changing. In the 1920s and 1930s, distributors who battled movie censorship in the courts lost case after case.[71] But in 1952, three years after Frank's timid concurrence, champions of movie freedom won their first important victory in the Supreme Court. The case, *Burstyn v. Wilson*,[72] concerned a short Italian movie, *The Miracle*.[73] In the movie, an ignorant woman is plied with drink and seduced. She gives birth, and comes to believe that St. Joseph was the father of the child. Local officials of the Catholic Church were outraged at the movie, which they condemned as offensive, blasphemous, and anti-Catholic. The New York censors banned it as "sacrilegious." Burstyn, the distributor, was a stubborn man, and he believed in the film. He went to court and fought his way up to the United States Supreme Court, which unanimously reversed the censorship action.

This was a significant victory, though in some ways a cautious one. New York, the Court held, could not ban a movie simply because it was supposedly "sacrilegious." That concept was, in the first place, impossibly vague. And in the second place, the government, in a country that separated church and state, had no business deciding whether a movie was or was not "sacrilegious." The Court left open the question of censorship on the grounds of obscenity. Still, the case struck a sharp blow against censorship of movies and the work of censorship boards.

In the next years, the Supreme Court overturned the ban in every case where a banned movie came before the Court. The French movie *La Ronde* (1950) was based on a novel by Arthur Schnitzler, an important figure in Austrian literature, and was directed by a famous director, Max Ophuls.[74] The movie tells the story of a series of eleven couples who have sex with each other. One of the two, in each segment of the film, then takes up with somebody else, and, at the end, the circle gets closed when a partner in the last segment takes up with one of the partners in the first. New York banned the movie as "immoral." The Supreme Court reversed, though with a teasingly short *per curiam* decision.[75] Still, the decision sent a message: "immoral" was no better grounds for censorship than "sacrilegious." Meanwhile, some local censorship laws had trouble in their home states. Ohio and Pennsylvania courts, for example, struck down censorship laws on constitutional grounds.[76] One thing was clear: the idea that "entertainment" did not deserve protection on the basis of free speech was gone with the wind.

Defiance of the Code and the church groups that backed it soon spread beyond art films and imported movies. In Hollywood, for example, the director Otto Preminger defied the Code and released a film, *The Moon Is Blue*, in 1953, without the benefit of industry approval. This harmless comedy used a word or two ("virgin," for example, in its sexual sense) that the Code did not permit. The movie, despite the ban (or because of it), was a resounding box-office success.[77] For the Code, and for censorship in general, the handwriting was on the wall.

In theory, as we said, the Supreme Court had held—and continues to hold—that obscenity is not protected speech; state and local governments have had and still have the right to control, or even prohibit, whatever is obscene.[78] In practice, however, this once-mighty power has, over the years, shriveled to a mere shadow of its former self. The *Ulysses* case in the 1930s was an early landmark.[79] Was *Ulysses*, the dense, difficult novel by James Joyce, obscene? Federal law banned importation of any "obscene" book. And, to be sure, parts of this book—especially the long monologue by Molly Bloom at the end of the book—were explicit and dealt with sex in a way that would have turned the hair of solid, respectable Victorians. *Ulysses* won its case, first in the federal district court, then on appeal. The *Ulysses* case has long been enshrined in the pantheon of great cases, cases that advanced the cause of freedom of expression. But it is important to remember that *Ulysses* is not at all easy reading; in fact, it is notoriously difficult. The monologue at the end is a lot more accessible than much of the rest of the novel, but not many people were likely to get that far.

Ulysses, in short, was obviously a work of serious literature. And tough going. No doubt this helps explain why the district court was comfortable with *Ulysses*; it did not appeal to prurient interests—it was not, as the judge put it, an "aphrodisiac." A true aphrodisiac had to be a lot easier to read. The appellate court agreed; the book did not promote mere "lust." In these opinions, it is hard to escape a strong whiff of elitism. If you are intellectual enough to read *Ulysses*—no easy matter—you are unlikely to be corrupted by it. In this period, in editions of the works of the Marquis de Sade, which were certainly scandalous enough, a reader might suddenly confront a passage in French, rather than English; similarly, in editions of the *Satyricon* of Petronius Arbiter, a late Latin classic, the text could abruptly lapse from English into Latin. The theory, presumably, is that anybody able to read French or Latin was an intellectual, and not part of the corruptible masses.[80]

This theme, of course, was not new. Laws against vice had long had this distinctly elitist flavor. It was the idea that underlay censorship of movies: the idea that some people in society were more corruptible than others. The most vulnerable, of course, were children. But in a way, the masses—people of small income and small education—were vulnerable, too. Like children, they stood in grave danger of moral corruption.

The *Miracle* case in 1952 had dealt a blow to movie censorship, despite its cautious language.[81] In the following years, some censorship boards went out of business. Some state courts, as we saw, ended movie censorship on their own. *Freedman v. Maryland* (1965) was a significant case at the level of the Supreme Court. Freedman, who owned a theater in Baltimore, was arrested for showing a movie, *Revenge at Daybreak*, without a license. The Supreme Court sided with Freedman, and almost (but not quite) ruled that *any* "prior restraint" on movies violated the federal constitution.[82] Censorship was by then quite pointless. Social change, as we said, finished the job; the old standards were now totally obsolete. The Production Code did not survive the 1960s. It was replaced by a voluntary rating system, administered by a Code and Ratings Administration. Movies rated G and PG could be seen by anyone. *PG*, however, stood for "parental guidance," and was meant to be a signal to parents that this film contains something a bit edgy. In 1984, a new category, PG-13, was introduced: parents are "strongly cautioned" that some material in the film might not be suitable for children under thirteen. If a movie was rated R, no child could attend without an adult in tow, and NC-17 was simply forbidden to anybody under seventeen; this replaced the X rating in 1990.[83] Most theaters (except for "adult" theaters) simply would not show an X-rated movie. NC-17 movies today are quite rare. But this is misleading. Social tolerance has shifted, and at lightning speed. By the beginning of the twenty-first century, movies were rated PG-13 that would have earned an X in an earlier period and would have been totally banned in the age of the Production Code. Take, for example, "Philomena," a highly regarded movie released in 2013. It would have run afoul of the Code, as an attack on the Catholic religion (the movie was highly critical of actions taken by Catholic nuns in Ireland); moreover, an important character was identified as a gay man who died of AIDS—a subject also once taboo but now very much in the open.[84] The movie was rated PG-13.

Censorship—"prior restraint"—was therefore essentially dead, at least as far as movies were concerned. In England, there were parallel developments. Book banning lasted into the 1950s; in 1954, there were 132 prosecutions under the Obscene Publications Act, but this was almost the end. In 1960, the Director of Public Prosecutions put Penguin Books in the dock for publishing D. H. Lawrence's famous novel *Lady Chatterley's Lover*. But Lady Chatterley and her randy lover won their case.[85] Censorship of plays, as we mentioned, ended in 1968; the Lord Chamberlain lost this thankless job. But even after censorship left the stage, so to speak, and in an age of rampant permissiveness, there is still something of a cloud hanging over the status of pictures and words that are sexually explicit.

The precise legal question is this: to what extent does the First Amendment, and the concept of freedom of speech, apply to "obscenity," that is, to words and images that are, frankly, openly sexual? The Supreme Court first addressed this issue in the 1950s. In *Roth v. United States*, the Supreme Court held that the First Amendment does not protect obscenity as such.[86] "Obscenity" meant material that "deals with sex in a manner appealing to prurient interests."[87] Material that appeals, in other words, to sheer lust or is deliberately titillating. This is hardly a bright-line standard. In this and in later cases, the Court struggled to develop doctrine that would allow states to exercise just the right amount of control, but not too much. Too much would violate the right of freedom of expression. But how much was too much? The Court never really worked out an answer.

In *Memoirs v. Massachusetts*, the Supreme Court confronted Fanny Hill, a famous lady in the world of pornography.[88] Fanny was the heroine—if that is the word—of a pornographic classic, John Cleland's book *Memoirs of a Woman of Pleasure*, which was written in the middle of the eighteenth century. The book had been banned in England, and pirated editions in the United States suffered the same fate. But in the early 1960s, Putnam's, a well-known and well-established publishing house, sensing that times had changed, brought out an unexpurgated copy of the book.

In a curious sense, the book itself, rather than its publisher or seller, was on trial: the Attorney General of Massachusetts had brought a civil suit in equity, asking the court to declare the book obscene (and thus have it banned). The highest court of Massachusetts agreed with the Attorney General: Fanny's book was in fact obscene. It is, in one sense, hard to argue with this holding. This book was frankly written to be pornographic; and throughout its long history everybody recognized the book for what it was: well-written, to be sure, but definitely and explicitly a dirty book.

The high court of Massachusetts brushed aside "expert testimony" to the effect that the book had "literary merit" insofar as it possessed "skill in characterization and a gift for comedy," that it had historical importance, and that it even contained a moral message. A book that "appeals to prurient interest and is patently offensive," said the court, can be banned as obscene, even if it is not "unqualifiedly worthless."[89]

But Justice Brennan, writing for the Supreme Court, disagreed; the Court reversed the Massachusetts court, and made Fanny, at last, if not an honest woman, at least a woman not totally beyond the pale. A "book cannot be proscribed unless it is found to be utterly without redeeming social value."[90]

This is true even for books that appealed to the dreaded "prurient interest." Brennan hedged a bit: evidence that the book was "commercially exploited for the sake of prurient appeal" might be relevant to the issue of legality. But the blanket ban on the book could not stand.

"Prurient appeal," however, as the be-all and end-all of obscenity law, was clearly weakened by this decision. Yet if one discarded the idea that a book that appealed to "prurient" interests was obscene, the whole concept of obscenity would collapse, and the war on pornography was as good as lost. Moreover, at one time, if any part of a book or play was offensive, the whole book or play could be banned. It did not matter if the work, as a whole, had some merit. Anything exposed to the public—a book, a play, a movie—was dangerous if it aroused sexual desire, in whole or in part. The overtly erotic had to be kept strictly private. Desire, lust, and sexual passion had to be contained, monitored, and controlled. Lust had to be kept safely underground, in a kind of psychological storage bin, to be opened and released only when a person married. But this was an idea whose time had passed. Pornography had probably always been more popular than society liked to admit; when it came out of the closet, its enormous popularity was plainly visible to the naked eye. *Deep Throat*, an out-and-out pornographic movie, made tons of money in 1972.[91] Pornographic websites today exist by the millions, and get millions of visits every day, from millions of visitors.[92]

The law, however, still fusses and worries about overtly sexual materials. The Supreme Court was unwilling to let go entirely of the idea that "prurient" material could be subject to legal restraints. In *Miller v. California*, the defendant had "conducted a mass mailing campaign" advertising the sale of "adult" books, including one called "Sex Orgies Illustrated," and a film called "Marital Intercourse."[93] The Court repeated its conviction that the First Amendment did not protect "obscenity" but that material was to be judged by "contemporary community standards." Furthermore, a work, to be obscene, must appeal to "prurient interest" in a "patently offensive way," and must be completely lacking in social, artistic, or scientific value. The court did offer some examples of "obscenity": "[p]atently offensive representations or descriptions of ultimate sexual acts" or of "masturbation, excretory functions, and lewd exhibition of the genitals."[94]

The formal law to a degree still thunders and pontificates against obscenity. The current Alabama statute makes it unlawful to "display in public any bumper sticker, sign or writing" that contains obscene language, and any obscene "description of sexual or excretory activities" is still unlawful.[95] State obscenity laws still condemn the appeal to "prurient" interests. The New York statute, for example, defines obscenity as material that, "considered as a whole," makes a "predominant appeal to the prurient interest in sex," and that "depicts or describes in a patently offensive manner actual or simulated sexual intercourse" or "sexual bestiality, masturbation, sadism, masochism, excretion or lewd exhibition of the genitals." But any such material must also lack "serious literary, artistic, political and scientific value."[96] The Virginia statute also defines obscenity in terms of "appeal to the prurient interest in sex," and goes on to explain what is meant: "a shameful or morbid interest in nudity, sexual conduct, sexual excitement, excretory functions or products thereof or sadomasochistic abuse," though only if this material goes beyond "customary limits of candor" and lacks "serious literary, artistic, political or scientific value."[97] Another traditional theme appears in the English law, the Obscene Publications Act of 1959; the statute applies to material that, "taken as a whole," would be such as to "tend to deprave and corrupt persons who are likely to hear, see, or read the stuff."[98]

These statutes seem pretty severe; but they give, on the whole, a wrong impression. They are in fact much weaker than the obscenity laws of the past, and much weaker than they seem. A book or magazine is obscene today only if it is obscene when taken "as a whole"; in the past, any obscene snippet could fatally injure a book. And "customary limits of candor" have changed dramatically in the past decades. In earlier times, literary merit did not save Fanny Hill—for that matter, even classics like Rabelais and Bocaccio were in trouble. Now, "four letter words" are as common as dirt in books and movies. Even the venerable *Oxford English Dictionary* has come around: the second edition is no longer bashful; the banned four-letter words have returned from exile and disgrace, and now enjoy full coverage. The Supreme Court of one state—Oregon—struck down its obscenity statute in 1984, as a violation of the state constitution.[99] The Supreme Court of the United States has not changed its tune officially, though the Court did strike down a law about internet indecency in 1997 on the grounds that it went too far.[100] The Court has never disclaimed the idea that there is such a thing as "obscenity," and that, whatever it is, it does not enjoy constitutional protection.

The Constitution does, however, extend its wings of protection to "expletives." *Hess v. Indiana* addressed a circumstance that occurred in the midst of turmoil over the Vietnam War; during an antiwar demonstration, Gregory Hess, in a fairly loud voice, said something about retaking the "fucking street."[101] The local sheriff "heard Hess utter the word 'fuck' . . . and immediately arrested him for disorderly conduct." The Supreme Court reversed his conviction; what Hess said could not be considered obscene, was not a breach of the peace, and could not be punished. Similarly, in *Cohen v. California*, the defendant had worn a jacket with the words "Fuck the Draft" emblazoned on it.[102] His conviction for "maliciously and willfully" disturbing the peace was overturned by the Court.[103] Obscenity means sex and words and phrases, no matter how vulgar, no matter how improper and rude they might be, in some contexts, cannot be the basis for criminal prosecution.

WHAT HAPPENED?

The law in this area has tracked and responded to a crucial change in the culture. People apparently no longer believe that letting the tiger out of its cage will end civilization as we know it. After a reputable publisher brought out an edition of *Fanny Hill*, a book full of tales of Fanny's sexual adventures, universities and libraries placed "an unusually large number of orders" for the book, as Justice Douglas pointed out in the Supreme Court decision that upheld *Fanny Hill.* Indeed, the Library of Congress "requested the right to translate the book into Braille."[104]

Fanny Hill, in the 1960s, was more than two hundred years old. The book was older, in fact, than the Bill of Rights. Yet for two hundred years, Fanny had led a more or less underground existence. Nobody, for most of this period, felt that she had rights under the First Amendment or the equivalent. Quite the contrary. Only in the 1960s did she come out of the closet, so to speak; only then did she ask for, and get, constitutional protection. Of course, the book had never really gone out of fashion; what was new was its demand for *legitimacy*—the right of an ordinary publisher to publish it, on decent paper—and the right of people to read it without hiding in a corner and pretending to be reading something else. This was the period, too, in which Hugh Hefner began to publish *Playboy* magazine. The magazine, which came out in 1953, was famous for its pictures of naked women, legitimated more or less by essays and fiction from the workshop of good writers, which were published in the rest of the magazine.[105] *Playboy* was on glossy paper, it was well-edited, and it was designed to be suitable for the coffee tables of young urban professionals, absolving them of any sense of guilt for displaying the magazine. *Playboy* was a ringing success, and not only in the United States. In this period, in short, some aspects of the private went resoundingly public. Explicit sexual material no longer lived in dark caves; it came into the sunlight and demanded a measure of acceptance. So much so, in fact, that even *Playboy* came to seem, well, a bit behind the times. Indeed, in 2015, *Playboy* decided to stop publishing images of naked women. This was not a sudden outburst of morality. If anything, it reflected the very opposite. The battle against prudery had "been fought and won," according to Scott Flanders, the chief executive of Hefner's company. "You're now one click away from every sex act imaginable for free"; *Playboy*, then, was no longer the flagship of appeals to "prurient interests" and was, perhaps, obsolete.[106] In 2017, the magazine changed course; the decision had been a financial mistake, apparently. Nude pictures would now be back in.[107] But Flanders' point was still, on the whole, completely valid: *Playboy* was no longer ahead of the curve.

The elitist flavor of censorship laws has been weakened, if not totally destroyed. This seems to be part of a larger trend. Morals have become more democratic (if that is the word). In the nineteenth century, ordinary people seemed to want to imitate their betters: dressing the way they dressed, acting the way they acted, and in general behaving like the better sort of people. To a certain degree, the late twentieth century turned this around; millionaires began to wear blue jeans (though possibly "designer" jeans) and kids paid premium prices for jeans that were pretorn and prefaded. Franklin D. Roosevelt famously served hot dogs to the English royal family when they visited Hyde Park. Musicians can make millions out of "gangster rap"; basketball players openly boast about how many women they have successfully bedded. Of course, the rich can still flaunt their wealth; they can wear diamonds and drive sports cars. But they also revel in a culture they once considered lower class.

It is also the age of celebrity culture, which we will discuss in a later chapter. And it is also the age of cohabitation, of gay rights, and now of gay marriage, which the Supreme Court validated for the entire country. Clearly, one factor is the sexual revolution and a whole series of interlinked cultural changes; underlying them seems to be the notion that the individual's wishes and wants—his or her desires and habits—have a kind of primacy and legitimacy that include sexual choices, in a way that would have shocked and horrified moral leaders in the nineteenth century. At one time, many people believed society would collapse unless sexuality were repressed and kept within limits. Today, the ruling notion is almost exactly the opposite and centers on the belief that sexual repression is no more natural than bulimia or anorexia, that it is psychically harmful to repress one's natural urges. In this cultural climate, it makes no sense to espouse Victorian prudery. Open displays and open discussions make sex much less mysterious, and much less inhibited. The public sphere has invaded the private sphere—at first on tiptoes, and then with a crash of hobnailed boots.

Are people more obsessed with sex than they were in the past? Do they *do* more sex than people did in the past? It is very hard to say. Certainly, *attitudes* have changed. Sex is no longer treated as completely private, secret, or even shameful in a way. Women's magazines no longer deal only with recipes and other household subjects; they also tell women how to have better sex, how to appeal to the "prurient interest" of men, how to have bigger orgasms, and the like. Of course, not everybody enlists in the army of the sexual revolution—there is resistance, disagreement, and backlash—but the basic lines of development seem abundantly clear, and, on the whole, the revolution has prevailed.

NOT IN FRONT OF THE CHILDREN

In essence, then, the campaign against obscenity is dead—at least for adults. Yes, under current doctrine, states probably still have the right to regulate or ban hardcore pornography; at least they still have obscenity statutes on their books. New York, for example, still has a law that talks about a "prurient interest in sex," and that makes the knowing possession of "any obscene material" an offense.[108] Yet in practice, especially in big cities and on the internet, there seem to be no meaningful controls.

What does survive and, indeed, may be more important than ever is regulation that focuses on children. The more permissive the adult world, the more people feel an almost desperate need to shield children from the facts of this big, bad world. Pornography might be all right for adults but certainly not for children. Indeed, in Illinois, for example, although obscenity is defined in terms of the standards of "ordinary adults," it has to be "judged with reference to children" if it appears "from the character of the material or the circumstances of its dissemination to be specially designed for or directed to such an audience."[109] Shielding children is also why television has to be controlled and why it is held to stricter standards than, say, the movies. After all, nobody stands at the door of the living room, the bedroom, or the family room taking tickets and making sure only grown-ups pass through. There is no practical way to filter children out of the audience. The only thing to do, then, is to keep offensive stuff off the screen altogether.

Ironically, part of the problem comes from the fact that, in our times, children have more privacy than they used to have. In middle-class families, each child has a room—and very likely a TV set, a smartphone, and some sort of computer. This makes it hard to police what they see. Poor families in the past had much less privacy. Whether this kept them pure is another question. When everybody is crammed into a small space, it is hard to keep the kids from hearing, or even seeing, the sex act. Poor people rarely undressed; in crowded tenements and farmhouses, without a lot of space (and without modern baths and stall showers), nudity was almost never experienced. Couples had sex, of course, but perhaps they waited until the children were safely asleep. On the other hand, in crowded cities, in poor neighborhoods, with brothels, saloons, and cheap hotels, many kids must have grown up street-smart and fast; on farms, children were exposed not just to the birds and the bees, but also to the sex lives of hogs, sheep, horses, and cattle. Even in the high and palmy days of formal, official prudery, Victorian society could not win its war against open acknowledgment of sex. Polite society struggled, with some success, to keep sex as private as possible.

Legally speaking, the war on smut ended with a truce; "freedom of speech," however, remained in firm control of the battlefield. Protecting children from hearing and seeing too much too soon is still an important policy goal. So, even though book censorship is dead, there are periodic outbursts of prudery aimed, for example, at high school libraries or curricula.[110] J. D. Salinger's *The Catcher in the Rye*, hardly a dirty book, was perhaps the most frequent target, at least in the 1960s. Even today, parents in many towns complain if their children are assigned, or even allowed to read, books with profanity, bad words, and references to sex. Not all of the protests come from the traditional wing of society. In some towns, parents complain about books that contain the "n-word," or that, in their view, slight or insult minorities.[111]

Parents and others, in short, feel a need to shield their children from the oceans of sexual material washing over society. It is obvious that teenage children are often more sexually active than their parents would want to admit. But it is one thing to be aware of this fact and quite another thing to give teenage sex the green light. Until fairly recently, in some high schools, school rules discriminated against married students. In many states, kids can marry at sixteen (with parental consent). School boards, one might think, would encourage these youngsters to keep on studying, and not to drop out of school. But in many schools, married students were treated almost as pariahs: they were barred from extracurricular activities and excluded from the prom, or from school events in general.[112] Why would a school adopt such a policy? Married kids have sex—legitimately of course; this makes their presence in school very dangerous; they might contaminate the other (presumably celibate) students. Sex was essentially for married people past high school age; teenage sex was deviant, even when it was legal; it had to be kept under wraps. These kids, then, could go to class—that was unavoidable. But nothing else: there was to be no fraternization with the others, if at all possible. The sexuality of these young people had to be kept private, at all costs. The same impulse produced rules against teachers who were obviously pregnant. A student's wedding ring, like a teacher's baby bump, too obviously advertised sex. Of course, all such measures were probably useless. All these rules are no doubt history today.

THINK OF THE CHILDREN: SEX EDUCATION IN THE SCHOOLS

The prudery of the Victorian era has gone away, in the age of sexual freedom, leaving aside the special and sensitive case of children. That remains, even with respect to information that is designed to inform and help students, rather than to appeal to their "prurient interests." Sex education in the schools is a delicate subject. In the 1960s, sex education programs in schools were widely attacked as immoral; by the 1970s, twenty states had decided to abolish or significantly restrict sex education, and only a few states still required sex education to be part of the school curriculum at all.[113] At that time, it appeared that the concept of sex education in schools was on the road to extinction.

But in the 1980s, the AIDS epidemic heightened the felt need to educate young people about safe sexual practices.[114] This led states to begin requiring schools to provide education on AIDS and other sexually transmitted diseases. Some programs included broad, comprehensive coverage of sex education, including information on contraceptive methods, while others primarily preached abstinence. In any case, the door was open in most states to include some form of sex education as part of school training in matters of health.[115]

In the 1980s and 1990s, comprehensive sex education programs had to do battle against abstinence-only programs. Conservatives, then and now, objected to anything that did not put the emphasis on abstinence, that is, on chastity before marriage. At least half of the states now include sex education in the curriculum; but many focus on abstinence, and most authorize parents to "opt-out" of sexual education entirely.[116] Parental rights have been continually reaffirmed by the Court[117] and are a firm basis for provisions allowing parents to opt out.[118]

Opting out has its limits. A father challenged a school health curriculum that featured six days of material on family life, sexual health, and the prevention of AIDS. The Second Circuit Court of Appeals considered his claim in 2003. The court held that a parent could utilize the state's opt-out provision to prevent his child from attending the six classes related to family-life instruction and AIDS education but that was all. He did not have the right to insist that the curriculum be changed for everyone. Even a parent's constitutional right to direct the upbringing and education of his child was not sufficient justification for opting out of health instruction beyond courses on family life and AIDS prevention.[119] Similarly, in 2005, the Ninth Circuit held that the constitutional rights of parents do not grant parents the ability to restrict the flow of certain information in public schools, including even information regarding sexual matters. In that case, a group of concerned parents challenged a questionnaire issued to students at school that included questions on sexual topics, claiming a constitutional right to control the provision of sexual information to their children.[120] The court held that parents have "no due process or privacy right to override the determinations of public schools as to the information to which their children will be exposed while enrolled as students"; parents, in other words, cannot entirely shield their children from instruction involving information related to sex.[121]

Many parents do object to some aspects of sex education programs, especially those pertaining to issues like sexual orientation, gender identity, and masturbation. In Ontario, Canada, the expansion of school sex education programs to include these issues caused a parent-led protest that resulted in over thirty-four thousand students being kept home from school.[122] Similar protests have also cropped up in the United States in response to programs designed to include topics like oral sex, anal sex, and homosexuality.[123]

Incomplete or inadequate sex education certainly has consequences. In the United States, the average adolescent has sex for the first time at age seventeen, but 44 percent of females and 49 percent of males between the ages of fifteen and nineteen have already had sexual intercourse.[124] Young people are certainly having sex, and where sex education fails to provide adolescents with comprehensive, accurate information, the likelihood of sexually transmitted infections (STIs) and other consequences rises; adolescents and young adults account for a large percentage of new cases of STIs in the United States each year, and this disproportionate distribution is likely due to age-based disparities in access to information and services that would or could prevent these diseases.[125] All states allow minors to get treatment for sexually transmitted ailments without their parents' consent. But in eleven states, this is true only for minors of a certain age. Minors who are younger than this—typically twelve to fourteen—are in trouble if they need treatment and do not want their parents to know.[126] Preventing adolescents from obtaining STI treatment doesn't reduce sexual activity, but it certainly makes it more dangerous; it discourages teenagers from getting treatment they need. Studies show that comprehensive sex education programs—which include information on contraceptive use and disease prevention—significantly reduce the risk of STI transmission and teen pregnancy.[127] Our society tends to protect the sexual privacy of *adults* but it has a way to go on matters of sex education and the sexual health needs of adolescents.

CHILD PORNOGRAPHY

In our times, since pornography is everywhere, it is hard to protect children from seeing and experiencing obscene material. Of course, actual sex with children was and is an extremely serious crime. It is a felony in California, for example, to commit any "lewd and lascivious act" on a child under age fourteen, "with the intent of arousing, appealing to, or gratifying the lust, passions, or sexual desires" of the perpetrator or the child.[128] But what about child pornography? Of course, to actually *use* children to produce pornography is a serious crime, and is clearly banned. But the campaign against child pornography goes further. Child pornography is linked, one might think, with pedophilia; arguably, it might nurture, encourage, or stimulate real sex with real children. Many people also simply find it sinful, disgusting, and unnatural. State after state has enacted laws meant to put an end, if possible, to child pornography, and to punish those who make, distribute, or use it. The Supreme Court confronted one of these statutes in 1982, in *New York v. Ferber*.[129] The New York law made it a crime to use a child under sixteen in a "sexual performance"—that is, a performance including "sexual conduct." "Sexual conduct" was defined to mean "actual or simulated" intercourse, masturbation, or "lewd exhibition of the genitals," among other things. It was a crime to make, sell, or distribute this kind of material.

The defendant in the case, Paul Ferber, ran a bookstore in Manhattan and sold two films to an undercover police officer—films which were "devoted almost exclusively to depicting young boys masturbating." That seems pretty hard-core, but the statute in question had a problem: it did not say explicitly that the "sexual conduct" had to be "obscene." It tells us something about how loose standards had become that this was an issue in the case (you can imagine how far the claim that the film was legal would have gotten in the nineteenth century). In the end, the Court upheld the statute—though somewhat cautiously, obviously anxious to avoid what it called the "heavy hand" of the censor. Society, said the Court, depends on the "healthy, well-rounded growth of young people into full maturity as citizens." The statute in question had an important purpose—so important that a state could make "sexual conduct" by children in a film illegal, even if the film had artistic or literary merit. Such a film would not be technically "obscene." After all, if a high-minded film needed to show sexual conduct by children, the filmmakers could always hire actors and actresses who simply *looked* young.

The federal government had its own version of the type of statute at issue in the *Ferber* case. But the unstoppable march of technology seemed to make such laws painfully inadequate—at least in the minds of members of Congress (much or most of the general public no doubt felt the same way). The rule laid down in *Ferber* seemed wishy-washy and inadequate. In 1996, Congress passed a new law, the Child Pornography Prevention Act.[130] This outlawed any "visual depiction" (including a "computer-generated image or picture") that showed, or *appeared* to show, a minor "engaging in sexually explicit conduct." The aim was to ban "virtual child pornography." And any movie, even if it didn't use *actual* child actors, was under the ban, if any actor "appear[ed] to be" a minor engaging in "actual or simulated" intercourse.

The law quickly ran into legal trouble. It was challenged by an organization called the Free Speech Coalition ("a California trade association for the adult entertainment industry"), and a number of other plaintiffs, including Bold Type Inc. (the "publisher of a book advocating the nudist lifestyle"). The Supreme Court, in 2002, agreed with the challengers; the Court thought the statute went too far.[131] The law banned any "depiction of sexually explicit activity," whether or not it would "appeal to the prurient interest." The law could apply, for example, to a "picture in a psychology manual, as well as a movie depicting the horrors of sexual abuse." The distinguished justices took note of the fact that some teenagers do have sex ("it is a fact of modern society"); minors (sixteen-year-olds) can marry, with parental permission, in many states, as we mentioned. And Juliet, in Shakespeare's *Romeo and Juliet*, was a mere thirteen years old. The play has "inspired no less than 40 motion pictures, some of which suggest that the teenagers consummated their relationship." Any statute that made Romeo a criminal, or Shakespeare, or the director of a movie version of *Romeo and Juliet*, was never going to pass a constitutional test. Congress, naturally, found this decision unacceptable. They responded by passing a new law, the PROTECT Act of 2003. The old law was defective, in that it banned material that was not legally obscene (if, for instance, it had literary or artistic merit). The PROTECT Act tried to plug this hole and avoid the constitutional issue. Under this law, it is a crime to produce or distribute a "visual depiction of any kind" that shows a "minor engaging in sexually explicit conduct" and that is "obscene" or "depicts an image that is, or appears to be," a minor doing various sexual acts, and that "lacks serious literary, artistic, political or scientific value." The minor need not "actually exist."[132]

Presumably, this law can pass muster, since obscenity laws, whatever their shriveled meaning, are still on the books. Federal law still makes it a crime to import, or to send across state lines, any "obscene" material—not just books, but any "paper, letter, writing, print, or other matter of indecent character."[133] In 2005, one Dwight Whorley, of Richmond, Virginia, was caught with pornographic Japanese cartoons on his work computer; these cartoons apparently showed young girls having sex. Whorley also, it seems, possessed other kinds of child pornography. He was convicted of violating the pornography laws. He appealed, lost in the Fourth Circuit, petitioned for his case to be heard by the full court en banc, and then lost again. The Chief Judge, Gregory, dissented from this decision: Whorley, he said, was convicted under the federal law "for communicating by email with consenting adults about their personal and private fantasies." The emails "were purely textual and did not include any images." No money was involved, and there was no "victimization or exploitation of actual children." He said it was a "difficult" case, and the whole panel, therefore, ought to hear it. He was troubled by the criminalization of "fantasies." Historically, of course, obscenity law did in fact try to criminalize "fantasies." This is just another way of describing a "prurient interest." In our times, "fantasies" have been decriminalized—for adults but not for children, or when children are involved. Even "fantasies" about adults having sex with children, or children having sex of any sort, are, to a degree, prohibited. Most adults, one would guess, would agree with this thrust of the law.

Despite doubts—by some people—about the validity of some laws aimed at child pornography, they remain on the books and there is definite enforcement. A first offender who produced child pornography faces at least twenty-five years in prison. Child pornography includes any image showing a minor engaged in sexual conduct. But even a photo or video of a naked child, if it is sexually suggestive, comes under the ban. In November 2019, a twenty-one-year-old substitute teacher for elementary schools in Fairfax County, Virginia, was sentenced to 150 months in prison, to be followed by twenty years of "supervised release," for violating the law against child pornography. The defendant was caught in a sting operation: an undercover detective had claimed to be the father of a seven-year-old who the defendant was led to believe was available for sex; the defendant also received and sent videos that constituted child pornography.[134]

A CONCLUDING WORD

For much of our history, and the history of the Western world in general, there were strict taboos against open and notorious discussion of sex, and taboos against images of sexual activity. It made no difference if the sex partners were married and were having perfectly legitimate, vanilla sex; it still needed to be kept strictly private. A vague, implicit, but powerful theory lay behind the legal and social ban on sexual expression. These taboos, it was believed, held society together; they prevented the kind of riotous sexual behavior that presumably could destroy an empire and a civilization. In the late twentieth century, for complex reasons, this theory lost its power; and a period of enormous permissiveness began. This is the period we live in right now. Not everyone, of course, is happy about the triumph of permissiveness; powerful forces would like to bring back the old way of life, though they have an uphill battle. Meanwhile, just about everybody would agree that children must be somehow sheltered from the awful facts of modern life. For them, the private must stay private until they are old enough, and mature enough, to handle the new world of sexuality.

NOTES

1. *See, e.g.*, Roy L. Sturgeon, "China's Homegrown Free-Speech Tradition: Imperial Past and Modern Present. And Post-Modern Future," *Fla. J. Int'l L.* 26 (2014): 291, 295–300; Rebecca Favret, "Comment: Back to the Bad Old Days: President Putin's Hold on Free Speech in the Russian Federation," *Rich. J. Global L. & Bus.* 12 (2013): 299, 301–05.

2. The Saudi laws requiring women to dress modestly and cover their hair are said to derive from Qur'anic requirements. Two Qur'anic verses in particular advise women to cover themselves; these verses form the basis of this legal requirement in Islamic nations like Saudi Arabia; these are Qur'an 24:31 and Qur'an 33:59.

3. Quoted in Walter Kendrick, *The Secret Museum: Pornography in Modern Culture* (Berkeley: University of California Press, 1987), 140.

4. J. Richardson Parke, *Human Sexuality: A Medico-Literary Treatise on the History and Pathology of the Sex Instinct for the Use of Physicians and Jurists*, 4th ed. (Philadelphia: Professional Publishing Company, 1909), 373–74, 380. Moreover, in Parke's opinion, "[t]housands of men . . . fail in business solely because they are masturbators." *Id.* at 375. Parke felt that many societies had fallen prey to this vile practice (not to mention such animals as camels). Since, in Parke's view, almost all men and many women indulged in "self-abuse," you have to wonder why the country did not contain countless millions of hopeless imbeciles.

5. The book was Harry Hascall Moore, *Keeping in Condition: Handbook on Training for Older Boys* (New York: The Macmillan Company, 1915), quoted in Patricia J. Campbell, *Sex Education Books for Young Adults, 1892–1979* (New Providence, NJ: R. R. Bowker Company, 1979), 38.

6. Lawrence Stone, *The Family, Sex and Marriage in England, 1500–1800* (New York: Penguin Books, 1977), 678. Stone adds that "'spending' had both sexual and economic meanings, both pejorative." What Victorians valued above all was "respectability," which included "moral asceticism." *Id.*

7. *Exodus* 20:14 (King James version of the Bible).

8. *The Book of Lawes and Libertyes Concerning the Inhabitants of the Massachusets* (1648).

9. *See* Lawrence M. Friedman, *Crime and Punishment in American History* (New York: Basic Books, 1993), 127.

10. Lawrence M. Friedman, "Name Robbers: Privacy, Blackmail, and Assorted Matters in Legal History," *Hofstra L. Rev.* 30 (2002): 1093, 1100.

11. Fla. Stat. § 798.02 (1868) (amended 2016).

12. *Thomas v. State*, 22 So. 725 (1897).

13. *See, e.g.*, Fla. Stat. § 798.01 (1971); Wis. Stat. § 944.16 (1955) (amended 2001).

14. *See Lawrence v. Texas*, 539 U.S. 558, 578 (2003).

15. Donna Dennis, *Licentious Gotham: Erotic Publishing and Its Prosecution in Nineteenth-Century New York* (Cambridge, MA: Harvard University Press, 2009), 182–190.

16. Tariff Act of 1842, ch. 270, § 28, 5 Stat. 566 (repealed 1846).

17. Lawrence M. Friedman, *Guarding Life's Dark Secrets: Legal and Social Controls Over Reputation, Propriety, and Privacy* (Stanford, CA: Stanford University Press, 2007), 147.

18. Comstock Act, ch. 258, 17 Stat. 598 (1873) (current version at 18 U.S.C. § 1461 (2018).

19. *See generally* Andrea Tone, *Devices and Desires: A History of Contraceptives in America* (New York: Hill & Wang, 2001).

20. *See* Neil Miller, *Banned in Boston: The Watch and Ward Society's Crusade against Books, Burlesque, and the Social Evil* (Boston: Beacon Press, 2011).
21. *Id.* at 157–67.
22. *See* Pamela Hunt Steinle, *In Cold Fear:* The Catcher in the Rye, *Censorship Controversies, and Postwar American Character* (Columbus: Ohio State University Press, 2002).
23. "Indictment for 'Sapho'," *New York Times*, Mar. 23, 1900, at 2.
24. "Jury Soon Acquits Miss Nethersole," *New York Times*, Apr. 6, 1900, at 7.
25. Lillian Hellman, *The Children's Hour* (New York: St. Martin's Press, 1934).
26. "Blame the Public for Immoral Plays," *New York Times*, Feb. 12, 1909, at 13.
27. "Censorship of Motion Pictures," *Yale L. J.* 49 (1939): 87, 89.
28. Dominic Shellard and Steve Nicholson, *The Lord Chamberlain Regrets: A History of British Theatre Censorship* (London: The British Library, 2004), 9–10.
29. *Id.* at 68.
30. G. Bernard Shaw, "The Censorship of the State in England," *North Am. Rev.* 169, no. 513 (1899): 251, https://www.jstor.org/stable/25104865.
31. Shellard and Nicholson, *supra* note 28, at 86.
32. Theatres Act, 1968, § 1 (Eng.).
33. *Block v. City of Chicago*, 87 N.E. 1011, 1013 (Ill. 1909).
34. *Mutual Film Corp. v. Industrial Comm'n of Ohio*, 236 U.S. 230, 240 (1915).
35. *Id.* at 243.
36. *The Birth of a Nation*, film, directed by David W. Griffith (San Fernando Valley, CA: David W. Griffith Corp., 1915).
37. *See* Lee Grieveson, *Policing Cinema: Movies and Censorship in Early-Twentieth-Century America* (Berkeley: University of California Press, 2004), 132–33; *see also* Lee Grieveson, "Fighting Films: Race, Morality, and the Governing of Cinema, 1912–1915," in *The Silent Film Reader*, eds. Lee Grieveson and Peter Kraemer (New York: Routledge, 2004), 169.
38. Ass'n of Motion Picture Producer, The Motion Picture Production Code of 1930 (1930), available at https://www.asu.edu/courses/fms200s/total-readings/MotionPictureProductionCode.pdf.
39. *Id.*
40. *Id.*
41. *Id.*
42. H. L. Mencken, *The American Language: An Inquiry into the Development of English in the United States* (New York: Alfred A. Knopf, 1945), Supp. 645.
43. Ass'n of Motion Picture Producer, The Motion Picture Production Code (1956), available at https://productioncode.dhwritings.com/multipleframes_productioncode.php.
44. *See* H. Franklin Robbins Jr. and Steven G. Mason, "The Law of Obscenity—Or Absurdity," St. Thomas L. Rev. 15 (2003): 517, 522–23; and Eric Jaeger, "Obscenity and the Reasonable Person: Will He 'Know It When He Sees It'?," *B.C. L. Rev.* 30 (1989): 823, 832.
45. Ala. Code 1928, ch. 75, § 3193.
46. Ariz. Code, §§ 43–3001, 56–118 (1919).

47. Miss. Code, § 97–29–47 (2010).

48. At the obscenity trial of *Ulysses*, Sam Coleman, representing the prosecution, felt that the only way to win the case was to shock the judge by showing him "the great number of vulgar four-letter words" Joyce used. But, Coleman said, "I can't do it," because "there is a lady in the courtroom." Kevin Birmingham, *The Most Dangerous Book* (New York: Penguin Books, 2014), 319.

49. It wasn't until 2008 that the "C" word appeared in the *Oxford English Dictionary* and 2014 for the "F" word.

50. Geoffrey Hughes, *Political Correctness* (Hoboken, NJ: Wiley-Blackwell, 2010), 46.

51. Mencken, *supra* note 42, at 646.

52. A provision of Michigan law made it a misdemeanor to use "indecent, immoral, obscene, vulgar or insulting language in the presence or hearing of any woman or child." Michigan's Penal Code § 750.337. That law was not repealed until 2016. A somewhat similar provision was once in Cal. Penal Code § 415, but has now been removed.

53. *See* U.S. Equal Emp. Opportunity Comm'n, *Facts about Sexual Harassment*, https://www.eeoc.gov/eeoc/publications/fs-sex.cfm (noting that "verbal . . . conduct of a sexual nature" may constitute sexual harassment when it affects an individual's employment; interferes with their work performance; or creates an intimidating, hostile, or offensive work environment).

54. *Chaplinsky v. New Hampshire*, 315 U.S. 568, 573 (1942).

55. Pub. Laws N.H. 1926, c. 378, § 2.

56. Tracey Tulley, "Debate Erupts at Rutgers Law School after White Student Quotes Racial Slur," *New York Times*, May 4, 2021, at A17. The article goes on to say that any "public use of a racial epithet can carry a risk of steep professional consequences," mentioning, for example, that it led to the firing of the head of the journalism department at Central Michigan University, who also quoted the word.

57. John Parascandola, *Sex, Sin, and Science: A History of Syphilis in America* (Westport, CT: Praeger Publishers, 2008), 91.

58. Eric Burns, *Invasion of the Mind Snatchers: Television's Conquest of America in the Fifties* (Philadelphia: Temple University Press, 2010), 206.

59. 18 U.S.C. § 1464 (2018).

60. Lilli Levi, *The FCC's Regulation of Indecency* 7 First Reports 1 (Apr. 2008), available at http://www.firstamendmentcenter.org/madison/wp-content/uploads/2011/03/FirstReport.Indecency.Levi_.final_.pdf.

61. 438 U.S. 726 (1978).

62. *F.C.C. v. Fox Television Stations, Inc.*, 556 U.S. 502, 530 (2009).

63. *Id.*

64. *Id.*

65. Obscenity, Indecency & Profanity, FCC document, https//www.fcc.gov/reports-research/guides/obscenity-indecency-profanity-faq.

66. FCC Consumer Guide, www.fcc.gov/consumer-governmental-affairs-bureau.

67. FCC, Quarterly Reports, https://www.fcc.gov/general/quarterly-reports-consumer -inquiries-and-complaints.

68. *In the Matter of WDBJ Television, Inc.*, FCC "Notice of Apparent Liability for Forfeiture," March, 2015, FCC 15–32.

69. *Roth v. Goldman*, 172 F. 2d 788 (2nd Cir. 1949).

70. *Id.* at 792 (Frank, J., concurring).

71. *See, e.g., Pathe Exchange, Inc. v. Cobb*, 202 A.D. 450 (N.Y. 1922), aff'd, 236 N.Y. 529 (1923)..

72. 343 U.S. 495 (1952). For a full treatment of the case, and what led up to it, *see* Laura Wittern-Keller and Raymond J. Haberski, Jr., *The Miracle Case: Film Censorship and the Supreme Court* (Lawrence: University Press of Kansas, 2008).

73. *L'Amore* (Finecine 1948).

74. *La Ronde* (Films Sacha Gordine 1954). Schnitzler's book was published in 1897.

75. *Superior Films, Inc. v. Dep't of Educ. of State of Ohio, Div. of Film Censorship*, 346 U.S. 587, 588–89 (1954).

76. On Ohio, see Wittern-Keller and Haberski, *supra* note 72, at 184–85; on Pennsylvania, *id.* at 187–88.

77. Wittern-Keller and Haberski, *supra* note 72, at 147–48.

78. *See Miller v. California*, 413 U.S. 15 (1973).

79. *United States v. One Book Called "Ulysses,"* 5 F. Supp. 182 (S.D.N.Y. 1933), aff'd sub nom. *United States v. One Book Entitled Ulysses by James Joyce*, 72 F.2d 705 (2d. Cir. 1934). For a full account of the trial, see Kevin Birmingham, *The Most Dangerous Book: The Battle for James Joyce's Ulysses* (New York: Penguin Books, 2014), 313–31.

80. *See* Lawrence M. Friedman, *American Law in the 20th Century* (New Haven, CT: Yale University Press, 2002), 563.

81. *See Joseph Burstyn, Inc. v. Wilson*, 343 U.S. 495 (1952).

82. *Freedman v. Maryland*, 380 U.S. 51 (1965).

83. *See* Motion Picture Ass'n, *Film Ratings*, https://www.motionpictures.org/film-ratings.

84. The movie was based on a book, which told the true story of Philomena Lee's search for her lost child, who was renamed Michael Hess by his adoptive parents in the United States. *See* Michael Sixsmith, *The Lost Child of Philomena Lee: The Mother, Her Son and a Fifty-Year Search* (New York: Macmillan, 2011).

85. Adrian Bingham, *Family Newspapers? Sex, Private Life & the British Popular Press, 1918–1978* (Oxford, UK: Oxford University Press, 2009), 30.

86. 354 U.S. 476 (1957). Justice Brennan, who wrote the majority opinion, described sex as "a great and mysterious motive force in human life." The use of the word "mysterious" is particularly interesting. It implies something hidden and strange, something uncanny, something private and dark.

87. *Id.* at 487.

88. 383 U.S. 413 (1966).

89. *Id.* at 419.

90. *Id.*

91. *Timeline of Greatest Film Milestones and Turning Points in Film History: The Year 1972*, Film Site, http://www.filmsite.org/1972-filmhistory.html (last visited Nov.

2, 2015). The exact amount is in some dispute but it may have been something on the order of $45,000,000.

92. Alexis Kleimann, "Porn Sites Get More Visitors Each Month Than Netflix, Amazon and Twitter Combined," *HuffPost*, Dec. 6, 2017.

93. 413 U.S. 15 (1973). Miller's conviction was vacated, and the case was remanded to the lower courts, but with no indication that Miller could not be convicted if the proper legal tests were used. Justice Douglas, dissenting, commented that the "Court has worked hard to define obscenity and concededly has failed." *Id.* at 37 (Douglas, J., dissenting).

94. *Id.* at 27.

95. Ala. Code § 13A-12–131 (2020).

96. N.Y. Penal Law § 235.00(1) (2020). Similarly, in Illinois: 720 Ill. Comp. Stat. 5/11–20 ch. 38, par. 11(b) (2020).

97. Va. Code § 18.2–372 (2014).

98. The Obscene Publications Act, 1959, 7 & 8 Eliz. 2, ch. 66, § 1(1) (Eng.).

99. *State v. Henry*, 732 P.2d 9 (Or. 1987).

100. *Reno v. ACLU*, 521 U.S. 844 (1997).

101. 414 U.S. 105 (1973).

102. 403 U.S. 15 (1971).

103. *Cohen v. California*, 403 U.S. 15 (1971).

104. *Memoirs v. Massachusetts*, 383 U.S. 413, 426 (1966).

105. *See* "Playboy in Popular Culture," *New York Times,* Sept. 28, 2017.

106. Ravi Somaiya, "Nudes Are Old News at *Playboy*," *New York Times,* Oct. 13, 2015, at A1. The magazine would still "feature women in provocative poses," but "no longer . . . fully nude."

107. *See* Derek Hawkins, "After a Nudity-Free Year, Playboy Will Again Run Pictures of Naked Women," *Washington Post*, Feb. 14, 2017.

108. N.Y. Penal §§ 235.00 and 235.20 (McKinney 2020).

109. 720 ILCS sec. 11–20 (c) (2020).

110. *See* Annie Julia Wyman, "What Kind of Town Bans Books?," *New Yorker*, Oct. 1, 2014.

111. In June 2017, it was discovered that the yearbook of a grade school in San Diego County had reprinted on the cover an old map, which, unfortunately, contained a place-name in which the n-word appeared. When this was discovered, the staff of the school had to go through each yearbook and scratch out the offensive name. Anne Claire Stapleton, "Students Get Yearbook with N-word on the Cover," *CNN.com*, June 7, 2017.

112. On this, see Lawrence M. Friedman, "Limited Monarchy: The Rise and Fall of Student Rights," in *School Days, Rule Days: The Legalization and Regulation of Education*, eds. David L. Kirp and Donald N. Jensen (London: Falmer Press, 1986), 238; see also *Cleveland Board of Education v. LaFleur*, 414 U.S. 632 (1974), striking down a rule requiring pregnant school teachers to step down, and mentioning the factor discussed in the text.

113. *See* Valerie J. Huber and Michael W. Firmin, "A History of Sex Education in the United States since 1900," *Int'l J. Educ. Reform* 23 (2014): 25.

114. *See, e.g.*, C. E. Koop, U.S. Dep't of Health and Human Servs., "Surgeon General's Report on Acquired Immune Deficiency Syndrome," *Pub. Health Rep.* 102 (1987): 1–3.

115. *See* Patricia Donovan, "School-Based Sexuality Education: The Issues and Challenges," *Perspectives on Sexual and Reproductive Health* 30, no. 4 (1998): 188–193; *see also* "History of Sex Education in the U.S.," Planned Parenthood, https://www.plannedparenthood.org/uploads/filer_public/3e/de/3edec4e8-3604-44f9-998b-6a7cff9d22ad/20170209_sexed_d04_1.pdf.

116. For additional information on state policies regarding sexual education, see "Sex and HIV Education: State Laws and Policies," Guttmacher Inst.; *see also* "Opt-Outs and Sex Ed: What Are the Percentages?," Sexuality Info. and Educ. Council of the United States.

117. The right of parents to control aspects of their children's education, without undue interference from the state, was recognized in *Mayer v. Nebraska*, 262 U. S. 390 (1923), and in *Pierce v. Society of Sisters*, 268 U.S. 510, 534–35 (1925), the Court recognized the fundamental "liberty of parents and guardians to direct the upbringing and education of children under their control."

118. *See, e.g.*, Ala. Code § 16–41–6 (LexisNexis 2012); Cal. Educ. Code § 51937 (West 2006).

119. *Leebaert v. Harrington*, 332 F.3d 134, 135–38 (2d Cir. 2003).

120. *Fields v. Palmdale Sch. Dist.*, 427 F.3d 1197, 1200–03 (9th Cir. 2005), *opinion amended on denial of reh'g sub nom. Fields v. Palmdale Sch. Dist.* (PSD), 447 F.3d 1187 (9th Cir. 2006).

121. *Id.* at 1200.

122. *See* Michelle McQuigge, "Ontario's Sex-Ed Curriculum: Hundreds of Kids Stay Home in Protest," *HuffPost*, May 4, 2015.

123. *See* "Parents Protest 'Graphic' Sex Ed Curriculum in Calif. Schools," CBS News, Mar. 30, 2017.

124. "Fact Sheet: Adolescent Sexual and Reproductive Health in the United States," Guttmacher Inst.

125. *Id.*

126. *Id.*

127. *See* "National Data Shows Comprehensive Sex Education Better at Reducing Teen Pregnancy Than Abstinence-Only Programs," Sexuality Info. and Educ. Council of the United States.

128. Cal. Penal Code, § 288 (2020). Other provisions are more specific, prohibiting "oral copulation" with anybody under eighteen, or under sixteen if one of the participants is over twenty-one. Cal. Penal Code, § 288a (2014).

129. 458 U.S. 747 (1982).

130. Child Pornography Prevention Act of 1996, 18 U.S.C. § 2252A, *invalidated by Ashcroft v. Free Speech Coalition*, 535 U.S. 234 (2002).

131. *Ashcroft v. Free Speech Coalition*, 535 U.S. 234 (2002).

132. 18 U.S.C. § 1466A (2018).

133. 18 U.S.C. § 1462 (2018).

134. Press release, Dep't of Justice, https://www.justice.gov/opa/pr/former-elementary-school-teacher-s-assistant-sentenced-150-months-child-exploitation-crimes.

Chapter 4

The Privilege of Silence

As we saw in chapter 1, you have a right to keep your body private; and, indeed, historically you *had* to keep it private. Nobody could force you to undress in public, nor would you be allowed to undress in public, even if you wanted to. Also, nobody could force you to talk about sex or use "dirty" words. Of course, all of us have conversations, about sex or anything else, that we consider private, and which we would like to keep private. And, as it turns out, the law does in fact protect the privacy of some types of conversation. These rules about confidentiality are part of the law of evidence. The rules protect certain private conversations; they stem from policies and motives that are very different from those that concern the body or the rules of censorship. The technical term for these rules is "privilege." What you tell your lawyer about your case is private. The lawyer cannot be forced to disclose what you said, even in court, even under oath. This chapter briefly describes this and other evidentiary "privileges." When do you have the choice to remain silent? When must you stay silent? When must you speak?

THEIR LIPS ARE SEALED

In 2001, a man named José Morales, who had spent thirteen years in prison in New York State, sued for a writ of habeas corpus.[1] If you read the words of the United States District Court for the Southern District of New York, it would be hard to resist feeling that Morales had been the victim of a monstrous miscarriage of justice.

Morales had been convicted of murder, but on very shaky evidence. A gang of teenagers had actually committed the crime. One eyewitness fingered Morales, while five others testified in such a way as to give him an alibi. The jury chose to believe the one eyewitness. Shortly after the trial, as sentence was about to be pronounced, a young man, seventeen-year-old Jesús Fornes, told at least four people that he was the actual killer and that Morales and his co-defendant, Ruben Montalvo, were innocent. The four people to whom Fornes confessed were a priest, Father Joseph Towle; Montalvo's mother; a lawyer for the Legal Aid Society whom he had consulted for advice; and the defendant Morales's lawyer, who Fornes had approached during Morales's sentencing. Fornes told the defendant's lawyer, "I did the crime, I will do the time. They did nothing. They weren't even there."[2]

None of these statements could be admitted in evidence at the trial, even though they clearly would have been sufficient to exonerate Morales. Some were barred by rules about confidentiality. Catholic practice sealed the priest's lips. Fornes's lawyer was not able to testify because of the attorney-client privilege. Fornes did not testify himself, invoking the privilege against self-incrimination. And what Fornes said to Moltalvo's mother was excluded from court on the grounds that it was hearsay. Morales and Montalvo went to prison.

Years went by. Fornes died in an accident. Father Towle wrestled with *his* conscience, and decided (somewhat legalistically) that Fornes's statement had not really been a "confession"; rather, it was just a "heart-to-heart talk," and therefore he was free to come forward.[3] The prosecution's case unraveled, though the state, for whatever reason, stubbornly continued to insist that Morales was guilty. The federal judge, Denny Chin, was convinced, however, that Morales was innocent, that Fornes was telling the truth when he confessed. He granted the writ of habeas corpus.[4]

This case can be read either as a story about the ultimate triumph of justice, or as a depressing tale of rank injustice perpetrated by the legal system. It illustrates, for one thing, the grim, misplaced tenacity of prosecutors, who often seem stubbornly reluctant to admit the prosecution has made a mistake.[5] It is also one more example of how easy it is for so-called eyewitnesses to be wrong.[6] But above all, it is a case about the power of confidentiality. It is a case about evidentiary privileges: rights to keep certain kinds of information private, to keep them out of court.

Privileges limit the flow of information from witnesses to the jury and other courtroom figures. English common law recognized a number of evidentiary privileges, and early American courts adopted them.[7] The law recognizes a number of different privileges. There is, for example, an attorney-client privilege. There are two privileges that apply to "pillow talk" between spouses. One is a testimonial privilege; in other words, one spouse cannot be forced to testify against the other. The other is a marital confidences privilege, protecting certain communications against even voluntary disclosure. What you tell your psychiatrist is also confidential, and hence privileged. These are the most generally recognized privileges, though a few states also recognize a general doctor-patient privilege, or even a parent-child privilege.

Probably the most important privilege is a more general one: the privilege against self-incrimination. This indeed is enshrined in both the federal and state constitutions. Under the Fifth Amendment to the federal Constitution, a defendant cannot be forced, "in any criminal case," to "be a witness against himself."[8] This clause protects two distinct rights: (1) a defendant's right not to take the witness stand in his or her own criminal trial and (2) a person's right not to answer any questions in any proceeding, civil or criminal, if his responses might be incriminating. This is a right to refuse to "respond to inquiries, not a prohibition against inquiries designed to elicit responses incriminating in nature."[9] The right against self-incrimination is considered so important that the police must inform an individual about it before questioning a suspect they have in custody.[10] The famous "Miranda warning" stems from the Supreme Court case of *Miranda v. Arizona*: a suspect must be told of the right to remain silent and reminded that the government can use a person's own words against them in court.[11] The warnings are familiar to virtually everyone who watches TV or goes to the movies, even though most people have never had to listen to a police officer giving them the warning. The right to *Miranda* warnings is "self-executing"; the suspect does not have to claim it specifically.[12] The right to remain silent can be waived—but unless and until an individual makes a knowing and voluntary waiver, the police must stop questioning the suspect.[13] If the police fail to read the *Miranda* warning to a suspect, they will not be allowed to bring into court any evidence they got during questioning, under the "exclusionary rule."[14] In other words, the privilege against self-incrimination gives people the right to keep information private, even at the cost of a certain amount of truth and justice. The elective privacy here is deemed (probably rightly so) important enough to be worth the cost. Privileges are justified on various grounds. The privilege against self-incrimination, for example, is presumably a bulwark against an over-mighty state; it goes far back in history.[15] In our own times, this privilege, and the others, can also be analyzed as aspects of *privacy*. Each separate privilege may protect privacy for a different reason. We will return to this theme.

The law of privilege is complicated; it is a confused tangle of rules and standards. Policies clash and change prismatically over time. Perhaps the main justification for evidentiary privileges is to allow relationships that depend on confidential communications to flourish. For the great evidence scholar Wigmore, this was the driving force behind these privileges. One of four conditions he deemed necessary to justify a privilege is that the "element of confidentiality must be essential to the full and satisfactory maintenance of the relation between the parties."[16] But notions of privacy are also invoked to justify privileges, especially in more modern cases, as courts decided whether particular communications should be treated as privileged.[17] Federal

Rule of Evidence 501, which was enacted in 1975, makes clear that courts can recognize testimonial privileges on a case-by-case basis.[18] This makes the reasoning behind privileges all the more important. A privilege might be justified based on an individual's claim of privacy—the "demand . . . that his private personal affairs shall not be laid bare to the world and be discussed by strangers."[19] Crucial concepts in privacy law are also relevant here: it is embodied in the phrase "reasonable expectation of privacy." Like pi in mathematics, this notion crops up in all sorts of places. Privacy is not and cannot be an absolute, in any of its senses. The phrase expresses one of the limiting notions. And it reflects general feelings, norms, and attitudes about privacy; these tend to harden over time into doctrine, and find their way into law.

The law of privileges, the subject of this chapter, may seem like a cluster of dry, doctrinal principles. Technically, privileges are exceptions to a general rule that relevant evidence is admissible in court. But like all other aspects of the law, the rules of privilege reflect social norms and attitudes. As the Supreme Court noted more than a century ago, the privileges are thought to protect certain interests, that are "more important than the interests served by the resolution of litigation based on full disclosure of all relevant facts."[20] "The public," after all, "has a right to every man's evidence."[21] There needs to be a pretty significant counterweight to justify ignoring relevant facts in a legal system that is supposedly premised on a search for truth. There is in society a vague but significant feeling that out of the many rooms and chambers that make up life in society, there are some into which the law must not be allowed to enter. In such spaces, either the government and its legal system are absolutely barred, or the law may enter only with a "warrant." The word "warrant" has two meanings. One, a quite concrete meaning, refers to a document issued by a judge. But there is also a less literal meaning: a warrant is a justified right.

It is the second meaning, primarily, which this chapter is concerned with. Privileges are doctrines that extend the cloak of privacy over certain kinds of discussions.

ATTORNEY-CLIENT PRIVILEGE

This is one of the most significant privileges; it is one of the oldest and best known. What you say to your attorney is "confidential." You cannot be forced to reveal it, even in court, even under oath. Without your permission, your lawyer cannot testify about anything you told her. What you say to a lawyer, in her capacity as a lawyer, is private: it is between you and her only. The California Evidence Code, for example, gives a client a "privilege to refuse to disclose, and to prevent another from disclosing, a confidential communication between client and lawyer."[22] The lawyer, of course, is the "other" who the client can prevent from talking. The Texas Rules of Evidence use analogous language: communications are privileged, when they are made to facilitate "the rendition of professional legal services."[23]

This is a strong privilege, but no privilege is absolute. When can it be overridden? Here is where the concept of a "reasonable expectation of privacy" comes in. What you say to your lawyer is not privileged if you say it in a room full of people. In that situation, one might say that you had "waived the privilege," but that is law talk. What this means in ordinary language is that, if you have an audience, you have no reason to think what you said was private and could or should be kept secret.

The attorney-client privilege is considered "indispensable"; it "may well be the pivotal element of the modern American lawyer's function as advocate."[24] The policy behind this privilege seems clear enough. Clients should be able to speak openly and frankly to their lawyers. Communication would be stifled if the lawyer could be forced to testify about these conversations. Only by promising complete silence can we encourage clients to communicate openly and honestly with their lawyers and only with such communication can lawyers serve the client's interests. The lawyer, after all, can "adequately prepare a case only if the client is free to disclose everything, bad as well as good."[25] As the Supreme Court noted, the "lawyer-client privilege rests on the need for the advocate and counselor to know all that relates to the client's reasons for seeking representation if the professional mission is to be carried out."[26] The privilege, by the way, belongs to the client, not the lawyer. The client can waive it; the lawyer cannot.[27] In the *Morales* case, young Jesús Fornes invoked the privilege. Fornes was dead at the time the action for habeas corpus was brought but, somewhat surprisingly, the attorney-client privilege is in some regards immortal; it survives the death of the client, at least as a general rule, though with a number of fuzzy exceptions.[28]

There is a rich harvest of cases on the privilege and a substantial literature of analysis. What the client said, in general, is protected only if it was intended to be confidential. And what the lawyer says to the client is not protected, unless the lawyer's advice is too tangled up with communications from the client to render the two inseparable.[29] As one court noted, "In practice . . . advice does not spring from lawyers' heads as Athena did from the brow of Zeus." Inevitably, attorney's opinions reflect an accumulation of education and experience in the law; the advice that is a reaction to what the client said "cloaks a communication from attorney to client 'based, in part at least, upon a confidential communication [to the lawyer from the client].'"[30]

The privilege only goes one way. The law is complicated: there are many subsidiary questions, and a flock of exceptions, big and small, some of them embodied in statutes. But the core of the privilege remains quite robust.

You don't have to be cynical to notice that lawyers benefit from the privilege, professionally and economically.[31] This has led to a certain amount of criticism. Jeremy Bentham, in the early nineteenth century, was one of the most famous (and oldest) of the critics; Bentham felt the privilege was harmful in that it protected guilty people. Getting rid of the privilege would make it harder for guilty people to concoct a false defense.[32] The privilege, nonetheless, survives. That it sometimes leads to injustice is undeniable. But it is important for the protection of clients—at least this is a plausible argument.

MARITAL PRIVILEGE

There are, in fact, two distinct privileges that flow from the status of husband and wife. The "spousal testimonial privilege" is one of the two; a married witness does not have to testify against his or her spouse in a criminal case.[33] This is true even if the testimony would concern something that happened before they were married. At one time, spouses could not give any testimony for or against each other in a court proceeding, whether the testimony was positive or negative. As Lord Coke pronounced in 1628, "[I]t hath beene resolved by the Justices that a wife cannot be produced either against or for her husband."[34] But this prohibition was tangled up with two rules that are no longer part of the law—a general ban on the testimony of interested parties and the doctrine of coverture, that is, the idea that a married woman had little or no legal existence separate from her husband. The privilege has survived, but in a changed form. Since the first half of the twentieth century, spouses have been allowed to testify *for*—but not against—the other spouse. The reason for the distinction is that hoary chestnut: fostering "family peace," which benefits the family, and society in general.[35] Jeremy Bentham wrote that permitting spousal testimony would veer from a world in which "every man's house is his castle" to one in which his house is "a den of thieves."[36] What would the breakfast table be like after one spouse took the stand and testified in a way that was adverse to the other? In most places, the privilege only applies in criminal cases.[37] And only legally married couples have access to the privilege—courts do not consider cohabitants to be eligible, no matter how much they act like a married couple.[38] Furthermore, couples who marry only to defraud or manipulate, such as a sham green-card marriage, may also not be protected.[39] Even a lawfully married couple loses the privilege if they divorce.[40]

In some states, the defendant holds the privilege; a married defendant can keep his or her spouse from giving harmful testimony, even if the spouse is perfectly willing to talk on the witness stand. In *Hawkins v. United States*, the Supreme Court held that the privilege belonged to both spouses—the defendant and the spouse who might be summoned as a witness.[41] But the Court rolled back the federal rule twenty-two years later; the states had trended in a similar direction: the privilege was vested only in the spouse called to testify. In California, for example, a "married person has a privilege not to testify against his spouse in any proceeding."[42] The Court reconsidered the evidentiary rule in federal court proceedings in *Trammel v. United States*.[43] Otis Trammel was on trial for smuggling heroin into the United States. His wife was part of the scheme; she was caught, and, in exchange for leniency, eagerly testified against her husband. She was essentially the entire case for the prosecution; and Trammel was convicted. He tried to invoke the privilege, arguing that he should be able to *prevent* her from testifying about his alleged role in a heroin distribution conspiracy, but he lost the argument. The Supreme Court, despite earlier case law to the contrary, held that the wife had discretion to invoke the privilege or not, as she saw fit; if she wanted to testify, her husband could not stop her. Her marriage to the defendant did not disqualify her as a witness; it simply gave her the privilege to elect to remain silent—or to speak, if what she had to say might be damaging. But what about the idea of preserving harmony between husband and wife? If one spouse was willing to testify against the other in a criminal case, the Court argued, then the marital relationship "is almost certainly in disrepair" already.[44] Trammell's conviction was upheld.[45] Whether the marriage survived is another question.

If Trammell's wife had information that might have helped him, rather than incriminated him, she could have been forced to testify. The privilege does give one spouse the option to withhold favorable testimony in a criminal case where the other spouse is the defendant.[46] But even if a spouse elects to remain silent, damaging statements made by the spouse may be admitted into evidence if they come from another source. Courts are split about whether other witnesses can repeat things the spouse has said, even when the spouse refuses to testify (and assuming there is no hearsay issue).[47]

The spousal privilege is somewhat controversial, and some states have abandoned it. Most states that have kept it have carved out an exception for domestic violence cases. It would, after all, be strange if a husband could prevent his wife from testifying at a trial where he stands accused of beating or abusing her.[48] Battered women, however, are often understandably leery about taking the stand, which presents a complex legal and social problem. One of the cornerstones of the defendant's right to a fair trial, in our system, is the right to confront the witnesses, and recent court cases have put special emphasis on this right.[49] But the right to "confront" is obviously obnoxious to witnesses who do not want to expose themselves to public scrutiny or to cross-examination, which can be quite harsh. Still, the duty to testify is, in general, an outstanding example of the limits of people's privacy rights. A person called as a witness cannot simply say, "I'd rather not."

There is also a separate privilege for pillow-talk, as it were: the so-called marital confidences privilege. A husband, for example, can refuse to reveal confidences between him and his wife, and he can also prevent her from revealing any such confidences; she has the same power. All of the states recognize this privilege. It applies, in most states, both to the spouse that uttered the words and to the spouse that heard the words. But the statement has to be intended to be confidential,[50] and it must be kept confidential afterward.[51] A spouse who discloses the information does not kill the other spouse's privilege; but if the spouse discloses to a third party, that spouse's privilege is lost.[52] The pillow-talk privilege applies in all types of proceedings—civil, criminal, and administrative. The privilege too only applies to lawfully married couples, but it can be invoked even after a marriage is over, as long as it pertains to communications that took place during the marriage.[53]

This privilege seems directly rooted in notions of privacy. A marriage is fundamentally a private relationship, and there are many doctrines that prevent the prying eyes of the government or private third parties from peeking inside the relationship. In family law, for example, the doctrine of marital privacy prevents one spouse from suing the other for support during the marriage, even though there is a duty for each one to support the other. Courts feel enforcement of the right to support is too much of an intrusion into the private space of marriage.[54] Similarly, in the famous case of *Griswold v. Connecticut* (1965), the Supreme Court held that the state could not prohibit the sale or use of contraceptives.[55] As Justice Douglas asked in the majority opinion, "Would we allow the police to search the sacred precincts of marital bedrooms for telltale signs of the use of contraceptives?" Obviously not. "The very idea," he said, "is repulsive to the notions of privacy surrounding the marriage relationship." The confidential communications privilege is thus in line with other legal principles that accord great respect for marital privacy.[56] The Supreme Court has recognized that the privilege granted to confidential communications is useful and benign; and has a firm place in the federal law of evidence.

> This rule of privilege for spousal confidences is founded on the deepest and soundest principles of our nature. These principles have grown out of those domestic relations that constitute the basis of civil society, and are essential to the enjoyment of that confidence that should subsist between those who are connected by the nearest and dearest relations of life. To break down or impair the great principles that protect the sanctities of husband and wife would be to destroy the best solace of human existence.[57]

Other modern decisions support this somewhat overblown praise for the privilege. As one court put it, marital confidences are "so essential to the preservation of the marriage relationship as to outweigh the disadvantages to the administration of justice."[58]

Despite all this laudatory language, the law recognizes a number of exceptions; one of them, more or less like the exception to the other marital privilege, cuts off the privilege if the defendant is charged with certain specific crimes or charged with a "crime . . . against the person or property of the other spouse or of a child of either."[59] It also doesn't apply to suits between spouses, including divorce actions and child custody suits.[60] Nor does it protect joint participants in a crime, at least to the extent of the communications that occurred during their criminal activity.[61] The policies behind the privilege "pale in the face of public concerns about bringing criminals to justice."[62] Some court opinions have held that the privilege does not apply to a troubled marriage or where the spouses have permanently separated.[63] The boundaries of this privilege are somewhat uncertain. It can apply not only to oral and written communications, but to expressive conduct as well.[64] The privilege plainly applies to a sealed letter written from husband to wife. But what about a postcard, which all the world can see? Anything blurted out in front of a third person is clearly not privileged, but what if someone overhears a husband and wife whispering to each other?

And what if the message is sent by email?[65] Consider the troubles of one Philip Hamilton. Hamilton was a member of the Virginia House of Delegates. He was also a part-time consultant for the public school system of the city of Newport News. He had financial problems, and this got him into serious trouble. He went on trial in federal court for bribery and extortion. The charge flowed from Hamilton's dealings with Old Dominion University, a public university in Norfolk, Virginia. Hamilton desperately wanted a job with the university, and he got one. But, according to the charge, this was a dirty deal: he would get the job—director of a new university Center for Teacher Quality—if he could get the legislature to fund the Center, which he did. A jury convicted him, and he appealed. In December 2012, the Fourth Circuit Court of Appeals turned down his appeal.[66]

Hamilton's lawyer raised a number of points, but the crucial one concerned the marital communications privilege. The trial court had admitted into evidence some fairly damning emails that he had sent to his wife. He had used a "workplace computer, through his work email account," and he did nothing in later years "to safeguard the emails."[67] The appellate court refused to apply the privilege. There was no "reasonable expectation of privacy"; therefore, the emails were not truly "confidential."[68]

The court cited a Supreme Court case from 1934, *Wolfle v. United States*.[69] In that case, the key question turned on a letter that the defendant wrote to his wife, "but [was] proved by the testimony of a stenographer" who read from her notes.[70] The defendant had been foolish enough to dictate the letter to his secretary. The Supreme Court decided that the communication was "not within the privilege," because he had voluntarily disclosed the communication to a third person, his stenographer.[71]

The *Hamilton* court thought this was relevant. It said that email "has become the modern stenographer."[72] Yet surely Hamilton *thought* these emails were private; he certainly was not such a fool as to want the world to became aware of these messages. He learned his lesson the hard way. It is a lesson most people are learning, slowly and painfully. Emails are never totally private. You cannot, for example, actually delete them, you cannot drive a stake through their hearts; they have some sort of shadowy existence, for ever and ever, somewhere out there in cyberspace. Technology is outstripping our "reasonable expectations." But of course, insofar as we really *do* learn the lesson, then, as a matter of fact, when we send an email, arguably we lack that all-important "reasonable expectation of privacy."

It is easy to get lost in technicalities, case law analysis, and doctrinal fine points. The real question is, what is the point of the privilege or does it actually have a point? Old chestnuts about marital harmony seem pretty feeble nowadays. Modern science can perform miracles, but it cannot tell us what does and what does not rock the boat of marital love. There may not *be* an answer, at least not a satisfying answer. The key—if there is a key—is not marital harmony but privacy, or, to be more precise, the changing notions of what is and what is not a "reasonable expectation of privacy."

Cases on overheard conversations are instructive. In a Florida case, Charles William Proffitt lived in a mobile home with two bedrooms. The second bedroom was rented out to a Mrs. Bassett. Proffitt told his wife he had stabbed a man to death. Mrs. Bassett heard him say this, although she admitted she only heard "segments" of the conversation. Proffitt was convicted, and one of his grounds for appeal was the marital confidence privilege. The Florida Supreme Court rejected this claim; Mrs. Bassett's testimony had been properly admitted into evidence.[73] Mr. and Mrs. Proffitt certainly did not want to be overheard, did not know they had been overheard, and certainly never waived the marital confidence privilege. The Florida court was, perhaps, unenthusiastic about the privilege and perhaps even considered it obsolete. There was no reason, then, not to nibble away at it. Moreover, Proffitt had killed a man and presumably deserved to be punished. This was surely not lost on the court.

Pillow-talk falls within the zone of the "reasonable expectation of privacy." Almost all of us would agree that nobody has a right to take pictures of husbands and wives having sex in their bedroom, or a right to force them to undress in public, or even a right to eavesdrop by listening in on their talk, at least not as a general rule. If you tell someone a secret, you always run the risk that they will pass it along to somebody else; the juicier the secret, the greater the temptation to your confidante, who might tell the secret to at least one other person, and this person might pass it along to one more, and so on and so on. The only fool-proof way to keep a secret is to keep it. But most people may think that what you say to a spouse—like what you say to a lawyer or to the priest in the confessional booth—falls into a different category. Nevertheless, there can be limits: confessing to a spouse that you committed murder might cross a line into "unprivileged" territory. An "expectation of privacy" has to be "reasonable," and society decides what is reasonable and what is not.

THE CLERGY

As we mentioned, a priest, minister, rabbi, or imam can refuse to testify about confessions or confidences made by a member of his flock. This applies especially to the confession booth. Some form of this privilege exists in every state. In some states, the privilege is shifted from the clergyman to the penitent: testimony about the confession or confidence is taboo, unless the penitent agrees. The California Evidence Code gives the privilege both to the penitent and to the clergy if the communication is confidential and is made to a "member of the clergy who . . . is authorized or accustomed to hear those communications," and who, under church rules, "has a duty to keep those communications secret."[74] There is a similar rule in other states as well, for example, Colorado.[75]

The California provision seems fairly narrow; it is aimed, perhaps, primarily at Catholics who tell tales to a priest in the confessional booth. Other statutes are broader. The Wisconsin statute protects a "confidential communication . . . to a member of the clergy in the member's professional character as a spiritual adviser."[76] Under Catholic doctrine, the privilege is pretty much absolute; the priest may not disclose whatever was confessed, law or no law. Father Towle, as we saw, found a way out of his dilemma but this would not normally be the case.

In general, under state law, clergy must report any case of suspected child abuse; thus, in Arkansas, for example, a clergyman must "immediately notify the Child Abuse Hotline" if the member of the clergy has "reasonable cause to suspect . . . child maltreatment."[77] But the Wisconsin statute makes an exception for "communications made . . . privately or in a confessional setting," if the "disciplines, tenets or traditions of . . . [the] religion" impose a duty "to keep these communications secret," an obvious gesture to Catholic doctrine.[78]

THE PSYCHIATRIST'S COUCH

There is a privilege not only for pillow-talk, but also for couch talk; any "confidential communication" made by a patient to a psychiatrist or psychotherapist is also privileged.[79] We want people, presumably, to seek professional help for their neuroses and psychoses, and the privilege is, therefore, supposed to be sound policy. How far does the privilege extend, and to which professions? In *Jaffee v. Redmond* (1996), Mary Lu Redmond was a police officer in the Village of Hoffman Estates in Illinois.[80] She shot and killed a man while she was on duty and, although she claimed self-defense, this fact was disputed. The estate of the dead man sued Officer Redmond. Redmond, it seems, had sat through fifty sessions with a "licensed clinical social worker." The plaintiff wanted to see the notes from these counseling sessions. Were they privileged?

The federal courts had never clearly signed on to the psychiatrist's privilege. In this case, however, the Supreme Court interpreted Federal Rule of Evidence 501 to include the privilege, bringing federal law in line with the courts of all fifty states. Moreover, it held that the privilege was broad enough to include the "licensed clinical social worker" involved in this case. In permitting her to protect the notes she took while meeting with the officer, the Court recognized a broad privilege for communications between patients and those administering psychotherapy. The possibility of future disclosures by the therapist would "impede development of the confidential relationship." Effective therapy "depends on an atmosphere of confidence and trust in which the patient is willing to make a frank and complete disclosure of facts, emotions, memories and fears."[81] Justice Scalia dissented in his customary biting and sarcastic way. He had his doubts about the privilege altogether. The majority opinion was "particularly unpalatable for those who love justice." He sneered at the whole idea of a counseling privilege. People had always tried to work out their difficulties by talking them out: to "parents, siblings, best friends and bartenders." It was ridiculous to extend the privilege to social workers. If you needed advice, you might as well go to a priest, a rabbi, or get "advice from your mom."[82]

Stevens, who wrote the majority opinion, and Scalia clearly lived in different cultural and moral worlds. To Stevens, counseling could be good for people; indeed, people should be encouraged to seek out advice and therapy from professionals. Scalia, on the other hand, had contempt for the whole counseling trade. For him, convicting the guilty was a paramount value and privileges were obstacles in the path of justice. For a law-and-order person like Scalia, the privacy of the couch (though presumably not the privacy of the confessional booth) had no particular social value.

The privilege is far from absolute, in any event. It took a beating in the well-known *Tarasoff* case in California (1976). A man named Prosenjit Poddar, who was in treatment at Cowell Memorial Hospital at the University of California, Berkeley, told his therapist, Dr. Lawrence Moore, about his wish to kill a woman "readily identifiable" as Tatiana Tarasoff. Poddar was committed to a mental hospital, and then released. He did in fact murder Ms. Tarasoff, and her family sued the University of California. Dr. Moore, they claimed, had a duty to warn—in other words, he had a duty to disclose Poddar's murderous intention. The California Supreme Court agreed. The decision sent the psychiatric profession, and ancillary professions, into a kind of panic. The ruling threatened to destroy the privilege, and it would have a negative effect (they argued) on the therapeutic process. Organizations of mental health professionals asked the court to grant a rehearing. State supreme courts rarely grant rehearings but in this case, the California Supreme Court agreed to rehear the case. On rehearing, the Court modified its opinion—but only slightly. There was no absolute duty to warn, but there was a duty to use "reasonable care," which *might* include a duty to warn.[83] Psychiatrists and others, who are, after all, not lawyers, probably still assume there is some sort of duty to warn. The holding of the second decision was extremely vague—what does "reasonable" mean? This kind of standard is impossible for professionals to follow or to work with. The *Tarasoff* case did, however, have an influence on the mindset of mental health professionals. They changed their behavior; they were and are keenly aware of the case, and they recognize a duty to warn in appropriate cases.[84] *Tarasoff*, of course, was a California case, and presumably did not apply elsewhere, but this kind of jurisdictional point, which is obvious to lawyers, is not obvious to lay people. In any event, there are statutes and cases in almost every state by now dealing with the *Tarasoff* issue.

ALL IN THE FAMILY

The *Tarasoff* case fits in with other developments in the law. For example, there is a statutory duty on doctors and others to report suspicions of child abuse; this duty trumps most of the privileges. Some states, however, leave the confessional privilege and the lawyer-client privilege untouched by this duty to report. Kentucky is one of these states.[85] In Michigan, any "legally recognized privileged communication" is "abrogated" with regard to the duty to report suspected child abuse, but here, too, the attorney-client privilege and confessional admissions are exceptions to this exception.[86] Statements made in the confessional booth are treated as sacred in Wisconsin.

Before the late twentieth century, a curtain of secrecy guarded most intimate behavior, whether good or bad, from the eyes of the world. Private life was exactly that: private. Only extreme violence broke through and received legal attention; a husband who beat his wife severely or who killed his wife forfeited, in theory and to some extent in practice, the protective privacy of family life. Yet, somewhat surprisingly, when a woman killed an abusive husband or lover, courts and juries were sometimes apt to forgive the defendant and find her not guilty.[87] Today, the curtain of secrecy is no longer quite so thick; there are a number of important rips and vents. Child abuse and domestic violence are considered serious social problems. The law, it is felt, must deal with these issues. "Privacy" is no longer the trump card here, if it ever was.

Child neglect has been a criminal offense for a long time. But in recent years, child abuse and child molestation have become issues as salient as neglect, if not more so. Catholic priests who abused children are the subject of a huge international scandal. The scandal of abuse drove the Boy Scouts into bankruptcy.[88] Sometimes the scandal is closer to home: the villain may be a family member. In 1987, lawyer Joel Steinberg beat to death six-year-old Lisa, a child he had illegally adopted. The incident, and the trial that followed, produced screaming headlines.[89] To mention another high-profile example, the former president of Penn State University was convicted of child endangerment for failing to stop Jerry Sandusky from molesting children attending a program on the campus.[90]

One might think that child abuse, child molestation, and the like have become a kind of modern epidemic, a disease rarely seen in the past, which has suddenly burst out into public. In fact, no one can say whether child abuse is more common today than in the past; there might be more, less, or the same amount today as, say, a century ago. But clearly, society now deals more seriously with the issue. The curtain of privacy is definitely less dense and protective than it was in the past.

The emphasis on child abuse is consistent with increased sensitivity to the rights of children and the wrongs done to them, as we saw in chapter 3. Prudery and censorship no longer shield children from the big bad facts of life. Arguably, then, they need more protection in other ways. In general, too, the walls of the home have become more porous. In an age of broken homes, high divorce rates, blended families, and cohabitation, many people feel that the family has entered a time of troubles or crisis. More and more, the home is less and less the castle that perhaps it once was. The law can penetrate its walls in defense of the children. Parents can forfeit their children if they fail to live up to legal standards. Crisis, here and elsewhere, trumps privacy. We will explore this theme in later chapters.

A GRAB-BAG OF PRIVILEGES

The common law did not recognize a general doctor-patient privilege. There is none under the federal rules of evidence, but many states have enacted statutes to provide at least some protection for information shared between patient and doctor. Like any other privilege, the point is to foster open communication so that the patient feels comfortable confiding in the doctor; in this way, the doctor will be better able to advise and treat the patient. The privilege would also "prevent physicians from disclosing information which might result in humiliation, embarrassment or disgrace to patients."[91] After all, doctors often end up with private information most patients would prefer to keep secret—whether it's something as simple as a patient's body weight, an unsightly rash, or, more seriously, information about a sexually transmitted disease or an overdose. The scope of this privilege varies by state. In California, for example, a patient can refuse to disclose a "confidential communication" made to a doctor, even a doctor like a podiatrist.[92] Texas has a privilege similar to California's.[93] In Colorado, the privilege extends to doctors as well as to any "registered professional nurse" who is assisting a doctor.[94] California also recognizes a limited privilege for confidential communications made by a victim to a "sexual assault counselor," a "domestic violence counselor," or a "human trafficking caseworker."[95] These privileges created by statute have a number of exceptions. In California, physician-patient privilege cannot be invoked in any "criminal proceeding" or in any tort action for injury or death.[96] The federal Health Insurance Portability and Accountability Act (HIPAA) is more important today in protecting medical information than state privileges. We discuss HIPAA in more detail later in this chapter.

Are communications to an accountant privileged? More than half of the states have passed laws creating such a privilege. Courts have tended to construe these privileges narrowly.[97] Jurisdictions do not agree on whether the privilege belongs to the accountant or the client. In some states, the accountant can refuse to divulge information even if the client consents.[98] In others, the client controls whether information is concealed or disclosed.[99] In Florida, for example, a client "has a privilege to refuse to disclose . . . the contents of confidential communications with an accountant" if made in the context of the accountant's professional capacity.[100] The privilege cannot be used to shield advice related to present or future wrongdoing.[101] In some states, the privilege also dies with the client; an accountant can be forced to reveal information in an estate proceeding.[102] There is no accountant-client privilege under the federal rules of evidence and the Supreme Court has expressly rejected the notion.[103] Congress has enacted a limited privilege; it protects communications with an accountant in civil tax cases to the same extent that communications with the taxpayer's lawyer are protected.[104]

Four states recognize a parent-child privilege on the grounds that it promotes family privacy.[105] However, most states do not, and there is no federal rule providing for such a privilege.[106] In a Fourth Circuit case (2014), a man was accused of owning unregistered firearms, including "two assault-style rifles, a WWII-style pistol, a loaded semi-automatic handgun, and an AK-47 assault rifle"; after a search, deputies discovered that the man was also growing marijuana plants in five-gallon buckets.[107] His nineteen-year-old son, who lived with him, tried to resist testifying; the District Court recognized a parent-child privilege on privacy grounds. But the appellate Court reversed.[108]

MEDICAL PRIVACY

In 1996, Congress passed HIPAA.[109] This is a complex law which takes up a number of issues. Title II of the act instructs the Secretary of Health and Human Services to set up national standards for the privacy and security of health information. These standards now govern hospitals, clinics, health maintenance organizations, and other health care facilities all across the country.

What information do these standards protect? Basically, HIPAA covers "individually identifiable health information." Information is "individually identifiable" if it includes such things as a patient's name, address, birth date, or social security number. This kind of information cannot be given out, publicized, or shared without the patient's consent. There are some exceptions, however.[110] Protected information, for example, can be used to comply with a court order, to identify the suspect of a crime, or for activities that relate to national security.[111]

To say that certain information is "protected" does not tell us, in itself, *how* it is protected, especially in an age in which information consists of electronic blips stored on some computer or server or off in the cloud. Complicated rules try to set up national standards for the protection of health information held or transferred in electronic form. Basically, health entities covered by the law must adopt appropriate administrative, physical and technical safeguards to guarantee the confidentiality and security of protected health information.[112]

Of course, as is always the case with a complicated law, the way ordinary people—nurses, doctors, and hospital staff—understand and carry out HIPAA is as important as the actual text of the statute, if not more so. When, for example, a person goes to a clinic, either to make an appointment or to report for an appointment, the patient might be asked to stand behind a line some six feet or so from the check-in desk while someone in front of him is checking in. The idea is to prevent the patient from seeing or hearing anything "identifiable" about the patient ahead of him in line. If a friend of yours has an operation, do not bother to call the hospital to ask how he or she is doing. They will refuse to tell anything to anybody outside the family, and if you ask why, the answer will be "HIPAA."

The doctor-patient privilege, if there is one at all, only applies to court proceedings. The HIPAA syndrome, of course, is vastly broader. It reflects an underlying norm: your health information is private; it is nobody's business but yours, unless you choose to waive your right of privacy. People claim "HIPAA violations" (often misspelled "HIPPA") in all sorts of contexts where it has no relevance at all.[113] The COVID-19 pandemic provoked a common misconception about the statute's protections—no, it doesn't prevent your employer or grocery store from inquiring about your vaccination status.[114] But when people overclaim the protections of HIPAA, they are revealing their underlying expectations about the privacy of medical information rather than making a precise legal argument. Perhaps the key issue here is consent, or, to put it another way, control. "Privacy" is the right to control access, the right to decide which elements of your self, what information about yourself, and which images of yourself can be kept entirely secret, as well as the converse right to decide what information *can* be shared and with whom.

This theme, in fact, ties together all of the various privileges. Whatever their original policy, they now depend on norms of privacy. Underneath the scholarly and philosophical cacophony about "privacy" is the central fact we have mentioned often: "privacy" is a *social* concept; it is an idea in the minds and hearts of ordinary people, something they value highly. But what it consists of, what its boundaries are, and what it applies to are matters that change over time and space.

Privacy, as it is understood today, is, above all, a norm of individualism; a norm of control; and a norm about people's right to lead their own lives, to make their own decisions, to blaze their own trail in life. This is not an absolute right, of course, but as much as is reasonably possible. Of course, people are social animals. Nobody can go through life as a totally "private" person. Except for hermits and some people who are mentally ill and live in a world of their own, all of us must deal with other people, in all sorts of ways; we must lean on and depend on others. We control our destiny only to a limited extent. Norms of "privacy" reflect the fact that people, no matter how strongly they believe in going it alone, eventually find themselves in the office of a doctor or a dentist or in an emergency room or talking to a priest, a psychiatrist, a tax lawyer, or an accountant. And most people will be talking also to people they are close with: friends, lovers, partners, spouses, mom and dad. People have secrets and they need to tell them to someone, either for psychological reasons, or for practical business and economic reasons. If not your wife or your husband, who can you tell? You cannot bottle up everything inside. The rules aim to let you depend on others, without giving up too much of your privacy or too much control.

The rules are technical; they seem muddled and vary from state to state. Is there a parent-child privilege? Most states say no. A few say yes. What is the issue here? That, too, varies from situation to situation. Most people would think it revolting to force a mother to testify against her child or a child against her mother or father. In the Soviet Union, if a child ratted on her parent, the state might label the child a hero. Most of us in democratic societies would strongly disapprove. If a sixteen-year-old tells her doctor she is sexually active or is pregnant, or if her brother tells the doctor he thinks he is HIV positive or is involved in a gay relationship, do the parents have a right to know? The bland word "privacy" conceals a range of sensitive social issues. And the same sensitive issues, cloaked in legal jargon, lie behind the rules of "privilege."

The HIPAA rules, as we said, may be annoying, and they may be overdone, but in essence, they conform to what people expect. Court privileges are also rooted in social norms. But the issues can be complicated. The rules, as we saw, can sometimes block evidence that would convict a killer or might free an innocent man. Historically, the benefits were felt to outweigh the costs. The privilege against self-incrimination was a check on big government. Confiding in your lawyer was a tool of due process. Spilling your guts to a psychiatrist is good for the soul and for mental health. Confessing to a priest might be your ticket to eternal life. Whether these privileges are still worth the costs is another question. The psychiatric privilege had to give way, in part, in the *Tarasoff* case; more generally, the duties to report child abuse, elder abuse, and the like now tend to trump various privileges. For each privilege, there will be some sort of balancing act. What must be private, and what must be revealed, are issues that have to be renegotiated every day, in court and in society. This will continue to be the case.

NOTES

1. *Morales v. Portuondo*, 154 F. Supp. 2d 706 (S.D.N.Y. 2001).
2. *Id.* at 713.
3. *Id.* at 710.
4. *Id.* at 732. The court did not order an immediate and unconditional release. The state was entitled to retry Morales. At any such retrial, however, the statements of Father Towle and the others would have to be admitted into evidence.
5. *See, e.g.,* Susan Bander, "Loyalty to One's Convictions: The Prosecutor and Tunnel Vision," *How. L. J.* 49 (2006): 475, 476; Alafair Burke, "Neutralizing

Cognitive Bias: An Invitation to Prosecutors," *N.Y.U. J.L. & Liberty* 2 (2007): 512, 517–18, which concluded that "tunnel vision" is a leading cause of wrongful convictions because investigators and prosecutors focus on one suspect and then search for evidence against that person, rather than searching for truth; Alafair S. Burke, "Prosecutorial Passion, Cognitive Bias, and Plea Bargaining," *Marq. L. Rev.* 91 (2007): 183, 211.

6. *See, e.g.*, Keith A. Findley and Michael S. Scott, "The Multiple Dimensions of Tunnel Vision in Criminal Cases," *Wis. L. Rev.* (2006): 291, 296–300, 318–19, 397, which notes, among other problems, that eyewitness error is a contributing factor in the majority of wrongful convictions; Amy L. Bradfield et al., "The Damaging Effect of Confirming Feedback on the Relation between Eyewitness Certainty and Identification Accuracy," *J. Applied Psychol.* 87 (2002): 112, 112–13; Gary L. Wells and Amy L. Bradfield, "'Good, You Identified the Suspect': Feedback to Eyewitnesses Distorts Their Reports of the Witnessing Experience," *J. Applied Psychol.* 83 (1998): 360, 360–62.

7. Philip A. Elmore, Comment, "'That's Just Pillow Talk, Baby': Spousal Privileges and the Right to Privacy in Arkansas," 67 *Ark. L. Rev.* 961, 964 (2014).

8. U.S. Const. amend. V, cl. 3.

9. *Garner v. United States*, 424 U.S. 648, 655 (1976); *Hiibel v. Sixth Judicial Dist. Ct.*, 542 U.S. 177, 189 (2004), explaining that privilege is available only when communication is testimonial, incriminating, and compelling; *U.S. v. Von Behren*, 822 F.3d 1139, 1145 (10th Cir. 2016), explaining that the privilege "is only properly invoked when the danger of self-incrimination is real and appreciable, as opposed to imaginary and unsubstantial, and this protection must be confined to instances where the witness has reasonable cause to apprehend danger from a direct answer."

10. The Supreme Court has considered when a suspect is "in custody" in several cases. *See, e.g., Orozco v. Texas*, 394 U.S. 324 (1969); *Stansbury v. California*, 511 U.S. 318 (1994); *Mathis v. U.S.*, 391 U.S. 1 (1968).

11. 384 U.S. 436 (1966); *Yarborough v. Alvarado*, 541 U.S. 652 (2004); *Pennsylvania v. Bruder*, 488 U.S. 9 (1988); *California v. Beheler*, 463 U.S. 1121 (1983); *Rhode Island v. Innis*, 446 U.S. 291 (1980).

12. *Roberts v. U.S.*, 445 U.S. 552 (1980).

13. *See Miranda*, 384 U.S. at 478–79, holding that an individual, after receiving warnings, "may knowingly and intelligently waive these rights and agree to answer questions or make a statement"; *Carnley v. Cochran*, 369 U.S. 506, 516 (1962), holding that waiver cannot be presumed from silence.

14. *See Miranda*, 384 U.S. at 479, stating that "unless and until such warnings and waiver are demonstrated by the prosecution at trial, no evidence obtained as a result of interrogation can be used against him."

15. *See* John H. Langbein, "The Historical Origins of the Privilege against Self-Incrimination at Common Law," *Mich. L. Rev.* 92 (1994): 1047.

16. *See* J. Wigmore, *Evidence in Trials at Common Law* § 2285(2) (1961), which sets out four prerequisites for recognition of a privilege.

17. *See generally* Bruce P. Brown, "Free Press, Privacy, and Privilege: Protection of Researcher-Subject Communications," *Ga. L. Rev.* 17 (1983): 1009.

18. Fed. R. Evid. 501 ("the privilege of a witness, person, government, State, or political subdivision thereof shall be governed by the principles of the common law as they may be interpreted by the courts of the United States in the light of reason and experience"); *see also Trammel v. United States*, 445 U.S. 40, 47 (1980), noting that in its adoption of Rule 501, "Congress manifested an affirmative intention not to freeze the law of privilege."

19. Roscoe Pound, "Interests of Personality," *Harv. L. Rev.* 28 (1915): 343, 362.

20. *See Hunt v. Blackburn*, 128 U.S. 464, 470 (1888).

21. *U.S. v. Bryan*, 339 U.S. 323, 331 (1950), which noted that testimonial privileges "contravene the fundamental principle" that evidence should be available.

22. Cal. Evid. Code § 954 (2020).

23. Tex. R. Evid. 503(b) (2020).

24. Geoffrey C. Hazard, Jr., "An Historical Perspective on the Attorney-Client Privilege," *Cal. L. Rev.* 66 (1978): 1061, 1061.

25. *Id.*

26. *Trammel v. U.S.*, 445 U.S. 40, 51 (1980).

27. There is a complicated set of rules about when the privilege has been expressly or impliedly waived. See generally Kenneth Duvall, "Rules, Standards, and the Attorney-Client Privilege: When the Privilege Is 'At-Issue' in the Discovery Rule Context," *N. Ill. U. L. Rev.* 32 (2011): 1, which explores the circumstances under which a client waives the privilege.

28. *Swidler & Berlin v. United States*, 524 U.S. 359 (1998); *Hearn v. Rhay*, 68 F.R.D. 574, 581 (E.D. Wash. 1975), which sets forth the leading test for implied waiver of attorney-client privilege; *Greater Newburyport Clamshell Alliance v. Pub. Serv. Co.*, 838 F.2d 13, 20 (1st Cir. 1998), which sets forth an alternative test for implied waiver of the attorney-client privilege;

29. 1 Attorney-Client Privilege in the U.S. § 5:2 (2021), which explains that the privilege provides direct protection only for communications from the client to the attorney, and derivative protection for communications going the other way if necessary to protect the client's confidences.

30. *In re Sealed Case*, 737 F.2d 94, 99 (D.C. Cir. 1984). The burden is on the party claiming the privilege to "demonstrate with reasonable certainty . . . that the lawyer's communication rested in significant and inseparable part on the client's confidential disclosure." *Id.*; *see also United States v. Silverman*, 430 F.2d 106 (2d Cir. 1970); *Radio Today v. Westwood One*, 1989 WL 2733, at *1 (S.D.N.Y. 1989).

31. *See* Charles L. Black, Jr., "Marital and Physician Privileges—A Reprint of a Letter to a Congressman," *Duke L. J.* (1975): 45, 50.

32. Jeremy Bentham, *Rationale of Judicial Evidence* 302 (1827).

33. *See, e.g., U.S. v. Brock*, 724 F.3d 817 (7th Cir. 2013).

34. *Trammel v. United States*, 445 U.S. 40 (1980) (citing 1 E. Coke, A Commentary upon Littleton 6b [1628]).

35. *Hawkins v. United States*, 358 U.S. 74, 77 (1958); G. Gilbert, *The Law of Evidence* 96 (1754).

36. Bentham, *supra* note 32, at 340.

37. *See* Eldred, "'Every Spouse's Evidence': Availability of the Adverse Spousal Testimonial Privilege in Federal Civil Trials," *U. Chic. L. Rev.* 69 (2002): 1319, noting that the weight of authority limits the testimonial privilege to criminal cases, although some scholars have argued for extending it to civil trials also. The privilege also applies in grand jury proceedings where one spouse is the target. *See In re Grand Jury Matter,* 673 F.2d 688, 692 (3d Cir. 1982); *In re Snoonian*, 502 F.2d 110, 112 (1st Cir. 1974); *U.S. v. George*, 444 F.2d 310, 313–14 (6th Cir. 1971).

38. *See, e.g., U.S. v. Acker*, 52 F.3d 509, 514 (4th Cir. 1995); *U.S. v. Snyder*, 707 F.2d 139, 147 (5th Cir. 1983); *U.S. v. Rhodes*, 569, 569 F.2d 384, 388–89 (5th Cir. 1978).

39. *See, e.g., Lutwak v. U.S.*, 344 U.S. 604, 614–615 (1953); *U.S. v. Saniti*, 604 F.2d 603, 604 (9th Cir. 1979); *In re Grand Jury Proceedings* (84–5), 777 F.2d 508 (9th Cir. 1985); *San Fratello v. U.S.*, 340 F.2d 560, 566 (5th Cir. 1965).

40. *See, e.g., Pereira v. U.S.*, 347 U.S. 1, 6 (1954); *U.S. v. Smith*, 533 F.2d 1077, 1079 (8th Cir. 1976); *U.S. v. Moore*, 604 F.2d 1228, 1238 (9th Cir. 1979); *U.S. v. Lustig*, 555 F.2d 737, 747 (9th Cir. 1977).

41. 358 U.S. 74 (1958).

42. Cal. Evid. Code § 970 (2020).

43. 445 U.S. 40 (1980).

44. *Id.* at 52.

45. *Id.*

46. *Id.* at 51.

47. *Compare U.S. v. Mackiewicz*, 401 F.2d 219, 225 (2d Cir. 1968), which admitted an out-of-court statement by the spouse because it was less likely to aggravate "marital frictions" because of the "convenient buffer" of the third party), and *U.S. v. Archer*, 733 F.2d 354, 359 (5th Cir. 1984), which held that the privilege extended to out-of-court statements by a spouse.

48. Quite a few states have also carved out an exception for child abuse cases as well.

49. R. Michael Cassidy, "Reconsidering Spousal Privileges after Crawford," *Am. J. Crim. L.* 33 (2006): 339. The Crawford case, *Crawford v. Washington*, 541 U.S. 36 (2004), "revitalized the Confrontation Clause in criminal proceedings by restricting the government's use of hearsay evidence" if the person who made the statement does not actually testify. This decision, according to Cassidy—with some empirical evidence to back him up—has had a major influence on cases of domestic violence; many of these cases now have to be dropped.

50. Cal. Evid. Code § 980 (2020) states "a spouse . . . whether or not a party, has a privilege during the martial relationship and afterwards to refuse to disclose, and to prevent another from disclosing, a communication if he or she claims the privilege and the communication was made in confidence between him or her and the other spouse while they were spouses." *See also Wolfle v. U.S.*, 291 U.S. 7, 17 (1934), which noted that spousal communications "voluntarily made in the presence of their children, old enough to comprehend them, or other members of the family within the intimacy of the family circle, are not privileged"; *U.S. v. Marashi*, 913 F.2d 724, 730 (9th Cir. 1990); *U.S. v. Montgomery*, 384 F.3d 1050 (9th Cir. 2004).

51. *See, e.g., U.S. v. Harper*, 450 F.2d 1032, 1046 (5th Cir. 1971), which held that the husband's disclosure to third parties removed any element of confidentiality; *U.S. v. Lilley*, 581 F.2d 182, 189 (8th Cir. 1978), which held that the privilege was waived when the communication was disclosed by the spouse claiming the privilege.

52. *See, e.g., U.S. v. Neal*, 532 F. Supp. 942, 947 (D. Colo. 1982), *aff'd*, 743 F.2d 1441 (10th Cir. 1984).

53. *See, e.g., U.S. v. Acker*, 52 F.3d 509, 514 (4th Cir. 1995), which refused to apply privilege to a couple because neither state they had lived in recognized common-law marriage; *U.S. v. Boatwright*, 446 F.2d 913, 915 (5th Cir. 1971), which refused to recognize privilege between a man and woman who lived together but were not married; *U.S. v. Hamilton*, 19 F.3d 350 (7th Cir. 1994), which refused to recognize privilege even though the man had a good-faith belief he was married to a woman who had never divorced her prior husband.

54. *See, e.g., McGuire v. McGuire*, 59 N.W.2d 336 (Neb. 1953).

55. 381 U.S. 479 (1965).

56. *See* Note, "Pillow Talk, Grimbribbers and Connubial Bliss: The Marital Communication Privilege," *Ind. L. J.* 56 (1980): 121, 139–42; *see also* Krattenmaker, "Testimonial Privileges in Federal Courts: An Alternative to the Proposed Federal Rules of Evidence," *Georgetown L. J.* 62 (1973): 60, 92.

57. *Stein v. Bowman*, 38 U.S. 209, 223 (1839).

58. *Wolfle v. U.S.*, 291 U.S. 7, 14 (1934); *see also* Louisell, "Confidentiality, Conformity and Confusion: Privileges in the Federal Court Today," *Tulane L. Rev.* 31 (1956): 101, 111–13; *U.S. v. Brock*, 724 F.3d 817, 820–21 (7th Cir. 2013).

59. Cal. Evid. Code § 985(a) (2020); *see also U.S. v. Breton*, 740 F.2d 1 (1st Cir. 2014); *U.S. v. Martinez*, 44 F. Supp. 2d 835, 836 (W.D. Tex. 1999); *U.S. v. Underwood*, 859 F.3d 386, 391–92 (6th Cir. 2017).

60. *Poppe v. Poppe*, 144 N.E.2d 72 (N.Y. 1957); *T.C.H. v. K.M.H.*, 693 S.W.2d 802, 804 (Mo. 1985).

61. *See, e.g., U.S. v. Estes*, 793 F.2d 465, 468 (2d Cir. 1986).

62. *U.S. v. Marashi*, 913 F.2d 724, 731 (9th Cir. 1990).

63. *See, e.g., In re Witness Before Grand Jury*, 791 F.2d 234, 238 (2d Cir. 1986), which held the privilege was unavailable for communications that occurred while husband and wife were living apart, and husband was living with another woman; *U.S. v. Murphy*, 65 F.3d 758, 761 (9th Cir. 1994), which held the privilege was not available where spouses had been separated for seven years and filed for divorce; *U.S. v. Treff*, 924 F.2d 975, 982 & n. 11 (10th Cir. 1991), which admitted a wife's diary entry with statements by her husband because they were separated and the privilege does not apply in a "failed or failing marriage"; *U.S. v. Singleton*, 260 F.3d 1295 (11th Cir. 2001), which convicted a wife based on statements she made to her husband as they were divorcing. On the application of the privilege after divorce or death of a spouse, see *Pereira v. U.S.*, 347 U.S. 1, 6 (1954), which held that divorce does not terminate the marital confidences privilege; *see also U.S. v. Brock*, 724 F.3d 817, 820 (7th Cir. 2013); *In re Grand Jury Investigation of Hugle*, 754 F.2d 863, 865 (9th Cir. 1985); *U.S. v. Burks*, 470 F.2d 432, 436 (D.C. Cir. 1972).

64. *See, e.g., U.S. v. Estes*, 793 F.2d 465, 467 (2d Cir. 1986), which excluded evidence that the husband poured out a saddlebag full of cash on the bed and indicated he had stolen the money, as his conduct "was intended to convey a confidential message from the actor to the observer."

65. *See* Mikah K. Story, "Twenty-First Century Pillow-Talk: Applicability of the Marital Communications Privilege to Electronic Mail," *S.C. L. Rev.* 58 (2006): 275.

66. *United States v. Hamilton*, 701 F.3d 404, 411 (4th Cir. 2012).

67. *Id.* at 407.

68. *Id.* at 408–9.

69. 291 U.S. 7 (1934).

70. *Id.* at 12.

71. *Id.* at 14.

72. *Hamilton*, 701 F.3d at 408.

73. *Proffitt v. State*, 315 So. 2d 461 (1975). Proffitt's case (he had been sentenced to death) went to the Supreme Court, on the issue of whether the Florida statute on death penalty cases met constitutional standards; the Court held that it did.

74. Cal. Evid. Code § 1032 (2020).

75. *See, e.g.*, Colo. Rev. Stat. Ann. § 13–90–107(c) (West 2020).

76. Wis. Stat. Ann. § 905.06 (West 2020).

77. Ark. Code Ann. § 12–18–402 (LexisNexis 2020).

78. Wis. Stat. Ann. § 48.981(2)(b) (West 2020).

79. *See, e.g.*, Cal. Evid. Code § 1014 (2020).

80. 518 U.S. 1 (1996).

81. *Id.* at 10.

82. *Id.* at 18–36. The California statute specifically mentions psychologists, anyone "licensed as a clinical social worker . . . when . . . engaged in applied psychotherapy of a nonmedical nature," marriage and family therapists, any psychological "intern . . . under the supervision of a licensed psychologist or board certified psychiatrist," and registered nurses with a "master's degree in psychiatric-mental health nursing," among others. Cal. Evid. Code § 1010 (2020).

83. The original case was *Tarasoff v. Regents of Univ. of California*, 529 P.2d 553 (Cal. 1974); the second case, "Tarasoff II," was 551 P.2d 334 (Cal. 1976).

84. See the study of the impact of the case, Daniel J. Givelber et. al., "Tarasoff, Myth and Reality: An Empirical Study of Private Law in Action," *Wisconsin L. Rev.* (1984): 443.

85. Ky. Rev. Stat. Ann. § 620.030(1)(3) (LexisNexis 2020).

86. Mich. Comp. Laws Ann. § 722.631 (West 2020).

87. Carolyn B. Ramsey, "Domestic Violence and State Intervention in the American West and Australia, 1860–1930," *Indiana L. J.* 86 (2011): 185; Carolyn B. Ramsey, "Intimate Homicide: Gender and Crime Control, 1880–1920," *U. Colo. L. Rev.* 77 (2006): 101.

88. Samantha Schmidt, "Boy Scouts Must Settle 95,000 Abuse Claims by Next Summer—or Risk Running Out of Cash," *Washington Post*, Nov. 19, 2020.

89. *See, e.g.*, Patricia Volk, "The Steinberg Trial: Scenes from a Tragedy," *New York Times Magazine*, Jan. 15, 1989.

90. *See* Will Hobson, "Former Penn State President Graham Spanier Sentenced to Jail for Child Endangerment in Jerry Sandusky Abuse Case," *Washington Post*, June 2, 2017. The conviction was initially overturned because the wrong version of a statute was applied, but later restored on appeal of that ruling. *See Spencer v. Director Dauphin County Probation Servs.*, 981 F.3d 213 (3d Cir. 2020).

91. *In re Bergamo Medical, P.C.*, 840 N.Y.S.2d 709, 713 (N.Y. Sup. Ct. 2007).

92. Cal. Evid. Code §§ 994, 998 (2020).

93. *See* Tex. R. Evid. 509 (2020).

94. Colo. Rev. Stat. Ann. § 13–90–107(d) (West 2020).

95. Cal. Evid. Code §§ 1035, 1037, 1038 (2020).

96. Cal. Evid. Code §§ 994, 998 (2020).

97. *See, e.g., Airgas Mid-America, Inc. v. Long*, 812 N.E.2d 842 (Ind. Ct. App. 2004).

98. *See, e.g., Brunton v. Kruger*, 32 N.E.2d 567 (Ill. 2015).

99. *See, e.g., Landau v. Bailey*, 629 N.E.2d 264 (Ind. Ct. App. 1994).

100. Fla. Stat. Ann. § 90.5055(2) (West 2020).

101. *See, e.g., Rose v. Commercial Factors of Atlanta, Inc.*, 586 S.E.2d 41 (2003).

102. *See, e.g., Brunton*, 8 N.E.3d at 536.

103. *See Couch v. U.S.*, 409 U.S. 322, 334 (1973).

104. *See* 28 U.S.C. § 7525(a)(1) (2018).

105. Those states are Idaho, Massachusetts, Minnesota, and New York.

106. *See In re Grand Jury*, 103 F.3d 1140 (3d Cir. 1997), noting that the Advisory Committee to the Federal Rules of Evidence did not think privacy in parent-child communications was sufficiently important to justify a privilege. *See generally* Hillary B. Farber, "Do You Swear to Tell the Truth, the Whole Truth, and Nothing but the Truth against Your Child?," *Loy. L.A. L. Rev.* 43 (2010): 551, which argues that parents should not be forced to testify against their children. Catherine Ross makes a similar argument, but on the basis of due process rights for minors. *See* Catherine Ross, "Implementing Constitutional Rights for Juveniles: The Parent-Child Privilege in Context," *Stan. L. & Pol'y Rev.* 14 (2003): 85.

107. *Under Seal v. United States*, 755 F.3d 213, 215 (4th Cir. 2014).

108. *Id.* at 221–22.

109. Health Insurance Portability and Accountability Act of 1996 (HIPAA), Pub. L. No. 104–191, 110 Stat. 1936.

110. 45 C.F.R. § 164.512 (2020).

111. *Id.*

112. *See* 45 C.F.R. pt. 160 (2016); *The Security Rule*, U.S. Dep't of Health and Human Serv., https://www.hhs.gov/hipaa/for-professionals/security/index.html (last visited Oct. 10, 2017).

113. *See, e.g.,* Paula Span, "HIPAA's Use as Code of Silence Often Misinterprets the Law," *New York Times*, July 7, 2015; Sara Morrison, "HIPAA, the Health Privacy Law That's More Limited Than You Think, Explained," *Vox.com*, April 20, 2021.

114. *See* Allyson Chiu, "Explaining HIPAA: No, It Doesn't Ban Questions about Your Vaccination Status," *Washington Post*, May 22, 2001.

PART II

Elective Privacy

Chapter 5

I Want to Be Alone: Privacy and Choice

Is it legal for a man to strap a camera to his shoe and secretly take pictures up the skirts of women on the subway or in a shopping mall? Has the government done anything wrong when it collects vast amounts of cell phone data without a warrant or consent? These are thoroughly modern problems, but they raise age-old questions about *privacy*. As we have seen, "privacy" is a difficult word, with many shades of meaning.

In a free society, among the many choices people have are choices about what to keep secret and what to reveal. This can be a personal, individual matter. Some people would not reveal how much money they make, even if you tortured them on the rack. Other people brag about their wealth and flaunt it. Most people hide their bodies. But others—exhibitionists or members of a nudist colony—are willing or eager to take off their clothes. Some people (mostly young people) send pictures of their naked selves to friends. In an earlier chapter, we discussed the legal and social issue of nudity. In another chapter, we discussed lawyer-client privilege, and other privileges: what matters can or must be kept private, out of the reach of court proceedings.[1]

People commonly talk about a "right" to privacy and about violations of that right—so-called invasions of privacy. Almost everybody would agree that a Peeping Tom is invading the privacy of whatever or whomever he is peeping at. Almost everybody recognizes the privacy of the bathroom and the bedroom. Privacy is enclosed space. It is where nobody can reach you, see you, or touch you without your specific invitation. This is one of the core notions of privacy. The Supreme Court has also, in a dramatic line of cases, sketched out a protected right of privacy, which the Court found hidden inside the Bill of Rights, where it had been lying, like the Dead Sea Scrolls, unknown and undiscovered, since the beginnings of the Republic. Expansion of this "privacy" right led to the famous abortion decision *Roe v. Wade*[2] and, in 2003, the Supreme Court invalidated, once and for all, statutes that punished sodomy, as we have seen in a previous chapter.[3] The so-called right of privacy was a factor here, too.

Many people, to be sure, found and still find these results wrongheaded or worse. The Republican Party is more or less committed to overturning *Roe v. Wade* and the constitutional doctrines protecting abortion rights. At this writing (December 2021), the case hangs by a thread in the Supreme Court: the Court has a strong conservative majority, thanks to the three seats filled during Donald Trump's presidency, and overruling *Roe v. Wade* now seems not only possible but likely.[4] Many scholars, and ordinary people, have wondered what on earth the right to have sex, with or without contraceptives, and with whatever kind of adult partner one chooses, plus the right to have babies or not, could conceivably have to do with "privacy." But the underlying idea seems to be this: the Constitution, as the Court interprets it, protects certain basic life choices. These choices must remain in the private sphere. Whether abortion is one of these protected choices is hotly contested, but other choices (e.g., of sexual partners or modes of contraception) seem pretty much conceded. The issue, then, is freedom of choice, whether you call it "privacy" or something else. Laws and social norms are invariably about choice: what you can or cannot choose. A trip to Sweden, or buying a refrigerator is up to you; robbing a bank (legally) is not. Privacy is also, in many regards, a *choice.* Secretly filming you in the shower would be a gross "invasion of privacy" but you can take nude pictures of yourself, if you wish, and send them to your sweetheart of the moment.

An enormous body of law has grown up around privacy, to establish what things you must keep secret and what things are up to you. In this chapter, we will discuss what you can but do not have to keep secret. We might call this "elective privacy." What legal consequences follow if things are disclosed *against* your will?

Elective privacy poses legal issues but it is also, and perhaps more fundamentally, an issue of social norms. These, of course, vary from place to place and time to time. What people normally wear on the beach today would have been considered indecent in 1900. Of course, nobody *forces* you to wear a skimpy bathing suit. But you can, if you wish. You can keep a secret diary or plaster the most intimate facts about yourself on social media, or you can keep no diary at all and avoid social networking like the plague. But can social media sites sell or pass along your data? The boundaries and the gray areas are where interesting questions arise.

In this chapter, then, we discuss privacy as a *choice*. All choices in life are constrained. We think we have absolute freedom to decide, for example, what to eat and what to wear. Yet we choose from a limited menu. In a restaurant, nobody forces us to order filet of sole. Yet we cannot choose something that isn't on the menu. Social life is a giant menu, but a restricted one. We can "choose" privacy, but only when privacy is on the menu.

And privacy is often, quite literally, *not* on the menu. Poor people who live in crowded flats; immigrant garment workers who live six to a room; rural peasants who share a hut with sheep, goats, and pigs—all these people have far less privacy than people with money, who give every child his or her own room, who have two or four or six bathrooms, and who live in gated communities or on two-acre lots. One might imagine that cities, with their huge populations, would severely restrict the privacy of people who live in them. On the other hand, cities gave us more anonymity than small towns—more of a sense of privacy within a crowd because nobody knows or cares who we are and what we do. In small towns, everybody knows everybody else's business, and life can be crushingly oppressive and intrusive.

Amitai Etzioni, for one, has argued that sometimes *less* privacy may be both desirable and protective; that is, it can "curtail the need for governmental control and intrusion."[5] What he means is that in small or closed communities, the community itself enforces the norms; this reduces the need for government to do so. Of course, Etzioni understands that people want and need privacy. But he draws attention to the vexed relationship between privacy and social control. Here, one might mention the famous book by Jane Jacobs, *The Death and Life of Great American Cities*.[6] Jacobs hated "urban renewal"; she rejected the idea that dense neighborhoods were evil, that they were swamps of blight to be eliminated. A dense neighborhood, she argued, is, among other things, a safe neighborhood; the very lack of privacy (she did not put it this way) could be a positive rather than a negative feature.[7] The eyes of neighbors, the people sitting on their stoops, and the crowds on the street were not signs of blight but signs of a vibrant, livable neighborhood. And many feminist writers have pointed out that stress on the "privacy" of the home very often gave a pass to violent husbands and boyfriends.[8]

The whole field of "privacy law" is more than a century old, at least from the standpoint of terminology. Traditionally, the initial development of a legal right of privacy is credited to a famous article by Charles Warren and Louis Brandeis, published in 1890 in the *Harvard Law Review*.[9] The article claimed (a bit disingenuously) that, in a way, there already *was* a right of privacy, only nobody had recognized it. They mentioned a case here, a case there, and stitched little fragments of common law together into a somewhat coherent fabric. Of course, in reality, they were proposing something new, which they felt *should* be recognized in law. In the background were social and technological changes—better cameras (the "Kodak"), for example. The "candid camera" made it possible, for the first time, to take a person's picture without their knowledge or permission. Yellow journalism was flourishing: cheap, sensational newspapers sold millions of copies every day and were full of gossip about the high and mighty. Respectable elites, men like Warren and Brandeis, shuddered at the way the press could invade, and did invade, the sacred privacy of the rich and well-born.

In one sense, Warren and Brandeis were right to claim that a right of privacy already existed, at least in some regards. The United States Constitution—to be precise, the Bill of Rights—gives people the right to be "secure" in their homes; searches require a warrant, issued by a judge on the basis of probable cause. The law of search and seizure is highly complex, and, in many ways, quite confusing. And it has changed greatly since the days of Warren and Brandeis. New social situations and technologies have complicated this area of law. The men who drafted the Bill of Rights could not foresee wiretapping or hidden recording devices, not to mention devices that can almost literally see through walls—all of the elaborate paraphernalia of modern snooping. Nor, for that matter, did they foresee suicide bombers, international terrorists, or drug cartels—aspects of contemporary life that, for many people, justify invasions of privacy. Arguments about privacy rights pit safety and security against the freedom to hide from the beady eye of the state. It is a conflict that cannot be definitively resolved.

In this chapter, however, we will sidestep some of these issues, and discuss instead some aspects of elective privacy: when, why, and how we can choose to conceal some of the bits and pieces that make up our lives. This chosen concealment is what we usually call "privacy," and, in many ways, it is a crucial value in society. A closely related value is *anonymity.* This, too, is important. At home, we have privacy, especially if we lock the door and pull down the shades. Home is the place where you can walk around in your underwear or naked if you choose. Obviously, Main Street is not such a place. When you walk down Main Street, you lack the kind of privacy you have at home, but you can and do have anonymity. Anonymity is the privacy we have in the midst of strangers. It is a sort of visible invisibility. The person rushing along on a busy street, pushing her cart in the aisles of a supermarket, strap-hanging on a bus, or strolling in the park has anonymity. Everybody sees her, in a way, but she is nonetheless invisible.

The legal system, for the most part, does not give explicit recognition to anonymity, but it can be nonetheless an important value. During the civil rights era, some southern states, anxious to find out who supported the NAACP so they could harass the members, ordered the organization to divulge the names of its members. In a case from Alabama, the Supreme Court refused to go along with Alabama's wishes; the Court spoke of the right of "privacy in group association." The Court was clearly aware of what really lay behind the tactic—Alabama wanted these lists made public so that the members could be more easily intimidated.[10] And in *Talley v. California*,[11] the Supreme Court struck down a Los Angeles ordinance which made it a crime to distribute any "hand-bill" without the names and addresses of the sponsors. Justice Tom Clark wrote a vigorous dissent. The Constitution, he argued, says nothing about "freedom of anonymous speech."[12] The majority, on the other hand, pointed out that "[a]nonymous pamphlets . . . have played an important role in the progress of mankind," and that even the Federalist Papers were published under pseudonyms.[13]

The Supreme Court made clear that anonymous speech ought to be protected. In *McIntyre v. Ohio Elections Commission*, the Court held that the election board could not impose fines for the distribution of anonymous leaflets, reasoning that "the interest in having anonymous works enter the marketplace of ideas unquestionably outweighs any public interest in requiring disclosure as a condition of entry."[14] The very decision to "remain anonymous . . . is an aspect of the freedom of speech protected by the First Amendment."[15] Indeed, "[a]nonymity is a shield from the tyranny of the majority" and "anonymous pamphleteering is not a pernicious, fraudulent practice, but an honorable tradition of advocacy and dissent."[16] Leaflets designed to "influence the electoral process deserve constitutional protection."[17] This is true, regardless of whether the person distributing pamphlets fears retribution, seeks to avoid social ostracism, or is motivated "merely by a desire to preserve as much of one's privacy as possible."[18] In *Watchtower Bible and Tract Society of New York, Inc. v. Village of Stratton*, the Court invalidated an ordinance that required door-to-door canvassers to obtain a permit that would then be available for public inspection in part because the process "necessarily results in a surrender of that anonymity."[19] Although this case involved the activities of Jehovah's Witnesses, the Court made clear that its rule against permits or registration applied not only to "religious proselytizing, but also to anonymous political speech and the distribution of handbills."[20]

Rules about the privacy of tax returns, medical records, and the like protect privacy but they also, in a way, protect anonymity. Governments can, for example, release *general* data about income; hospitals can compile *general* data about mortality rates and other medical results. The individuals behind the statistics remain anonymous parts of the mass.

Most people take a high degree of anonymity for granted. They have always assumed that they can live most of their lives, and do most of their activities, in complete anonymity, even when they are "in public"; examples include walking down the street, sitting in a movie theater, or buying groceries. But in the contemporary world, this assumption no longer holds. We live today in what we might call a "surveillance society." Millions of cameras watch us in various settings. Cameras on the street see us driving by (possibly speeding or running a red light), watch us as we enter a bank or use an ATM, or even record us getting on a bus. At airports, we have to go through electronic security. The level of surveillance varies from place to place.

London alone has millions of surveillance cameras; small towns in Iowa might have few or none. On the whole, people seem to accept these cameras. They assume that nobody actually watches these films, that attention will be paid only in the event of some kind of crisis or crime. They also assume that the tapes are erased after some reasonable period of time. Hence, for the most part, they think of these cameras as a potential, but not actual, threat to anonymity. But, as Jeffrey Rosen observes, new technologies enable "strangers" to see and watch over "more and more aspects of our lives." Inevitably, too, this means that these "strangers" will be able to evaluate those same aspects of our lives.[21]

Surveillance cameras are not the only ways in which modern technology encroaches, or can encroach, on anonymity. Many simple, everyday activities are recorded and stored somewhere. At one time, shopping for groceries was anonymous, especially in a large supermarket. No longer. But this is not only true of grocery stores. Today, "[i]nvisible scanners automatically record the stores you visit, the magazines you browse, the pages you linger over, and the time that you linger over them."[22] More and more, our lives are an open book. Amazon knows which publications we like to read. Facebook and other social media sites know all sorts of things about millions and millions of users. What we like to eat, drink, and enjoy is subject to electronic monitoring, in various ways; presumably this information can be made available to businesses willing to buy it. Stores might use new apps that stalk people while they shop with targeted ads and promotions.[23] An article in the *New York Times* told this story: the chain store Target guessed (correctly) that a teenage girl was pregnant based on what she bought, and started sending relevant coupons and other material to her home address. Her irate father stormed into Target to complain only to have to admit days later that his daughter had finally revealed she was pregnant—something she had been carefully hiding from her parents.[24]

People, we think, also feel a right to something rather vague that we might call the "right to evanescence": the right to have things, words, and actions forgotten. This is the right, as it were, to have the tapes erased. If you march in a parade protesting something or other, you expect a certain amount of anonymity, at least if the parade is big enough. You also expect evanescence; you expect the parade to end. If someone focuses a video camera on the parade, this expectation is violated. It might make at least some of the marchers queasy. In general, most of us would like a great deal of what we say or do to vanish with the wind. Memories fade, and, in many ways, this is all to the good. Would anybody really be happy if a giant camera recorded everything we did all day, every day, and kept these (mostly boring) rolls of film forever, so that our families—or big business, or the government or friends or just random people—could find these films and replay them whenever they liked?

In other words, we want to decide what parts of our past we feel like preserving. Those old sepia photographs of grandma can be precious. People paste familiar pictures in albums, and treasure them. On the other hand, most people would prefer to delete unflattering pictures or pictures of themselves as naked babies (this was once a popular theme of home photography). We can keep old letters or throw them away. All of this has become more complicated. The computer age is a threat to evanescence, as well as to privacy and anonymity. Surveillance cameras could, one supposes, indefinitely preserve what their pitiless eyes perceive. Email, we are told, is indestructible. We think we get rid of these messages by pressing the "delete" key; but apparently we are wrong. Our emails get warehoused somewhere, somehow—mysteriously, in some strange, magical cloud or storage bin in the sky, where they are housed forever. What is worse is that they are also in some way retrievable, at least by people who know how to do such things.

Government, of course, is not the only "big brother." Big business is scooping up information on a level that probably exceeds the data-collecting activities of the government. We mentioned Facebook and Amazon. The "Googleization" of identity means that enough information has been collected that "could allow government agents to single out any individual from the crowd and reconstruct his or her movements, purchases, reading habits, and even private conversations for any period of time."[25] Maybe that information is not lying in plain sight like an autobiography, but it *can* be assembled from what Daniel Solove terms one's "digital dossier."[26] But the big tech companies are certainly not the only organizations that collect and use data about their customers. In short, privacy, though most people value it highly, is definitely under siege.

HOW WE GOT TO WHERE WE ARE

Human beings have been around for thousands of years. For most of those years, people on earth were born, lived, and died without leaving anything behind—not a trace, not even a memory. An occasional body is found, left over from the ice age, mummified or somehow preserved in the tundra, or in glaciers in the Andes. We have no name for the man who owned this body, no idea about his life, his hopes, his dreams, his sex life, his hunting skills, whether he loved his mother, or any other aspect of his short existence on earth. We can see if his teeth had cavities and sometimes we can figure out how he died or speculate about how he lived. One recent study suggested that Neanderthals were "neat freaks" who shunned clutter.[27] Anthropologists can invent a name for some rare person, sole survivor of his period (in a sense), a man or woman who left behind a skull, a molar, a loose tibia, or the like.

The rest of the population remains anonymous and forever gone. The same is true of whoever cooked food in the broken pots that archeologists unearth and of the name and way of life of the unknown artist who used the wall of a cave as his canvas.

The invention of writing changed everything. The Chinese, the Sumerians, and perhaps the Mayans invented writing, probably independently. From these three sources, it spread to other cultures. In written documents, a few actual names began to emerge from the primal mists. Mostly, these were names of kings, queens, and other nobles; for some rulers, early chronicles survive. But for the mass of Egyptians who broke their backs building the pyramids and the Chinese who labored on the Great Wall, nothing—or almost nothing—remains. In ancient times, few people could read and write. Gradually, we begin to find records of people who were not kings, queens, or nobles, people who scrawled inscriptions on walls, scribes who wrote letters, and the like. But deep into early modern times, information about ordinary people was rare and random. Overwhelmingly, people on earth left no trace behind. We have no record of their faces, no record of the sound of their voices.

This was not only true of the poor and downtrodden. Do we really know what Shakespeare looked like? A few portraits, or supposed portraits remain; but can we be sure? Roman emperors had portrait busts. But when the Roman empire ended, so did this practice. Was Charlemagne handsome? Or Attila the Hun? How did they wear their hair? In the seventeenth century, rich Dutch burghers commissioned portraits to hang on their walls. By this time, members of the upper class, who could afford it, hired artists to paint them and their families. More and more people knew how to read and write. In England, the practice of keeping diaries became common from the sixteenth century on, at least among members of the upper class. The reason was, perhaps, a growing "habit of self-examination encouraged by Protestantism," and a "growing interest in public affairs."[28] The quote is from the introduction to an abridged edition of the famous diary of Samuel Pepys, written in the seventeenth century.

The camera was invented in the early nineteenth century. Early cameras were unable to capture motion. People who wanted to be photographed had to sit still, in rather stiff poses. Matthew Brady took arresting photographs showing dead bodies on a Civil War battlefield. As the technology improved, photographs became extremely popular; there were shops everywhere in the cities, and certain kinds of photographs—for example, the "cartes de visite," which were the size of ordinary visiting cards and were printed on cardboard—became cheap and accessible. The camera recorded the faces of ordinary people, and ordinary families. Portrait painting had always been, for obvious reasons, a luxury; camera portraits were within the range of millions.

Thousands of nineteenth-century photographs survive, showing men, women, and children staring fixedly into the eye of the camera.

The invention of the "candid camera" in the late nineteenth century was another fateful technological step. Now the camera could, in fact, deal with objects and people in motion. Cameras were produced on a vast scale; millions of families bought small box cameras. Now photographs multiplied enormously: countless pictures were generated of picnics, family gatherings, children playing. The faces and bodies of almost anybody could now be recorded, kept in albums and scrapbooks, and treasured in families. Future generations could see what great-grandma actually looked like.

Great-grandma probably posed for her picture; perhaps she went to a professional photographer to have it taken. But the "candid camera" could take pictures of people who had *not* posed, including people who were not even aware that someone was taking their picture. In fact, as we mentioned before, the candid camera was one factor underlying Warren and Brandeis's famous article in 1890 on the right of privacy. The camera was invading the private lives of elites, respectable people like Warren and Brandeis themselves. The camera could act as an accomplice to that other villain of the late nineteenth century: the yellow press.

More than a century has gone by since then. The technology that permits invasion of privacy has mushroomed. Controlling these invasions is a major issue of public policy. One thing is clear: the America of Warren and Brandeis is gone with the wind. Warren and Brandeis did not know about wiretapping, surveillance cameras, or paparazzi. Their descendants live in a different world. They live in what has been called the Facebook Nation. Or perhaps it is the Surveillance Nation, the nation of eyes that never sleep.

THE SILVER SCREEN

The Truman Show, a remarkably successful movie, was released in 1998.[29] The main character was a young man named Truman Burbank. Truman was completely unaware that he was—and had been since birth—the main character in a television show. Every move he made was captured by a cluster of hidden cameras, and broadcast, live, to a huge, unseen audience. He was, in fact, part of what we would now call reality TV, except that Truman himself did not know this. Rather, he thought of himself as an ordinary guy, living an ordinary life, and cushioned (as most of us are) in a warm cocoon of anonymity. What he considered his hometown was actually a giant television set, and the people he met and interacted with were, in fact, actors and actresses, merely playing a part. The movie tells his story as he slowly and gradually realizes the awful truth and, in the end, breaks free from his life, a life in which he was basically a prisoner, the captive of a huge, voracious public, a kind of animal in a huge and barless cage.

Of course, *The Truman Show* is fantasy—or, perhaps, a kind of nightmare—but the nightmare is only a short distance beyond the border of reality. The movie is about an ordinary person who believes he has both privacy and anonymity, but in truth has neither; technology has stolen them from him. What the movie only hints at is the dreadful possibility that we could all become characters in a "Truman Show" of our own. In this regard, the movie was perhaps prophetic. Of course, people today are not living on a stage set, but they are more and more often recorded, filmed, and observed—often in ways they are unaware of. It is an age of powerful, runaway technology. What hope, then, is there for privacy and anonymity? In a way, the debate about privacy asks whether legal and social norms can protect us from the fate of Truman Burbank.

Truman Burbank was a victim. He never chose his peculiar role in life. When he began to realize who he was, he tried to escape. An important aspect of the movie was the point that the "Truman Show" was immensely popular. It enthralled and fascinated the public; millions watched the show. One can ask *why* the show was so popular. Truman was an ordinary person. Yet he was turned into a genuine celebrity. Did this give the public some sort of claim or right with regard to Truman? As we shall see, the legal answer is a qualified yes.

ORDINARY PEOPLE

When Warren and Brandeis argued for a common law right of privacy, they were thinking primarily of people like themselves, that is, well-to-do and prominent people. They hated the intrusion of gossipy newspapers and the actions of the proto-paparazzi. The action of the gossipy, irresponsible press was one factor that inspired them to write their article. Since they wrote, the right of privacy, legally speaking, has traveled down a kind of bumpy, zigzag road. The newly minted tort was quite slow to catch on. Some states simply rejected it. This was true, for example, in New York, in a case decided in 1902.[30] A flour company and a box company had plastered pictures of the plaintiff, a young woman, all over their advertising posters. She had never given them permission. She claimed the situation humiliated her, subjected her to "scoffs and jeers," and gave her a "severe nervous shock" that sent her to bed. The New York Court of Appeals was unsympathetic. But the New York legislature took notice; it passed a statute creating a cause of action against any company that used the "name, portrait or picture of a living person" for advertising purposes without getting that person's permission.[31]

A few courts reached this result without the benefit of a statute. In a Kansas case decided in 1918, Stella Kunz shopped in a dry-goods store.[32] The store's owners took "moving picture films . . . of her face, form, and garments" without her knowledge and used these to advertise their business "by public exhibition in a moving-picture theater in the neighborhood where she lived."[33] As a result, she said she had become "the common talk of the people in the community"; people thought she had "for hire permitted her picture to be taken and used as a public advertisement." The trial court basically held she had no cause of action. But the appeal court reversed. The store had violated her right of privacy.

In a well-known California case, *Melvin v. Reid*, decided in 1931, the plaintiff was a woman named Gabrielle Darley Melvin.[34] Ms. Melvin had led quite a life. She was at one time a prostitute. In Los Angeles, she shot to death a man named Leonard Tropp, her pimp and former lover. Her trial in 1918 was a total sensation. She hired a skillful lawyer, Earl Rogers, who argued that she had acted in self-defense. Her claim, which was completely bogus, was that she had been "as pure as . . . snow" until Tropp lured her to Los Angeles "under promise of marriage" and enlisted her in a life of shame. The jury obviously found her story convincing; she was acquitted in short order.[35]

Years later, in 1927, Hollywood made a movie about her life called *The Red Kimono*.[36] It used her actual name: Gabrielle Darley. It was sentimental and largely (but not entirely) fictional. The movie, by the way, was totally sympathetic to Gabrielle, and yet Gabrielle, who deserved some sort of Academy Award for chutzpah, brought a lawsuit against the filmmakers. She claimed she was now a respectable married woman, a housewife, and a lady of "culture and refinement"; the movie, she said, had invaded her privacy, causing her enormous grief, to the tune of $50,000. Her self-portrayal, by the way, was a complete fabrication; she was, as a matter of fact, still working as a prostitute but the court had no way of knowing this. The court swallowed her story hook, line, and sinker, agreed that her privacy had been invaded, and accepted her cause of action.

The image of a repentant sinner, a fallen woman who had reformed and was intent on living down her past, clearly dazzled the court. There was no obvious statute or precedent that the court could cite to bolster its decision, but the court brushed this consideration aside. The California constitution used the phrase "pursuit of happiness" and that was enough to sustain Gabrielle's claim.[37] Today, the California Constitution and a number of other state constitutions *do* use the word "privacy" in their bills of rights. Yet, on the other hand, today the case would probably come out differently. Gabrielle Darley Melvin would likely be considered some sort of public figure, and, as we will see, this would severely limit her right to privacy.

Two types of distinction emerge from the tangled history of privacy law. The first is the distinction between public and private figures (with all sorts of gradations in between). The second are the distinctions between sources of invasions of privacy: is the source the government, a business corporation, a private citizen, or the media? The precise *situation* also matters. You have the most protection if you are not a public figure, if other people are the source of the invasion of privacy, and if most people would consider the place, the time, or the event something you have a right to keep private. So if your neighbor plants a hidden camera in your bedroom or bathroom, you are likely to have a cause of action. If the invader is a newspaper, this is probably still true, but freedom of the press might complicate the issue. What the police or the government (state or federal) are allowed to do is a most complicated issue; a lot depends on the kind of invasion, what was invaded, and why. And in each case, whether or not you are a public figure makes a considerable difference. In a later chapter, we will discuss the privacy rights of public figures. This chapter is mostly about the rest of us.

MALL RATS AND OTHER RODENTS

Privacy issues have given rise to an immense literature on the applicable law. William Prosser, for many years the leading guru of the law of torts, systematized the existing law, as he understood it, in 1960. Prosser divided cases on invasion of privacy into four distinct causes of action or, if you will, four separate torts.[38] The Restatement (Second) of Torts, a treatise that describes (and to a certain extent molds) the law, codified Prosser's description in 1977.

The first type of tort protects against unreasonable intrusion upon the seclusion or private affairs of another. As defined in the Restatement (Second) of Torts, "One who intentionally intrudes, physically or otherwise, upon the solitude or seclusion of another or his private affairs or concerns, is subject to liability to the other for invasion of his privacy, if the intrusion would be highly offensive to a reasonable person."[39] No particular harm need come from the intrusion—the intrusion itself is the actionable harm; nor is malice required. All that is necessary is proof of (1) an intentional intrusion (2) into a matter the target has the right to keep private (3) through a method that would be objectionable to a reasonable person.[40] Most states follow some version of this rule.[41]

This tort is the embodiment of the elective aspect of privacy. The action is defined by what reasonable people expect when they have chosen (permissibly) to keep something private. They have the right to expect solitude and respect for the boundaries they have established. The second common privacy tort is a corollary to the first one: the right against public disclosure of private life or facts. According to the Restatement's version of the rule, "One who gives publicity to a matter concerning the private life of another is subject to liability to the other for invasion of his privacy, if the matter publicized is of a kind that (a) would be highly offensive to a reasonable person, and (b) is not of legitimate concern to the public."[42] It does not matter how these private facts are gathered, only that they not be made public. This is so even if the facts shared are true; unlike a defamation case (libel or slander), truth is not a defense. The truth is the very thing the victim wants to keep from public knowledge.

This particular tort—revealing private facts—does not cover gossip in the traditional sense; a person can share secrets with one or even a few people without risking liability for this tort. The test is truly whether the information has been "made public, by communicating it to the public at large, or to so many persons that the matter must be regarded as substantially certain to become one of public knowledge."[43] The individual's interest in privacy is balanced against the public's right to know; this tort only covers situations in which the public has no natural and proper interest in the disclosed facts.[44] And if the facts are already part of the public record—say, a mugshot or arrest report—further dissemination or disclosure is not actionable. This is one of the rules that is different for the famous. As we discuss in chapter 9, public figures, whether they chose to be public figures or had it thrust on them, have a special position in the law. The public seems to want to know everything about celebrities and other public figures; they want to be able to peek through the window, so to speak, and see and hear everything about that person; the law protects that impulse to a certain degree.[45]

The third privacy tort protects a person against publicizing information that would place the person in a "false light."[46] This type of disclosure is actionable if the false light would be highly offensive to a reasonable person—and if the person who disclosed the information either knew that the information was false or that it would create a false impression. Not every state recognizes this claim; Florida, Texas, and North Carolina have rejected it, and other states have been cagey about their comfort with it.[47] Edith Rapp sued for "false light" invasion of privacy after her stepson, an employee of Jews for Jesus, Inc., wrote an article for the organization's newsletter in which he suggested that Edith, who was Jewish, had accepted Jesus as her savior. The Florida Supreme Court refused to recognize the false light tort under Florida law.[48] Although the court recognized that presenting someone in a false light can be harmful, it felt that defamation law in Florida was broad enough to cover situations in which true statements create a false impression ("defamation by implication"). But a plaintiff in a defamation case has to show a harm to reputation or other interests, while false light cases merely need to show that the actions were "highly offensive" to the subject. The Florida court felt that the false light tort gives too much weight to offensiveness, at the expense of freedom of expression. As for Edith, her claim was remanded for a determination of whether the statement was indeed false and of a nature that could render her the object of "hatred, distrust, ridicule, contempt or disgrace" in the eyes of a "substantial and respectable minority of the community."[49]

Finally, Prosser outlined a fourth privacy tort—unwarranted appropriation of name or likeness, also known sometimes as the "right to publicity." A person has the right to choose to keep aspects of their lives and identity private but also to exploit the value of their names, lives, and identities, if they so choose. The Restatement defines this fourth tort as follows: "One who appropriates to his own use or benefit the name or likeness of another is subject to liability to the other for invasion of his privacy."[50] This tort applies when someone has appropriated or exploited another person's face or name for profit—by using it in advertising, for example. More than half the states recognize this tort. In California, for example, a statute makes it unlawful "for the purpose of advertising or selling, to knowingly use another's name, voice, signature, photograph, or likeness without that person's prior consent."[51] This protection lasts for fifty years after a person's death. Celebrities like Bette Midler, Johnny Carson, and Kareem Abdul-Jabbar have used laws of this type to protect against misappropriation of their names, images, and catch phrases. A portable toilet company could not use the phrase "Here's Johnny" to introduce its product without violating Johnny Carson's right of publicity, even though the company did not use his name or likeness in their marketing materials.[52] The company admitted that it used the phrase because it was associated with Carson, a host on late night television; this violated Carson's exclusive right to profit off his celebrity.

Prosser's work was useful and important for courts struggling to cope with privacy doctrine and many courts found his categories useful. But privacy law, like privacy practice, has been shaped by technology, by social norms, and by the culture of modernity. The world is quite different than it was in 1960 when Prosser first outlined his analysis of privacy law; the world is also different from the way it was in 1977 when the Restatement adopted Prosser's formulation (to say nothing of how different the world is today, compared with the world of Warren and Brandeis in the 1890s).

The role of technology, namely, the ubiquitous camera, and other devices that can and do impinge on privacy, is obvious. Technology, however, merely provides tools or instruments. The key questions remain: what is an "intrusion" or "invasion"? And what is the "privacy" that has been invaded or intruded upon? Where and when do people actually have a "reasonable expectation of privacy"? This vague phrase has spread like an infection from statute to statute. In fairness, since some of the statutes that prohibit invasions of privacy are in form criminal statutes, courts are fussy about these laws and resist expanding them beyond the situations to which they clearly apply.

Take, for example, the law relating to an unholy new practice called "upskirting," which seems to flourish at shopping malls and on buses and trains. "Upskirters" use small but powerful cameras to try to take photographs or make videos under women's skirts. In a case reported in 2010, "upskirting" was the practice of a man in Tennessee named Jesse. Jesse had "created a contraption whereby a camera was attached to the inside of a binder with velcro."[53] Jesse would then put the binder inside a shopping bag, and if he held the bag under a woman's skirt at a "good angle," he hoped to get the pictures he wanted. He was pursuing his distasteful hobby at the Cool Springs Mall in the Nashville area when somebody called the police and he was arrested. Worse luck followed: the police got a warrant to search his house, and there they found evidence of another hobby in the form of "a white, zippered, plastic bag" full of marijuana.

The marijuana was big trouble for Jesse. But, he argued, the police had no right to use the bag of marijuana as evidence against him because the search warrant was illegal. And why? Because, he said, "upskirting" was not a crime. Under a local statute, it was an an offense to photograph a person if this would "offend or embarrass an ordinary person," and the photo was taken "for the purpose of sexual arousal or gratification."[54] So far, this clearly applied to Jesse; but the mischief had to be done in a place where there was a "reasonable expectation of privacy."[55] The female victims were in a "public place," a mall; thus, Jesse argued, they could not have had a reasonable expectation of privacy. The Tennessee court agreed: Jesse won his case.[56]

Other courts, somewhat surprisingly, came to the same conclusion. In Washington State in 1999, Sean Glas "took pictures up the skirts of two women . . . at the Valley Mall in Union Gap, Washington."[57] A woman "working in the ladies' department at Sears" saw him "squatting or sitting on the floor" with a "small, silver camera in his hand." He also took pictures of the "undergarments" of Shantel Phillips, another employee of the mall. In Washington State, too, the local statute used the phrase "reasonable expectation of privacy."[58] The court reversed Sean's conviction.[59] To the court, a mall was a public place, and "casual intrusions occur frequently when a person ventures out in public."[60] A "public place," therefore, could not "logically constitute" a location where a "person could reasonably expect to be safe from casual or hostile intrusion or surveillance." Not that the court approved of this "disgusting" and "reprehensible" behavior; but the behavior did not violate the local statute. And in a Virginia case, one Charles L. C'Debaca practiced his "upskirting" at the Fairfax County Fairgrounds. His behavior was "contemptible," but not criminal. The victim "had no reasonable expectation of privacy while standing on the public fairgrounds."[61] And in 2014, the Supreme Judicial Court of Massachusetts ruled in *Commonwealth v. Robertson*[62] that the state's voyeurism law did not prohibit a man from surreptitiously videotaping up the skirt of a woman sitting across from him on a Boston trolley.[63] An undercover police officer had caught the man as part of a sting operation to catch him in the act after complaints from female riders. He filmed up the officer's skirt, just as they had predicted he would; he was then arrested. But the charge was dismissed. According to the court, the statute only applied to situations where the victim was in a private place—her home, for example—where she would "normally have privacy from uninvited observation."[64] The trolley car was an extremely public place, a place, in fact, where users are routinely photographed and videotaped for security purposes. The Commonwealth argued that the "private" place was not the trolley car, but rather the "private" place was the part of the woman's body that was videotaped. The court thought this was too much of a stretch. The law was drafted with Peeping Toms in mind. Hence, a crucial element of the crime was lacking; the trolley was a place the statute was never meant to cover. Robertson had not committed a crime.[65] Danielle Citron felt cases of this sort showed that privacy law can seem ill-equipped to handle modern, technology-fueled invasions of privacy.[66] This is particularly the case, she argues, with regard to sexual privacy, which "deserves special recognition and protection given its foundational relationship with sexual autonomy, intimacy, and equal opportunity."[67]

After decisions of this type cited here, some legislatures reacted by changing the wording of their statutes. Nevertheless, the phrase "reasonable expectation of privacy" stuck like a barnacle to the texts of the laws. The courts had been paying too much attention, arguably, to *where* the act took place. A mall is not private but, as the Commonwealth argued in the Massachusetts case, the body *is* private. Underwear is private. And there is a "reasonable expectation" that people can choose (as almost everybody does) to keep underwear private. Moreover, even in a mall or on a trolley, there is a reasonable expectation, if not of "privacy," then certainly of anonymity, which the defendants violated. Most ordinary people would be shocked to learn that "upskirt" practitioners went unpunished in these cases. In a mall, you expect attention from salespeople (or not); you definitely do not expect to be accosted, photographed, or stalked—and you certainly do not want or expect some sleazy creature to take pictures of your underwear and put the pictures on the internet. Clearly, a man who groped women in a mall would be arrested, and "upskirting" is, in a way, a form of groping. As awareness of "upskirting" increased, and as it became clear, from decisions, that the current laws against voyeurs did not provide a remedy, legislatures tried to plug the gaps. Washington State, after the *Sean Glas* case, amended its law in 2003.

The new version defined voyeurism to include photographing or filming "the intimate areas of another person without that person's knowledge and consent and under circumstances where the person has a reasonable expectation of privacy, whether in a public or private place."[68] In Massachusetts, the legislature took less than a week to pass a bill titled *An Act Relative to Unlawful Sexual Surveillance*,[69] which makes it a criminal invasion of privacy to film or photograph "under or around the person's clothing to view or attempt to view the person's sexual or other intimate parts when a reasonable person would believe that the person's sexual or other intimate parts would not be visible to the public and without the person's knowledge and consent."[70] This law made clear that upskirting is a crime even if the victim is fully clothed and in a public place. In Canada, "upskirting" is punished as a form of illegal "voyeurism" and an act of the English parliament, which went into effect in April 2019, the Voyeurism (Offences) Act, made "upskirting" specifically a crime; during 2019, ten men were convicted of sixteen offenses; many more were reported to the police.[71]

An Ohio court in 2012 had seemed to get the point, though in this case the victims were nude men instead of women in their underwear.[72] Paul Dennison took "nude photographs of men" in the locker room of the YMCA in Bryan, Ohio. An Ohio statute made it a crime to "surreptitiously invade the privacy of another . . . in a state of nudity" if done "for the purpose of sexually arousing or gratifying the person's self."[73] Dennison argued that men who used the locker room to change clothes, shower, and the like had no "reasonable expectation of privacy." The three men he photographed "knowingly disrobed in front of him" and the "locker room was open and accessible"; this made it a "public place for which no right of privacy applies."[74] The court refused to buy this argument. True, the men had to change clothes and use the shower at the YMCA gym; but this did not "remove all expectations of privacy." These men certainly did not expect someone to hang around with a camera and take pictures of them in the nude. This makes sense; but technically speaking, it was not "privacy" that was invaded here, but anonymity, and what we have called the right to evanescence. Yes, the men undressed and showered in the YMCA, and, yes, this was not the same as undressing and showering at home. But there are norms of locker room behavior and Dennison's creepy and disturbing behavior clearly violated those norms.[75] The men did not expect to have their naked bodies photographed and preserved for posterity or for Dennison's sexual gratification.

The essence of the offense, perhaps, was that photographs are, or can be, permanent. If Dennison, instead of taking pictures, had simply quietly and discreetly taken a peek at the naked bodies around him in the locker room and in the showers, he would have committed no crime. If he stared brazenly at the naked bodies in the locker room, he would have definitely violated a social norm; he would have risked losing his membership at the YMCA and risked also, perhaps, a punch in the nose. Photographs and videos are another and more serious story. They violate anonymity—and evanescence. And, of course, a photograph is not only permanent, it can also be copied and circulated.

If Dennison had gone to a nude beach with his camera, and taken pictures to satisfy his prurient interests, would he have been guilty of a crime? In an Ohio case in 1994, James Frost sat in his car, near a beach, and watched "two bikini-clad females" through binoculars.[76] A state park manager, who saw him, then approached and found Frost with his "pants around his ankles," masturbating. A court dismissed the complaint: the "young ladies had no right of privacy at a public beach, and they probably expected to be observed in their bikini bathing suits." There was "neither a trespass nor an invasion of privacy." Frost was guilty of no crime.

But suppose instead of secretly peeking at these women through binoculars, Frost had actually photographed them: would the case come out the same way? Obviously, a woman who puts on a bikini and goes to a beach lacks some of her usual "expectation of privacy." But here, too, the issue is not so much privacy as anonymity, and what we called evanescence. Our woman in a bikini might or might not be pleased if people at the beach admired her figure; she might or might not mind it if people looked at her (but no staring, please). Photographs, on the other hand, would have made at least some women distinctly uncomfortable and increased the chance that the images might be used in a way they didn't reasonably expect.

To stare at a person—on the street, in an elevator, or in a restaurant—is not a crime but it violates a social norm. It is also not a crime to follow somebody on the street but at some point, following in a persistent and menacing way becomes "stalking," and this can indeed constitute a crime under a number of modern statutes.[77] Privacy norms and privacy law overlap, but they are not identical. This does not mean that the law somehow "lags" behind social norms but rather that to punish *some* social norms is either felt to be not worth the trouble or might be thought to do more harm than good, either by violating a *different* social norm or by giving the government more power than we think is good for society. A man who stares and stares obsessively at women in bathing suits is acting rudely and is violating beach etiquette; most of us would think of him as at least somewhat pathological. Still, putting him in prison might seem too harsh a punishment. Or it might raise difficult issues of law enforcement. Making something a "crime," after all, means giving local police a power we do not always want them to have.

HIJINKS IN LOWER MERION

In one rather extraordinary case, the school district of Lower Merion, a Philadelphia suburb, issued laptops to high school students.[78] What the students, and their parents, did not know is that the school district had secretly loaded a device onto these computers that allowed the district to activate a tiny camera and take pictures of the students wherever they happened to be with their laptop. And the district proceeded to do this, at least in the case of a sophomore named Blake J. Robbins. The district confronted Robbins, and disciplined him, on the basis of what these secret photos told them. Robbins sued in federal court.[79] In October 2010, the school district settled out of court.[80]

Exactly what the camera saw Robbins doing is not very clear. The school authorities thought it had something to do with drugs; apparently they were wrong. They did take pictures of Robbins sleeping and coming out of the shower shirtless. People in the community were outraged. The question is, what exactly was it that shocked the good citizens? Was it the raw fact that the school district was spying on its students? Or was it this plus the vague hint of a Peeping Tom school board, gawking at naked bodies, or watching to see what sorts of sexual behavior the students were indulging in, if any? Here, as elsewhere, the (not-so-faint) odor of sex pervades the law of personal privacy. One's sex life is the last frontier of privacy, for most people, that is. And the history of privacy law is bound up with the history of the sexual revolution in more ways than most people suspect.

In 2010, the parents of Lower Merion could not have dreamt of one result of the 2020 pandemic: students taking exams at home, while the computer's camera watches their every move, scans the room for other people and notes, and tries to re-create, through remote surveillance, the way a teacher might monitor a class for cheating. Circumstances alter the concept of privacy and the *expectation* of privacy, a key concept in both law and social norms.

Myra Creel was a white-collar worker in a hospital. She was married to Claude Creel, pastor of the Huntsville Evangelistic Community Church in Huntsville, Indiana. Myra was in an auto accident; a dispute arose between her and the insurance company. The company hired a private detective to snoop on Myra and find out more about her condition. The investigator, J. D. Renner, "presented himself as a worshipper" at church services conducted by the Reverend Creel. He "wore a sling on his arm that concealed a video camera" and videotaped the Reverend and his wife as she played the piano during church services. The insurance company denied Myra's claim. But she found out about the secret videotaping and she and her husband filed suit in 1999 for invasion of privacy.[81]

The Creels argued that during church services, they had a "reasonable expectation of privacy, solitude, or seclusion."[82] But they were "neither alone nor secluded," and the church services "were open to the general public."[83] What Renner taped was hardly secret; the whole congregation saw the same thing he saw—that much was surely true. Consequently, the Creels had no "reasonable expectation of privacy"; but surely they did not expect to be filmed in church and their feelings about anonymity and evanescence were definitely violated. So far, at least, these values are not recognized or protected in law. Many people, however, perhaps even most people, would consider the action of the insurance company disreputable and intrusive, and many of these people might feel "there ought to be a law."

THE SPY IN THE BEDROOM

The Creel case at least lacked strong sexual overtones. These overtones, however, are pervasive in privacy situations. Case in point is a 1964 decision in New Hampshire, *Hamberger v. Eastman*. Carl Hamberger claimed that his landlord, Clifford Eastman, "installed and concealed 'a listening and recording device'" in the bedroom where Mr. and Mrs. Hamberger slept. The device was "concealed in an area adjacent to the bed" and connected to the landlord's house "by means of wires capable of transmitting and recording any sounds and voices" coming from the bedroom.[84] Hamberger sued for invasion of privacy. He claimed he was distressed, humiliated, embarrassed, had become "extremely nervous and upset," and had been "unable to properly perform his normal and ordinary duties as a father and as a husband," not to mention his inability to perform his "duties at his place of employment" (these presumably did not involve sexual intercourse). His wife also filed suit, advancing claims of her own.

This was the first case in New Hampshire on the so-called right of privacy. The defendant moved to dismiss the case. The appellate court denied this motion. The court, not surprisingly, had little sympathy for the defendant. Nobody, according to the defendant, had actually listened or overheard anything going on in that bedroom, but this was irrelevant in the court's opinion, even if true. What people did in their bedrooms was their business, and nobody else's. Eastman's intrusion was one "that would be offensive to any person of ordinary sensibilities."[85]

True enough. Almost everybody would be outraged to discover a "bug" under the bedroom mattress. The Hambergers were not only outraged, they also claimed, in effect, that they were suffering mentally and physically. Mr. Hamberger hinted strongly that this horrific discovery made him impotent. We have no way of knowing if this was true or simply a way to maximize a sense of outrage and increase the claim for damages. Plaintiffs can and sometimes do allege wild amounts of psychic harm and picture themselves as extremely sensitive plants to bolster their case. Still, the sexual machine *is*, for many people, delicate and easily disturbed; how many people, for example, could bring themselves to perform in front of an audience?

Or to undress in front of an audience? "Sabrina W.," was twenty-three, a single mother who lived in Nebraska, and brought suit in a case reported in 1995.[86] She bought a "membership in a tanning facility" from Ron Willman who owned a hair salon that also contained a tanning room. According to Sabrina, Willman "secretly watched and photographed her while she was in various stages of undress and nude in the tanning room."[87] He took the photos to be developed. An employee of the developing facility told the police about the photos. The police "confiscated the photographs" when Willman came to get them. A police lieutenant told Sabrina W. about the photos; she went to the police station and identified herself as the subject of the photographs. She said she felt "shocked, humiliated . . . embarrassed . . . and . . . degraded." The news somehow got out. People told jokes. Men made "indecent proposals." Her co-workers harassed her and she felt compelled to leave her job. Her former husband tried to take her child away. She "started drinking. . . . She was afraid to use a public dressing room or stay in a motel room. The incident affected her attitude toward men, her interest in them, and their interest in her." Her physical health was affected and she "gained weight."[88] The trial court had directed a verdict for the defendant on the grounds that she had "failed to show that she suffered severe emotional distress," but the appellate court disagreed and reversed. Once an invasion of privacy of this sort is shown, then the trier or fact (court or jury) can assess damages.[89]

Tanning salons seem to be dangerous places as far as privacy is concerned. David Paro, owner of a tanning salon in Buffalo, Missouri, secretly videotaped his women clients, who were lying naked under tanning lights. People in town learned, to their horror, that this Peeping Tom videographer had recorded more than one hundred women. This was, apparently, not illegal in Missouri; Paro, however, ultimately pleaded guilty to child abuse because some of his clients, including the sheriff's daughter, were underage. In 2002, the Missouri legislature passed a law to plug the statutory gap: it became an offense to photograph someone in a "state of full or partial nudity" in a place where the person has a "reasonable expectation of privacy"; disseminating any such photograph bumps the offense from misdemeanor to felony. The state's own governor would end up indicted under this law; the governor was accused of taking pictures of his mistress against her will. These photographs of the woman, partially nude, were supposedly to be used as a blackmail tool, to keep the woman quiet about the affair.[90] The charges were eventually dropped; prosecutors were unable to locate the alleged photos and the woman in question refused to cooperate.[91]

Incidents of this sort awakened the sleeping congressional giant. What concerned the government, above all, was sexual and bodily privacy. Congress enacted a law, the Video Voyeurism Prevention Act of 2004,[92] which was specifically meant to outlaw the abusive use of hidden cameras and video recorders. The Act made it a crime to "capture an image of a private area of an individual," without that person's consent, "under circumstances in which the individual has a reasonable expectation of privacy." A person's "private area" was defined to mean "the naked or undergarment clad genitals, pubic area, buttocks, or female breast," and "female breast" was further defined as "any portion of the female breast below the top of the areola." The statute was, obviously, quite limited; it did not apply to invasions of privacy except for those that have a sexual tinge. And the statute exempted "any lawful law enforcement, correctional, or intelligence activity."[93]

There are similar or analogous statutes in many states. In California, for example, it is a crime to "secretly videotape, film, photograph, or record by electronic means" a person's body or underwear, without that person's knowledge, in order to "gratify the lust, passions, or sexual desires" of the person doing the recording, if done without the victim's consent and under "circumstances in which the other person has a reasonable expectation of privacy."[94] Here, too, the sexual element in the invasion of privacy is paramount. And in Canada, also, a provision of the criminal code prohibits secret observing or recording of a person who is "nude, is exposing his or her genital organs or anal region or her breasts, or is engaged in explicit sexual activity," provided the person is in a situation that gives rise to that familiar concept, "a reasonable expectation of privacy."[95]

The cases and statutes, quite obviously, are designed to protect sexual and bodily privacy. The people who are "invading" the victim's privacy are almost always men and almost always have sex on their mind. They are pursuing their own rather creepy need for this kind of gratification. The plaintiffs typically claim that they were traumatized—that the defendant's actions humiliated them, ruined their reputation, made them an object of gossip, or curdled their sex lives. A rabbi in New York got into a mess of trouble when it turned out he was peeking at women in the mikveh, the ritual bath used by Orthodox women. He pleaded guilty to fifty-two counts of voyeurism and was sentenced to six-and-a-half years in prison. Like Sabrina and the Hambergers, the women who were spied on claimed the experience was traumatic. One of them testified that she felt as if she had fallen "off the edge of this earth" when she learned that she had been watched during her ritual bath.[96]

In 2010, a Rutgers student, Dharun Ravi, spied on his roommate, Tyler Clementi, who was gay.[97] Ravi and another student secretly set up a web cam and circulated live images of Clementi "making out with a dude." When Clementi found out about this, he was tremendously upset; he tried to change his room assignment, and then, in desperation, committed suicide by jumping off the George Washington Bridge. An angry storm erupted directed at Ravi and his friend. They were arrested, and in March of 2012, Ravi was found guilty of a number of crimes, including invasion of privacy. He was sentenced to a short jail sentence plus three years' probation, three hundred hours of community service, and a fine of $11,000.[98]

Tyler Clementi committed suicide because his privacy had been invaded and because of the shame and humiliation that followed. He was a shy, introspective, and private young man. He was, obviously, not about to march in gay pride parades; and of course he had a perfect right to "stay in the closet." His death touched off a national debate about "cyberbullying." Bullying itself is as old as the hills, and, particularly in the hands of adolescents, it can be merciless. No doubt, there have been college students and teenagers who killed themselves after relentless bullying, even without the benefit of modern technology. But the webcam made things worse for Tyler: it meant that embarrassing images could be sent out to friends, family, classmates, and perhaps the whole world.

REVENGE PORN

There are all sorts of ways to harm a partner—or former partner. Privacy is more and more a complex issue in this age of new technology and the explosive growth of social media. People are in constant communication with each other. Their conversations are not simply words: they are punctuated with "selfies," videos, and recordings. People in romantic relationships have new ways to express love and lust; partners can supplement chocolates, flowers, and valentines with more explicit and graphic messages. This has led to a new phenomenon—"sexting" between partners.[99] In a healthy, trusting romance, this might be harmless. But what happens when relationships sour and two lovers become "exes" or even enemies?

One result at times is so-called revenge porn. Generally, this term is used to describe sexually explicit or naked pictures or videos of a person that someone posts online without the subject's consent; this practice has vast potential for harm. The term "revenge" refers to the background of the posting: the source of the pictures is usually a former partner who puts the photos or videos out there in order to shame, humiliate, or embarrass an ex-lover. In the most objectionable form, the poster shares not only images but also identifying information—such as the victim's name, address, and social media profiles. Websites have sprung up that are expressly designed to make revenge porn possible—these are sites that have as their purpose the sharing of such images and information. The victims of revenge porn are mostly women who are more likely to have been pressured into sharing images in the first place and are more likely to be harmed by "slut shaming."[100] Revenge porn is a type of cyber harassment that can ruin a person's life. According to a 2014 article in *The Economist*, there have been at least three thousand revenge-porn sites worldwide; more of them come into being all the time.[101] To be sure, some of the most notorious of these have been taken down.

Revenge porn is one of the unsavory downsides of the internet. The internet makes invasions of privacy costless to the invader, instantaneous, damagingly widespread, and almost impossible to undo. But revenge porn, like upskirting, does not obviously violate most privacy statutes or privacy doctrine in general. Revenge porn is tricky; the images, after all, were generally consensual when they were produced. Sometimes they were taken by the "victims" themselves—as "selfies" perhaps—and sent in digital form to a partner, who has since become an ex-partner and a tormentor.

In the age of "sexting," revenge porn has become a modern hazard of romances that have floundered and sunk. In some cases, hackers have used illicit, or deceitful, means to get hold of compromising photos and share them with the world; sometimes they demand money in exchange for removing these photos from the public eye.[102] But more commonly, it is a disgruntled "ex" who shares explicit videos or images of a former lover—images originally meant to be private. Cybercrime laws and laws about invasion of privacy can deal with some situations, but "revenge porn" as such needed special legislation. For example, in 2013, Adriana Batch discovered that Ian Barber (described as her "boyfriend") had not only posted naked pictures of her online but had also emailed them to her sister and her employer. This surely ruined the Barber-Batch relationship, if it was not ruined already; Batch complained, and her complaint led to criminal charges against Barber. But a New York court held that his conduct, while "reprehensible," did not violate any existing state law.[103]

Federal and state governments play a game of catch-up; legislators and advocates try to draft laws that can deal with revenge porn and similar matters. This is not easy. There is, to begin with, the little matter of the First Amendment and the right of free speech and free expression. It is hard to craft laws that ban just enough conduct, not too much, and not too little.

Still, a number of states have passed laws specifically aimed at revenge porn.[104] California's law dates from 2013. The law made it a misdemeanor to "intentionally distribute the image of the intimate body part or parts of another identifiable person, or an image of the person depicted engaged in an act of sexual intercourse, sodomy, oral copulation, sexual penetration, or an image of masturbation by the person depicted or in which the person depicted participates, under circumstances in which the persons agree or understand that the image shall remain private." But this is only a crime if the person distributing the image "knows or should know that distribution of the image will cause serious emotional distress, and the person depicted suffers that distress." This is a fairly vague standard. If a student shows his girlfriend's selfie to his fraternity brothers after a break-up, has he violated the law? Does it depend on whether her feelings have been hurt? If she, after the break-up, shows *his* selfies to her friends, can he do the same? Does the law—or society—assume that a naked photo of her is more harmful than a naked photo of him? Most of the complaints have come from women, complaining about the actions of men. But a woman in Virginia was arrested for violating a Virginia law that made it an offense to put a nude photo on the internet without the consent of the owner of the body. The woman had gotten hold of an explicit picture of her ex-boyfriend's new girlfriend and posted it on Facebook.

California has not only passed a revenge porn law but also created a special prosecution unit to focus on crimes facilitated by internet technology, including revenge porn. In 2014, California also added a civil provision; now the victim can sue for damages someone who distributes a photo that was supposed to be private and that causes harm to the victim.[105] The first man convicted under the revenge porn law (in December 2014), was Noe Iniguez, a thirty-six-year-old man in Los Angeles. Noe was definitely the ex-boyfriend from hell. His anger was limitless—his victim felt compelled to get a restraining order against him at one point. He then turned to revenge porn, posting derogatory comments on her employer's Facebook page, and then a topless photograph, together with a message calling her a "slut" and a "drunk," and encouraging the company to fire her. The topless photo had been taken while the pair were still dating, and the victim had never intended for anyone other than Iniguez to see it.[106] He was arrested, prosecuted, convicted, and sentenced to a year in jail.[107] Justice was done but only after tremendous pain had been inflicted on the victim of Iniguez's rage.

Iniguez's behavior was, of course, disgraceful, but before the passage of the revenge porn law, he could have argued that nothing he did was illegal. After all, he was in possession of that photo because she sent it to him. Invasions of privacy do not usually start with something consensual. Nobody invites a Peeping Tom to do the peeping; nobody invites the work of the paparazzi with their zoom lenses. A person who is foolish enough to send off an embarrassing photo knows or should know that she or he is taking a risk. Whoever gets a picture or a letter or an email can normally do what they want with it. Revenge porn laws carve out a kind of exception to this general rule.

Sadly, there is something of a revenge porn industry. It depends on stolen photos. General cybercrime rules, privacy laws, or rules against blackmail and extortion can be used against this business, against those who hack into computers and steal nude images. Hunter Moore, the so-called king of revenge porn, ran a website called "Is Anyone Up." His website raked in substantial amounts of ad money. Hunter's glory days did not last, however. In 2015, he was arrested, tried, and sentenced to a term in prison.

Hunter of course was not alone; there are others in this business. Some revenge porn websites are little better than blackmail machines. The site is happy to delete material—so long as the victim is willing to pay. Craig Brittain, who operated a revenge porn site, settled with the Federal Trade Commission, agreeing to take his website offline and delete all the images and personal information he collected. Besides his traffic in revenge porn, he acquired revealing photos of women through trickery, then tried to get them to pay money to have the images removed. The FTC shut him down. In general, the fight goes on. A law firm based in Pittsburgh recruited fifty lawyers who volunteered, together with advocacy groups, to fight to "empower" victims to stand up for their rights. The most solid weapon, of course, is statutory.[108]

Here, too, we might mention "doxxing," the practice of gathering personal data and using it for nefarious purposes—another grim device that the internet, hacking, and the new dark skills of technology make possible. The Korean "dog-poop" girl was perhaps the first known victim of doxxing; she was identified and cyber-harassed after not cleaning up her dog's poop on the subway. This and other stories illustrate the explosive power of the new media that can be used to destroy reputations. "Right-to-lifers" can, for example, compile personal information on doctors and clinics that perform abortions, spread this information broadly, and stimulate campaigns of terror against these doctors and clinics. In this age of political polarization, people in public life (on the right or the left) who take positions that extremists disapprove of are certain to be exposed to risks to reputation or to personal safety; death threats spring up like mushrooms. The possibilities of weaponized computer technology, in this day and age, are endless. Not all of them, of course, are malignant. But many of them are.

It seems like a paradox that in our times, which is so much more permissive than the Victorian era, norms of modesty and privacy, including sexual privacy, need protection from attack. But perhaps this is not a paradox at all. Privacy is harder to maintain in a permissive age. Material intended to be kept private can go public in the blink of an eye; what is thought to be temporary and forgotten turns out to be permanently stored in some permanent electronic warehouse. Privacy in the internet age is more and more endangered. In the Victorian era, prudery acted as a kind of shield, protecting privacy. Books never used dirty words. Buying or selling dirty pictures was illegal. Pornographers could be arrested. They sold their goods in the proverbial plain brown wrappers. People covered their bodies, even at the beach. Many married people had intercourse without undressing beyond the irreducible minimum. Most people rarely bathed. Homes did not contain stall showers. Except for boys at the swimming hole, nudity was fairly uncommon. People were not supposed to think dirty thoughts (though of course they did). Freud had not yet burst upon the scene. People in novels got married and had children but the authors never talked about how these children were actually produced.[109] Sex was treated as a dirty little secret. What went on underneath the Victorian surface was clearly much more complicated; still, the surface reflected a powerful ideology of restraint and modesty.

A lot had changed even before the so-called sexual revolution of the late twentieth century. In the 1920s, people complained about the "flappers," and about dissolute and immoral young people. Today, sex is everywhere. Traditional morality struggles valiantly against the tide but so far it seems to be losing the battle. Most forms of sexual behavior between consenting adults have been legalized. Gay sex has come bursting out of the closet. The strict movie code is history. Movies that would have been banned as totally immoral in the past can be shown even to children. Adolescents take nude pictures of themselves and send them via smartphone to their friends. Pornography is almost out of control. TV programs and movies chatter away about abortion, contraception, and subjects that once were taboo. Women's magazines have given up on recipes for apple pie, and instead run articles on sexual positions and how to have bigger and better orgasms. An Olympic star, once a man, becomes a woman thanks to hormones and surgery and lands on the cover of national magazines. There are a few limits—prime-time network television does not show hardcore pornography, for example. The #MeToo movement stormed into public consciousness in 2017; it ripped apart the iron curtain that had shielded the private predatory sexual behavior of the rich and powerful. Many rich and powerful men lost jobs and careers because of their sexual misconduct—men like the movie mogul Harvey Weinstein and even stars of the world of classical music like James Levin and Placido Domingo. When Jeffrey Toobin exposed himself during a work meeting on Zoom in 2020—mistakenly toggling back from a video sex site to an election preparation meeting—he was suspended by the *New Yorker* magazine.[110] There may not be many limits left, but this is one of them. The norms have changed dramatically and the tiger of sex is out of its cage, but still there are definite rules, and these rules privilege willingness and consent.

The twentieth century of course did not invent sex, orgasms, and the like. Humans have been zestfully reproducing since the dawn of time. Whether people are now having more sex than before, and whether the amount of "prurient interest" has gone up, are open questions since we know so little about actual sexual behavior before the days of survey research. Perhaps there *is* more sex: young couples now live together freely; perhaps, in the past, "free love" or an active sex life for the unmarried was harder to manage and to consummate, as it were. But modesty has not been abolished. Most people are, in fact, still quite modest, at least for themselves, if not for others. Their modesty, however, is a choice, not a legal requirement; if they choose not to be modest, there are fewer social consequences. Permissiveness means that lines, boundaries, and limits have to be carefully redrawn. Precisely because there is so much sex, and so much chatter about sex, people feel that children need special protection. And grown-ups still have the right to opt out of the permissive society—to wear clothes, as it were, at the nude beaches of modern society.

TWO FACES OF SOCIETY

Modern society is, in fact, curiously two-faced. In the developed world, most people cling for dear life to their privacy—Tyler Clementi died of shame when his secret was revealed. People cling to anonymity as well. They bitterly resent "invasions" of privacy, or even of anonymity; they detest "upskirters" and the like. Yet a small but significant segment of society is only too eager to wash dirty linen in public. The two groups, no doubt, are grossly unequal in size: one very large group consists of people who, at most, love to watch other people on "reality TV" or otherwise, but for themselves cling to privacy and anonymity; the second is a noisy, but much smaller, group that would do anything to get on reality TV and who seem to value privacy and anonymity very little if at all. Most people would never dream of stripping off their clothes in public or taking a picture of themselves in the nude and forwarding it to a friend. But some do exactly that. And they get an audience. For every Lady Godiva, there are thousands of Peeping Toms.

What people generally want, in short, is the freedom to be private; yet a great many people also seem to want access to the other class of people—the people who blithely abandon their privacy. For the majority, privacy is the shield that protects them when they choose to be modest. Yes, you can go to a nudist colony or stretch out on a blanket at a nude beach. You can audition for a slot on a reality TV show. Most people choose not to. But the *choice* in itself is significant. Laws and social norms will protect that choice, either way. The larger group is the audience; the smaller group is the performers. Society is made up of both exhibitionists and voyeurs.

Of course, there have always been audiences—the "groundlings" who watched Shakespeare's plays at the Globe Theater, more than four hundred years ago, the kids and their grown-ups who went to the Barnum and Bailey circus and watched lion-tamers and trapeze artists, the fans of the great soloist musicians Paganini and Clara Schumann in the nineteenth century, the audiences at Vaudeville or the audience for Harry Houdini and other magicians and escape artists. The mass media expanded enormously; the reading and watching public expanded tremendously as well. The mass-market newspapers of the nineteenth century covered "public figures" and supplemented their words with woodcuts of trials, murderers, sports stars, and beautiful women. A picture is worth a thousand words, as the saying goes; its influence is certainly greater. The movies were a huge leap forward (or backward, if you will). Very soon after movies began, they were attracting an amazingly large audience. Movies were everywhere; they were entertainment for the masses. Television was another quantum shift in sheer size, scope, and attractiveness. And now we have the internet: YouTube, Facebook, WhatsApp, and the rest. We are a world of watchers and the watched.

Who are the exhibitionists? Who are the people who clamor for their fifteen minutes of fame, for a spot on TV, perhaps on one of the "reality" programs? Who are the "litigants" in Judge Judy's "court"? Who are the people who spill their guts on the "trash talk shows"? These people are, in a way, "defecating in public"; in exchange for a free trip and a short stint on television, they reveal "deep secrets and intimate life experiences," and they do it in a way that is "exaggerated, loud," and very often in poor taste.[111] Some do it no doubt as an adventure, like boys who climb rooftops or men who scale Mount Everest; some may see it as their only chance to express themselves. This has been true, for example, of some members of sexual minorities who had long been shut out of conventional ways to express themselves in public and who now march in gay pride parades and fly rainbow flags. In short, some people—no accurate count is possible—reject core notions of privacy, unlike the majority, which cherishes them. The very *existence* of the smaller troop of people surely influences both the law and the norms of privacy. If people who cheat on their partners, people who are human pack-rats, people desperately trying to lose weight, single people looking for mates, and a host of nonconformists willingly expose themselves to millions on TV (and even more on the web), this phenomenon, and this behavior, very likely influences public opinion, social norms, and, ultimately, law.[112] Nobody is in fact an island—not the talk show guests, the litigants, or the reality-mongers; what they do and think has ripple effects, whether they like it or not.

THE INVASION MARKET

Thankfully, not many people have landlords who bug their mattresses, roommates who record their sexual behavior, or owners of tanning salons who peek on their customers. The chief threats to privacy today do not come from dirty-minded *individuals*, but from businesses, and from the government itself.

As the *Creel* case illustrates, many businesses are willing to intrude on clients, claimants, or customers. Sometimes this is done for dubious motives but mostly it is the normal pursuit of profits. Businesses crave information that can help them sell their products. Amazon, the giant bookseller, suggests books you might want to buy based on what you bought in the past, and what they think these buying habits say about your likes and dislikes. Other companies do the same sort of thing. The worst threat to privacy, perhaps, comes from Big Brother, government itself. Autocratic governments censor the news and suppress dissent. Democratic societies are supposed to abide by the rule of law; they are supposed to value and protect citizens from invasions of privacy (of one sort or another). There are, however, both formal and informal exceptions. Governments all over the world—including the most democratic ones—maintain agencies to spy on other governments, even friendly ones, and to eavesdrop electronically on foreign leaders. They resort to various dirty tricks, even if their tactics are in fact against formal law. The key justification, or excuse, for much of the invasion of citizens' privacy is security, especially the war against terror. And the public, by and large, accepts this excuse. We will deal with this issue in a later chapter.

NOTES

1. These issues are explored in chapter 1.
2. 410 U.S. 113 (1973).
3. *Lawrence v. Texas*, 539 U.S. 558 (2003). Ellen Alderman and Caroline Kennedy explore the range of constitutional notions of privacy in *The Right to Privacy* (1995).
4. *See, e.g.*, Mary Ziegler, "With a Conservative Court, Abortion Foes Could End Roe—and Go Even Further," *Washington Post*, Sept. 23, 2020. The Supreme Court agreed to review a Mississippi law that bans abortions after the fifteenth week of gestation. This will be an opportunity for the newly composed court to repeal or roll back the abortion precedents. *See Dobbs v. Jackson Women's Health*, 2021 WL 1951792 (May 17, 2021) (granting certiorari).
5. Amitai Etzioni, *The Limits of Privacy* (New York: Basic Books, 1999), 213.
6. Jane Jacobs, *The Death and Life of Great American Cities* (New York: Vintage Books, 1992).
7. *Id.* at 200–20.
8. *See, e.g.*, Reva B. Siegel, "'The Rule of Love': Wife Beating as Prerogative and Privacy," *Yale L. J.* 105 (1996): 2117. Siegel argues that the husband's right to discipline his wife gave way in the nineteenth century to a doctrine of marital privacy that effectively insulated domestic abuse.
9. Samuel D. Warren and Louis D. Brandeis, "The Right to Privacy," *Harv. L. Rev.* 4 (1890): 193.

10. *See Nat'l Ass'n for the Advancement of Colored People v. Alabama*, 357 U.S. 449 (1958). The court held that the order to disclose names of members infringed on a right of association protected by the First Amendment to the Constitution.
11. 362 U.S. 60 (1960).
12. *Id.* at 70.
13. *Id.* at 64.
14. 514 U.S. 334, 342 (1995).
15. *Id.*
16. *Id.* at 357.
17. *Id.* at 344.
18. *Id.* at 341–42.
19. 536 U.S. 150, 166 (2002).
20. *Id.* at 153.
21. Jeffrey Rosen, *The Naked Crowd: Reclaiming Security and Freedom in an Anxious Age* 12 (New York: Random House, 2004).
22. Jeffrey Rosen, *The Unwanted Gaze: The Destruction of Privacy in America* (New York: Vintage Books, 2001), 165.
23. *See* Anita Ramasastry, "Stalking Us as We Shop: HP's New Smartshopper App," *Justia: Verdict*, Apr. 8, 2014.
24. Charles Duhigg, "How Companies Learn Your Secrets," *New York Times Magazine*, Feb. 19, 2012, at MM30.
25. Rosen, *supra* note 21, at 19.
26. Daniel J. Solove, "Digital Dossiers and the Dissipation of Fourth Amendment Privacy," *S. Cal. L. Rev.* 75 (2002): 1083; *see also* Daniel J. Solove, *The Digital Person: Technology and Privacy in the Information Age* (New York: New York University Press, 2004).
27. *See* Julien Riel-Salvatore et al., "A Spatial Analysis of the Late Mousterian Levels of Riparo Bombrini," *J. Canadien d'Archéologie* 37 (2013): 70; the Neanderthals, they conclude, "were indeed able to organize their use of space in patterned and somewhat predictable manners."
28. Samuel Pepys, *The Shorter Pepys,* xxxiii (Robert Latham, ed. 1985). The Pepys diary was, however, quite unusual in its scope, breadth, and frankness. And Pepys, who died in 1703, was an important government official.
29. *The Truman Show* (Paramount Pictures 1998). The film was directed by Peter Weir. It was much admired by movie critics and was also a box office success. The actor Jim Carey played Truman.
30. *Roberson v. Rochester Folding Box Co.*, 64 N.E. 442 (N.Y. 1902).
31. 1903 N.Y. Laws, ch. 132.
32. *Kunz v. Allen*, 172 P. 532 (Kan. 1918).
33. *Id.*
34. 297 P. 91 (Cal. Ct. App. 1931).
35. *See* Alfred Cohn and Joe Chisholm, *Take the Witness!* (New York: Garden City Publishing Company, 1934), 259–69 (a book about Earl Rogers).
36. *The Red Kimona* (Fine Arts Studios 1925).

37. *See Melvin*, 297 P. at 93: "the fundamental law of our state contains provisions which, we believe, permit us to recognize the right to pursue and obtain safety and happiness without improper infringements thereon by others."

38. For a discussion of all four causes of action, see William L. Prosser, *Law of Torts*, 4th ed. (Eagan, MN: West Publishing Company, 1978). On Prosser's influence, see Neil M. Richards and Daniel J. Solove, "Prosser's Privacy Law: A Mixed Legacy," *Cal. L. Rev.* 98 (2010): 1887.

39. Restatement (Second) of Torts § 652B (1977).

40. *See* 62A Am. Jur. 2d Privacy § 39.

41. Illinois may be the exception. *See Muick v. Glenayre Elecs.*, 280 F.3d 741, 743–44 (7th Cir. 2002), noting that it is unsettled whether Illinois recognizes this tort. For a standard articulation of the test, see *Valenzuela v. Aguino*, 853 S.W.2d 512, 513 (Tex. 1993).

42. Restatement (Second) of Torts § 652D (1977). Most states recognize this cause of action; Indiana and North Carolina are the exceptions. *See Doe v. Methodist Hosp.*, 690 N.E.2d 681, 685–86 (Ind. 1997); *Broughton v. McClatchy Newspapers, Inc.*, 588 S.E.2d 20, 27 (2003).

43. *Id.* § 652D cmt. a.

44. 62A *Am. Jur.* 2d Privacy § 100.

45. *Id.* at § 106.

46. Restatement (Second) of Torts § 652E (1977).

47. *Cain v. Hearst Corp.*, 878 S.W.2d 577, 578 (Tex. 1994); *Broughton v. McClatchy Newspapers, Inc.*, 588 S.E.2d 20, 27 (N.C. 2003); *Jews for Jesus, Inc. v. Rapp*, 997 So. 2d 1098 (Fla. 2008).

48. *Rapp*, 997 So. 2d at 1114.

49. *Id.* at 1114–15.

50. Restatement (Second) of Torts § 652C (1977).

51. Cal. Civ. Code § 3344 (2020).

52. *Carson v. Here's Johnny Portable Toilets, Inc.*, 698 F.2d 831, 835–37 (6th Cir. 1983).

53. *State v. Gilliland,* No. M2008-02767-CCA-R3-CD, 2010 WL 2432014, at *1–2 (Tenn. Crim. App. Jun. 17, 2010).

54. Tenn. Code Ann. § 39–13–605 (West 2014).

55. *Gilliland*, 2010 WL 2432014, at *1.

56. *Id.* at *5.

57. *State v. Glas*, 54 P.3d 147, 149 (Wash. 2002). Glas's case was consolidated with the case of one Richard Lynn Sorrells, who had the nasty habit of "videotaping underneath little girls' dresses." *Id.*

58. Wash. Rev. Code Ann. § 9A.44.115 (West 2010).

59. *Glas*, 54 P.3d at 154.

60. *Id.* at 150.

61. *C'Debaca, v. Commonwealth*, No. 2754–97–4, 1999 WL 1129851, at *3 (Va. Ct. App. Feb. 2, 1999). Not all upskirters were in the clear, however, even before legislatures stepped in. A Pennsylvania lawyer, Clayton Boulware, pleaded guilty to two counts of upskirting; he was arrested for upskirting two females at a shopping

mall, one of whom was only sixteen. He was reportedly trying to find a substitute for the "swinging lifestyle" he had had with a prior girlfriend. He was suspended from the practice of law for six months, but then reinstated. *See* Debra Cassens Weiss, "Lawyer Wins Reinstatement after Suspension for Taking Upskirt Photos," *ABA Journal*, Apr. 29, 2014.

62. 5 N.E.3d 522 (Mass. 2014).

63. *Id.* at 523.

64. *Id.* at 528.

65. For more on this case, *see* Joanna L. Grossman and Lawrence M. Friedman, "A Private Skirt in a Public Place: The Surprising Law of Upskirting," *Justia: Verdict*, Mar. 12, 2014.

66. Danielle Keats Citron, "Mainstreaming Privacy Torts," *Cal. L. Rev.* 98 (2010): 1805.

67. Danielle Keats Citron, "Sexual Privacy," *Yale L. J.* 128 (2019): 1870, 1960.

68. Wash. Rev. Code Ann. § 9A.44.115(2)(a)(ii) (West 2010).

69. Mass. Ann. Laws ch. 272, § 105 (LexisNexis 2010).

70. *Id.*

71. www.bbc.com/news/uk-England510761749, visited January 20, 2020.

72. *State v. Dennison*, No. WM-10–019, 2012 WL 1580610 (Ohio Ct. App. 2012).

73. *Id.* at *2.

74. *Id.* at *3.

75. Note that it is simply assumed, quite plausibly, that Dennison made the photos "for the purpose of sexually arousing or gratifying" himself. *Id.* at *1–4.

76. *State v. Frost*, 634 N.E.2d 272, 272 (Ohio Ct. App. 1994).

77. *See, e.g.*, Cal. Penal Code § 646.9 (West 2010) (a person who "willfully, maliciously, and repeatedly follows or willfully and maliciously harasses another person and who makes a credible threat with the intent to place that person in reasonable fear for his or her safety," is guilty of stalking).

78. "Lower Merion School District Settles Webcam Spying Lawsuits for $610,000," *HuffPost*, Dec. 11, 2010.

79. *Id.*

80. *Id.* The Lower Merion School District admitted to capturing thousands of webcam photographs and screenshots from student laptops in an effort to locate missing computers. *Id.* The school agreed to pay $610,000 to settle the lawsuits. *Id.*

81. *Creel v. I.C.E. & Assoc.*, 771 N.E.2d 1276, 1277–79 (Ind. Ct. App. 2002).

82. *Id.* at 1280.

83. *Id.* at 1281.

84. *Hamberger v. Eastman*, 206 A.2d 239, 239–40 (N.H. 1964).

85. *Id.* at 242.

86. *Sabrina W. v. Willman*, 540 N.W.2d 364 (Neb. Ct. App. 1995).

87. *Id.* at 367.

88. *Id.* at 368.

89. Plaintiff had wanted to testify that she overheard a conversation in the post office. Three men were talking about the case; these men felt that Willman was having sex with women he photographed, and that some of them were angry and

jealous because "he was giving more sexual attention to one woman." The trial court excluded this evidence, but the appeal court felt it was "prejudicial" to block this testimony. *Id.* at 372.

90. *See* Joanna L. Grossman and Lawrence M. Friedman, "Misgoverning Missouri: Sex, Privacy, and the Leering Eye of the Camera," *Justia's Verdict*, Mar. 26, 2018.

91. *See* Alvin A. Reid et al., "Gov. Eric Greitens's Charge Is Dropped, for Now, in Missouri," *New York Times*, May 14, 2018, at A14.

92. Video Voyeurism Prevention Act of 2004, Pub. L. No. 108–495 (2004), 118 Stat. 3999 (codified at 18 U.S.C. § 1801 [2018]).

93. 18 U.S.C. § 1801(c) (2018).

94. Cal. Penal Code, § 647(j)(2) (West 2020).

95. Criminal Code, R.S.C. 1985, c C-46 (Can.) § 162(1).

96. John Clarke, "Rabbi Barry Freundel Gets 6 1/2 Years for Mikveh Peeping," *Forward*, May 16, 2015.

97. Lisa W. Foderaro, "Private Moment Made Public, Then a Fatal Jump," *New York Times*, Sept. 30, 2010, at A1.

98. Kate Zernike, "Rutgers Webcam-Spying Defendant Is Sentenced to 30-Day Jail Term," *New York Times*, May 21, 2012, at A1. Ravi's friend agreed to testify against him, and was spared punishment. Sue Epstein, "Molly Wei, Defendant in Tyler Clementi Case, Is Accepted into Pretrial Intervention Program," *NJ.com*, May 6, 2011.

99. *See* Sasha Harris-Lovett, "In Survey, 88% of U.S. Adults Said They Had Sexted and 96% of Them Endorsed It," *L. A. Times*, Aug. 10, 2015.

100. *See* Danielle Keats Citron, *Hate Crimes in Cyberspace* (Cambridge, MA: Harvard University Press, 2014), 17.

101. "Misery Merchants," *Economist*, July 5, 2014.

102. *See, e.g.*, Press Release, "FTC Approves Final Order in Craig Brittain 'Revenge Porn' Case," Fed. Trade Comm'n, Jan. 8, 2016.

103. *See People v. Barber*, 992 N.Y.S.2d 159, at *1–2 (N.Y. Crim. Ct. 2014). Although the state of New York still lacks a statute specifically criminalizing revenge porn, the New York City Council took action to make the conduct criminal in 2017. *See* Antonia Blumberg, "New York City Council Votes to Make Revenge Porn Illegal," *HuffPost*, Nov. 16, 2017.

104. In states without a revenge porn law, revenge porn might still expose a person to civil or criminal liability through other means—laws and doctrines against stalking, harassment, conspiracy, cyberhacking, and copyright infringement. (Selfies, in particular, can be protected by copyright laws, though only if the "photographer" is willing to register the images with the federal Copyright Office.)

105. Cal. Civ. Code § 1708.85 (2020).

106. *See People v. Iniguez*, 202 Cal. Rptr. 3d 237, 240–42 (Cal. App. Dep't Super. Ct. 2016).

107. Jill Stewart, "Revenge Porn Conviction Puts Noe Iniguez, L.A.'s Douchebag Boyfriend, in Jail," *LA Weekly*, Dec. 14, 2014.

108. Not everybody is on board. The ACLU felt the California bill went too far: it criminalized speech, even when the speech was no threat to the victim's safety.

109. Courtni E. Molnar, "'Has the Millennium Yet Dawned?': A History of Attitudes toward Pregnant Workers in America," *Mich. J. Gender & L.* 12 (2005): 163, 165.

110. *See* Katie Robertson, "Jeffrey Toobin Is Fired by the *New Yorker*," *New York Times*, Nov. 11, 2020, at B7.

111. Joshua Gamson, *Freaks Talk Back: Tabloid Talk Shows and Sexual Nonconformity* (Chicago: University of Chicago Press, 1998), 7.

112. What these people reveal to the world can have disastrous consequences. A man named Scott Amodure appeared as a guest on the *Jenny Jones* show (the session was taped, but never shown). He confessed to a secret crush on a friend, Jonathan Schmitz. Schmitz, who had a history of mental illness, somehow found out, was extremely upset, and killed Amodure. He was convicted of second-degree murder. Amodure's family sued the program, but lost on appeal. *Graves v. Warner Bros.*, 656 N.W. 2d 195 (Mich. Ct. App. 2003). *See* Keith Bradshaw, "Talk Show Guest Is Guilty of Second Degree Murder," *New York Times*, Nov. 13, 1996. This was of course an extreme case and Schmitz perhaps was not just reacting to a confession; the circumstances of the crime are unclear—Amodure may have made some sort of pass at Schmitz.

Chapter 6

They Led Two Lives

INTRODUCTION

There was a great deal of public sympathy for Notre Dame football player Manti Te'o over the news that his girlfriend, Lennay Kekua, had tragically died of leukemia. The sympathy, it turns out, was misplaced. Kekua never died because she never lived.[1] She was an internet hoax—a woman Te'o thought he loved, and with whom he had communicated over a long period, but who in fact had been created by jokesters.[2] Te'o appears to have been "catfished"—a modern term for being duped. In a 2010 documentary, *Catfish*, a man meets a woman online and falls for her, only to learn later that her true identity was a far cry from the one portrayed on the internet.[3] In a TV series also called *Catfish*, we see more unsuspecting people lured into online dating hoaxes; viewers are entertained by the excitement and then the humiliation of the victims.[4] "Catfishing" had trapped Manti Te'o in its net.

The internet has made this sort of hoax more feasible, but it did not invent the sport of fake seduction and humiliation. A Connecticut watchmaker and part-time judge fell for Gladys Wilson, an imaginary woman who, he thought, had written him scores of love letters over fourteen years. Gladys was the creation of a man intent on swindling the watchmaker out of his earnings. After the swindler decided the well was dry—he had induced the watchmaker to send him $6,000 in total—he killed off Gladys in one final letter.[5] At the heart of "catfishing," whether accomplished with new technology or not, is a basic life problem: how do we ever know whether people are who they say they are? How real are the images a person projects? For some men and women—for example, spies and con men—the image is deliberately and intentionally false. Most of us do not fall into these extreme categories. But all of us are impostors, at least in a mild sort of way. All of us in a sense lead two lives—in fact, more than two. There is, at a minimum, a personal, private life, lived largely behind closed doors, and a public open life, a life on the streets, in the office, at school, and so on. But people in general play many roles and show many faces. In reality, all of us are actors and much of our behavior in everyday life can be called a "performance." This was Erving Goffman's insight.[6] We play roles—even when we walk on the street or drive a car: we act in such a way as to make ourselves "readable."[7] And of course, we are also "reading" the other people we meet or see or interact with. Part of our job in life is to manage our roles and our identities as much as we can. And, of course, we must also "read" the messages other people send out; we must scan them and react to them.

The earlier chapters of this book considered situations where privacy is mandatory—the naked body is the classic example. This chapter deals with two other types of situations: one where privacy (or concealment of identity) is either wrongful or downright criminal and one where privacy is elective, where, in other words, we can choose how much privacy we want or need. There are times where full disclosure will bring about hurtful consequences. Here we may be allowed, for the most part, to keep some aspect of our identity private; the law may even punish those who violate our expectations.

For all of us, there is surely a private core, a zone of privacy, where outsiders are not supposed to enter. Some of it is so personal that we can and do keep out absolutely everybody. Nobody is allowed to intrude and nobody will in fact intrude, unless, in some dystopian future, science develops ways of reading minds and hearts. In some aspects of our lives, we let in one or a few selected outsiders: a spouse or "significant other," for example, or, more prosaically, a tennis partner or a partner in bridge. The law, in some ways, acts to protect the zone of privacy. It does this by virtue of the tort of "invasion of privacy,"[8] but also by virtue of the privilege against self-incrimination, the attorney-client privilege, the rules against unlawful searches and seizures, and so on.

Basically, we have a right to play our roles. There is no truth serum. There is no mind-reading machine (as yet). We are perfectly free to say one thing and mean another; to present ourselves in one way or another way; to wear a different dress, so to speak, on different occasions; to behave differently behind closed doors from the way we behave out in public. Behind my smiling face, I may be hiding, or trying to hide, my bitter, nasty personality. I may love some people, I might daydream erotically about some of them, other people I may hate; some bore me, some people even disgust me. I know better than to let people know my "true" feelings. As sociologists and psychologists recognize, to ask which roles and aspects of the self are the "real" person, and which are not, is a question that has no answer. Almost all of your roles, in one way or another, are aspects of the "real" you; even when an actor plays Hamlet, his performance might be in some ways an outgrowth of his "real" personality. Or perhaps the real you is the composite of all the various roles you play and the identities you assume.

Telling white lies (or even nonwhite lies) is not a crime in most instances, not part of the criminal code. We are allowed, in other words, to live two lives (or three lives, or *n* lives). In our culture, and probably in most cultures, we tend to think of some roles as "authentic"; that is, they reflect what people are "really" like. Others we consider false or contrived. "Real" performances are seen as "an unintentional product of the individual's unself-conscious response to the facts in his situation" while "contrived" performances are "painstakingly pasted together, one false item on another."[9] Matters, however, are not really that simple, as Goffman points out. Since we are all role-players, since we all go through life like actors and actresses playing now this part and now that part, it is hard to draw a line between the "authentic" self and the spurious self—if, indeed, these are concepts that make sense at all. Sometimes, when we drop the mask, or when we blurt something out, or when somebody overhears us saying something they were not meant to hear, we find ourselves in a situation that is personally embarrassing or even harmful. Other people do not always appreciate candor. Candor can have consequences—for example, when a political candidate, unaware that a camera or an open microphone is recording, drops the political mask and says something sincere but politically harmful. This happened to Mitt Romney when he was running for president in 2012 and claimed that 47 percent of Americans were mooching off the government; this was a damaging remark, made at what he thought was a private and friendly gathering of Republicans.[10] Another example was the old video of Donald Trump that surfaced in which he bragged about being able to "grab women by the pussy" just because he was famous.[11] A candidate who thinks the microphone is dead when actually it's "hot" can blurt out something candid but unfortunate. Canadian Prime Minister Justin Trudeau was overheard, together with other world leaders, making fun of Donald Trump.[12] Yet what we hear when the live microphone is on or in the private gathering, is (we think) more authentic than the canned speech—more authentic than careful responses to questions by reporters, and other "performances." But just as it is no crime to be open and honest, it is generally no crime *not* to be open and honest.

A person growing up in society learns what the rules of conduct are and how we are supposed to behave in different contexts. These are, in a sense, rules about managing roles; they are for the most part fairly general rules that apply to everybody or to everybody in some particular category. The rules about role-playing are subtle and complex. There are rules about which roles can and should be kept private, which ones must be kept private, and which ones cannot be kept private—which ones are legitimate and which ones are not.

There are also rules about *when* one can play certain roles. In many societies, there are special events or periods—carnivals, festivals, and the like—when certain rules of behavior are relaxed. People are allowed to role-play in ways that would not be socially tolerated at other times. Halloween costumes are a mild form of this kind of role-playing. Suspension of rules is more pronounced for Mardi Gras and equivalent festivals in other societies. Manuel

Gomez studied the culture and the rules of the game in Burning Man, the city that arises out of nothing in the Nevada desert every year. At Burning Man, participants are allowed a "certain degree of release or licensed elision . . . from their everyday lives"; they can wear costumes, can adopt a "temporary identity—their playa name—and other imaginative elements," which help "conceal their default world identity."[13]

Whether at a festival or not, we can, in most respects, project a spurious self on the world—to live, as it were, two lives. Not only is this sometimes harmless but in some situations, law and society extend their blessing to a kind of fictional identity. When a child is adopted, for example, a new birth certificate might be issued, which in a sense remakes the child's identity. The certificate replaces the names of birth parents with the names of the adoptive parents. In this way, the adoptive parents can present the child as their own biological child if they choose to do so. In the past, the records were then permanently sealed so that no one could be the wiser. In a similar vein, a transgender person in many states can obtain a new birth certificate reflecting a gender identity created by hormones and surgery rather than chromosomes.[14] A young person with a juvenile record can have the past expunged on reaching majority, so that in a sense the delinquency never happened. Or a person who has helped prosecute a dangerous criminal can be offered a new safe identity as part of the witness protection program. In each of these situations, one is allowed, with the blessing of the law, to suppress a "real" or at least an original identity. These are extreme examples of what all of us can do to molt or suppress a self and move on in life. But there are limits. This chapter is about those limits. It is about situations where it is, or was, considered wrong or illegal to live two lives or where the "false" or outer life is a lie, and a lie, moreover, that is considered gravely and impermissibly deceptive, at least by some people. Spies project a false, patriotic identity to steal government secrets. Con men assume a false persona to swindle people out of their money or possessions. A married man might falsely pretend to be a bachelor to take another wife, in violation of law, social convention, and, most likely, the preferences of both of these women. In each case, the double life makes a kind of theft possible—of secrets, of money, of affections. Here the law makes false and double lives a crime.

A PATRIOTIC PERFORMANCE: THE WORLD OF THE SPY

Spying is one of the oldest professions. The spy betrays one country, usually his own, on behalf of another. No doubt every major country today has a network of spies to ferret out some of the secrets of its enemies, often even some of the secrets of its friends. Spying is a dangerous occupation. A wartime spy is liable to be executed. Peacetime spies in autocratic countries are definitely risking their lives. And even in the United States, spying can be a dangerous occupation. Julius and Ethel Rosenberg were convicted of passing atomic secrets to the Soviet Union; they were executed in 1953.[15] The Soviets, of course, had no qualms about executing citizens found guilty of spying.

For the spy or mole, it is a crime to hide their real job. The modern ambiguity about "true" identity is perhaps more pronounced for spies than for anyone else. A spy who broadcast his real identity, his real job, would be immediately arrested, and of course would be useless as a spy. The classic spies have always lived two lives. The best spies are those whose surface identity puts off suspicion and who are able to infiltrate high levels of government in order to steal government secrets. A notorious British spy ring, the Cambridge five, consisted of men from impeccable and even upper-class origins; it was broken up in the 1950s; some of the members fled to Russia, but another member of the group, Anthony Blunt, went undetected for years (and pursued a career as an art historian).[16]

Why does anyone become a spy? Sometimes the motive is simple: money. Aldrich Ames had been an employee of the CIA. He sold CIA secrets to the Soviet Union. Among other things, Ames blew the cover of certain Americans inside the Soviet Union; this cost them their lives. The Soviets paid Ames handsomely for his work. Soviet money allowed Ames to pursue a lavish style of life.[17] Other spies have betrayed their country out of ideology or conviction. This was true of the Cambridge five and of many Soviet agents during the Cold War. Klaus Fuchs was a scientist who was German by birth and worked for the British, but passed atomic secrets to the Soviet Union. He was a committed Communist. The Cambridge five were devout Marxists who admired the Soviet Union. Ideology also probably explains the behavior of Julius Rosenberg.[18] Eli Cohen, a famous Israeli spy, was able to infiltrate the highest circles of the Syrian government; he provided the Israeli government with vital military information, before he was caught, tortured, and executed in 1965.

Spying, as we said, goes back quite far in history; the Bible mentions spies. In Europe, for centuries, kings and governments maintained spies and informants in other countries. But spying became a much more serious and important business in the nineteenth century. Partly, this was because war technology was developing rapidly; this led to a kind of arms race among European powers. A spy who learned secrets about new weapons or army plans was of incredible value to the country he was working for, and incredibly dangerous to the country he betrayed. Major powers began to pay more attention to the spy business. The English Parliament passed an Official Secrets Act in 1889.[19] In 1909, after a report pointed to the possible threat of German spies, the British formed a Secret Service Bureau.[20] In the United States, an Espionage Act was passed in 1917, during the First World War.[21] The Act made it a crime to gather information "respecting the national defense with intent or reason to believe that the information is to be used to the injury of the United States, or to the advantage of any foreign nation."[22] In the 1950s, a new law, the Internal Security Act, was passed in response to the perceived threat of Communism.[23] That law prohibits the communication of national defense information to anyone not entitled to receive it.

In the early days, the Espionage Act was used primarily to prevent foreign moles from infiltrating American society.[24] But currently, it is also used to prosecute ex-government employees who have leaked classified information to the press.[25] In a recent scandal, Edward Snowden, a former employee of the National Surveillance Agency, released to the public damaging information about the way the United States collects information about foreign governments, as well as information about its own citizens. A hero to some and a traitor to others, Snowden faced potential prosecution under the espionage and security laws even though his leaks forced the government to limit surveillance; Snowden had revealed that the government was secretly collecting enormous amounts of cell phone data.[26] Snowden fled the United States, claimed asylum in various countries, and ended up in Russia; in 2020, he applied for Russian citizenship.

There is a fine line between spies and whistle-blowers. Indeed, in an interview with journalist Amy Goodman in September 2019, Snowden described himself as a "whistle-blower." Snowden's work was out in the open—at least initially. Other whistle-blowers try to keep their identity secret. Whistle-blowers are, on the whole, men and women eager to expose wrongdoing on the part of government or large institutions. The identity of the "whistle-blower" who revealed what Donald Trump had said to the president of the Ukraine in 2019, in contrast, was kept secret from the public, even though the leaked information ultimately led to impeachment proceedings against the president in the House of Representatives (the Senate failed to convict).[27]

Spies are also staples of popular culture. Spy novels in Britain date from the late nineteenth century.[28] Some of the authors have been wildly successful: Eric Ambler and E. Phillips Oppenheim are examples. More recently, John le Carré's novels about British intelligence have been enormous best sellers. Readers seem to find spies fascinating—and particularly "moles," spies deeply imbedded in government institutions. *Tinker, Tailor, Soldier, Spy*, one of le Carré's most successful books, turns on the search for a "mole" at the very highest levels of the British secret service; the job of le Carré's hero, George Smiley, is to find out the mole's identity and unmask him.

In a famous movie, *The Manchurian Candidate* (1962), based on a novel by Richard Condon, the main character, Raymond Shaw, is a kind of inadvertent "mole." He had been a prisoner of the Chinese communists during the Korean War. The Chinese brainwashed him and programmed him to respond unconsciously to their commands after receiving a certain signal—the Queen of Diamonds appears in a game of solitaire. Their ultimate object, in the rather complicated and convoluted plot, was to take over the government of the United States and transfer power to the hero's evil mother and stepfather, murdering the legitimate candidate for president along the way. In the end, the plot fails and the hero kills his own mother—and then himself.

The main character in *The Manchurian Candidate* was a mole but did not realize this fact. There are, however, real-life moles. In 2010, a network of moles working for the Russian government came to light in the United States. Two Russian spies, Richard and Cynthia Murphy, lived in suburban Montclair, New Jersey, carrying on lives "far from the James Bond image. . . . They joined neighbors at block parties, school picnics and bus stops." The Murphys had two daughters and grew vegetables in their back yard garden. They were in "deep cover," living lives of "mundane, suburban anonymity."[29] Their job was to become thoroughly Americanized, "infiltrate" American institutions, and presumably provide their Russian handlers with insights into the way American civil society worked.[30] Before they came to the United States, they had been trained in techniques and language. They were given a false identity and, as an email explained (the United States intercepted it), they had been sent to this country on a "long-term service" mission. Education, bank accounts, car, house, and so on were meant to serve one goal: "to search and develop ties in policymaking circles in the US" and send intelligence reports to their handlers.[31] When they were exposed, they faced charges of conspiracy to act as unregistered agents of a foreign government and conspiracy to commit money laundering.[32]

These "moles" almost seemed like a joke, a caricature. When the truth came out, their neighbors were flabbergasted. To think that their neighbors, with their kids and their vegetable garden, were actually spies, under deep cover, secretly biding their time, less like the "moles" that burrow in the ground and eat earthworms than like spiders hiding in their web, ready at some point to pounce on hapless victims or harm a careless nation. This was a chilling and fascinating notion. It was a spy novel come to life. The "Murphys" inspired a popular television series, *The Americans.* The "Murphys," themselves, along with others in "the illegals" program, were eventually sent back to Russia as part of a prisoner swap.[33]

The suburban moles in Montclair were a reminder of how little we may actually know about the "real" selves of people we see every day. Sometimes, after someone is revealed to be a brutal, pathological killer, neighbors tell the world on TV interviews how shocked they were to learn that Mr. X, such a quiet and ordinary man, had buried dead bodies in his cellar year after year, or had crept out at night to murder almost at random. The identity of "Jack the Ripper," responsible for a number of grisly murders in late nineteenth-century London, has never been determined. Whoever it was succeeded in hiding his real and murderous self; it is not at all unlikely that "Jack the Ripper" was a member of the middle class or even of the aristocracy. The United States maintains its own network of spies in other countries; very likely it has its own "moles" living in suburban Moscow or Beijing. Countries also spy on their own people. They try to infiltrate extremist organizations—or what they consider extremist organizations.[34] The Federal Bureau of Investigation has tried to infiltrate criminal organizations—and it has also actively worked against left-wing groups, and any organization it considered to be dominated by Communists.

There is a good deal of ambivalence about spying on friendly countries; the revelation, in 2013, that the American government had bugged the cell phone of the prime minister of the Federal Republic of Germany touched off something of an international incident.[35] Jonathan Pollard spied on the United States, but for the benefit of Israel, an ally and friend. There is no such ambivalence about spying on enemies. Of course, those who spy on us are villains but *our* spies in enemy countries are heroes—those who, for example, were insinuated into Nazi Germany or occupied France during the Second World War. In May 2012, the United States foiled a plot to blow up an airplane bound for this country. The tip came from a Saudi Arabian, who had infiltrated the terrorist group, and then betrayed the group to Saudi Arabian and American authorities.[36]

The old game of spying is, in short, very far from dead. What is new, however, is a different kind of "spy." Technology has revolutionized spying. Many modern "spies" are quite unlike the heroes and villains in spy novels. These "spies" never run any personal risk. They sit in rooms and examine tons of data brought in by surveillance devices. These spies might still lead double lives if they conceal from family or friends what they actually do for a living. Controversy is not about the spies, but about what they are spying on and their involvement in the struggle between privacy and the war on terror and crime, which we discuss in more detail later. This controversy was at the heart of the dispute over Edward Snowden's whistle-blowing.

WITCH HUNTING

That people are not always what they seem is an old and obvious idea. In the Faust legend, Faust sold his soul to the devil. People in, say, the sixteenth or seventeenth centuries believed in witches and devils; they felt that there were women and some men who had gone over to the dark side and whose surface identity concealed another, more sinister identity; they were part of a satanic throng. The moral panic in seventeenth-century Salem led to a series of notorious witchcraft trials and brought the expression "witch hunt" into the language.[37]

A "witch hunt" today is rarely a literal search for witches. Rather, it describes actions in response to modern paranoia about spies, agents of foreign countries, jihadists, communists, and any other enemies of the state or of the people. During the Cold War, and particularly during the McCarthy period, millions of people in the United States came to believe that Soviet spies had penetrated every branch of government and were working their evil magic on such American institutions as Hollywood, the state department, elite universities, and even the armed forces. Egged on by Senator Joseph McCarthy and right-wing members of Congress, there was a massive campaign against "reds" and their fellow-travelers. Those on the other side labeled the campaign a witch-hunt, with considerable justice. There were, in fact, Soviet agents in the country but the campaign against "un-American activities" vastly magnified the problem and ruined dozens and dozens of lives and careers. Fear of spies, Communists, terrorists, and aliens from outer space may be a specific pathology of our times. In the notorious McMartin case in Los Angeles, people came to believe that a day care center for kids, run by the McMartins, was in fact a festering hive of Satanic practices.[38] The Protocols of the Elders of Zion, a famous hoax that was first printed in 1903, purports to describe a secret plot of Jewish leaders to control the world.[39]

The paranoia that gripped the country during the McCarthy period has passed into history. Under the Trump regime (2016 to 2020), it was not Communists but Muslim extremists, jihadists, and criminal immigrants that evoked the most fear and loathing. Fear of terrorism, after the attack on the Twin Towers and the Pentagon in 2001, led to a burst of legislation and a whole new cabinet department, the Department of Homeland Security, which, among other things, was concerned with detecting and foiling "terrorists."[40] Witches were human only on the surface; for many red-blooded Americans, spies and Communists also lacked some of the essential aspects of humanity. In the well-known movie *Invasion of the Body Snatchers* (1956), creatures from outer space arrived on planet Earth.[41] Secretly and quietly, they usurped the bodily forms of actual people. After a while, it became impossible to tell who was human and who was not; aliens and Americans looked exactly the same. The original movie, directed by Don Siegel, was based on a novel published in 1954. The movie is "conventionally interpreted in a cold war context"; the "pod people/body snatchers" were "seen as a metaphor for the 'communist threat.'"[42] The original and two later versions of this movie reflected "the fear that one's closest associates and relatives are not who they appear to be."[43]

Hardly anybody in developed countries believes literally in witches. But quite a few apparently believe that earth can be, or even has been, invaded by aliens from outer space. The underlying theme of *Invasion of the Body Snatchers* is an exaggerated form of a common psychological feeling or worry: who is this person, really, this person that I think I know, this person I imagine is my friend or my teacher or my companion? Who is this person I married, the person I sleep with, the person I see every day? Do I—can I—really know him or her? In Alfred Hitchcock's 1941 movie *Suspicion*, a young English woman marries a slightly disreputable man; she begins to suspect he is trying to kill her to get her money. In fact, the husband is innocent (the studio insisted on a happy ending). But the plot turned on the wife's inability to know who or what her husband really was.[44] The exploding divorce rate in country after country is at least indirect evidence that people marry people who are, or become, total strangers to them in one sense or another.

Both science fiction and reality rest, of course, on an aspect of life (and not only modern life) that is undeniable: people have a private core that can be hidden and suppressed but that may also at times burst forth. The underlying notion, then, is simply the mystery of identity. Who are we, anyway? The private core may be different from the public role, and even from the semi-private roles people play within the family, at work, and at the office. In the modern, complex world, people may come to trust only the people in their immediate circle. Outside is a dark and mysterious void. And at times, that void is even closer to home.

FALSE HONESTY

The term "confidence man," often shortened to "con man," dates from the nineteenth century. The *Oxford Dictionary* traces it to 1849. Herman Melville published a novel called *The Confidence Man* in 1857. A confidence man is, essentially, a swindler or a crook, somebody who wins the confidence of a victim (the "mark") and then proceeds to cheat him. Cheating and fraud are of course not new in human life. But in the nineteenth century, swindling reached some sort of social climax: this was the high-water mark, perhaps, of the confidence game. The confidence game was what we might call a "crime of mobility," that is, a crime that "depended on anonymity, ambiguity of identity, and the fluidity of lines that separated strata and classes in the population."[45] These were not, as we pointed out, conditions easily met in small societies, in traditional societies, or in small towns with a fixed population.

But the bustling, boiling flux of nineteenth-century life was fertile soil for clever men and women, a stage on which to practice their dark talents.

The con man essentially does his work through lies, through pretending to be something he or she is not, and prying money out of his victim with some more or less clever scheme. James Crawford, dressed as a priest, went from house to house in 1902 asking for money; Mrs. Emma Meyer, who wore the "garb of the Little Sisters of the Poor" did the same.[46] Fake doctors, army officers, and noblemen plied their dubious trade at a time when people moved freely about from place to place and could shed identities the way a snake sheds skin. The con man continued his work well into the twentieth century, if not the twenty-first. There was, for example, the man who, in 1935, called himself "Commissioner Laynar of the State Tax Department" in New York, and collected money for "needy families that could not get on the relief rolls." In fact, the only needy "family" he was collecting for was his own.[47] And one "Ramon Padilla" claimed in 1928 to be the son of the Spanish ambassador; he wheedled money out of "incautious persons" in Washington, DC.[48]

Impostors are an especially flamboyant kind of con man. Some have been astonishingly successful at role-playing. In France, a man who called himself the Marquis de Roquefeuil became "one of Paris's most popular society men . . . lionized in the best society." The charming "Marquis" wooed and married a Countess who was twenty years his senior. The real members of the De Roquefeuil family unmasked him and he ended up facing prison in 1911.[49]

A few skillful (and pathological) people have in a sense made a career of impostorship. One Stephen Weinberg was a notorious example. For fifty years, he adopted all sorts of roles: he passed himself off as an ambassador, a doctor, a lawyer, a naval officer, a "Serbian diplomat and a smooth-talking reporter at the United Nations." In 1921, he "talked himself into the White House . . . by posing as a State Department protocol officer." At one point, he spent time in a federal prison. Ironically, he met his doom working at a legitimate job—night manager of a motel. A hold-up man shot him to death and escaped with $200.[50]

An even more striking example was Ferdinand Demara. He was a man of many names and many identities: a civil engineer, a sheriff's deputy, a prison official, a doctor, a lawyer, a teacher, even a Trappist monk. Most remarkably, during the Korean War he posed as a surgeon named Dr. Joseph Cyr. The fake Dr. Cyr served on a destroyer of the Canadian navy. The ship picked up dozens of injured men who needed medical treatment. Demara quickly read a few pages from a medical textbook and then carried out a series of complicated operations. The parents of the real Dr. Cyr, unfortunately, got wind of this and the false surgeon was exposed as a fake.[51]

Frank Abagnale was another impostor who at one point practiced medicine, posing as a pediatrician in a Georgia hospital. Abagnale also pretended to be an airline pilot. He later moved to Louisiana, armed with a forged degree from Harvard Law School, and practiced law. Abagnale did time in prison, but in the 1970s, he was released after promising to help the FBI with advice about scam artists. He became a successful businessman, acting as a consultant on fraud prevention. Apparently, it takes one to know one. In 2000, he published a book about his exploits, *Catch Me If You Can*, later made into a Hollywood movie starring Leonardo DiCaprio.[52] And in 1988, a promising young man named (he said) Alexi Indris-Santana was admitted to Princeton University. Actually, this was James Hogue, a thirty-one-year-old who was in prison at the time for bicycle theft. Released, he jumped parole and proceeded to Princeton. At Princeton, he was an A student, a track star, and was even accepted into the exclusive Ivy Club. Unfortunately, at a track meet, a Yale student recognized him; he was arrested a few days later on a warrant as a fugitive. When he got out of prison again, he somehow managed to convince a museum at Harvard to hire him as a security guard; a jewelry theft tripped him up once more.[53] Hogue was charged with forgery, wrongful impersonation, and falsifying records. He had borrowed $22,000 in financial aid, which he was ordered to pay back.[54]

An impostor figured in one of the most sensational trials of nineteenth-century England. The man claimed to be Roger Tichborne, the heir of a baronet, James Tichborne. Roger Tichborne had disappeared in 1859 and was presumed lost at sea. His mother refused to give up hope; she was sure her son had somehow survived and managed to reach Australia. She advertised in the Australian press; sure enough, a man turned up, claiming to be the long-lost heir. Even though elements of his story were clearly preposterous, she believed him, and so did many other people. In all likelihood, the Tichborne claimant was one Arthur Orton, the son of a butcher from Wagga Wagga. After a sensational trial, he was found guilty of perjury and sent to prison. He died in poverty.[55] A twentieth-century analog was "Anastasia," who claimed to be one of the daughters of the last Russian czar, Nicholas Romanov. The whole Romanov family had been murdered by order of the Soviet authorities but it was rumored that "Anastasia" had somehow mysteriously and miraculously survived.[56]

As we pointed out, the con game is a crime of mobility. The crime consists of pretending to be somebody we are not for fraudulent purposes. It consists of concealing a private self. It is also a crime of what we might call the "credentialed society." Credentials are a key to social mobility: the college degree, the license, the diploma, the ordination as a priest, the swearing in of the police officer. This is, in a way, a modern paradox: supposedly, anyone can rise in society, no matter what their background—but you must do it in patterned ways, and you have to earn the right credentials. It is against the law to take a short-cut, to pass yourself off as something you are not; it is a crime to practice law or medicine, or many other professions, without a license. Many states have laws against identity fraud, for acts as insignificant as falsifying a driver's license.[57] Yet it is not against the law to tell lies, so long as you are not claiming a credential, and so long as there is no attempt to squeeze money out of a victim. The First Amendment protects the right to lie about one's own identity—up to a point. Congress tried to make it a crime to claim, falsely, that you had been awarded the Medal of Honor. But the Supreme Court struck down this "Stolen Valor" law; it was framed too broadly and therefore (in the opinion of the majority), it violated the right of free speech.[58]

The same period that gave birth to the con man gave birth to his nemesis, the detective. Police officers work to maintain order in public places; they wear uniforms and badges, which clearly identify them as police. The detective wears plain clothes. His job is to ferret out hidden, clandestine criminals, including, notably, confidence tricksters. As a contemporary wrote in 1895, it is "second nature" for detectives to "unravel plots, unmask falsehoods, and extort the truth." A skilled detective has a "wonderful memory" and can recognize the faces of known crooks, "however altered or disguised."[59] By the end of the nineteenth century, every city had a detective force. Business was also thriving for private detectives. The most famous in his day was Alan Pinkerton; his organization was the Pinkerton Agency. In a way, there was a kind of arms race between the con men and their enemies, the detectives: the con men worked to devise more and better ways to fleece people; the detectives worked to figure out more and better ways to catch the con men and put an end to their schemes.

Another "crime of mobility" was blackmail: you can only blackmail someone with a guilty secret; and guilty secrets—secrets about one's private life—grow more frequent when and where people move about, shifting from place to place, ending up, particularly, in big cities. Blackmail went hand in hand with the confidence game. New York in the nineteenth century was described as a city "full of adroit rogues," some of whom practiced black mail "as an art." Blackmailers (men and women) were adept at trapping foolish tourists and visitors to the big city. A man might come to New York from some small town and visit one of New York's many brothels—something he might not dare to do back home. Alas, sometimes our poor visitor got more than he bargained for: he might fall into the clutches of blackmailers, who demanded money as the price of their silence.[60]

Some of the cruder forms of the confidence game are now obsolete but the problem is still very much alive. John Meehan wormed his way into the life of a very wealthy woman in Southern California. He pretended to be a rich anesthesiologist and a war veteran; he kept hidden his life as an often-homeless grifter with an opiate addiction and a criminal record.[61] Meehan's con ended dramatically: he was stabbed to death after he attacked the daughter of his target. She was perhaps about to succeed in convincing her mother that John was not who he said he was and that they were all in danger. In this she was completely right. Serialized in a television show and a very popular podcast, both aired under the name *Dirty John*, Meehan's story is a modern-day reminder that people are still vulnerable to the con—even though technology provides tools for uncovering the truth. Indeed, the woman's daughters had tracked his movements with GPS, done background checks online, and found many holes in his self-presentation. But what technology could not undo was their mother's weakness and her strong desire to see only what she wanted to see.

As Meehan demonstrated, it is still possible to take on a false identity; the social conditions that gave birth to the con man continue in modern society. The confidence game, and its many variants, are still crimes under state laws, which define them as frauds. In California, for example, it is a crime, punishable by a prison sentence, to defraud "any other person of money, labor, or property," "knowingly and designedly, by any false or fraudulent representation or pretense."[62] The con game, as we saw, was a crime of mobility: yet the social background is still one that fosters such crimes; indeed, the conditions of modern life make it even easier to cheat, swindle, and bilk people through the use of false identities. Modern technology gives the con man ways to troll for victims on a mass scale. The classical con man might have to go door to door, pretending to be something he was not; his modern descendant can flood the inboxes of millions of potential victims, at very little cost in money and time. In contemporary times, scams multiply. Thousands got calls from callers who claimed to be from the Internal Revenue Service; the caller threatened arrest for tax evasion unless the target arranges to pay up.[63] The scammers prey on everyone's fear of the IRS (and the reality that lots of people have cheated on their taxes and have some reason for fear); modern technology makes it harder and harder to know if a call is real or a scam. A robocaller can be used to make millions of calls. And the scam can be a roaring success, even if only a few of the millions fall for the scheme.

Just as the "victim" of blackmail was often not exactly blameless, neither are the various victims of internet scams. As the old saying goes, you can't cheat an honest man. Only fools will believe that they can earn a fortune by advancing money to help someone (say, a supposed Nigerian businessman) who needs to transfer funds to a foreign bank account.[64] The contemporary world is a world full of lotteries, Ponzi schemes, and other arrangements that seem to promise quick and painless wealth—some of these are legal (the lottery), some illegal, some simply too good to be true. Great rascals can make temporary millions with these schemes. Bernard Madoff lived the good (and luxurious) life; he passed himself off as a shrewd and successful businessman but in reality, he was working a Ponzi scheme. But he was caught, charged, convicted, and eventually sentenced to 150 years in prison.[65] He died in prison in 2021.

This is the age, then, in which people worry about "identity theft." Men and women have found technological ways to pass themselves off as somebody else. The point, of course, is to siphon off the victim's money or make some other use of aspects of their identity.[66] Cunning identity thieves are like spiders, lurking in the corners of an artfully spun web, in which they can catch their victim and take over their financial lives. "Phishing" is another new tactic: playing on people's trust in some organization they know, in order to pry information out of the victim. The perpetrators are clever people; they are getting better all the time at imitating logos, letterheads, and other ways to make people think the message is coming from a place they know and trust. We think we have ways to guard the privacy of our personal information; the identity thieves are out to prove that we are wrong.

Of course, all of their activity is illegal. In California, for example, anyone who "willfully obtains personal identifying information . . . of another person" and uses that information "for any unlawful purpose" without that person's consent is guilty of a crime.[67] Congress in 1998 enacted an "Identity Theft and Assumption Deterrence Act," which makes it a federal crime to steal personal information with the intent to commit an unlawful act.[68] But enforcement of this law is a challenge. There is a constant, never-ending arms race between the crooks and the gullibles (and not-so-gullible). In this intercontinental, global world, "crimes of mobility" have expanded from the city streets to the entire globe.

PROCLAIMING INNOCENCE

In a sense, most criminals lead double lives—a criminal life and an ordinary life. Even burglars have families, go to restaurants, pay rent, watch TV, play games, and try to get a night's sleep. They must, of necessity, keep their other life, the burglary life, a secret, at least from the authorities. Success depends on secrecy, and, to some degree, on the constitutional right against self-incrimination. Each form of criminality has its own way of maintaining this double life—from the ski mask of the armed robber to the elaborate bookkeeping tricks of the "wolves of Wall Street" who violate the Securities Act and the mysterious hackers and "phishers" of the world wide web. Each period and society defines crime in its own way, and each has its own forms of criminality. So, for example, corruption and bribery are, in a way, conspicuously modern. Selling public offices, or handing them over to favorites or family members, is against the law in the United States and other developed countries; bribery is also a crime. But what we consider bribery and corruption was simply normal and expected behavior in, say, the France of Louis XVI or the England of Henry VIII. The king handed out lucrative jobs to his favorites; clerks did the actual work and the concept of a "public servant" hardly existed. Nor was there, in that period, anything remotely like "investigative journalism," a staple of the modern press. The nobles and landed gentry had no need to lead double lives. Edwin Edwards ended up in prison for behaving, as governor of Louisiana, as if he was living in the days of Louis XVI. He was convicted of taking nearly $3 million in payments—including oodles of cash left in trash bins—for helping companies who wanted casino licenses in New Orleans. His assistant tried to explain that "this is the way it's done in Louisiana," but the prosecutors and jurors were unmoved.[69]

Of course, the old days had their crimes as well; the highwaymen wore masks and the sneak thieves worked in quiet and at night. The nineteenth century, as we indicated, brought in new forms of criminality—particularly crimes of mobility and crimes of identity. The crisis of identity also lies at the core of that nineteenth-century invention, the mystery story or novel. Edgar Allan Poe is often given credit for inventing this literary form; his short story, *The Murders in the Rue Morgue* (1841), is sometimes cited as the very first example of this genre.[70] By the end of the nineteenth century, "mysteries" poured out of the world's presses. The most famous detective of them all, Sherlock Holmes, the brainchild of Arthur Conan Doyle, made his appearance in the 1880s. Since then, literally thousands and thousands of "mysteries" have been published.[71] It seems impossible to say anything general about the endless diversity of these books and stories. Yet for the most part they do follow a common pattern: a crime (mostly murder) is committed. But by whom? The reader does not know. Clues may be scattered throughout the text; most readers will fail to see them. In the well-crafted mystery, we learn who committed the crime only at the end of the book. And, if the book is successful, the unmasking comes as a complete surprise. It is the person we least suspect. Thus, the story turns on concealment of a "true" identity: the killer has succeeded in fooling us for two or three hundred pages—fooling all of us, that is, except the "detective."

Many of the big criminal trials, the trials that make headlines, have a similar element of mystery. This is one reason why these trials so fascinate the public. Is this man in the dock innocent or guilty? For example, consider Claus von Bulow, a suave member of European nobility and defendant in a famous trial: did he really try to kill his wealthy wife, Sunny von Bulow? Or was he innocent, despite appearance; was he the victim of trumped-up charges? In short, who was he really? Was he a more or less honorable husband, or did he have a dark side, a secret, more authentic, identity?[72] Did Lizzie Borden, in Fall River, Massachusetts, in the 1890s, really take an axe and kill her father and stepmother?[73] Lizzie was a spinster, a member of the upper middle class, and a regular churchgoer. But was she also in fact a cold-blooded and perhaps pathological killer, hiding violence, pathology, and frustration under a bourgeois exterior? In fiction, the villains are revealed at the end for what they truly are. Real life is much more uncertain. The trial, like the detective story, usually ends with a definitive verdict: guilty or innocent (a few trials, of course, end with a hung jury). The verdict is definitive for the defendant but the public may remain unconvinced. For many trials, the shadow of a doubt remains.

In general, the persistence of crime, despite changes in shape and definition, means the persistence of double lives. But the arms race, so to speak, continues between society (meaning police and detectives), on the one hand, and criminals, on the other. Forensic tools, DNA testing, fingerprinting, analysis of hairs and fibers: these modern tools make it possible to find, identify, and punish criminals who might have escaped in the past. Science marches on. Even cold cases can be defrosted at times. In 2018, Joseph James DeAngelo, aged seventy-two, was arrested in connection with a string of murders and rapes that were committed between 1976 and 1986; "genetic genealogy" was used to identify DeAngelo and prove he was the notorious "Golden State Killer."[74] Detectives used DNA from those old crime scenes to create a fake profile on genealogy websites, hoping to smoke out relatives that would lead them to the actual killer. It worked; this was the first time this technique was used to solve a big case. After almost forty years, DeAngelo ended up in prison. In theory, these forensic techniques also shield innocent people who only seem guilty and DNA has vindicated men who were convicted of crimes and, in some cases, were rotting on death row. Researchers estimate that at least 4 percent of those sentenced to death were wrongly convicted.[75] So-called innocence projects have played an important role in drawing attention to these errors—and in freeing some of those wrongly convicted.[76] Complex rules of criminal procedure are at least theoretically in place; their task is to balance the interests of state and accused. Of course, whole books can and have been written about whether and how this balance works. The point made here is that the forensic techniques—DNA, for example—are ways to decide on identity: what is this person's actual self? Is he a killer? A rapist? The father of this child? And the rules on the other side—rules about search and seizure, for example, or about warrants or admissibility of evidence are rules of due process. But they are also rules that allow even guilty people to protect some precious core of identity in the interests of freedom, rights, and the greater good of society.

THE FICTIVE FAMILY

British intelligence faced a puzzle: why were staff people who worked at Soviet Bloc embassies so interested in "cemeteries and country churchyards"? Eventually they figured out the reason: they "were looking for the gravestones of dead children, in order to obtain their birth certificates and then apply for passports, driving licenses," and so on.[77] Spies, after all, need to construct a phony identity and this seemed like an excellent way to do the job. Indeed, Donald Heathfield, a Russian agent in the United States, "used the stolen birth certificate of a Canadian baby who died in 1963."[78] (This was also one technique of the Russian spies like the Murphys, who infiltrated suburbia with fake American identities.)

Spies, however, are not the only ones who have used this, or a similar ploy, to build a false identity for themselves. Many Chinese immigrants constructed "fictive families" as a way to get into the United States. From about 1880 on, American laws—as "harsh as tigers"—barred almost all Chinese from entering the country; the law also prevented Chinese residents from becoming naturalized citizens. On the other hand, under the Fourteenth Amendment, anyone actually born in the United States was automatically a citizen—so-called birthright citizenship.[79] This made the birth certificates of dead Chinese babies who had been born in the United States extremely valuable. A fair number of Chinese, arriving by ship in San Francisco during the era of Chinese exclusion, claimed to be citizens by birth. Consular officials thought most of these people were lying. Most of them, in fact, *were* lying. But the gambit sometimes worked; federal courts were at least willing to listen sympathetically to these claims.[80] In 1906, the great earthquake and fire destroyed much of San Francisco—and, incidentally, reduced to ashes virtually all of Chinatown and destroyed most municipal records; this opened another door to claims of birthright citizenship by claiming that documents had been lost; local officials were skeptical, and justifiably so. Chinese immigrants, knocking on the doors of America, felt compelled to lie—forced to tell a fib because of racist and discriminatory laws.[81] Other immigrants, too, have tried to create fictive families to get around immigration law. Spouses of American citizens may have a more or less automatic right to citizenship; but the suspicious souls at Immigration and Customs Enforcement (ICE) try to thwart what ICE considers "sham" marriages.[82]

In *Lutwak v. United States*, the defendants were anxious to bring male relatives, who survived World War II, into the United States. They arranged for these men to become male "war brides," by marrying them off to former US servicewomen.[83] The marriages were to be "in form only," and the brides were paid for their services. The government prosecuted, the "brides" turned state's evidence, the defendants were convicted, and they lost their appeal to the Supreme Court. The marriages, incidentally, were technically valid under Illinois law, where they took place, and under the law of France, the home country of the men. The United States government insisted nonetheless that such a marriage was genuine only if a couple planned to live on indefinitely as husband and wife and that view prevailed in the Supreme Court. The Chinese in fictive families were telling an outright lie; the marriages in the *Lutwak* case were, on the other hand technically valid—the couple went through the usual forms. We do not usually inquire into *why* A marries B. But the government in this case insisted that, if the point of a marriage was simply to evade the immigration rules, then the marriage is fraudulent. A marriage usually implies an intention to form a family (and sexual) unit. Still, if we looked too closely into *why* people marry, we would find a cluster of motives—money, position, convenience—and other motives, some perhaps quite suspect.

The *Lutwak* case grew out of conditions in the mid-twentieth century. But the United States government is still eager to sniff out marriages that it considers to be tainted by immigration fraud. Under the Immigration Marriage Fraud Act of 1986, spouses married less than two years have only conditional residence rights. They have to wait two more years; during this time, the citizen and the immigrant must petition jointly to get rid of the conditional status. They must also show that the marriage is bona fide, that the couple really lived together, and that the marriage was not a sham.[84] The ominous "Stokes unit" in New York subjects couples who have failed an initial screening interview by the immigration authorities to separate and invasive questioning.[85] Couples are asked all sorts of questions, ranging from "where's the hamper" to "who's the boss." Their answers are then compared. If the answers of the partners are too different from each other, this can derail the quest for a green card and the immigrant "spouse" is liable to be deported. In the end, ICE denies less than 1 percent of the petitions, on the grounds that the marriage was fraudulent. One wonders how many "genuine" spouses would also fail the tests imposed by the ICE.[86]

In fact, even for citizens, a marriage based on fraud or a serious lie is legally precarious. It may lay the basis for an action of "annulment"; that is, the marriage can be declared void, as if it had never happened. But the lie or the fraud has to be fairly extreme; it must affect what the state deems the "essentials of the marriage."[87] Lies about sex and procreation are treated seriously. In one example from 2008, Lilia Llamas claimed her husband had concealed from her his intimate relationship with Lilia's sister—a relationship he planned to continue after the wedding. Lilian won an annulment in California.[88] A promise of monogamy is "essential"; lies about sexually transmitted infections, intent to consummate a marriage, intent to have a child, or pregnancy by another man may also be considered "essential" and the basis for annulment. But most lies—especially those about character, financial condition, and personal habits—are generally not enough. A certain amount of role-playing, even outright fabrication, is an expected part of courtship and indeed of any and every relationship. Divorce (or "dissolution of marriage"), rather than annulment, is the remedy for expectations dashed once the honeymoon is over, when the partners reveal their "real" selves.[89]

BIGAMY

Bigamy is a type of family fiction that has grown no less odious over time. Bigamy very likely became more common in nineteenth-century America. People came and went; they moved freely from place to place. Indeed, starting over, going off to find one's fortune, was part of the American dream, or myth, or experience. Still, one was supposed to play by the rules. A married man from, say, New Hampshire, who moved on (by himself) to Ohio, was not supposed to pretend to be a bachelor and woo a woman in Ohio, hiding his former life. But some men did. This was the banal, sordid story behind dozens of bigamy cases. A bigamous marriage was and is invalid under the law in every state and in federal territories; it is also a crime. Bigamy is another classic crime of mobility. In a small village, it would be next to impossible to pull this off: everybody would know if you were married or not. But the nineteenth century was a restless period, as we pointed out; it was a century of immigration from abroad and tremendous coming and going inside the country. This situation made the con man possible and it was also fertile soil for bigamy. The cities and towns were environments full of strangers. People were constantly reinventing themselves, often for other, less sinister reasons. There are no accurate statistics about bigamy and other family frauds. And for every actual bigamist, no doubt there were countless men who only dreamed if not of bigamy, at least for a sex life broader than Victorian convention deemed acceptable.

In a popular British movie, *The Captain's Paradise* (1953), starring Alec Guinness, the main character runs a ferry between Gibraltar and Morocco; he has a wife in both places and leads a true double life. He asks the crew on each journey to tell him when the ship is halfway between the two ports, at which time he flips the picture over his bed to display the appropriate wife. The wives serve different roles for the captain. His Moroccan wife is young and sexy; with her, he goes out dancing and drinking every night and never has a home-cooked meal. His Gibraltar wife is his helpmate, and the mother of his children. He chafes when each tries to step out of the role he sees for them. He tells his exotic wife, when she dons an apron and starts to boil water, that "if you cook, all that beauty will vanish." And, after an uncomfortable night at a club into which his traditional wife has dragged him, he tries to make her promise never to go dancing again.

A similar plot was at the center of *Boeing-Boeing*, a French play that, translated into English, was a great hit in London in 1962. Bernard, a businessman in Paris, is engaged to three beautiful women, from three different countries, all of them flight attendants. Bernard chose them because of their incompatible flight schedules; they were never in Paris at the same time. Bernard describes his scheme to a friend as "mathematical, geometrical, and poetic." The slapstick comedy gets its farcical plot from a simple turn of events—Boeing develops a jet that can fly faster, and the women began showing up in Paris ahead of schedule; one night, they are all in town. In the end, Bernard finds himself abandoned by all three but not because they discovered his betrayal. One of the women is herself a two-timer, one runs off with his best friend, and the third decides to try the single life. In *The Captain's Paradise*, too, Alec Guinness ends up alone, even though his secret is never revealed. His insistence that his wives be one-dimensional brings an end to both relationships. His traditional wife leaves him to marry her cousin, who takes her drinking and dancing. His Moroccan wife says that sometimes she just wants to cook and eat dinner at home; she leaves him for a cab driver who wants a traditional wife.

The movie and play were both comedies, both fiction, but real life has a way of imitating if not outdoing fiction. A medical school professor at Stanford University, Norman Lewiston, died suddenly in 1991 at the age of fifty-two; only then did it come out that this noble and caring doctor, an expert on cystic fibrosis, in fact had three wives: two in the Bay Area and one in San Diego. He told the second wife that he was divorced; he told the same story to his colleagues, who knew his first wife, but were invited to the second wedding; for the third, he forged two sets of divorce papers to prove to her that he was free to marry. He spent his after-work hours with wife 2; then he went to wife 1, telling wife 2 that he had to sleep at the hospital. He went out of town to see wife 3, claiming he frequently had to attend medical conferences. After he died, wife 2 found out his secret when the hospital told her another wife had already come to claim the body.[90] His third wife had discovered his secret a few months before his death; they had reached an agreement to get the marriage annulled, but the paperwork had never been filed. The strain of juggling this triple life might have hastened his death.[91] Dr. Lewiston's first wife was the only one his will provided for; she also had community-property rights in his earnings. She sued the other two wives to claim the property he held jointly with the other two women. The third wife told a reporter that she had no intention of making claims on his estate: "The only thing I want to inherit is his frequent-flier miles."[92]

Gordon Getty, a billionaire and a prominent citizen of San Francisco, had a wife, Ann, and four sons. This was, apparently, not enough for him. It turned out he had another family in Los Angeles—a female partner (they weren't married) and three daughters. The news of his second family broke when the Los Angeles daughters filed a petition in court in 1999 to change their last name to Getty.[93] Was Getty's double life really a secret? Perhaps not. An article in the *Los Angeles Times* spoke of "open secrets and closed mouths, about a man with a double life and the singular city that has sheltered him."[94]

In 2009, while he was governor of South Carolina, Mark Sanford dropped out of sight. He had gone on a trip with his Argentine mistress, lying to the public and even to his staff about his whereabouts. His wife, the mother of his four children, divorced him. In a book she later wrote, she expressed regret that she had not seen the writing on the wall—he had insisted that the clause about fidelity be removed from their wedding vows.[95]

These are extreme cases but there are many such private secrets, tens of thousands no doubt, some open, some closed; sometimes they stay secret, sometimes chance or fate reveals them. In Chile, in 2010, the world was electrified by the saga of thirty-three men, trapped 2,300 feet underground for more than two months in a gold and copper mine. They went seventeen days without any communication from rescuers. Finally, to great global joy, the men were rescued. Their families had been keeping vigil nervously, waiting anxiously for rescue. For some men, however, secrets rose to the surface along with the men themselves. At least five of the rescued miners had double lives: a secret mistress or a second wife and, in some cases, two sets of children. The government offered compensation to the miners' families but this set off a furious controversy. Sometimes two women showed up to claim the money for the same man; this exposed the bitter truth about their man's infidelity and betrayal. At least one wife and mistress came to blows.[96] One wife took the high road; she stayed home on rescue day and let her husband's mistress meet him as he came to the surface. The wife told a reporter that she was "happy for him, and if he remakes his life, good for him."[97] The government toyed with the idea of sending word down to the trapped miners that each would have to send up one name—and only one—to avoid the headache of sorting out benefits. Without this mine disaster, the double lives of these miners might not have come to light.

Bigamy is probably not a common crime. True double lives like the Stanford doctor's are even rarer.[98] More prosaic forms—married people who carry on affairs—surely occur more often. What these situations have in common is the double life—the life divided into compartments, each of which is (usually) sealed off from the others, at least in most societies. But not in all. In some societies, elite men are expected to have mistresses, or the situation is at least tolerated. High-level Chinese men, in classic times, were expected to have concubines. In some Mexican states, a man can legally have a concubine—a woman who does not have the rights of a wife but who is in a recognized relationship with him nonetheless. Men in such systems have no need for a double life, in the sense used here. But in the United States, a married person can have only one partner; the rest must remain shrouded in secrecy from the state, if not also from the legitimate spouse.

Role-playing is common, in large ways and small, and nobody tells the truth about themselves all of the time. Jill Hasday speaks about the legal consequences of "intimate lies." Many of these "lies" are commonplace and almost unavoidable. At the beginning of a relationship, no doubt countless men and women puff themselves up and try to sell themselves in ways that are, well, frankly lies[99] In some situations the "intimate lies" verge on fraud or worse: the son who overstated his college expenses to wheedle more money out of his mother or the woman who told her ex-boyfriend she was pregnant with his child when she was not, thereby destroying his marriage.[100]

Most "intimate lies" are not crimes. But throughout much of our history, adultery, a classic "intimate lie," was indeed a crime and severely punished. In about twenty states, adultery is still nominally against the law. The governor of New York, David Paterson, admitted in 2008 that he had had extramarital affairs but claimed that he hadn't broken the law (in fact he had: adultery was still illegal in New York). The most recent famous adulterer from New York is surely Donald Trump, who has bragged about his exploits; he was not prosecuted but was in fact elected president of the United States. But today the law in New York and other relict states is hardly ever enforced.[101] Yet adultery is not exactly a victimless crime: a person who commits adultery is said to be "cheating" on the spouse. And "cheating" is felt by countless spouses as intolerable, as a mortal wound to a marriage. Social attitudes toward adultery, which have changed over time, determine whether an adulterer feels driven underground, whether the adulterer feels forced or induced to lead a double life, one of which is kept private and secret. At one time, interestingly, the formal law practically encouraged a double life. Under many nineteenth-century statutes, adultery per se was not illegal: it was a crime only if was "open and notorious."[102] A one-night stand, or a secret fling, was not a crime at all. "Cheating" was only a crime when it flew in the face of community standards.

The second wife of a bigamist is, as we said, an actual victim. This was especially true under the moral code of the nineteenth century. If and when the truth came out, she discovered, to her horror, that she was not a respectable married woman but a woman sharing a bed with a married man. The marriage was legally void, of course. She was then left high and dry. She was "ruined goods"; she had lost years of her life, perhaps, and her status in the marriage market was seriously if not fatally impaired. Today, her situation is much less dire. But she has lost those legal rights that flow from a regular marriage. Only the bigamist's first spouse has full rights that include protection against disinheritance, community property (in some states), and so on. The other spouses might have to settle for whatever protection a state might accord a "putative spouse" who believed in good faith that she had a valid marriage.[103]

A married person who is involved in an extramarital affair is violating the law, technically speaking, in the states that still make adultery a crime. In other states, under modern criminal codes, no crime has been committed. Adultery has been "decriminalized"; that is, the state no longer even tries to enforce honesty in marriage. It is left to individual choice—left to families to work things out. The lying goes on, but not as a way to avoid going to jail. "Cheating" on a spouse was always grounds for divorce and no doubt is still a prominent reason why people get divorced, even though, under no-fault statutes, either party can get out of a marriage for any reason or no reason at all. Indeed, as Jill Hasday argues, the law often exempts intimate partners from otherwise available remedies for deceit.[104] Rather than give partners any special protection against lies by the person they are supposed to trust most, it gives them even less.

Of course, fraud is still fraud. Spying is still betrayal. Bigamy is still a crime. The confidence game is still against the law. The hidden private life can land a person in jail. But in many other regards, we can live two or three or many lives—all of them legally, if not morally, legitimate. Bigamy may be a crime; infidelity is generally not. In most instances, the hidden private life is not the government's business. There are, however, some important and interesting in-between cases—cases that we could call cases of "passing." We will deal with them in the following chapter.

NOTES

1. Erik Brady and Rachel George, "Manti Te'o's 'Catfish' Story Is a Common One," *usatoday.com*, Jan. 18, 2013; Mary Pilon, "In Te'o Story, Deception Ripped from the Screen," *New York Times*, Jan. 17, 2013, at B11.

2. Some doubters still think Te'o may have been behind the hoax himself in an effort to gain attention during a triumphant football season for his team.

3. *Catfish* (Hit the Ground Running Films, 2010).

4. *Catfish: The TV Show* (Catfish Picture Company, 2012).

5. "Wooed a 'Marjorie Daw' for Fourteen Long Years," *New York Times*, Oct. 2, 1910.

6. Erving Goffman, *The Presentation of Self in Everyday Life* (New York: Anchor Books, 1959), is the classic exposition of this point of view.

7. Erving Goffman, *Relations in Public* (New York: Basic Books, 1971), 11.

8. The tort is usually, and conventionally, traced to a famous 1890 article, written by Samuel D. Warren and Louis D. Brandeis, "The Right of Privacy," *Harv. L. Rev.* 4 (1890): 193. Warren and Brandeis thought there ought to be a right of privacy, and they argued, on the basis of doctrinal odds and ends lying about in the storehouse of the common law, that the courts had whatever material they needed to develop such a right. Today privacy torts are the subject of a huge, complex body of law. See further, in chapter 5.

9. Goffman, *supra* note 6, at 70.

10. The full comment was: "There are 47 percent of the people who will vote for the president [Obama] no matter what. All right, there are 47 percent who are with him, who are dependent upon government, who believe the government has a responsibility to care for them, who believe they are entitled to health care, to food, to housing, to you-name-it. . . . My job is not to worry about those people. I'll never convince them they should take personal responsibility and care for their lives." Amy Davidson, "Mitt's Forty-Seven-Per-Cent Problem," *New Yorker*, Sept. 18, 2012.

11. *See* Emily S. Rueb, "Is This Thing On? A Look Back at Political Hot Mic Moments," *New York Times*, Apr. 5, 2019.

12. "Transcript: Donald Trump's Lewd Comments about Women," *New York Times*, Oct. 8, 2016.

13. Manuel Gomez, "Order in the Desert: Law Abiding Behavior at Burning Man" *J. Dispute Resolution* 2 (2013): 349.

14. *See generally* Lisa Mottet, "Modernizing State Vital Statistics Statutes and Policies to Ensure Accurate Gender Markers on Birth Certificates," *Mich. J. Gender & L.* 19 (2013): 373.

15. *See* William R. Conklin, "Pair Silent to End," *New York Times*, Jun. 20, 1953, at 1.

16. *See* Anthony Boyle, *The Climate of Treason: Five Who Spied for Russia* (London: Hutchison of London, 1979).

17. *See* Tim Weiner et al., *Betrayal: The Story of Aldrich Ames, an American Spy* (New York: Random House, 1996).

18. *See* Betty Burnett, *The Trial of Julius and Ethel Rosenberg: A Primary Source Account* (New York: Rosen Publishing Group, 2003).

19. The Official Secrets Act of 1889 (52 & 53 Vict. C. 52).

20. Stephen Twigge, Edward Hampshire, and Graham Macklin, *British Intelligence: Secrets, Spies and Sources* (New York: Bloomsbury Academic, 2008), 64–65.

21. 18 U.S.C. §§ 792–99 (2018).

22. 18 U.S.C. § 793 (a) (2018).

23. 50 U.S.C. § 797 (2018). A spy might face an elevated charge of capital espionage and treason on the basis of "(a) prior convictions for treason or espionage, for which death or life in prison was authorized; (b) knowingly creating a grave risk to national security; (c) knowingly creating a grave risk of death to another person; and (d) any other aggravating factor for which notice has been given." 18 U.S.C. § 3592(b) (2018). A defendant may face the death penalty if "the offense . . . directly concern[s] nuclear weaponry, military spacecraft or satellites, early warning systems,

or other means of defense or retaliation against large-scale attack; war plans; communications intelligence or cryptographic information; or any other major weapons system or major element of defense strategy," or if any members of the intelligence services were identified and killed as a result of the defendant's treasonous activity. *Id.*; *see also* Ryan Norwood, "None Dare Call It Treason: The Constitutionality of the Death Penalty for Peacetime Espionage," *Cornell L. Rev.* 87, (2002): 820, 828.

24. A typical case is *Gorin v. United States*, 312 U.S. 19 (1941).

25. *See, e.g., United States v. Drake*, 818 F. Supp. 2d 909 (D. Md. 2011).

26. *See* Peter Baker, "Moves to Curb Spying Help Drive the Clemency Argument for Snowden," *New York Times*, Jan. 4, 2014.

27. *See* Sharon LaFraniere et al., "Trump, Ukraine and Impeachment: The Inside Story of How We Got Here," *New York Times*, Nov. 11, 2019, at A1.

28. David A.T. Stafford, "Spies and Gentlemen: The Birth of the British Spy Novel, 1893–1914," *Victorian Studs.* 24 (1981): 489.

29. Bob Drogin and Geraldine Baum, "A Spy Story Set in Suburbia," *L. A. Times*, June 30, 2010, at A1.

30. Jerry Markon and Philip Rucker, "The Spies Next Door," *Washington Post*, June 30, 2010, at A1.

31. *Id.*

32. The criminal complaint against them is available at http://documents.nytimes.com/criminal-complaints-from-the-justice-department?ref=Europe.

33. *See* Thom Patterson, "The Russian Spies Living Next Door," *CNN.com,* July 19, 2017. The children were apparently unaware of what their parents actually did for a living. At least this is what one of them claimed when applying for Canadian citizenship.

34. See, for example, Rob Evans and Paul Lewis, *Undercover: The True Story of Britain's Secret Police* (London: Faber and Faber, 2013), for a vivid account of the way in which the "Special Demonstration Squad" inserted moles into extremist organizations—for example, ecoterrorist groups. The main character in a recent American movie, "The East," was a woman recruited by a private company (on behalf of various corporations) to infiltrate and expose an ecoterrorist group.

35. Tom Cohen, "Top Senator: Obama Didn't Know of U.S. Spying on Germany's Leader," *CNN,* Feb. 1, 2014, The program was authorized under Section 215 of the Patriot Act, with the main goal of thwarting domestic terrorism.

36. Scott Shane and Eric Schmitt, "Double Agent Disrupted Bombing Plot, U.S. Says," *New York Times*, May 8, 2012, at A1.

37. *See* Earle Rice, *The Salem Witch Trials* (San Diego, CA: Lucent Books, 1996).

38. *See* Robert Reinhold, "The Longest Trial—A Post-Mortem," *New York Times*, Jan. 24, 1990.

39. *See* George Johnson, "The Infamous 'Protocols of Zion' Endures," *New York Times*, July 26, 1987, at D6.

40. Notably, Congress passed, in almost indecent haste, the U.S.A. Patriot Act, 115 Stat. 272 (Oct. 26, 2001). The Act was extended in 2011.

41. A lesser-known movie, from 1958, has the intriguing title *I Married a Monster from Outer Space*. In this movie, directed by Gene Fowler Jr., a young woman,

Marge, finds her husband, Bill, acting more and more strangely. She discovers that this person is not really Bill at all, but an alien who has taken over Bill's body. He and the other men in town—also taken over by aliens—come from a planet where the woman are extinct and they have come down to mate and save their own kind from extinction.

42. Ray Pratt, *Projecting Paranoia: Conspiratorial Visions in American Film* (Lawrence: University Press of Kansas, 2001), 32.

43. *Id.* at 35.

44. In another well-known movie, *Gaslight*, directed by George Cukor and released in 1944, Paula, the niece of a murdered woman, marries Gregory, who is secretly the man who murdered her aunt and who tries to drive Paula mad for his own nefarious purposes. Of course, he is revealed as a villain by the end of the movie.

45. Lawrence M. Friedman, *Crime and Punishment in American History* (New York: Basic Books, 1993), 195.

46. *Id.* at 196.

47. "Impostor Is Hunted in Fake Relief Plea," *New York Times*, Nov. 20, 1935, at 18.

48. "Envoy Warns of Impostor," *New York Times*, Feb. 21, 1928. There was an actual Ramon Padilla, who was the son of the ambassador, and had nothing to do with the scheme.

49. "Unmasked Impostor Posed as a Marquis," *New York Times*, Apr. 9, 1911, at C3. The real name of the Marquis was Paul Reiss, the son of a wine seller and "wanted by the police" in France and elsewhere for "bankruptcy, swindling, and bigamy."

50. "Notorious Impostor Shot Dead, Defending Motel in Hold-Up," *New York Times*, Aug. 28, 1960, at 1.

51. A movie, *The Great Impostor* (1959), was based on his exploits. See also Joe McCarthy, "The Master Impostor: An Incredible Tale," *Time*, Jan. 28, 1952, at 79.

52. The book was Frank W. Abagnale with Stan Redding, *Catch Me If You Can: The True Story of a Real Fake* (New York: Broadway Books, 2000).

53. James Barron and M. A. Farber, "Tracing a Devious Path to the Ivy League," *New York Times*, Mar. 4, 1991.

54. *See* "Top 10 Imposters," *Time,* Feb. 1, 2014.

55. On this famous case, see Douglas Woodruff, *The Tichborne Claimant: A Victorian Mystery* (New York: Farrar, Strauss, and Giroux, 1957); Geddes MacGregor, *The Tichborne Impostor* (Philadelphia: Lippincott, 1957).

56. *See* Michael Specter, "Moscow Is Almost Certain: Anastasia Died with Czar's Family," *New York Times*, Sept. 6, 1994.

57. *See, e.g.,* Okla. Admin. Code §10–1–101 (2020). Oklahoma has a general identity theft statute, Okla. Stats. Tit. 21, sec. 1533.1, which makes it illegal to "willfully and with intent to defraud" obtain "personal identifying information." There is also an "Anti-Phishing Act" (Okla. Stat. tit.15, sections 776.10–1776.11 et. seq.), which makes it illegal to create a webpage or use a trademark and the like without the authorization of the real owner of the site in an attempt to squeeze personal identifying information out of the victim.

58. *United States v. Alvarez*, 567 U.S. 709 (2012).

59. Helen Campbell et al., *Darkness and Daylight: or Lights and Shadows of New York Life* (Hartford, CT: The Hartford Publishing Company, 1895), 524.

60. Matthew Hale Smith, *Sunshine and Shadow in New York* (Berkeley: University of California Libraries, 1869), 128.

61. Kenny Herzog, "How Dirty John Actors Compare to Their Real-Life Counterparts," *Vulture,* Dec. 13, 2018.

62. Cal. Penal Code § 532(a) (2020). There are also many specific frauds that have their own code section, for example, 532b, impersonating a veteran; 537, getting food or lodging at a hotel or restaurant without paying and with intent to defraud the owner; or 538d, impersonating a police officer.

63. *IRS Warns of New Phone Scam Using Taxpayer Advocate Service Numbers*, irs.gov (Mar. 15, 2019).

64. *See* FBI—Common Fraud Schemes, available at http://www.fbi.gov/scams-safety/fraud.

65. *See* Stephanie Yang, "5 Years Ago Bernie Madoff Was Sentenced to 150 Years in Prison—Here's How His Scheme Worked," *Business Insider*, July 1, 2014.

66. *See, e.g.,* Matthew B. Kugler, "From Identification to Identity Theft: Public Perceptions of Biometric Privacy Harms," *UC Irvine L. Rev.* 10 (2020): 107.

67. Cal. Penal Code 530.5 (2020).

68. 18 U.S.C. § 1028 (2018); *see also* Kurt M. Saunders and Bruce Zucker, "Counteracting Identity Fraud in the Information Age: The Identity Theft and Assumption Deterrence Act," *Cornell J. L. & Pub. Pol'y* 8 (1999): 661.

69. Kevin Sack, "Former Louisiana Governor Is Indicted in Extortion Case," *New York Times*, Nov. 7, 1998, at A7; Kevin Sack, "Former Louisiana Governor Guilty of Extortion on Casinos," *New York Times*, May 10, 2000, at A1.

70. On the early history of the genre, see T. J. Binyon, *"Murder Will Out": The Detective in Fiction* (Oxford, UK: Oxford University Press, 1989).

71. Twelve of them, it might be noted, have been written by one of the co-authors of this book, all of them featuring a fictional California lawyer, Frank May. *See, e.g.,* Lawrence M. Friedman, *The Book Club Murder* (New Orleans, LA: Quid Pro Books, 2013); *Death of a One-Sided Man* (New Orleans, LA: Quid Pro Books, 2013); *A Body in the Yard* (New Orleans, LA: Quid Pro Books, 2018).

72. On this case, see Alan M. Dershowitz, *Reversal of Fortune: Inside the Von Bulow Case* (New York: Random House, 1986).

73. *See* David Kent, *Forty Whacks: New Evidence in the Life and Legend of Lizzie Borden* (Dublin, NH: Yankee Books, 1992); Cara Robertson, *The Trial of Lizzie Borden: A True Story* (New York: Simon & Schuster, 2019).

74. *See* Michael Levenson, "Golden State Killer Sentenced to Life in Prison without Parole," *New York Times*, Aug. 21, 2020.

75. *See* Samuel R. Gross et al., "Rate of False Conviction of Criminal Defendants Who Are Sentenced to Death," *PNAS* 111 (2014): 7240.

76. *See generally* Keith A. Findley, "The Pedagogy of Innocence: Reflections on the Role of Innocence Projects in Clinical Legal Education," *Clinical L. Rev.* 13 (2006–2007): 231.

77. Edward Lucas, *Deception: The Untold Story of East–West Espionage Today* (New York: Bloomsbury, 2013), 162.

78. Lucas, *supra* note 77, at 153.

79. See U.S. Const. Amend. XIV ("All persons born or naturalized in the United States, and subject to the jurisdiction thereof, are citizens of the United States and the State wherein they reside.").

80. On this issue, see Estelle Lau, *Paper Families: Identity, Immigration Administration, and Chinese Exclusion* (Durham, NC: Duke University Press, 2007); Lucy E. Salyer, *Laws Harsh as Tigers: Chinese Immigrants and the Shaping of Modern Immigration Law* (Chapel Hill: University of North Carolina Press, 1995).

81. For about a century, the typical divorce petition in the United States was a kind of family fiction. The law did not allow couples to get a divorce, even if both parties wanted one: there had to be "grounds" for divorce. This led to a system of collusion: the plaintiff in a divorce action—usually the wife—accused the other spouse of adultery or cruelty (depending on the jurisdiction); whatever the reality of the life of the family, the particular story that the petition told was simply not true. Indeed, family law in general was shot through with these fictions. Today, in the era of no-fault divorce, these family fictions are no longer necessary. See, in general, Joanna L. Grossman and Lawrence M. Friedman, *Inside the Castle: Law and the Family in 20th Century America* (Princeton, NJ: Princeton University Press, 2011).

82. *See generally* Kerry Abrams, "Immigration Law and the Regulation of Marriage," *Minn. L. Rev.* 91 (2007): 1625.

83. 344 U.S. 604 (1953).

84. Immigration Marriage Fraud Amendments of 1986, Pub. L. 99–369, § 216(g), 100 Stat. 3537, 3541 (codified at 8 U.S.C. § 1186a(g) (2018); Abrams, *supra* note 82, at 1682–94.

85. See Nina Bernstein, "Do You Take This Immigrant?," *New York Times*, June 11, 2010, at MB1.

86. As Kerry Abrams points out, the federal marriage fraud rules are also designed to prevent unilateral marriage fraud "where a foreign man or woman tricks a citizen into marriage . . . only to divorce the unlucky spouse once permanent residency has been obtained." Abrams, *supra* note 82, at 1683 n. 267

87. The "essentials" test was set forth in *Reynolds v. Reynolds*, 85 Mass. 605 (1862) and was adopted in many states.

88. *See In re Marriage of Ramirez*, 165 Cal. App. 4th 751 (2008).

89. Annulments are, in general, uncommon, and hard to get. But in New York, during the period when adultery was the only practical grounds for divorce—well into the twentieth century—many couples sought annulments and the New York courts were sympathetic; consequently, annulments were more common than in other states. *See* Grossman and Friedman, *supra* note 81, at 180–87. Devout Catholics, who are not allowed to divorce, also prefer annulment, which the Church allows in certain cases.

90. Richard C. Paddock, "Doctor Led Three Lives with Three Wives," *L. A. Times*, Oct. 14, 1991.

91. *Id.*

92. "Doctor's Polygamy Surprising," *Daily News*, Oct. 9, 1991.

93. Maria L. LaGanga and Jocelyn Stewart, "2nd Getty Family an Open Secret," *L. A. Times*, Aug. 30, 1999.

94. *Id.*; *see also* Stacy Finz and Jaxon Van Derbeken, "Getty's Secret Double Life," *sfgate.com*, Aug. 21, 1999. Even after the story broke, Ann Getty did not divorce her husband.

95. Jenny Sanford, *Staying True* (New York: Ballantine Books, 2010), 28–29.

96. Fiona Govan, "Mistresses and Wives Clash over Trapped Chilean Miners," *Telegraph*, Sept. 2, 2010.

97. Bonnie Goldstein, "Wronged Wife of Chilean Miner Out-Classes Jenny Sanford," *Politics Daily*, Oct. 14, 2010.

98. Bigamy laws are not routinely enforced, except for raids on polygamous communities—in which the plural marriages are in any event hardly a secret.

99. Jill Elaine Hasday, *Intimate Lies and the Law* (Oxford, UK: Oxford University Press, 2019).

100. *Id.* at 158, 188.

101. On the current landscape and historical enforcement patterns, see Joanne Sweeny, "Undead Statutes: The Rise, Fall, and Continuing Uses of Adultery and Fornication Criminal Laws," *Loyola U. Chi. L. J.* 46 (2014): 127.

102. *See* Lawrence M. Friedman, *Private Lives: Families, Individuals, and the Law* (Cambridge, MA: Harvard University Press, 2004), 85; see also Cal. Penal Code § 266a (1872).

103. *See, e.g.*, *Spearman v. Spearman*, 482 F.2d 1203 (5th Cir. 1973).

104. *See* Hasday, *supra* note 99.

Chapter 7

In the Closet

In chapter 6, we explored instances of double lives that were illegal, or close to illegal—double lives that involved cheating, fraud, and downright theft. But there are or have been people who led double lives for a whole range of other reasons. A professor at George Washington University, Jessica Krug, confessed on social media that she had been falsely claiming several different black identities throughout her career. Although she was a white, Jewish woman born in the Midwest, she had "assumed identities within a Blackness that I had no right to claim: first North African Blackness, then US-rooted Blackness, then Caribbean-rooted Bronx Blackness."[1] As a historian who studied politics and culture in Africa and the African diaspora, her feigned blackness gave her a certain authenticity and perhaps access to academic positions she would not otherwise have held. Another professor in the field criticized Krug for taking up "some of the very few—very few—resources and spaces that there are available to Black and Latino scholars and use those to her advantage."[2] Krug had successfully "passed" for black, a valuable identity for her to assume in her line of work. But historically, whiteness was the prize, and the history of racial passing was largely about people who pretended to be white.

When people "pass," their "true" identities and traits are kept hidden because these identities and traits carry a social and sometimes legal stigma. A light-skinned person, with some African American ancestry, has been historically labeled black, socially and legally in the United States. To have that label was a source of enormous social disadvantage—and even physical danger. If light-skinned people "passed"—that is, if they crossed over into white society—these disadvantages would disappear and the white world and all its advantages would lie open. Similarly, the closeted gay could often pass for straight. There are other less common forms of "passing," for example, the occasional case of a woman who pretends to be a man to get the professional advantages open only to men. "Passing" might be considered by some as downright dishonest, or even as a kind of theft. The person who "passes" is stealing privileges that don't belong by right to that person. But our views about these double lives have been more changeable than views about the double life of spies, for example. Even at the height of American racism, not everyone wanted to deny blacks the rights and privileges of whites. And as social and legal norms evolved to embrace racial equality, the need to pass all but dried up; reducing the incentive for light-skinned "blacks" to pass. A similar story might be told about the gay closet, although that evolution is still incomplete and underway; the same is true for people who change or try to change the gender they were born with.

"Passing," then, in the broadest sense of pretending to be someone you're not, is an important social phenomenon. And, as we have said, in many ways all of us lead two lives, or many lives: inner and outer lives. All of us are "passing," in some sense. Social and legal norms tell us when we can legitimately "pass," and when we cannot. The right to pass is an aspect of privacy. Each form of "passing" has its own special history, its own characteristics. But each also reflects the special character of the modern world, a world in which identity is blurred, ambiguous, contested, in which identity can be more easily simulated than in past and traditional societies.

Contemporary society is more permissive, less (officially) racist, more committed to social equality. What was once taboo—like same-sex behavior—has sometimes become more legitimate. The movement in law and society has been toward more openness, and less need to conceal a "true" or more authentic self. In the age of civil rights and affirmative action, there is less reason to pass for white. Indeed, there may be reasons to come out of the racial closet and even the closet of sexual orientation. In our times, too, adopted children have often been able to look for and find their biological families as "open" adoption has become more common. Children of parents who are not married have less cause to "pass" for legitimate children. In this day and age, nobody much cares whether your parents had a marriage license or not.

PASSING FOR WHITE

Race relations in the United States have a long and tortured history. A vicious and deep-seated racist strain has strongly colored relationships between black and white. During the colonial period, there were black slaves in every colony; after the Revolution, slavery was abolished in the northern states but persisted in the southern ones and, indeed, slavery was a vital element in the southern economy and in southern culture and politics. In some parts of the south, slaves outnumbered free whites. After slavery was abolished, the system of white supremacy did not die; eventually, a severe and oppressive system of Jim Crow and apartheid became the norm in southern states.[3] As Michelle Alexander has put it, once slavery was gone, there was "no longer a formal mechanism for maintaining racial hierarchy," but southern society continued to be a society of white supremacy; African Americans were considered "intrinsically inferior and vile. . . . [T]he development of a new racial order became the consuming passion for most white Southerners."[4] Jim Crow was the result. Under this system, African Americans were oppressed and suppressed; those who violated the code of white supremacy even ran the risk of violent death at the hands of a lynch mob. In the north, white supremacy was also a powerful force, though in a less formal and less violent way.

Because race carried with it such dire consequences, it was important to define who was "black" and who was not. In American law—and American society—race is in many ways a social rather than a biological category. A person who is one-eighth black, and seven-eighths white, is "black" or "African American" and will be treated as such, for better or for worse. In part, this practice goes back to the days of slavery. Under the slave codes of the colonial period, and afterward, the status of the mother determined the status of the child.[5] Slave-owners were notoriously free to have sex with their helpless female slaves; light-skinned children who were born to these slave mothers would themselves be slaves from birth. The white father usually paid no attention to these children. In any event, if the story repeats itself in the next generation, the children of a light-skinned slave would be even lighter. After a few generations, there were slaves in some households who simply looked white.

At all points in American history, there were at least some free persons of color. They were free, but in no southern state were they treated as equal to whites. State laws defined how much black blood it took to get a person classified as black, and when slavery ended, these laws applied to the ex-slaves as well. The Virginia code of 1887 defined a person as "colored" if they had "one-fourth or more" black blood. In the code of 1924, anyone with one-sixteenth or more was "colored." This then morphed into the infamous "one drop" rule. In the code of 1942, every person "in whom there is ascertainable any negro blood shall be deemed . . . a colored person."[6]

Since blackness was so disadvantageous, both legally and socially, light-skinned "blacks" who could "pass" were tempted to try to cross over into white society. Mark Twain's novel *Pudd'nhead Wilson* pivots on the existence of "blacks" who could pass for white. In the novel, a slave owner's baby and a slave woman's baby are somehow exchanged at birth. The slave grows up thinking he is a master, and the master grows up thinking he is a slave. This plot, of course, would make no sense, unless the slave child could "pass" for white and the white child could be thought of as simply a light-skinned slave. Obviously, many "blacks" could pass for white, especially after the end of slavery, and especially in states where a person who was one-sixteenth black was legally black, and even more egregiously in, say, Virginia, under the "one-drop" rule. Under the Virginia rule, which was exceptional in this regard, it was "simply not possible to know whether you had one drop of black blood—to know whether you were a real white person or an imitation. . . . The one-drop rule made whiteness imaginary."[7]

"Passing" of course meant hiding a social identity; it meant living a second life. Thomas Jefferson freed the children of his slave Sally Hemmings—they were certainly his children as well; the two oldest, William Beverley and Harriet, "left Monticello as white people"; they were obviously light enough to pass.[8] The saga of the nineteenth-century Healy family is one of the most astonishing stories of "blacks" who passed for white. The Healys were the children of a white Irish immigrant and a slave woman, with whom Healy was in a long-term relationship. Their father sent the children north, to be educated in Catholic schools. Most of them, although not all, were light enough to pass for white. The ones who passed were brilliantly successful in their new lives as white people. One became a priest and later rose to be Bishop of a diocese; another was captain of a ship. A third, also a priest, became president of Georgetown University. All of these positions would have been out of the question if the secret of their mother's status had come to light.[9] In some families, after generations of "passing," descendants lost all memory of their African American ancestors. Daniel Sharfstein, in his book *The Invisible Line*, tells the vivid story of three families that, over the course of time, crossed the line from black to white. Indeed, one descendant fought as a white man in the Confederate Army.[10]

For those who "passed," and for their families, life could be precarious. A person who "passed" was awkwardly balanced between two worlds, and perhaps not really at home in either one. In a 1949 movie, *Pinky*, directed by Elia Kazan, the main character was a light-skinned woman, Patricia Johnson, who passed for white and became a nurse in the north. In the end, she decided in a sense to give up her whiteness; she resolved to stay in the south and work for the black community.

An interesting California case turned on the estate of a San Francisco lawyer, Ernest Torregano. Torregano was born in New Orleans to an African-American family. But he himself was light-skinned enough to "pass." He married and had a daughter, Gladys. Then he took a job as a Pullman porter (a traditional job for blacks); afterward, he moved to San Francisco, where he passed for white, studied law, and became a member of the bar. His mother, from New Orleans, visited him at one point, and told him his wife and daughter were dead. She then went back to New Orleans and told the wife and daughter that Torregano himself was dead. No explanation is given for these extraordinary lies; the best guess is that she saw him living in San Francisco as a white man and was afraid the truth about his black family in New Orleans would hurt his career. That truth never came out during his lifetime. But after he died, his daughter, Gladys, somehow discovered the truth. In his will, Torregano stated that he had no children (of course he thought this was true) and he left a nominal amount ($1) to anyone who claimed a relationship. This is a standard "no-contest" clause, and usually effective. In this case it was not. The California courts gave the estate to the long-lost daughter, despite Torregano's will, under a rule designed to protect children against accidental disinheritance.[11]

Cross-racial marriage was forbidden in many states throughout the nineteenth century, and well into the twentieth century; the Supreme Court eliminated the last of these laws in 1967.[12] Racial identity could often be confused and confusing—there were no genetic tests; a lot depended on how people behaved, who they associated with, and how the community defined them. Sometimes lawsuits turned on whether or not one party or another was black or white.[13] This issue arose, for the most part, in southern communities. The well-known *Rhinelander* case, however, in New York, in the 1920s, turned on the racial identity of a woman named Alice Jones. Kip Rhinelander, from a prominent and wealthy family, had married Jones, a girl from the other side of the tracks.[14] His family was bitterly opposed to the marriage. Kip, under their influence, left Alice and brought a lawsuit to annul the marriage. His wife, he said, had black blood, but had hidden this fact from him. This deception, he argued, was a fraud on the marriage and constituted grounds for annulment. The case turned on whether he had really been deceived about her racial identity. In one dramatic moment during the trial, Alice Jones stripped in front of the jury, so that they could see for themselves whether her body looked black or white. In the end, Rhinelander lost his case. The jury, in all likelihood, did think Alice was partly African American. But they perhaps also felt that Rhinelander must have known this fact, even before the marriage. The annulment action failed. Nonetheless, Alice and Kip never lived together again.

A person whose skin is quite light can "pass" for white and, by the same token, a white person can conceivably "pass" for a light-skinned black person. This is, of course, a much rarer situation. But it is not unknown. One remarkable case involved Clarence King, a famous explorer, geologist, and author in the nineteenth century, a man who led a spectacular double life. In one life, as the great Clarence King, he mixed with high government officials and other luminaries. But King had fallen in love with a black woman, Ada Copeland. He married her, lived with her, and had children, all the while telling her his name was James Todd, supposedly a light-skinned black man. Todd, he explained, was a Pullman porter, which is why he was so often away. This grand deception lasted many years. Only when King was dying did he reveal the truth to his wife.[15] Another remarkable case involved Rachel

Dolezal, an outspoken activist and professor of African studies who claimed to be black, but was "outed" as white by her white parents in 2015. Dolezal had built a world around her claimed identity; then it came crashing down. She was dismissed from her teaching position, forced to resign from her position as president of the local NAACP branch, and aggressively chastised by the media and society worldwide. However, Dolezal was unfazed, and remained staunch in her insistence that she was, in fact, truly black, though "on the inside"; in 2017, she legally changed her name to Nkechi Amare Diallo, and wrote a controversial memoir about her experiences.[16]

"Passing" had enormous consequences in American society. In other situations, in other societies, it could even be a matter of life and death. In the Third Reich, to be an "Aryan" was extremely beneficial. To be Jewish was dangerous in every way; ultimately, to be Jewish was to be consigned to the death camps and slaughtered. Laws defined what quantum of Jewish blood took you out of the realm of Aryan society. To hide a non-Aryan blot on family history could be a matter of sheer survival.[17] Many Jews were in hiding during the Nazi period or "passed" for gentile with fake identity papers. In the United States, Jews were never hunted down and slaughtered like animals, but a genteel form of anti-Semitism was quite common and many Jews found it worthwhile to "pass" into Christian society. Medieval Spain had been home to a large and flourishing Jewish community, but in 1492 King Ferdinand and Queen Isabella ordered Jews to convert or be expelled from Spain. Thousands left but some remained and converted to Christianity. Of these, a fair number continued to practice the Jewish religion, but in secret; in public, they "passed" for Catholics. Over the generations, descendants of these "conversos" often lost all memory of Jewish ancestry, but certain "family" customs that were, in fact, originally Jewish, continued to be observed in these families. A researcher who investigated descendants of "conversos" in New Mexico told about family members who told him things like "so-and-so lights candles" on the Sabbath and "does not eat pork." A few descendants of conversos in New Mexico have even returned to the Jewish faith.[18]

In 1900, a white southerner who discovered black ancestors would most likely be appalled. A Catholic in Mexico or Spain who discovered Jewish or Arab ancestry was unlikely to be pleased. But in the twenty-first century, the social meaning of these discoveries is radically different. The stigma has faded and the need to "pass" has faded as well.[19] Some Spaniards speak proudly of their "Jewish ancestry," even though this "fact" no longer has any religious meaning. Similarly, to discover that some ancestor was illegitimate no longer has the power to shock. Australia, as we know, was once a penal colony. Modern Australians who can trace their line back to a convict ancestor are unlikely to hide their heads in shame, if they ever did.

PASSING FOR LEGAL

We have mentioned in a previous chapter how Chinese immigrants constructed "fictive families" to gain a foothold in America—a country that did not want them to come. Their descendants no longer need to hide their background. Yet today, millions of men, women, and children living in the United States still have a desperate need to "pass." These are the undocumented aliens, the people who secretly crossed the Mexican border, or who floated on a rickety boat to some beach in Florida, or simply overstayed a visa. These immigrants try to keep their heads down; they need to be invisible, to melt into the mass of the population. This is much easier in the United States than in many countries, where strangers from strange countries stick out like a sore thumb. The United States is a nation of immigrants; millions of legal foreigners are already in the country and there is nothing—accent, skin color, dress—that unambiguously says to the outside world, "This person has no papers."

No one has an exact count of the numbers of aliens who "pass." The Department of Homeland Security in 2018 estimated there were roughly 11.4 million.[20] Each one of these millions has his or her own story—a story about living two lives. Harold Fernandez, for example, came to the United States when he was thirteen. His parents were already here illegally. Harold and his brothers fled from Medellin, Colombia; they flew to the tiny island of North Bimini. They boarded a wooden boat packed with other immigrants and made the treacherous sea voyage to Florida. Harold turned out to be a terrific student. He was valedictorian of his high school class. He entered Princeton with a fake green card and social security number. Eventually, he was exposed, but his story, unlike so many others, had a happy ending: Princeton and its lawyers came to his rescue. Today, Harold is a graduate of medical school and practices as a cardiac surgeon.[21]

People like Harold Fernandez are of course not typical. The so-called DREAM Act, which has bounced about in Congress and in the executive branch, would open a path to citizenship for young people who came in illegally as minors, and who graduated from college or served in the military, and have no criminal record.[22] Congress never enacted the DREAM Act. President Obama, however, announced in July 2012 that his government would in effect behave as if the act was law: immigrants who were "Dreamers" would not be deported.[23] Shortly thereafter, the Obama administration implemented an additional immigration policy: the Deferred Action for Childhood Arrivals (DACA) program. Under DACA, eligible young people could apply for work permits and would be safe from deportation. This gave "Dreamers" peace of mind and the right to get jobs or go to school in this country. The Trump administration, however, undid Obama's action, plunging roughly 800,000 "Dreamers" into a sea of uncertainty.[24] The Trump administration's decision evoked strong public outcry, along with lawsuits. The Supreme Court ultimately held that the withdrawal of the program was arbitrary and capricious and thus did not comply with the federal Administrative Procedure Act.[25] Trump's administration at one point seemed willing to trade protection to "Dreamers" in exchange for big money for Trump's wall on the Mexican border.[26] This never happened. Trump is out of office and the new president, Joseph Biden, wants to do something for the "Dreamers."[27] Both parties seem to agree, but politics is a messy business, and as of this writing (December 2021), Congress has actually done nothing.

Many undocumented immigrants, moreover, would not qualify as Dreamers, did not graduate from Princeton, and do not work as cardiac surgeons. They are poor, sometimes very poor; they have low-level jobs cleaning latrines, washing dishes in restaurants, picking strawberries, plucking chickens, or standing on street corners waiting for jobs as day laborers. They often live in squalor and they are easily exploited—they have no vote, no power, and none of the benefits of citizenship. They are also, moreover, in constant fear of "la migra," or Immigration and Customs Enforcement (ICE), a controversial arm of the Department of Homeland Security, which was created in the wake of the terrorist attacks of September 11, 2001.[28] Undocumented immigrants are subject, in a number of states, to draconian laws. Life as an undocumented immigrant is difficult to navigate, requiring near-constant vigilance and avoidance of many of the institutions of civil society that citizens and documented immigrants take for granted, like schools and hospitals.[29] Nor was the Obama administration as kind-hearted as one might think; in 2011, the administration deported 396,906 men and women—a record number[30]—though it later showed a certain amount of commitment to immigration reform. Everyone agrees that the law could use some reforming, but there is little or no agreement as to what and how and how much. It is easy to imagine some sort of compromise: border controls would remain, and perhaps be tightened; at the same time, there would be a path—probably long, slow, and hard—for undocumented immigrants to follow, leading to the emerald city of citizenship. Yet Congress, so far, seems gridlocked on the issue.

PASSING FOR STRAIGHT

Historically, gays were mostly "in the closet"; that is, they hid their sexual orientation from public view and at work, and sometimes even at home and even in marriage. Strong social taboos against homosexual behavior made the gay closet necessary. The law reflected these taboos; same-sex behavior was a felony for most of American history, a crime that could earn long prison terms for a violator who was caught.

McCarthyism in the 1950s was not only a crusade against alleged communists and communist sympathizers; it also included an effort to purge gays from the federal civil service.[31] Even the American Civil Liberties Union (ACLU), the most ardent defender of civil rights, distanced itself from gay rights; a policy statement in 1957 expressed the view that sodomy laws were constitutional if state and local governments considered them "socially necessary or beneficial."[32] The federal government, meanwhile, mounted an antigay campaign of its own.[33] At the State Department, the campaign began in 1947 and targeted hundreds of alleged communists and gays; many people were fired. The effort spread to other federal agencies. A Senate resolution of 1950 ordered an investigation of gays and "other sex perverts" in government service. Employing them in government was "undesirable."[34] The danger did not come from so-called latent sex perverts, men and women who kept their "perversion" under control; the problem was the "overt" homosexuals. Just as in the military in later years, there was a policy for a while that was called (colloquially) "don't ask, don't tell," the idea here was to insist on the closet: on the maximum amount of concealment of behavior. Leading two lives was the only way for gays to survive in federal service.

National security was the excuse for the campaign.[35] Homosexuals were "outcasts" in society; they were security risks.[36] Gays would be obvious targets of blackmailers, who would threaten to expose them to the world and to their employers, unless the target passed along classified information. Gays, after all, supposedly had weak "moral fiber"; besides, "perverts" tended to "congregate at the same restaurants, night clubs, and bars" where any spy could find them and develop a relationship.[37] Agencies were encouraged to wake up and get rid of these dangerous and unstable men and women.[38] Dwight Eisenhower's campaign for the presidency included a slogan, "Let's Clean House"; this was a promise to rid the federal government of a "host of problems, including communism, corruption and sexual perversion."[39]

This war against gay people lasted for two decades; then it gradually began to crumble. In 1969, a federal appellate court, in *Norton v. Macy*, questioned whether it was "appropriate" for the federal bureaucracy to enforce "conventional codes of conduct in the private lives of its employees." This was "at war with elementary concepts of liberty, privacy, and diversity."[40] In this particular case, a budget analyst for NASA had been dismissed because he had made an off-duty homosexual advance in a private car. At a minimum, the court reasoned, the civil service commission would have to show a direct relationship between his conduct and the efficiency of the service. Moral condemnation or "transitory institutional discomfiture" by NASA because "one of its own was caught *in flagrante delictu*" was not enough to justify the firing.[41] That same week, the Stonewall Riot occurred, an event that is widely, if inaccurately, credited as the start of the gay rights movement. In 1975, the Civil Service Commission abandoned regulations that barred people who were guilty of "immoral conduct" from working for the national government; these regulations had been the formal excuse for the purge of gays and lesbians. In 1998, President Clinton issued Executive Order 13087, which prohibited discrimination based on sexual orientation in the civilian federal workforce.[42] In 2014, President Obama signed Executive Order 13672, which expanded protections by adding "gender identity" to the list of categories insulated from discrimination in the civilian federal workforce.[43] The Trump administration was hostile to the LGBT community. Among other actions, the administration withdrew a guidance designed to help federal agency managers respect the rights of transgender federal workers.[44] The Biden administration, however, reversed course, and an openly gay man with a husband was appointed to the cabinet.

For most of American history, gays were barred from military service.[45] The military pursued a policy of getting rid of gay soldiers, sometimes even using sting operations to ferret out closeted gays; often, gays who were dismissed were given a dishonorable discharge. During the years of the draft, 1940–1973, appearing gay was in fact a way to avoid the draft. One of the longest-running gags on the popular TV series *M*A*S*H* involved a corporal in the Korean War, Maxwell Klinger, who dressed in drag in the hopes of being discharged from service. Protest singer Phil Ochs released *Draft Dodger Rag* in 1965, a satiric critique of the Vietnam War, in which he recites all the standard excuses given to draft boards.

As the litany begins,

> I got eyes like a bat, my feet are flat, and my asthma's getting worse
> Yes, think of my career, my sweetheart dear, and my poor old invalid aunt

He continues with two more golden excuses.

> Besides, I isn't no fool, I'm a-goin' to school
> And I'm working in a DEE-fense plant

And brings it home with a chorus that trots out the ultimate excuse: "I always carry a purse." Carrying a purse was, of course, a sign of acting gay.

The ban on gays and lesbians in the military lasted until 1993. Under Clinton's policy of Don't Ask, Don't Tell (DADT), gay and lesbian service members could be discharged or barred entry into service only if they openly acknowledged their sexual orientation or engaged in same-sex conduct.[46] "Keep your homosexuality a secret" was, in short, a condition of service.

DADT did not end discrimination; over 14,500 service members were dismissed under DADT.[47]

DADT was abolished in December 2010, during President Barack Obama's first term in office. Public opinion had begun to shift dramatically in favor of gay rights generally, including military service.[48] The military was also, finally, embracing full participation by female soldiers; a long-standing ban on women's service in combat was lifted in 2015.[49] A federal district court ruled against DADT and, before the case could be appealed, Congress got rid of the policy.[50] DADT was replaced with a policy of nondiscrimination, effective September 2011. In 2016, President Obama opened the military to transgender individuals. The Trump administration, however, reinstituted the ban on transgender servicemembers except for those already serving in the military and serving in "their biological sex." The Supreme Court held by a vote of five to four that the policy could take effect pending the resolution of lawsuits about its validity; it remains in place.[51] The Biden administration reversed course again: transgender servicemembers are again eligible for military service.[52]

RIGHTS IN GENERAL

For most of U.S. history, same-sex behavior was a officially a serious crime. Sodomy was a felony.[53] An openly gay lifestyle was not legally possible. Gays and lesbians had to remain, as the saying goes, in the closet, for fear of arrest.

These laws were rarely questioned before the late twentieth century. In *Bowers v. Hardwick* (1986), in a five-to-four decision, the Court upheld anti-sodomy laws against the argument that these laws violated the constitutional right of privacy.[54] It remained risky business to be openly gay. Robin Shahar, a lawyer, learned this lesson the hard way. After receiving an offer to work in the Georgia attorney general's office, Shahar went through a "commitment" ceremony with her lesbian partner. The attorney general revoked her offer of employment; he quite logically took the ceremony as an admission that Shahar planned to violate the state law against sodomy. A federal appellate court upheld this decision.[55]

But public opinion was rapidly changing. Many states got rid of sodomy laws on their own. Sodomy laws survived mainly in the south and in a few other states (for example, Utah). Gay characters began to appear in favorable depictions in movies and on television. The creaking door of the closet began to open more and more. In *Lawrence v. Texas* (2003),[56] the Supreme Court struck down a Texas criminal law very much like the one the Court had upheld in *Bowers* only seventeen years earlier. Sodomy laws were unconstitutional. Adults had a right to have consensual personal relationships "in the confines of their homes and their own private lives."[57] *Lawrence*, on the surface, as usual, took the form of an interpretation of the text of the constitution, but of course the constitution had nothing in reality to say about the subject; the real force behind the opinion was a dramatic change in the culture: social acceptance of gay and lesbian behavior by a larger and larger percentage of the population. First one state (Massachusetts) and then a dozen more began to allow same-sex marriage.[58] And in 2015, in *Obergefell v. Hodges*,[59] a bare majority of the Supreme Court struck down all state bans on same-sex marriages.

Religious and social opposition to gay rights has diminished sharply but is far from dead. Social stigma is still a reality for gays and lesbians in many places, many situations, and many walks of life. Despite *Obergefell*, Kim Davis, a Kentucky county clerk, blatantly refused to issue marriage licenses to same-sex couples. This was, she said, against her religious convictions; ultimately, she chose a jail cell over compliance with the Supreme Court.[60] Many public officials—and many members of the general public—supported Davis's view. The Religious Freedom Restoration Act of 1993 subtly embodied this view.[61] Many states passed their own laws to protect religious freedom (freedom, that is, to dispense with the general law). And many devout people claimed a religious right to deny goods and services to LGBT people.[62] The war over gay rights goes on; the closet may ultimately go the way of pay phones, but it hasn't yet been boarded up. The whole country took part in the legal debate over the rights of a devout (and extremely talented) cake-baker who refused to bake a wedding cake for the wedding of a gay couple. The Supreme Court decided in favor of the cake-baker, but on very narrow grounds, and left the bigger issue open.[63]

The right to be openly gay in the workplace was another point of contention. Title VII of the Civil Rights Act of 1964 prohibits employers with at least fifteen employees from discriminating on the basis of race, color, religion, sex, or national origin.[64] Courts that considered the issue tended to hold that "sex" did not include "sexual orientation.[65] But change was coming.[66] The Supreme Court held in 1998 that Title VII could be applied to a situation in which a gay man was harassed by other workers.[67] Clearly, the court was responding to changes in the culture. But efforts since the 1970s to include, in federal anti-discrimination law, a prohibition against discrimination on the basis of sexual orientation, failed repeatedly.[68] Many states, however, added sexual orientation to local laws against discrimination. And even without a specific law, many large employers have adopted company policies against discrimination on the basis of sexual orientation.

Thus change was clearly on the way—in a period in which gay rights had made astonishing gains. In 2017, the Seventh Circuit Court of Appeals held in *Hively v. Ivy Tech Community College of Indiana* that Title VII prohibits workplace discrimination based on sexual orientation.[69] An openly gay professor sued her former employer, Ivy Tech Community College, for discriminating against her because of her sexual orientation. Kimberly Hively had been repeatedly denied advancement opportunities at Ivy Tech; she claimed that her status as a gay woman was the reason. The court held that Title VII prohibits discrimination on the basis of sexual orientation and gender identity.[70] This was the handwriting on the wall.

In 2020, the Supreme Court, in an important decision, adopted this point of view. The Court held in *Bostock v. Clayton County* that the word "sex" in Title VII did in fact refer to sexual orientation and gender identity. Gerald Bostock, who worked for Clayton County, Georgia, was fired after he joined a gay softball league. Aimee Stephens, who worked for a funeral home, was hired as a male, but she lost her job when she told her employers she planned to "live and work . . . as a woman."[71] Developments in the law, and in society, have sharply reduced the need for gays and lesbians to live double lives, but they do not eliminate the need by any means. A gay couple now has the right to marry, but, in many states, could lawfully be fired by a private employer for doing so. Prejudice remains. Families still reject some gay and lesbian children. Hate crimes still exist. It's no surprise that many gays and lesbians still feel that they had better stay in the closet—on the job, at home, and in the public sphere.

PASSING FOR MALE (OR FEMALE)

Gender impostors—the man who passes for a woman or the woman who passes for a man—are a rare but spectacular form of double life. A famous confidence artist in New Zealand, Amy Bock, in 1909 pretended to be a man named Percival Redwood. As "Percival Redwood," Amy even got herself engaged to a young woman. An elaborate wedding was planned but the bride found out Percy's secret; the marriage was annulled and Amy Bock was arrested.[72]

Billy Tipton was a famous jazz musician, a well-known figure in the music world of the twentieth century. In reality, Billy Tipton, the man, did not exist. Billy was really Dorothy Lucille Tipton. Dorothy wanted a career as a jazz artist but the field, she felt, did not welcome women. For this reason, she tried on a male identity and it worked. Later, she moved to Mississippi, and simply passed herself off as a man. Tipton even had sex as a man: she wore bindings that covered her breasts, made love in the dark, and used an artificial penis. Her partners apparently never guessed the truth. She lived with several women and adopted three boys. They had no inkling that their "father" was really a woman. In 1989, Tipton died at the age of seventy-four; when the body was examined, Billy's secret finally came out.[73]

A gender impostor was at the core of a well-known play, *M. Butterfly*, which was based on a real event. A French diplomat in China, Bernard Boursicot, in the 1960s, fell in love with a performer in Chinese opera, Shi Pei Pu. Shi Pei Pu looked like a man but convinced Boursicot that he was actually a woman who had been raised as a man to please his parents, who desperately wanted a boy. Bernard and Shi Pei Pu had sex, and Shi Pei Pu even claimed to give birth to a son; the child was, of course, not her biological child. This weird deception lasted some sixteen years; Boursicot engaged in espionage, passing secrets to the Chinese; the French government arrested him and his "wife," and only then did Boursicot learn that he had been living, in fact, with a man.[74]

The movie *Yentl*, with Barbara Streisand (1983), tells the story of a girl who posed as a man to penetrate the masculine world of Talmudic studies.[75] A man who posed as a woman in order to find work as an actor was the subject of the popular movie *Tootsie* (1982), starring Dustin Hoffman; there was a similar theme in *Mrs. Doubtfire* (1993), in which Robin Williams dressed up as a dowdy middle-aged woman and got himself hired as a housekeeper for his own family, in order to spend more time with his children after a divorce. Men, in Shakespeare's day, played women's roles, since women were barred from the stage. Thus, Lady Macbeth, Cleopatra, and all the rest of his heroines were played on the stage by men who specialized in women's roles.

In these examples of gender-bending (real and fictional), a new identity is assumed for professional, religious, or romantic ends. In most cases, no laws were broken. (Boursicot and his "wife" were in trouble for espionage, not for crossing the boundaries of gender.) Gender confusion is probably an old phenomenon. But modern medical technology, and modern sensibilities, have made it possible to cross over—or try to cross over—the line between male and female, to make up for what a person might think was a dreadful biological mistake. In some cases, the "man" in question becomes a "woman" through the surgical knife, hormones, and new ways of dressing and acting. The "woman" in question becomes a "man"; this is more difficult to do, but it too is possible. Is the person's new self the "true" identity—at least in the eyes of the law? In a Texas case, *Littleton v. Prange* (1999), Christie Littleton had her male sex organs removed; female ones were constructed.[76] In 1989, Christie married Jonathan Littleton. He died in 1996 and Christie brought a medical malpractice suit. The defendant, a doctor, claimed Christie was not a wife and could not be a wife under Texas law, and therefore had no right to bring any such lawsuit. The Texas court agreed. Christie Littleton was legally a man. Her marriage to Littleton was invalid and the lawsuit failed.

The Kansas Supreme Court adopted a similar posture in 2002.[77] J'Noel Ball, born a man, went under the knife to become an anatomical woman. She then married a rich old man, Marshall Gardiner. When Marshall died, she claimed a widow's share of the estate. No luck. To the Kansas Supreme Court, once a man, always a man. J'Noel of course looked like a woman, presumably behaved like a woman, and talked and dressed like a woman. To the court, however, J'Noel had a hidden, private essence, imprinted at birth, that could not be changed, no matter how much surgery was done, how many hormones swallowed, or how much role-playing was practiced.

Nonetheless, many states strike a more tolerant attitude toward transgender individuals, and do their bit to make the transition to new gender identity legal. In more than half of the states, the state will issue a new birth certificate to a transsexual who has undergone sexual reassignment surgery or has met other medical criteria; the new certificate will reflect the new name and the new sex, as if they had been assigned at birth.[78]

A transgender person in one of these permissive jurisdictions has gone through an interesting *social* process, as well as a psychological and medical one. This person began as two lives, in a sense: on the surface, a male life and underneath, a female sensibility (or vice versa). Then, after surgery and therapy, a new identity emerges, and the old life is relegated to the past. Lastly, in a sense, the old life is expunged from the records, as much as can be done. This may seem extreme: how can you wipe out the past? But the law allows second lives in other cases, too: records of juvenile delinquency can be expunged at the age of majority,[79] as can some kinds of criminal records as well. In many situations, then, people can live two lives—but serially, rather than simultaneously.

Modern medical science can, through the alchemy of medical technology, transform male into female and female into male. But this is only part of the story. A world of fluid identities opens up a world of possibilities. People are no longer required (socially speaking) to be "binary." Fluid identities also give wider scope for *choice*. Unlike in traditional societies, people in our society can shift aspects of their identity that were once more fixed—socially, if not legally. A born Catholic can become a Buddhist. A Buddhist can become a Muslim. In an age of expressive individualism, people are allowed—perhaps even encouraged—to change their styles of dress, their habits, their jobs, their religion, and their ways of life. And now, in cases of gender dysphoria, boys and girls may even be able to exchange their birth gender for something that fits more closely with their sense of who they are. Conservatives react in horror. To them biology is all. To change a person's sex is, in a sense, tampering with the natural order. Whatever private feelings a boy or girl may feel about sexual identity, those feelings must remain private. They cannot legitimately be acted upon, at least not in public.

Thus, in recent years, transgender individuals have been thrust into the political limelight; this particular minority group is now at the very center of political controversy. Bathroom use by transgender people has become a big issue. In conservative states, so-called bathroom bills aim to force transgender individuals to use the bathroom of the gender they were born with.[80] These bills have led to a storm of protest from civil liberties groups. The bills have led to boycotts and protests; for this reason, business groups have also entered the lists against them. Another huge controversy turns on membership in sports teams and sporting events. Can a person born male compete as a female? Unfortunately, this too has turned into a major political wedge issue that sharply divides liberals and conservatives.[81]

Gavin Grimm, a transgender high school student, born female, found himself embroiled in a dispute with his high school and school board in Virginia over bathroom policies in 2014; the high school had previously allowed Gavin to use the boy's restroom without incident, but the school board adopted a new policy after receiving complaints from parents and residents of the surrounding Gloucester County. The new policy required transgender students like Gavin to use "alternate" restroom facilities separate from those used by the general student population. Gavin teamed up with the ACLU to challenge the school board's action under Title IX, and the case made its way to the Fourth Circuit Court of Appeals. The district court had denied issuing an injunction; the appellate court overturned this decision and Gavin was thus able to use the boy's restroom at school.[82] The case was headed to the Supreme Court. But before the Court could hear the case, the Trump administration stepped in. Under President Obama, the Department of Education had issued guidelines that would require schools to let transgender students use the restrooms of their choice. The administration now rescinded these guidelines.[83] The Supreme Court dodged the issue, sending the case back to the Fourth Circuit for further consideration in light of the changed state of the guidelines.[84] Ultimately, Grimm won his case. He has a constitutional right to have a school identification card that reflects his correct gender—and a right to use the corresponding bathroom.[85]

PASSING FOR FAMILY: ADOPTION AND SOCIETY

In a 1996 British film, *Secrets and Lies*, Brenda Blethyn plays the role of Cynthia, a working-class woman whose somewhat pitiful life is changed dramatically by a phone call. The call is from a grown woman, who claims to be the daughter she gave up for adoption many years before.[86] The powerful story revolves around the sudden unraveling of secrets and lies of the past. One significant point in the plot: the daughter is black and the mother is white. But the secrets and lies relate mostly to the adoption itself—and the out-of-wedlock birth that precipitated it—rather than to the race of the biological father. In *Philomena*, a movie nominated for an Academy Award in 2014, the main character is an Irish woman who gave birth out of wedlock. She was sent with her baby to an institution run by nuns; the child was given away (or sold) to adoptive parents from America. Years later, Philomena sets out with a journalist to try to find the son she had been forced to give up.

At the nation's founding, the common law did not recognize legal adoption. The first general statute providing for adoption through a regular court proceeding was enacted in Massachusetts in 1851.[87] Every state eventually passed laws along more or less the same lines. These statutes made "parent-child relationships possible where blood could not."[88] Early in the twentieth century, states began to set up a process for establishing whether the prospective parents and the child were suitable for each other; some states allowed adoptive parents to back out if the child turned out to have some disease or defect that had been hidden at the time of the adoption.[89] Adoptions became more professionalized, with greater involvement of agencies, child welfare authorities, and private brokers.

In the early years of legal adoption, adoptions were a matter of public record. Many of the children were orphans. This was a time when many women died in childbirth, and both men and women were often carried off by disease. Frequently, relatives took in these orphan children. Later on, sex and shame, rather than death, were the source of the crop of babies needing adoption. It was at that point that adoption become shrouded in secrecy. The law made it possible to hide the very fact of adoption, and all the details, from the outside world. Both sets of parents were able to keep the adoption a deep, dark secret. Court records could be sealed and a new birth certificate issued, listing the adoptive parents as the natural parents. A 1930s Illinois law, for example, gave adoptive parents the right to a "clean" birth certificate, listing them and only them as the parents. The registrar was not permitted to indicate adoption or illegitimacy on the new record of birth.[90] Secrecy—or, perhaps more accurately, confidentiality—became the norm by the middle of the twentieth century. By the 1950s, every state followed procedures similar to those in Illinois. Thus, adoption in the twentieth century was characterized by "exclusivity, secrecy, and transposition"; the child was "taken from one family and given to another," the first family disappeared into the ether, and everyone proceeded "as if the first family never existed and the second was created through an act of nature."[91]

A second turn in adoption law extended the shroud of secrecy even further. Biological parents (usually just the mother) surrendered a child to an intermediary who selected adoptive parents and shepherded the child through the legal adoption procedures. The adoption was, in short, anonymous. The law protected the secret by sealing all information, even from the parties themselves. By the middle of the twentieth century, virtually all adoptions, if no relative or stepparent was involved, were "closed" and permitted "no disclosure or sharing of the identity" among the parties.[92] Philomena was never to know where her little boy had gone and the new parents never knew who the birth mother actually was.

Under this arrangement, the norm in adoption law and practice was a cluster of secrets. The system provided a clean slate for everyone concerned. Ideally, the birth mother resumed her life without the stain and shame of illicit sex and an illegitimate child; the child began a new life, free from the stain and shame of bastardy. The adoptive parents could decide who or what to tell about the birth of the child, but they had no cause to worry that a birth parent would suddenly show up. Indeed, the adoptive parents had no idea who the birth parents were and the birth parents had no idea who was raising their child. The state would deny any requests for information—from anyone. Adoptive placements also aimed to produce what we might call "biological plausibility." Infants were placed with younger women, who seemed like likely mothers. White children went with whites, black children with blacks, Catholic children with Catholic parents, and so on—all this to create an "as-if" family—"families in which children to all appearances might have been born to the adoptive parents."[93]

By the end of the twentieth century, this system had fallen apart. Many factors led to this change. Perhaps the most powerful was the passion of adopted children to know and find their roots. Adopted children grew up to be men and women who learned they had double lives, though not by choice. By the late 1970s, some of these children were demanding access to their original birth certificates; they wanted to know the names of at least one birth parent. They filed lawsuits claiming a constitutional right to know about their origins. These early lawsuits were, by and large, unsuccessful. Secrets were a protective shield for all concerned, according to the New Jersey Supreme Court. Sealed records saved the child "from any possible stigma of illegitimacy" and shielded a "loving and cohesive" relationship against the "invasion" of a "natural parent," who later on decided to "intrude into the relationship"; meanwhile, the birth parents are "free to move on and attempt to rebuild their lives."[94]

But social attitudes have changed and the law changed correspondingly. Under pressure from groups like Bastard Nation—the name tells a story in itself—and from birth mothers' groups like Concerned United Birthparents, many states took steps to make disclosure possible. Many have created registries to allow adopted children to find their birth parents—if the birth parents were willing. There are also private registries that help match up children and birth parents (again, with mutual consent); the largest is run by the Adoptees' Liberty Movement Association.[95] The first law to require disclosure without consent of the birth parent came in Oregon, through a voter referendum in 1998. Under this law, adopted persons born in Oregon who are twenty-one years of age or older have the right to request a copy of their original birth certificates, including the names and addresses of birth parents, as well as other identifying information.[96] A group of birth mothers unsuccessfully challenged the law.[97] They had various reasons for keeping their secrets: for example, some did not want to identify a rapist father or to reveal an unwed pregnancy. A few states now allow disclosure once an adopted child is legally an adult, or require birth parents to opt-out of disclosure.[98]

The closed, anonymous adoption has also now been almost entirely replaced by the so-called open adoption. That phrase can mean any number of things, but at its core it describes an adoption in which the birth parents know, and often select, the adoptive parents. There are no secrets.[99] Although most adoptive parents prefer the old, secret style of adoption, birth mothers prefer openness, and they call the shots. As the stigma of illegitimacy fades, socially as well as legally, many more unwed mothers keep their babies. Meanwhile, contraception and abortion are widespread and available; the result is a serious shortage of babies. Birth mothers who want to give up a baby for adoption can have dozens, even hundreds, of families to choose from. They often make openness a condition of the arrangement. They sometimes include the right to have contact with the child after the adoption. This, more than any effort to unseal old records, has driven the old system of secrets and lies out of adoption law. The adopted child and the birth mother no longer lead two lives. They lead a single life, punctuated with one significant event and its consequences.

The twists and turns in adoption law reflect, of course, social change. As we mentioned, illegitimacy no longer is a source of social stigma, at least to any appreciable degree. Nor is it any longer much of a *legal* stigma, either; thousands of couples cohabit and have children, without bothering to get married at all. This loss of stigma, as we mentioned, has affected the supply of babies and has driven many childless couples to seek adoption overseas. A high divorce rate means that huge numbers of children live with stepparents in "blended" families; huge numbers live in single-parent households or in gay households; some are the children of sperm donors and some have egg mothers and womb mothers, and so on. Very little of all this is secret; why, then, should adoption produce double lives? In addition, there is the modern passion for "roots," for knowledge of background, ethnicity, and family histories. The adoptive child shares this passion. And, last of all, advances in medical genetics gives adopted children yet another reason to want to explore their genetic backgrounds: they want to know more precisely what fates and what facts lie hidden in the genomes.

PASSING FOR HEALTHY

It is not only adopted children who want to know more about their genetic selves. The body today has given up some of its secrets. Scientists can now map the human genome. This information is also for sale. For example, 23andMe, a private company, will provide genetic information to customers based on their DNA, for a price.[100] The company can, it claims, uncover many hidden and private things about ourselves—secrets hidden in our genes and chromosomes. "Many Americans," the company tells us, "who consider themselves white or of European ancestry have African ancestry." This might well come as a shock to some people (fortunately, the "one-drop" rule is history). The company can reveal other aspects of the self, large and small: it has discovered "two genetic variants associated with whether a person's big toe or second toe is longer." It can also show a person the genetic factors that produce chin dimples, freckles, and "attached and unattached earlobes." More significant are genetic features related to disease: an "association between inherited variation in the JAK2 gene and rare blood cancers," and connections to Parkinson's disease and hyperthyroidism.[101] This can be vital information about someone's medical future. Are they carrying, inside their bodies, markers for some chronic or fatal disease? Many people, presumably, will want to know this information, coded inside their cells; others will prefer not to know.

Is there a downside to this kind of knowledge? If it became public, or semipublic, would it open the door to discrimination on the basis of genetics? Could employers use genetic information as an excuse not to hire a job applicant? In general, does a person have the right to keep this information secret? When people apply for insurance or a job, *must* they reveal what they know about their genes—*must* they reveal the risk of getting some awful disease? Should couples share this information with each other before they get married or have a child? People promise at the altar to stay together in sickness and in health, but do they really mean what they say? Can we live two lives in this new sense: a surface, healthy life, with a secret genetic time-bomb ticking underneath?

At the moment, this is less of a problem than one might think.[102] So far, it turns out, very few diseases are genetically inevitable. One dreaded example is Huntington's disease, a truly awful condition. Only people with a certain genetic defect will get this disease. There is no treatment and decline and death are unavoidable. But this is exceptional. There are other unavoidable conditions that, unlike Huntington's disease, can be treated. And in most cases, the genes are not destiny; they merely imply a certain increase in the risk—of Alzheimer's or diabetes or some other condition, for example. This is disturbing, of course, but it is not a death sentence. Life is full of risks. States forbid insurance companies from discriminating on the basis of genetics and genetic discrimination is not allowed in employment decisions.[103] Of course, no law forbids a young man or woman from breaking off an engagement after learning bad genetic news about a potential partner. How often this is likely to happen, to be sure, is unknown, and hard to predict.

Work on the human genome is in its infancy. As we find out more, predictions of disease and early death—or of chronic diseases or dementia—might become more precise and more unsettling. There are two privacy questions here: first, should we allow people to keep their genetic information to themselves, even if this has an influence on other people—for example, on an employer or a prospective mate? And second, should we prevent doctors, scientists, researchers, businesses, and law enforcement agencies from ferreting out genetic information, storing it, using it, or (worst of all) selling or promulgating it?

Most people, we feel, would say yes to both of these questions: keep this stuff private. Whether this is possible is another question. There are norms designed to protect the privacy of medical information. These norms, however, apply to hospitals, clinics, and other such institutions. It is a different question in the job market and in personal life. If the skeleton in your closet is a defective skeleton, should you be entitled to keep this private, to keep it a secret, under any and all circumstances? Can you be forced to tell the world, or some part of the world, or the government, about the hidden facts locked within your genome? If technology can unlock these secrets, who will hold the keys to this technology? These questions, today, are largely theoretical; tomorrow this may no longer be the case.[104] Ironically, then, in an age when light-skinned "blacks" can choose to be part of the white world or the black world as they choose, when thousands of gays and lesbians have come out of the closet, and where "open" adoption is the norm, a new closet may be forming: the genetic closet—the hiding place for the secrets stored inside our genes and chromosomes.

People's sexual lives are usually their own personal business as a matter of elective privacy, something they can and probably should keep to themselves. But an active sex life means partners, after all, and there are situations that may override the norm of privacy. Philippe Padieu, a Texas man diagnosed with AIDS, was charged in 2010 with six counts of aggravated assault with a deadly weapon. The deadly weapon was his own infected body. When his physician gave him the bad news about his HIV status, Padieu was warned of the risk of infecting others; he was told either to abstain from sex or to take measures to protect his partners. But Padieu ignored those warnings and had unprotected sex with six women, all of whom later tested positive for HIV. Worse, Padieu knew that he had infected some of the women, but continued to have unprotected sex with new partners, without telling them the facts. A local health department in 2007 ordered him to "cease and desist" sexual encounters without prior disclosure of his HIV status. But even that did not stop him; he had sex with another woman who was unaware of his condition.[105] He was eventually stopped by a posse of women; two former partners, having discovered that he had infected them, set out to identify and warn all his other victims. They watched his house, rifled through his trash, and approached women they saw coming or going. Eventually, they gathered enough evidence to interest police and prosecutors, who used an old law to tackle a new problem.[106] He was convicted and sentenced to a total of seventy years in prison for keeping his sexual history—and its consequences—secret.

The sudden eruption of the AIDS epidemic led states to pass laws relating to sexually transmitted infections (STIs or, in more dated parlance, STDs). Congress adopted the Ryan White Comprehensive AIDS Resources Emergency Act of 1990;[107] this law, later extended and reauthorized, provided federal money to states and communities to be used for low-income and uninsured people suffering with AIDS. One condition was that the states were required to pass laws making it a crime for infected people to transmit the virus in prohibited ways. Ryan White, a hemophiliac who was infected through a blood transfusion as a young adolescent, was an early victim of AIDS. He fought for the right not to be treated like a leper—to attend school and live as normal a life as possible, despite having a deadly disease with no known treatment. His fight drew attention to transmission of the virus and prompted significant legal, social, and medical changes to reduce the risk of exposure. Many HIV-specific laws were adopted during this period. Some criminalized all sexual acts between an HIV-infected person and a noninfected person.[108] But others only focused on those who passed for healthy but were secretly infected. The crime consisted of having sex without disclosing HIV status. An Arkansas law, for example, makes it a felony to engage "in sexual penetration with another person without first having informed the other person of the presence of [HIV]."[109] A countertrend has emerged since 2014, reflecting a decrease in stigma; six states have decriminalized the failure to disclose HIV status to sexual partners.[110]

Texas passed a statute on disclosure of STIs in 1989 but repealed it in 1993, long before Padieu infected anyone. But there was precedent in the state for using general criminal laws to stop the knowing spread of HIV. The development of antiretroviral drugs transformed HIV infections into a chronic but controllable disease, but before this development HIV was a death sentence. An HIV-positive prisoner, Curtis Weeks, was charged with attempted murder after he announced his status and then spit twice in the face of a correctional officer who was transferring him from one unit to another.[111] Weeks was agitated, fighting his restraints, and cursing and threatening the correctional officers. The jury found that Weeks, when he spat on the officer, intended to kill the officer. There was testimony at trial that Weeks "told everybody that he had AIDS and that he was going to take as many with him as he could." Experts testified that transmission of HIV through saliva might be possible, especially at more advanced stages when bleeding gums made it more likely that the saliva was laced with blood. Ultimately, Weeks was convicted of attempted murder and imprisoned for life; the sentence was affirmed in 1992.

HIV is not the only infection covered by some of these transmission laws. Many cover the whole spectrum of STIs. Florida's law makes it a crime to have sex without disclosing to a prospective partner "chancroid, gonorrhea, granuloma inguinale, lymphogranuloma venereum, genital herpes simplex, chlamydia, nongonococcal urethritis (NGU), pelvic inflammatory disease (PID)/acute salpingitis, . . . syphilis" or HIV infection.[112] And some of the laws cover activities other than sex—such as sperm donation or blood donation—where transmission of disease might be thought possible.[113]

Tort law reinforced the criminal laws that discouraged transmission without consent. Courts held that a person who knowingly transmits an STI, particularly if it results in significant harm, can be sued for damages. In the 1980s, a Minnesota man sued his former wife because he claimed she kept secret the fact that she had genital herpes before they began having sex. An appellate court in Minnesota agreed with him: people with genital herpes "have a duty either to avoid sexual contact with uninfected persons or, at least, to warn potential sex partners that they have herpes before sexual contact occurs."[114] The wife argued that a duty to disclose her infection constituted "an undue invasion of the law into the most private aspects of personal life."[115] On balance, the court felt, "society's interest in preventing the spread of a dangerous, incurable disease justifies some intrusion into personal privacy."[116]

The idea of a duty to disclose infectious diseases goes back more than a century. In Wisconsin, in the late nineteenth century, a father sent a servant to care for his sick child without telling her that the child had typhoid fever and then, after the servant discovered the truth, falsely reassured her that the disease was not contagious; the Wisconsin Supreme Court upheld a jury verdict against the father in 1896.[117] It was not much of a stretch to apply a similar principle to the transmission of venereal disease. Lacy Crowell prevailed in a lawsuit, reported in 1920, against her husband, who contracted a "vile and loathsome disease" (the traditional legal euphemism for an STI) by associating with "lewd and profligate women" (sex workers) and then infected her with it.[118]

In *Martin v. Ziherl* (2005), Muguet Martin sued a former sexual partner, Kristopher Ziherl, for infecting her with genital herpes.[119] He knew he was infected and failed to tell her, with predictable consequences. Kristopher filed a demurrer. At the time, it was illegal under Virginia law, he argued, for unmarried people to have sex. She had no right to sue, since she had committed an act that was against the law. In response, Muguet argued that Virginia's fornication law was obsolete; under modern privacy doctrine, the state could not make the simple act of sex before marriage a criminal offense. The Virginia Supreme Court agreed, clearing the way for the lawsuit.

Men like Kristopher Ziherl, Robert B., and the rest of this motley crew had done something that harmed their sex partner, in as obvious and literal a way as if they had committed rape, sexual battery, or, for that matter, any form of abusive behavior. "Privacy" was an issue only insofar as they (or more likely their lawyers) tried to use either the constitutional right of privacy, or some general notion about personal and intimate privacy, to get them off the hook. Those attempts failed. Nonetheless, there *is* a general right to keep secrets, to conceal a secret self, and even a right to lie; lying about a communicable disease, or failing to disclose it, is an egregious exception. A woman can pretend to have an orgasm, a man or woman can pretend to be in love, both can lie about sexual histories, about their bank accounts, about almost anything; and while all this might be reprehensible, the law has nothing to say about these aspects of personal privacy: they can be kept as private as one wishes. To be sure, getting married under false pretenses may lay the groundwork for an annulment, but that, too is somewhat exceptional. The general rule remains: telling a lie about one's private life is for the most part privileged.

A DUTY TO DISCLOSE

There are, however, exceptions to this general rule. Sometimes, disclosure of personal information—information about intimate details of life—may actually be required. Early in the twentieth century, couples who wanted to marry were obligated under the law in some states to first get a medical examination. People with venereal diseases were forbidden to marry in many states; some state laws called for specific laboratory tests for such diseases as syphilis and gonorrhea.[120] In the days before antibiotics, there were strong reasons for such requirements. Men, for example, often contracted the diseases from prostitutes; they could then pass the diseases on to innocent partners. In Ibsen's powerful play, *Ghosts*, written in the late nineteenth century, a leading citizen who led a secret life of sin, transmitted this fearful and incurable disease to his family. The powerful anti-vice laws of the late nineteenth and early twentieth century drew part of their strength from the fact that private sin had public consequences and that secrecy in sex put the health and lives of innocent women and children in danger. Courts generally upheld statutes on premarital testing. Society, said the Chief Justice of Wisconsin in a case decided in 1914, "has a right to protect itself from extinction and its members from a fate worse than death."[121] Requirements for blood tests and the like are now history, though as late as the 1970s, Ohio still required a doctor's statement affirming, based on a "standard serological test," that the applicants either did not have syphilis, or that the disease was "not in a state of that disease which is communicable."[122] In the late 1980s, Illinois briefly required marriage license applicants to undergo an HIV-AIDS test, but later backed off because of the cost, public objection, and the fact that residents of Illinois could and did go out of state to get married.[123] By the early 2000s, only a few states still required blood tests or other health certifications before marriage; in Mississippi, for example, a couple still had to take a blood test for syphilis.[124] In Indiana, a woman under age fifty had to provide a statement to show whether or not she was immune to rubella, a disease that can lead to birth defects if contracted by a pregnant woman. In Idaho, couples who wanted a marriage license were required to take a "confidential AIDS educational pamphlet" and "certify" that they had read it; they also had to answer a "confidential questionnaire" on the subject.[125] But Pennsylvania dropped the requirement of a test for syphilis in 1997, Oklahoma dropped it in 2004, and the District of Columbia dropped it in 2008.[126,127]

After antibiotics took away much of the terror of syphilis, fear of AIDS partially replaced it. Many states began to require HIV testing for pregnant women because of the assumed risk to newborn babies. In some states, testing is a standard component of routine prenatal care for pregnant women.[128] It is not required but women are strongly encouraged to do this. They may also be provided with information about the risks they might face. And even where a mother refuses testing and chooses to keep her HIV status unknown, some states require testing of newborns immediately following delivery.[129] A pregnant woman may not even be aware of her HIV status—or may not *want* to know it—but the state will pressure her to learn it, in order to share the information with her physician and other hospital staff members prior to giving birth

Moreover, if a patient tests positive for STIs, a clinic or testing facility is required to report those results to the relevant state health department, which sends a report, with personal information suppressed, to the Centers for Disease Control and Prevention. State laws may add a separate layer of protection by requiring those who test positive for certain diseases to notify their sexual partners, or, alternatively, may require healthcare providers to report the names of those partners if an infected patient refuses to report that information himself or herself. Here intrusion upon one person's privacy may be justified by the chance to mitigate the risk of harm to others.

This chapter and the previous chapter have been about role-playing in law and society, and about double lives—when and why these occur, how the law responds, and something of the social meaning of these double lives. The people who adopt a false identity constitute a diverse crew, a jumble of people and characters, all the way from spies and bigamists to people who are "passing" in one way or another. The choice to lie, cheat, steal, and manipulate identity, or, less negatively, to hide or simulate identity, is especially salient—and possible—in modern society, especially urban society. In a small, traditional village, roles are fixed, people know each other, and double lives are difficult and rare. Of course, people do role-play—they lie, they dissemble, they hide embarrassing facts. This has always been part of the human condition, but within limits. The modern world, on the other hand—the world since, say, 1800—is the golden age of duplicity, the high point of double living. Today, we may be on the brink of another major change, a full turn of the wheel—a world where a secret life is less and less possible, where all private selves can be exposed. It is still too early to tell.

In these chapters, we saw how social and geographic mobility make double lives—"passing" in the broadest sense—possible. In big cities, in the world of mass immigration, with shifting, restless populations, people bump elbows with strangers day in and day out. It is easier to hide one's "real" identity under these conditions. And it is harder to tell who people really are: their true names, place of birth, or status in society. It made "passing" a valuable strategy for those who were able to do so. It also opened the door to various kinds of fraud and chicanery.

Victorian society, and its American analogue, were famous for their rigid codes of morality and etiquette. But underneath it lay a more complex reality—a hidden world, for example, of very un-Victorian sexuality.[130] Victorian literature in its own way often exploited this duality. In Robert Louis Stevenson's famous novella, *The Strange Case of Dr. Jekyll and Mr. Hyde* (1886), the main character had two identities, one of them respectable, the other implacably evil. There are many ways to explain the meaning of this novella. But at the very least, the book presumes a society in which a double life is *possible*, and can be hidden from the world, perhaps forever.

We also mapped the direction of social change. "Passing" is surely less common today for certain groups: gays, for example. Is there movement in the other direction? Toward more "passing," rather than less? Perhaps not more—but different. Nobody in the nineteenth century worried about "identity theft." Today, people do. There are people, in short, who live two lives, one of them simply stolen from somebody else. In general, too, people can live many lives on the internet, and in social networks. Some of these lives are purely fanciful. A famous New Yorker cartoon showed a dog in front of a computer. The caption had the dog making this remark: "On the Internet nobody knows you're a dog." Blogs and social networks are, in some ways, like carnivals, where people wear masks and hide their identity. On the internet, nobody knows you are a dog or an imaginary person or a troll or a hacker; the internet provides a cloak of privacy, and at the same time, it can act as the deadly enemy of other people's privacy.

NOTES

1. "George Washington Professor Who Reportedly Faked Being Black Resigns," *NPR.org*, Sept. 10, 2020.
2. *Id.*
3. *See generally* C. Vann Woodward, *The Strange Career of Jim Crow* (Oxford, UK: Oxford University Press, 1955).
4. Michelle Alexander, *The New Jim Crow: Mass Incarceration in the Age of Colorblindness, 10th anniversary ed.* (New York: New Press, 2020), 33–34.
5. So, for example, as early as 1662, Virginia (Laws Va. 1662, Act xii) provided that "all children borne in this country shall be held bond or free only according to the condition of the mother."
6. *Va. Code Ann.* § 1–14 (1942) (repealed 2005); *Va. Code Ann.* § 67 (1924) (repealed 1976); *Va. Code Ann.* § 49 (1887) (repealed 1910). Also, in the section of the 1942 code dealing with miscegenation, a white person can only marry another white person, and a white person is a "person who has no trace whatsoever of any blood other than Caucasian," *Va. Code Ann.* § 5099a(5) (1942) (repealed 2005). *See also Loving v. Virginia*, 388 U.S. 1, 13 n.4 (1967).
7. Scott L. Malcomson, *One Drop of Blood: The American Misadventure of Race* (New York: Farrar, Straus and Giroux, 2000), 356. On "passing" in general, see Allyson Hobbs, *A Chosen Exile: A History of Racial Passing in American Life* (Cambridge, MA: Harvard University Press, 2014).
8. Annette Gordon-Reed, *The Hemingses of Monticello: An American Family* (New York: W. W. Norton & Company, 2008), 285. Three of the Hemings children "would live in the white world," and only one in the black world. *Id.* at 660.
9. The story is told in James M. O'Toole, *Passing for White: Race, Religion, and the Healy Family, 1820–1920* (Amherst: University of Massachusetts Press, 2002).
10. Daniel J. Sharfstein, *The Invisible Line: Three American Families and the Secret Journey from Black to White* (New York: Penguin Press, 2011).
11. In re *Torregano's Estate*, 352 P.2d 505 (Cal. 1960).
12. In *Loving v. Virginia*, 388 U.S. 1 (1967), the Supreme Court struck down Virginia's ban on interracial marriage, and, by implication, all such laws. *See generally* John DeWitt Gregory and Joanna L. Grossman, "The Legacy of Loving," *How. L. J.* 51 (2007): 15.
13. *See* Ariela J. Gross, *What Blood Won't Tell: A History of Race on Trial in America* (Cambridge, MA: Harvard University Press, 2008), 1–6.

14. On the *Rhinelander* case, see Earl Lewis and Heidi Ardizzone, *Love on Trial: An American Scandal in Black and White*, (New York: W. W. Norton & Company, 2001); Angela Onwuachi-Willig, *According to Our Hearts:* Rhinelander v. Rhinelander *and the Law of the Multiracial Family* (New Haven, CT: Yale University Press, 2013); Elizabeth M. Smith-Pryor, *Property Rites: The Rhinelander Trial, Passing, and the Protection of Whiteness* (Chapel Hill: University of North Carolina Press, 2009). Leonard Rhinelander appealed, but the trial court judgment was affirmed. *Rhinelander v. Rhinelander*, 219 N.Y. Supp. 548 (1927); the New York Court of Appeals affirmed without issuing an opinion, 157 N.E. 838 (N.Y. 1927).

15. Martha A. Sandweiss, *Passing Strange: A Gilded Age Tale of Love and Deception across the Color Line* (New York: Penguin Books, 2009).

16. *See* Adeel Hassan, "Activist Who Identified Herself as Black Takes an African Name," *New York Times*, Mar. 7, 2017.

17. This is the theme of the movie *Europa, Europa*, a 1990 film directed by Agnieszka Holland; it is about a young Jewish boy in Nazi Europe who successfully "passes" as an Aryan.

18. Kathleen Teltsch, "Scholars and Descendants Uncover Hidden Legacy of Jews in Southwest," *New York Times*, Nov. 11, 1990.

19. On pressure for racial assimilation in the modern workplace, see Devon W. Carbado and Mitu Gulati, "Working Identity," *Cornell L. Rev.* 85 (2000): 1259.

20. Dep't of Homeland Security, Office of Immigration Stats., Estimates of the Illegal Alien Population Residing in the United States: January 2015–January 2018, at 3 (2018).

21. Joseph Berger, "An Undocumented Princetonian," *New York Times*, Dec. 29, 2009.

22. David M. Herszenhorn, "Senate Blocks Bill for Young Illegal Immigrants," *New York Times*, Dec. 18, 2010.

23. Julia Preston and John H. Cushman, Jr., "Obama to Permit Young Migrants to Remain in U.S.," *New York Times*, June 15, 2012.

24. *See* "Memorandum on Rescission of Deferred Action for Childhood Arrivals (DACA)," U.S. Dep't of Homeland Sec., Sept. 5, 2017; Vanessa Romo et al., "Trump Ends DACA, Calls on Congress to Act," *NPR,* Sept. 5, 2017.

25. *Dep't of Homeland Security v. Regents of the University of California*, 140 S. Ct. 1891 (2020).

26. *See* Susan Davis and Scott Detrow, "White House Outlines Trump's Immigration Proposal," *NPR,* Jan. 25, 2018.

27. Press Release, Statement by President Biden on the American Dream and Promise Act of 2021, White House (Mar. 18, 2021), https://www.whitehouse.gov/briefing-room/statements-releases/2021/03/18/statement-by-president-biden-on-the-american-dream-and-promise-act-of-2021.

28. Since 2018, there has been a growing movement to abolish ICE, spurred by concern about its tactics and the over-criminalization of immigration issues. *See* Sean McElwee, "It's Time to Abolish Ice: A Mass-Deportation Strike Force is Incompatible with Democracy and Human Rights," *Nation*, Mar. 9, 2018.

29. *See generally* Angela S. Garcia and David G. Keyes, "Life as an Undocumented Immigrant: How Restrictive Local Immigration Policies Affect Daily Life," Ctr. Am. Progress, Mar. 26, 2012, https://www.americanprogress.org/issues/immigration/reports/2012/03/26/11210/life-as-an-undocumented-immigrant/.

30. Jose Antonio Vargas, "Not Legal Not Leaving," *Time*, June 25, 2012.

31. Mark Blasius and Shane Phelan eds., *We Are Everywhere: A Historical Sourcebook of Gay and Lesbian Politics* (Milton Park, UK: Routledge, 1997), 239.

32. "ACLU, 'Homosexuality and Civil Liberties' (1957)," in Mark Blasius and Shane Phelan, *supra* note 31, at 274–75.

33. For a comprehensive history on this subject, see David K. Johnson, *The Lavendar Scare: The Cold War Persecution of Gays and Lesbians in the Federal Government* (Chicago: University of Chicago Press, 2004); see also Margot Canaday, *The Straight State: Sexuality and Citizenship in Twentieth-Century America* (Princeton, NJ: Princeton University Press, 2009).

34. Interim Report, Sen. Comm. on Expenditures in the Executive Departments by Its Subcommittee on Investigations, "U.S. Senate, 'Employment of Homosexuals and Other Sex Perverts in Government' (1950)," in Mark Blasius and Shane Phelan, *supra* note 31, at 242.

35. *Id.*

36. *Id.* at 243.

37. A federal regulation provided that a civil service employee could be removed for "infamous . . ., immoral, or notoriously disgraceful conduct" and for "any . . . other disqualification which makes the individual unfit for the service." *See* 5 C.F.R. §§ 731.201(b), (g) (2012).

38. "ACLU, 'Homosexuality and Civil Liberties' (1957)," in Mark Blasius and Shane Phelan, *supra* note 31, at 250.

39. Johnson, *supra* note 33, at 121.

40. *Norton v. Macy*, 417 F.2d 1161 (D.C. Cir. 1969).

41. *Id.* at 1167.

42. E.O. 13087, 3 C.F.R. 13087 (1998).

43. E.O. 13672, 79 Fed. Reg. 72985 (2014).

44. For a list of anti-LGBT actions taken by the Trump administration, see Nat'l Ctr. for Transgender Equality, The Discrimination Administration, https://transequality.org/the-discrimination-administration.

45. On this history, see Allan Bérubé, *Coming Out Under Fire: The History of Gay Men and Women in World War Two* (New York: Free Press, 1990). As early as 1778, a man was dismissed on the basis of same-sex behavior.

46. National Defense Authorization Act of 1994, Pub. L. No. 103–160, 107 Stat. 1547 §571, codified as amended at 10 U.S.C. § 654 (2006).

47. About "Don't Ask, Don't Tell," Servicemembers Legal Def. Network, http://www.sldn.org/pages/about-dadt.

48. Military Readiness Enhancement Act (MREA) of 2007, H.R. 1246, 110th Cong., 1st Sess. (Feb. 28, 2007). Rep. Martin Meehan (D-Mass.) first introduced the MREA in the 109th Congress in March 2005; the bill gained 122 bipartisan cosponsors but failed to get past the House Armed Services Committee. See H.R. 1059,

109th Cong., 1st Sess. (Mar. 2, 2005). Rep. Meehan became Chairman of the House Armed Services Personnel Subcommittee and reintroduced the bill with 110 original cosponsors. A repeal bill passed the House in May 2010, but was voted down in the Senate. *See* 156 Cong. Rec. H4062-63 (daily ed. May 27, 2010); 156 Cong. Rec. S7246 (daily ed. Sept. 21, 2010).

49. Cheryl Pelleran, "Dept. Def., Carter Opens All Military Occupations, Positions to Women," *DOD News*, Dec. 3, 2015.

50. Don't Ask, Don't Tell Repeal Act of 2010, Pub. L. No. 111–321, §2(a)(2)(C), 124 Stat. 3515 (2010).

51. *See Trump v. Karnoski*, 139 S. Ct. 950 (2019), which stayed a lower court's injunction and allowed the ban to take effect pending litigation on the merits.

52. "Executive Order on Enabling All Qualified Americans to Serve Their Country in Uniform," White House, Jan. 25, 2021, https://www.whitehouse.gov/briefing-room/presidential-actions/2021/01/25/executive-order-on-enabling-all-qualified-americans-to-serve-their-country-in-uniform/.

53. *See, e.g.*, Ga. Code Ann. § 16–6–2 (West 2016), which authorized imprisonment for up to twenty years for a single act of consensual sodomy.

54. 478 U.S. 186 (1986).

55. *Shahar v. Bowers*, 114 F.3d 1097 (11th Cir. 1997). The Georgia Supreme Court struck down the state sodomy law in 1998, on the grounds that the right of privacy, under the state constitution, was broader than the federal right. *See Powell v. State*, 510 S.E.2d 18 (Ga. 1998).

56. 539 U.S. 558 (2003).

57. *Id.* at 567.

58. *See* Joanna L. Grossman, "From Zero to Fifty in Eleven Years: The Supreme Court Declares the Right of Same-Sex Couples to Marry in *Obergefell v. Hodges*," *Justia's Verdict*," June 26, 2015.

59. 576 U.S. 644 (2015).

60. Tamar Lewin, *Clerk in Kentucky Chooses Jail Over Deal on Same-Sex Marriage* (Sept. 3, 2015).

61. See 42 U.S.C. § 2000bb-1 (2018).

62. *See* Mahin Aminian et al., "Legal Recognition of Same-Sex Relationships," *Geo. J. Gender & L.* 18 (2017): 711, 737–41.

63. *Masterpiece Cakeshop v. Colorado Civil Rights Commission*, 138 S. Ct. 1719 (2018).

64. 42 U.S.C. 2000e *et seq.* (2018).

65. *See, e.g., Simonton v. Runyon*, 225 F.3d 122 (2d Cir. 2000).

66. In 1989, in *Price Waterhouse v. Hopkins*, the Supreme Court held that using sex stereotypes, say, by insisting a woman should not be "macho," or show up at work without makeup, is a form of sex discrimination. 490 U.S. 228 (1989). Antonio Sanchez was a gay, effeminate waiter. His co-workers mocked him for carrying a serving tray "like a woman" and for being a "faggot" and a "female whore." They called him "she," in Spanish and English. He sued for sexual harassment and won. The 9th Circuit upheld the verdict; the abuse was aimed at Sanchez because he did not act "as a man should act" and did not conform to "gender-based stereotypes"

but Antonio had a right to be himself at work. See *Nichols v. Azteca Restaurant Enterprises, Inc.*, 256 F.3d 864 (9th Cir. 2001).

67. *Oncale v. Sundowner Services*, 523 U.S. 75 (1998).

68. *See, e.g.*, S.811, A Bill to Prohibit Employment Discrimination on the Basis of Sexual Orientation or Gender Identity, 112th Cong., 1st Sess. (2011); H.R. 1397, A Bill to Prohibit Employment Discrimination on the Basis of Sexual Orientation or Gender Identity, 112th Cong., 1st Sess. (2011).

69. *Hively v. Ivy Tech Cmty. Coll. of Indiana*, 853 F.3d 339, 349 (7th Cir. 2017).

70. *Id.* at 341–42. The court argued that sexual orientation discrimination did fall within the realm of sex discrimination prohibited by Title VII, stating "[a]ny discomfort, disapproval, or job decision based on the fact that the complainant . . . dresses differently, speaks differently, or dates or marries a same-sex partner, is a reaction purely and simply based on sex. That means that it falls within Title VII's prohibition against sex discrimination." *Id.* at 347.

71. *Bostock v. Clayton County*, 140 S. Ct. 1731 (2020).

72. The story of Amy Bock is told in Jenny Coleman, *Mad or Bad? The Life and Exploits of Amy Bock* (Dunedin, New Zealand: Otago University Press, 2010).

73. Her story is told in Diane Middlebrook, *Suits Me: The Double Life of Billy Tipton* (London: Virago Press, 1999).

74. Joyce Wadler, "The True Story of M. Butterfly: The Spy Who Fell in Love with a Shadow," *New York Times Magazine*, Aug. 15, 1993.

75. *Yentl* was based on a play of the same name, which was in turn based on a short story by Isaac Bashevis Singer.

76. 9 S.W.3d 223 (Tex. App., 1999).

77. *In re Estate of Gardiner*, 42 P.3d 120 (Kansas, 2002).

78. *See generally* Dean Spade, "Documenting Gender," *Hastings L. J.* 59 (2008): 731.

79. On this issue, see T. Markus Funk, "A Mere Youthful Indiscretion? Reexamining the Policy of Expunging Juvenile Delinquency Records," *U. Mich. J. L. Reform* 29 (1996): 885.

80. These bills appeal to (completely unfounded) fears of male sexual predators disguising themselves to gain access to women's restrooms. In fact, transgender people are actually the ones at risk of assault. This has not stopped some states from passing or threatening to pass these "bathroom bills."

81. On recent efforts to exclude transgender girls from girls' sports teams, see Joanna L. Grossman and Saraswati Rathod, "Trashing the Playing Field: State Legislators' Misguided Move to Ban Transgender Women and Girls from Competing in Women's Sports," *Justia's Verdict*, April 27, 2021.

82. *G.G. ex rel. Grimm v. Gloucester Cty. Sch. Bd.*, 822 F.3d 709, 726 (4th Cir. 2016), *cert. granted in part*, 137 S.Ct. 369 (2016), and *vacated and remanded*, 137 S.Ct. 1239 (2017).

83. *See* Jeremy W. Peters et al., "Trump Rescinds Obama Directive on Bathroom Use," *New York Times*, Feb. 23, 2017, at A1.

84. *Gloucester Cty. Sch. Bd. v. G.G. ex rel. Grimm*, 137 S. Ct. 1239 (2017).

85. *Gloucester Cty. Sch. Bd. v. G.G. ex rel. Grimm*, 972 F.3d 586 (4th Cir. 2020).

86. *Secrets and Lies* (Channel Four Films 1996).

87. Laws Mass. 1851, ch. 324, p. 815.

88. Chris Guthrie and Joanna L. Grossman, "Adoption in the Progressive Era: Preserving, Creating and Re-Creating Families," *J. Am. Leg. Hist.* 43 (1999): 235; see also Stephen B. Presser, "The Historical Background of the American Law of Adoption," *J. Fam. L.* 11 (1971): 443; Joanna L. Grossman and Lawrence M. Friedman, *Inside the Castle: Law and the Family in 20th Century America* (Princeton, NJ: Princeton University Press, 2011), 305–29.

89. A 1917 Minnesota statute, for example, required the state board of control to consider whether the child was a "proper subject for adoption" and allowed the parents to annul the adoption if the child unexpectedly developed "feeble-mindedness, epilepsy, insanity or venereal infection as a result of conditions existing prior to the adoption." 1917 Laws Minn. ch. 22.

90. 1931 Laws Ill., p. 734; 1937 Laws Ill., p. 1006; Ill. Rev. Stat. 1939, ch. 111 ½ secs. 48a, 57.6.

91. Annette Ruth Appell, "Blending Families through Adoption: Implications for Collaborative Adoption Law and Practice," *B. U. L. Rev.* 75 (1995): 997; *see also* Adam Pertman, *Adoption Nation: How the Adoption Revolution Is Transforming America* (New York: Basic Books, 2000); E. Wayne Carp, *Family Matters: Secrecy and Disclosure in the History of Adoption* (Cambridge, MA: Harvard University Press, 1998).

92. Joel D. Tenenbaum, "Introducing the Uniform Adoption Act," *Fam. L. Q.* 30 (1996–1997): 333, 334.

93. Mary Lyndon Shanley, *Making Babies, Making Families: What Matters Most in an Age of Reproductive Technologies, Surrogacy, Adoption, and Same-Sex and Unwed Parents* (Boston: Beacon Press, 2001), 12.

94. *Mills v. Atlantic City Dep't of Vital Statistics*, 372 A.2d 646, 649 (N.J. 1977).

95. On this and other aspects of adoption in the United States, see the extensive materials of the Adoption History Project, https://pages.uoregon.edu/adoption/about.html. On advocacy for birth parents, see also Nadine Brozan, "Parents Who Gave Up Babies Organize to Gain New Rights," *New York Times*, Jan. 23, 1978.

96. Oregon Ballot Measure 58 (1998).

97. *See Doe 1 v. State*, 993 P.2d 822 (Ore. 1999).

98. *See* Alaska Stat. § 18.50.500 (2016); Kan. Stat. Ann. § 65–2423 (2005); Tenn. Code Ann. §§ 36–1–125 to 129 (2017); see also M. Christina Rueff, "A Comparison of Tennessee's Open Records Law with Relevant Laws in Other English-Speaking Countries," *Brandeis L. J.* 37 (1998–1999): 453. Alabama granted a child a blanket right to see the original birth certificates upon reaching adulthood but then changed the law. Now there is an automatic right only to nonidentifying information about background and circumstances of birth. Information revealing who the birth parents were, however, can be granted by court order or if the birth parents, after an intermediary contacts them, give their consent. Ala. Code § 26–10A-31 (LexisNexis 2016). For an example of an opt-out approach, see 2009 Ill. H.B. 5428 (enacted May 21, 2010). Before this Act, an adoptee could find his or her birth parents only if they had signed up for the state's Adoption Registry and Medical Information Exchange.

99. See, for example, Susan Livingston Smith, *Safeguarding the Rights and Well-Being of Birth Parents in the Adoption Process* (New York: Evan B. Donaldson Adoption Institute, 2007), 6, 19.

100. Human beings all have twenty-three chromosomes; hence the name of the company.

101. This information is from the company's website, https://www.23andme.com/genetic-science.

102. See, for a discussion, Henry T. Greely, "Genotype Discrimination: The Complex Case for Some Legislative Protection," *U. Pa. L. Rev.* 149 (2001): 1483.

103. Henry T. Greely, "Banning Genetic Discrimination," *New England J. of Medicine* 353 (2005): 865.

104. Obviously, there are many occasions where people are forced to swear an oath and tell the truth—witnesses in court, for example, who are supposed to tell the truth, the whole truth, and nothing but the truth, on pain of prosecution for perjury.

105. *See Padieu v. State*, No. 05–09–00796-CR, 2010 WL 5395656 (Tex. Ct. App. 2010), which upheld Padieu's conviction by a jury.

106. *See* Shana Druckerman and Susan Welsh, "How Women United to Stop HIV-Positive Man," *ABC News,* Sept. 11, 2011.

107. Pub. L. No. 101–381, 104 Stat. 576 (1990).

108. *See, e.g.,* Md. Code Ann., Health-Gen. § 18–601.1 (LexisNexis 2020) (which makes it a misdemeanor to knowingly transfer HIV to another person); N.Y. Pub. Health Law § 2307 (McKinney 2020) ("Any person who, knowing himself or herself to be infected with an infectious venereal disease, has sexual intercourse with another shall be guilty of a misdemeanor").

109. Ark. Code Ann. § 5–14–123 (2020).

110. *See* Jenny Whidden and Nara Schoenberg, "Illinois Legislators Approve Bill that Would Decriminalize HIV Transmission," *Chicago Tribune*, May 25, 2021.

111. *Weeks v. Texas*, 834 S.W.2d 559 (Tex. App. 1992), which upheld Weeks's conviction.

112. Fla. Stat. Ann. § 384.24 (West 2020).

113. *See, e.g.*, Tenn. Code Ann. § 39–13–109 (2020), which provides that a person commits a crime if he or she "[t]ransfers, donates, or provides blood, tissue, semen, organs, or other potentially infectious body fluids or parts for transfusion, transplantation, insemination, or other administration to another in any manner that presents a significant risk of HIV, HBV, or HCV transmission."

114. *R.A.P. v. B.J.P.*, 428 N.W.2d 103, 108 (Minn. 1988). The doctrine of inter-spousal tort immunity, hanging on in some jurisdictions, no longer seems to bar these types of suits. *See, e.g.*, *S.A.V. v. K.G.V.*, 708 S.W.2d 651 (Mo. 1986), which held that spousal immunity was not a bar to a cause of action for negligent transmission of herpes; *G.L. v. M.L.*, 550 A.2d 525 (N.J. Super. Ct. Ch. Div. 1988), which held that a wife's claim for transmission of herpes was not barred by interspousal immunity.

115. *R.A.P.*, 708 S.W.2d at 109.

116. The duty to disclose is for single as well as married people. In *Kathleen K. v. Robert B.*, 198 Cal. Rpt. 273 (Cal. Ct. App, 1984), a woman sued a former sexual partner who, she alleged, had lied about his STD status and infected her with genital

herpes. He argued that constitutional protection for privacy meant the court could not get involved in the private sexual matters of consenting adults. But, the court said, the right of privacy "is not absolute" and must give way to the social interest in protecting peoples' health. Robert also argued that he had no duty to disclose because he and Kathleen were not in a trust relationship, one that required honesty. The court disagreed, however; all intimate relationships involve "a certain amount of trust and confidence" and require the telling of truth.

117. *Kliegel v. Aitken*, 69 N.W. 67 (Wis. 1896).

118. *Crowell v. Crowell*, 105 S.E. 206, 207 (N.C. 1920). The court rejected the husband's claim that interspousal tort immunity prevented the suit from going forward. "Wives are no longer chattels. There are half a million women voters in North Carolina. They do not need to beg for protection for their persons, their property, or their characters." The rule of immunity "is not, and never has been" embodied in a statute, according to the court; it was, rather, "an inference drawn by courts in a barbarous age, based on the wife being a chattel and therefore without any right to property or person." *Id.* at 210.

119. *Martin v. Ziherl*, 607 S.E.2d 367 (Va. 2005).

120. *See* Note, "Pre-Marital Tests for Venereal Disease," *Harv. L. Rev.* 53 (1939): 309.

121. *Peterson v. Widule*, 147 N.W. 966 (Wis., 1914).

122. Ohio Rev. Code § 3101.5 (1972).

123. *See* Isabel Wilkerson, "Illinoisans Fault Prenuptial AIDS Tests," *New York Times*, Apr. 16, 1988, at 6.

124. Miss. Code Ann. § 93–1–5(e) (2010) (repealed 2012).

125. Idaho Code Ann. § 32–412A (2010); *see also* Georgia Code Ann. § 19–3–35.1 (2010).

126. Pa. Cons. Stat. Ann. §§ 23–1304 and 1305 contained the requirement until abolition. *See* Okla. Laws 2004, c. 333, § 3, which repealed 43 Okla. St. § 31; D.C. Law 15–154 (2003).

127. *See, e.g.*, Idaho Code Ann. § 32–412A (2010); Mont. Code Ann. § 40–1–203 (2017).

128. *See, e.g.*, Mont. Code Ann. § 50–16–1015 (2017); N.J. Stat. Ann. § 26:5C-16 (West 2007); Va. Code Ann. § 54.1–2403.01 (2013).

129. *See, e.g.*, Kan. Stat. Ann. § 65–6018(b) (2017).

130. *See generally* Ronald Pearsall, *The Worm in the Bud: The World of Victorian Sexuality* (New York: Penguin Books, 1983).

Chapter 8

The Eyes That Never Sleep: Surveillance and Society

A shocking crime made headlines all over the country on April 15, 2013. Bombs went off at the Boston Marathon, near the finish line. Three people were killed and more than 250 were injured.[1] Who could have committed this awful crime? No individuals or groups claimed credit. Yet the persons responsible for this crime were identified quickly: two young brothers of Chechneyan descent. The key evidence was provided by surveillance cameras. A massive manhunt followed. In the end, one of the brothers was killed; the younger brother was captured, put on trial, convicted, and sentenced to death.

Surveillance cameras were, in short, the heroes of this particular tale. These cameras (closed circuit television [CCTV]) are more and more of a presence in our cities. No one could have been surprised (unless the two brothers were) that these cameras, with their beady electronic eyes, were keeping watch over the finish line of the Boston Marathon. In our day, these cameras seem to be everywhere: in the lobbies of apartment buildings, in banks, in subway stations, in most public buildings, and, notably, on streets and highways. The constant presence of these cameras, these watching eyes, does not seem to bother the general public. They accept these cameras almost without question. A poll in 2007 showed that more than 70 percent of Americans were in favor of putting more cameras in public places as part of the battle against crime. Only about 25 percent of the respondents seemed to express any doubts.[2] The Boston Marathon incident helps explain why. It is a question of protection and security. We live in a dangerous world. We need ways to find, identify, and punish criminals—like the Boston Marathon bombers. This is exactly what the cameras are supposed to accomplish and what, in this particular case, they actually did.

People also use cameras and other devices to protect their homes. One company, which markets "hidden cameras" for monitoring homes and offices, boasts that some of its products feature "night vision, motion activation, and portability"; you can also take the device with you on the road and use it to "monitor a hotel room while on a business trip."[3] Little cameras can be hidden virtually anywhere: in smoke detectors, wall outlets, and even wristwatches. Retailers like Home Depot sell a wide range of cameras, which customers presumably buy to protect their homes from whatever it is that they fear. You can find all sorts of these devices online, everything from tiny cameras disguised as alarm clocks or concealed inside a photo frame. On the other hand, you can also buy "bug detectors" to detect the presence of a covert recording device. Home Depot even has fake security cameras for sale; these are marketed as affordable and effective alternatives that give your home the appearance of being monitored.[4]

Nobody finds it objectionable if a family installs cameras in the home to watch over a sleeping baby or to be on the lookout for intruders; after all, countless families have burglar alarms, which nobody questions. But if certain movies and TV shows are to be believed, surveillance devices can be used for less defensible purposes. They can be, for example, secretly installed in somebody else's home and used to spy on the people who live there. More on this later.

The general point, though, seems solid: people are more and more willing to accept cameras—and other devices—in public places and public institutions as a way of preventing crime and catching criminals. They accept body scanning devices at airports, and metal detectors in courthouses. Fighting crime—and fighting terrorists—have become among the paramount goals of public policy, important enough that people are willing to bargain away some of their privacy rights to achieve these objectives. Many people, in fact, would like even more protective surveillance.[5] And people are getting what they want. The pendulum has swung very far—perhaps too far—in this particular direction.

What direction is that? In the direction toward what has been called the surveillance society—a term that came into use most likely in the 1980s.[6] There is a large literature on the subject. Tons of books and articles pour off the presses—not to mention more transient materials. Ordinary people, too, are talking about the pros and cons of massive surveillance.

But first, we should distinguish between *overt* and *covert* surveillance. Cameras placed on street corners and in banks are open and obvious. By contrast, wire-tapping and the actions of the Central Intelligence Agency (CIA), the Federal Bureau of Investigation (FBI), the National Security Agency (NSA), and foreign equivalents are covert; their actions are closely held state secrets. We should also distinguish between *state* and *private* surveillance. And perhaps also between what we could call *pinpoint* surveillance (for example, wire-tapping a single individual) and *mass* surveillance and data-mining (gathering information on whole classes of people, or perhaps even an entire population).

HOW DID WE GET TO THIS POINT?

We begin with a consideration of the threat to privacy from the state.

Invasion of privacy by Big Brother has been a concern since the beginning of the American republic, and of course much earlier. The Constitution does not use the word *privacy* (at the time, nobody did, at least not in its modern sense), but the Fourth Amendment to the Bill of Rights guaranteed the right of the people "to be secure in their persons, houses, papers, and effects, against unreasonable searches and seizures." Search warrants were to issue only "upon probable cause," and the warrant had to describe what was to be searched and which persons or things could be seized.[7]

The Constitution, naturally, reflects its period, the concerns of its period, and also the technology of its period. The Constitution was drafted long before the technological revolution in modes of communication—and modes of search and seizure. George Washington had no telephone. The invention of the telephone led, perhaps inexorably, to the invention of wire-tapping. In *Olmstead v. United States*,[8] the Supreme Court had to consider the issue for the first time: was tapping a person's phone a violation of the Fourth Amendment? The case was decided during the Prohibition era. The defendant in the case, Olmstead, was a big-time violator; he was part of a "conspiracy of amazing magnitude" bringing liquor into Washington State from Canada. This conspiracy employed fifty people; various boats; a ranch; a "large underground cache for storage" along with smaller caches in Seattle; a "central office manned with operators"; and "executives, salesmen, deliverymen, dispatchers, scouts, bookkeepers, collectors, and an attorney."[9] The government's case against Olmstead, however, depended in large part on evidence gathered through a rather elaborate and extensive wire-tapping scheme; by virtue of this scheme, the government compiled a huge dossier, which they deployed in an effort to destroy Olmstead's crime ring and put him in jail.

A bare majority of the Supreme Court voted to uphold Olmstead's conviction. To Chief Justice Taft, the Fourth Amendment could not "be extended and expanded to include telephone wires. . . . There was no searching. There was no seizure. . . . There was no entry of the houses or offices of the defendants."[10] Four justices, however, dissented. Justice Oliver Wendell Holmes Jr. called wire-tapping a "dirty business." And Justice Brandeis made a comment that was remarkably prescient: the "progress of science," he said, "in furnishing the government with means of espionage is not likely to stop with wiretapping." Brandeis also pointed out that when a telephone is tapped, "the privacy of the persons at both ends of the line is invaded, and all conversations between them upon any subject . . . may be overheard." Also, tapping one person's phone "involves the tapping of the telephone of every other person whom he may call, or who may call him."[11]

Perhaps the background of the case—the Prohibition era—was significant. Prohibition was, politically speaking, a failure. It was unpopular, difficult to enforce, and, in the cities at least, evasion was epidemic. The avid "drys" were eager to ramp up enforcement. Heroic measures, they thought, could make Prohibition work; technical niceties should not be allowed to stand in the way. As violations flourished, the "drys" demanded a more vigorous crackdown. Later, "wars" on drugs, crime, and terror tempted the government to take even more drastic steps. And Brandeis's comment—that tapping A's phone has the effect of tapping the phones of many people—is applicable to data-gathering from phones and other sources in our own times.

Olmstead was a narrow, five-to-four decision; Congress, in the Communications Act of 1934, criminalized wiretapping and made wiretap evidence inadmissible in federal courts.[12] Some cases in the 1940s read the Fourth Amendment in a rather pinched and narrow way. In *Goldman v. United States*[13] (1942), the government had secretly used a Dictaphone to pick up conversations in another room. But since there was no physical intrusion, this act did not, in the Court's judgment, violate the Fourth Amendment.

The wheel turned dramatically in *Katz v. United States* (1967), which explicitly overruled the Olmstead case.[14] Charles Katz was running an illegal gambling business. To get evidence against him, federal agents tapped a public phone booth that Katz used to transact business. They had no warrant. The Court found this unconstitutional. As Potter Stewart put it, "[T]he Fourth Amendment protects people, not places"; what a person "seeks to preserve as private" should be protected, even if it takes place "in an area accessible to the public."[15] The government had pointed out that this particular phone booth was partly glass, and therefore plainly visible to the outside world. But, Stewart said, the case did not turn on the "intruding eye," but rather on the "uninvited ear." John Marshall Harlan, concurring, took an even broader view. Harlan stressed the importance of one's "actual (subjective) expectation of privacy," assuming, of course, that this expectation was "reasonable."[16]

"Reasonable expectation of privacy" has become a key concept in the law of privacy. Oceans of ink have been spilled over the meaning of this notion. It remains, however, as slippery as an eel. How can we know when and where people expect their privacy to be protected? How can we guess the parameters of the privacy they want to protect? How can we decide whether their views and opinions are "reasonable?" And, of course, what counts as "reasonable" changes over time? Little by little, privacy erodes and people hardly notice the process. What was once a reasonable expectation gradually becomes unreasonable, like the proverbial frog that boils to death, wholly unaware of its fate, in water that only slowly gets hotter. There's no question that travelers in the old days had a reasonable expectation of bodily privacy in airports, and might have objected strongly to luggage searches, body scans, pat-downs, and the like. But would that expectation still be considered reasonable today?

Kyllo v. United States (2001) illustrates how tricky these issues have become.[17] In 1991, a government agent, William Elliott, suspected that Danny Kyllo, who lived in a triplex on Rhododendron Drive in Florence, Oregon, was growing marijuana in his home. To grow this crop indoors, you need high-intensity lamps. One night, Elliott and another agent equipped themselves with an "Agema Thermovision 210 thermal imager" and drove to the street outside Kyllo's place; seated in the agent's car, they scanned the triplex from two angles. The imager was designed to "detect infrared radiation" and convert the radiation "into images based on relative warmth—black is cool, white is hot." The scan convinced Agent Elliott that Kyllo was "using halide lights to grow marijuana." A judge issued a warrant; Kyllo's home was searched, and the agents found more than one hundred marijuana plants. Kyllo was indicted for violating drug laws. He moved to suppress the evidence seized from his home. The issue was whether the use of thermal imaging constituted a "search" under the Fourth Amendment.[18]

A bare majority of the Court came to the conclusion that it did, and that the Fourth Amendment had been violated. The opinion laid heavy stress on the "sanctity of the home." The dissent argued that "observations of the exterior of the home" made with a "fairly primitive thermal imager" did not invade the right of privacy. The case added a point to an already vast storehouse of case law, theory, and discussion about the Fourth Amendment and the technical requirements of the law on warrants. Two points, however, can be made about cases like *Kyllo*. First, Brandeis was right: technology that can invade privacy advances by leaps and bounds. And second—Brandeis hinted at this—as that technology advances, the willingness (and indeed eagerness) of authorities to use that technology for their own ends also advances and grows. After all, *Kyllo* simply held that thermal imaging was an actual search; if, in the next case, the police went to the trouble of obtaining a warrant *before* using the thermal device, there would be no legal problem. Hence the question would be how much it would take to persuade a judge to issue a warrant. Presumably, not very much. Hence, *Kyllo* in a way put a stamp of approval on one device, and perhaps all devices, that can see or hear or smell or sense what goes on inside a private home.

Olmstead came out of a Prohibition context, *Katz* involved gambling, and *Kyllo* dealt with marijuana and drug laws. In all of these cases, the government was trying to enforce laws that were at least somewhat controversial or even unpopular. The war on drugs is not as savage a war as the war on terrorism, but it invokes a certain amount of zeal on the part of authorities. In 2013, the Supreme Court had to decide whether the Fourth Amendment allowed authorities to bring a dog, trained to sniff out drugs, onto a homeowner's porch.[19] The police had gotten a tip that Joelis Jardines (like Kyllo) was growing marijuana in his home in southern Florida. A detective took a "drug-sniffing dog" on a six-foot leash onto Jardines's porch. The dog detected the odor of drugs and then sat at the base of the front door, which it had been trained to do "upon discovering the odor's strongest point." On the basis of the dog's behavior, the police got a warrant and (no surprise) found marijuana plants inside the house. Was taking the dog onto the porch to sniff around a "search?" A majority of the Supreme Court said yes; thus it required a warrant. A concurring opinion added that it was also an invasion of privacy. Again, as in *Kyllo*, the warrant was the issue. Had a judge issued a warrant, there would have been no problem with the dog.

In these cases, the government (usually meaning the police) arguably invaded a person's privacy in a precise and overt way. There is a long and rather shameful history of government, and not just the police, amassing files, documents, dossiers, and mounting surveillance on large numbers of people. Notoriously, the FBI, under the leadership of J. Edgar Hoover, kept files and conducted surveillance on whomever Hoover defined as dangerous or as an enemy of the people. The FBI, under Hoover's powerful but somewhat paranoid leadership, cast its beady eyes on bank robbers and other common criminals, but also on communists, fellow travelers, and leftists in general. Hoover and his immediate successors also made war on pornography and pornographers.[20] Hoover's list of "enemies" included such unlikely targets as civil rights leaders, including even Martin Luther King Jr. Since Hoover's death, the FBI has presumably toned down some of its most egregious behavior, but surely not all of it. And the FBI plays a significant role in the "war on terror."

It would be wrong to think of Hoover as a kind of rogue elephant. He was probably more sinister, and more powerful, than his counterparts, both here and abroad. But countries typically spy on, or at least monitor, whoever the regime in power considers its enemies. This practice is certainly not confined to the United States of America. One example out of many is the egregious campaign of the West German government against leftists in the 1970s under the so-called Anti-Radical Decree. This campaign, like Hoover's, straddled the border line between individual and mass surveillance. The German government, in 2020 and 2021, has mounted a campaign against the opposite end of the political spectrum: neo-Nazis and fringe elements of the right wing, particularly in the army and local law enforcement units.

The Supreme Court took up this issue again in 2018 when it considered whether the government's use of cell-site location information (CSLI) to determine whether several robbery suspects were at the scene of the crime. Cell phones work by connecting to "cell sites"—radio antennas that now blanket the country. Each time a phone "pings" a cell site, it creates a time-stamped record with the CSLI. Wireless carriers continuously collect this data, which they use for a variety of business purposes. In *Carpenter v. United States*, the FBI got a court order to obtain CSLI for several robbery suspects (ironically sought for robbing cell phone stores) whose cell phone numbers it had identified.[21] The order was authorized by the Stored Communications Act, a federal law passed in 1994 to permit the government to compel disclosure of telecommunications records if there is a reasonable belief they are "relevant and material to an ongoing criminal investigation." The information received under the order revealed 12,898 location points for one suspect's movement—over 100 "pings" per day. That suspect, Carpenter, moved to suppress the evidence on grounds that the government's seizure of the CSLI records constituted a search, which had been conducted without a warrant and probable cause. The Court was sympathetic to Carpenter's claim that the CSLI records revealed an alarming amount of information about a person. It provides "an intimate window into a person's life, revealing not only his particular movements, but through them his 'familial, political, professional, religious, and sexual associations.'"[22] And all of this is revealed to the government "at practically no expense," meaning the government has almost no deterrent to accessing "each carrier's deep repository of historical location information."[23] This technology gives the government the power to conduct a retroactive search, in effect: "Whoever the suspect turns out to be, he has effectively been tailed every moment of every day for five years."[24] People, the majority reasoned, have a reasonable expectation of privacy in their physical location. Thus the government can obtain CSLI data for a suspect only after making a showing of probable cause necessary to obtain a warrant. The majority claimed that its decision was a "narrow one," designed to ensure it did not "embarrass the future."[25] But with the rapid advances in technology, we can be sure that this is not the last case of its kind.

MASS INVASIONS OF PRIVACY

Indeed, particularly in the last two generations, mass invasions of privacy have proliferated. Here, too the image of the frog slowly boiling to death is not out of place. Consider all those cameras on the streets of major cities and in public buildings. At one time, people surely would have felt a bit queasy at the very idea: that is, eyes watching them everywhere, recording their behavior, storing it, and perhaps even using it if the occasion arose. In 2015, New York City launched what it called the Lower Manhattan Security

Initiative, an "integrated" approach to security. The initiative included deploying more police officers, as well as "closed circuit televisions owned by the NYPD [New York Police Department] and its various private and public partners, license plate readers, and chemical, biological, radiological, and nuclear detectors." To be sure, NYPD also issued "Public Security Privacy Guidelines" to "limit" the use of these "counterterrorism technologies."[26] Nevertheless, the initiative represents a massive data-gathering effort, and, as NYPD is well aware, it is something of an encroachment on the privacy—or perhaps, more accurately, the anonymity—of everyone who enters the zone to which the initiative applies. One of the inspirations for the Lower Manhattan Security Initiative was London's "ring of steel," the Traffic and Environmental Zone, a technological cordon around the financial district of central London.

These cameras are excused, or justified, as a weapon against crime; they deter criminal activity and make it possible to find criminals who failed to be deterred. The manhunt following the Boston Marathon bombing demonstrated how useful they could be. In the greater London area, there are hundreds of thousands of cameras; but New York and London, of course, are not the only cities that make heavy use of these cameras. In big cities, they are fast becoming universal. By 2011, there were some 20,000 cameras on the lookout in France, and there were plans to increase their numbers dramatically. Nice had announced it was the "CCTV capital of France," with a "state-of-the-art" system consisting of five hundred cameras; the goal was to install one camera for every five hundred residents of the city. These cameras "allow the municipal police to keep an eye on large gatherings such as demonstrations and public events, such as the city's carnival." A poll showed that 71 percent of the French public approved of video surveillance in public places.[27] In Mexico City, the "nerve center" of the "Ciudad Seguro," called "the world's most ambitious urban security programme," is housed in a "concrete bunker, three stories high," built in 2011, and whose "eyes are 13,000 cameras arrayed throughout" Mexico City's core.[28] These cameras do serve a protective function but it is selective. In Chicago, it was reported in 2019 that there were "more than 32,000 video cameras that can feed directly to police stations and even into officers' laptops while they're sitting in a squad car." But this vast network of cameras does not cover most of the neighborhoods where "impoverished" people live—neighborhoods with a great deal of crime, but not much in the way of fancy restaurants, hotels, and office buildings.[29]

The use of these surveillance cameras in cities is increasing rapidly. By the end of 2021, it has been estimated, there will be more than a billion of them in use. Cities in China and India are the most densely covered but the practice is worldwide. Most people, as we said, like the idea of cameras that can keep the lid on crime—and might even favor greater use of this kind of protection. More controversial—and potentially more dangerous and pervasive—is surveillance and data-gathering conducted by the central government that is aimed not at monitoring traffic, catching the occasional robber, trying to keep the streets safe, and perhaps thwarting possible terrorists in airports and courthouses, but at fighting and frustrating a worldwide terrorist *movement*. Legally, this is a gray area. In 1968, a major federal statute that banned wiretapping and other forms of technological eavesdropping specifically stated that it did not "limit the constitutional power of the president" to take measures to protect the country from foreign attack, or to protect information vital to national security, so long as the president deemed these measures "necessary."[30] This was long before the "war on terror" broke out. But the language and the concepts the Act expressed are now used to justify very dark practices such as wholesale data gathering—including telephone and email information—by means of vast operations that invade the privacy of millions and millions of people. This is a dense and complex subject. It is embodied in a thick fabric of laws, rules, regulations, and practices. What makes this area of law and its implementation (or evasion) even denser and more complex is the fact that the fabric is made up of layers upon layers, all tightly wrapped in a cocoon of secrecy. And often, too, with an additional, effective covering, made up largely of lies.

The literature is enormous. Here, we can only touch on a few salient features relating to government surveillance and data gathering. The main points are roughly these: first, the war on terror is an effective—and mostly popular—cover; second, the law governing this "war" is complex; it generally authorizes surveillance and data-gathering, but it also expresses limits and controls over surveillance and data-gathering; third, the laws have become progressively more permissive, in response to increased hysteria over terrorism, and the increased demands by security agencies for access to data; and fourth, the agencies and the government increasingly disregard the laws and institutions that supposedly limit and control them. Government on the whole does what it feels like doing, and there seems to be little appetite or will to curb the war on privacy or, alas, little power to do so; the curtain of secrecy makes it difficult for courts or any other institutions to limit the work of surveillance and data-gathering.

The point of so much surveillance and data-gathering is the war on terror, as we said. There are, it is believed, enemies lurking here and abroad who are ready, willing, and able to launch vicious terror attacks on American citizens and the citizens of other countries. The danger may be exaggerated, but it is, after all, not a total fantasy. There are, in fact, terrorists and terror organizations. To fight them, the CIA and the NSA have been at work in recent years and the public, as we mentioned, is in general quite happy that the federal government has launched a "war on terror." The "war" metaphor is significant. In war, after all, it is acceptable to spy on the enemy and killing the enemy is not only acceptable, it is positively laudable. The Obama administration was proud to announce the death of Osama bin Laden in 2011. And the Trump administration boasted of killing the Iranian general Qasem Soleimani on January 3, 2020, with a drone strike.

Spying on foreign enemies is not a breach of American privacy, either in law or in fact. However, for some time, the NSA has engaged in domestic surveillance, and in a fairly massive way. After September 11, 2001, the "vast snooping powers" of the NSA focused "inward on US citizens, monitoring calls and e-mails with potential Al Qaeda links." The Foreign Intelligence Surveillance Act (FISA) had established a system that allowed wire-tapping based on the issuance of warrants. However laudable the system seemed on paper, the reality was quite different. In fact, the Bush administration "secretly circumvented" this system, and instead simply did whatever it pleased.[31]

Indeed, the FISA story is not unique. It seems pretty clear that laws meant to establish some sort of executive or judicial control over security agencies are basically failures—not in theory, but in practice. And there is abundant evidence that governmental officials feel free to tell bald-faced lies about mass surveillance and that they lie not only to the public, but also, at times, to Congress.

For example, the president authorized the NSA to collect metadata on telephone calls and internet use in 2001. Metadata is "information that describes who is communicating; potentially where they are located; the origin, path, and destination of each communication; and the length of the exchange."[32] In other words, metadata is everything except the actual *content* of the message. But, in the first place, it is naïve to think that collecting metadata does not invade privacy, simply because the actual content of the messages is not recorded. If somebody knows who we called, where we called, how long we spoke, and so on, they can often make a pretty good guess as to the content of the call. If a camera sees a man going into a brothel and records how long he stayed there, that "metadata" provides a pretty good idea of the "content" of his visit to the brothel.

So metadata is bad enough. But in 2013, it was revealed that the NSA and the FBI were actually collecting much more than metadata. The law, or at least the way the law was interpreted, allowed security agencies to listen in on messages sent or received from people outside the United States to someone inside the United States whenever there was some suspicion, however vague, that a foreigner had some connection to terrorism or terrorist groups. Data could also be collected about people who were connected with others outside the United States deemed to be suspicious in any way. And perhaps also about people connected to people who were, in turn, connected to others who had spoken to any foreigner with some sympathy for, connection with, or allegiance to terrorists or terrorist groups. As a result, it seems clear that government agencies were up to their necks in a massive data operation, collecting information about American citizens, peeking into their messages, and spying on them, even though they were inside the United States, and even when they were talking to other American citizens. This occurred even though the law "explicitly prohibited the knowing collection of domestic communications."[33]

Much of this data collection was secret, as far as the public was concerned. It was sometimes even a secret from members of Congress. In 2013, the Senate Intelligence Committee had a public hearing on national security issues. James Clapper, director of National Intelligence, was a witness. A senator asked him point blank whether the NSA was collecting "any type of data at all" on "millions or hundreds of millions of Americans?" Clapper said no, at least "not wittingly." This was simply a lie—and it was a lie delivered to the Senate, and, beyond this, to the public.[34]

Hence, there was a situation in the United States of "secret law," which, as Jennifer Granick puts it, "is almost like no law at all. Government officials can change it in secret." They can "violate it in secret" without consequences. Secret law, she feels, is "anathema to a democracy." How can elected officials be accountable to voters if the voters (and the officials, perhaps) have no idea what is actually going on?[35]

But secrets do not always stay secret. In June 2013, Edward Joseph Snowden "leaked" a dramatic and voluminous trove of information. Snowden had worked for the CIA and for other companies that had contracts with the NSA. He leaked thousands of classified NSA documents, which were then made public. These documents told a dismal story about a worldwide surveillance program run by the NSA and agencies of certain allied countries, notably Great Britain and Australia. Articles based on the leaked documents were published in an English newspaper, *The Guardian*.[36]

Snowden's documents were the stuff of headlines and they created a sensation. Officially, the government of the United States was horrified—although not by what was revealed but by the fact that it was revealed at all. As far as the administration was concerned, Snowden was not a whistle-blower; rather, he was a traitor and he had committed treason. His passport was revoked, and he fled the country to avoid arrest and possible punishment. Ultimately, he asked for and got asylum in Russia. Not everybody, by any means, considered Snowden a traitor to his country. Many people, to the contrary, considered him a hero and even a true patriot—a whistle-blower who deserved credit for exposing evil acts that the government was engaged in. For these people, Snowden was not the villain: the villains were the government snoops, with their vast and dangerous network and their egregious invasions of privacy. To be sure, Snowden had broken the law. But perhaps it was a law that, in this case, should have been broken. Whatever Snowden's motives, good or bad, he did pull aside a curtain that hid from view a sinister empire of government surveillance. What Snowden did may have been against the law—but so was the government program. Some of the information that came to light was deeply embarrassing for the United States government. Snowden's leaks revealed that the United States was spying on foreign leaders. It was listening in on the conversations of heads of government—Angela Merkel of Germany, very prominently. But the main thrust of the revelations was exposure of the fantastic scale of data collection by NSA—data not just on terrorists and possible terrorists but data on more or less everybody; the leaks showed that the NSA was a "giant, insatiable, deep-pocketed spy agency rummaging through the world's e-mails, texts, phone calls, video calls, Internet searches, and social media activities."[37]

Whatever one thinks of Snowden's actions, he beamed a spotlight on mass surveillance and mass data-gathering. Also, by implication, the spotlight was on the weakness of institutions that were supposed to control this activity. The NSA was clearly violating all sorts of laws. The laws, of course, could be changed—in either direction—if the government chose to change them, or was forced to by public opinion. A more basic question is whether, realistically, there is any hope of enforcing the laws, or any laws on the subject, or any hope of controlling the agencies. The texts of the laws hardly matter if the agencies simply do what they want to do, and what the government tells them to do, and if secrecy prevents any real chance of control.

The major powers, including the United States, run, in effect, two governments. There is the normal government: the government of laws and of elections. And then there is the national security government, which is huge, secret, powerful, and in many ways out of control. Those who work inside this giant machine and defend its actions insist that their tactics are necessary. We live in a world full of dangerous enemies who are plotting to destroy the Western way of life. People who criticize what the security forces do are naïve, soft-headed, or gullible. The new enemies cannot be fought with conventional weapons. And this may well be true. But mass surveillance and data-gathering go far beyond merely monitoring and ferreting out "enemies," even under the broadest definition of the word. The current system is like something out of a science-fiction movie in which human beings create intelligent robots that ultimately turn on their makers, destroy them, and set out to rule for themselves.

In fact, every major country is probably spying on other countries—and perhaps on its own citizens as well. Angela Merkel, the German chancellor, expressed anger and dismay when she learned that the NSA had been listening in on her conversations. She was quoted as saying something to the effect that friends were not supposed to spy on friends. But, according to an article in *Der Spiegel*, the pot was calling the kettle black: Germany was itself spying on its allies and friends—including the United States—not to mention France, the United Kingdom, Sweden, and many others, including the Vatican.[38] Dictatorships and semidictatorships use whatever tools they have to spy on their own citizens, let alone people in other countries. But then again, democracies do the same.

Secret surveillance is an issue in many countries. Roman Zakharov, "editor-in-chief of a publishing company and of an aviation magazine," and chair of a nongovernmental organization that monitors "the state of media freedom" in Russia, brought an action before the European Court of Human Rights (ECHR), which interprets the European Charter, in 2015. Zakharov claimed the government was interfering "with his right to the privacy of his telephone communications." He also claimed that mobile network operators, under orders from the government, had installed equipment that allowed the government to "intercept all telephone communications without prior judicial authorisation."[39] The Russian government, for its part, argued that Zakharov had no case; he could not show that the government had actually *used* the equipment to spy on him. Zakharov won his case and was awarded money damages, but only someone very naïve would think that the Russian government, having lost the case, would actually stop spying on its citizens—especially citizens like Zakharov, who seemed like a pestiferous dissident.

The Hungarian government was the defendant in another ECHR case decided in 2016.[40] The complaint closely paralleled the complaint in the Russian case. The plaintiffs were "staff members of . . . a non-governmental, 'watchdog' organisation voicing criticism of the Government." The National Security Services of Hungary were authorized, in the name of the battle against terror, to "search a dwelling secretly," and to "open and check postal mail and any closed parcel," among other things. ECHR, in this case, too, found a violation of the European Charter, and awarded money damages to the plaintiffs. In these cases, for obvious reasons, the plaintiffs could not actually prove that the beady eye of the authorities had been spying on them but the ECHR held that the nature of secret surveillance is such that a person can be a victim "even if he cannot point to any concrete measures specifically affecting him."[41] In the Hungarian case, the plaintiffs "thought they were at particular risk of having their communications intercepted," because they worked for "civil-society organisations criticizing the Government."[42] The Court felt that this risk could not be discounted. Courts should strictly scrutinize surveillance rules because of the potential for abuse. In this and other cases, the ECHR developed a noble and progressive set of doctrines. But, again, a skeptic can wonder if these decisions make any difference. Did the Hungarian government change its behavior? Did any government?

At the root of the problem is the breathtaking power and range of the modern technology of spying. The core *technical* fact is that Brandeis's prediction has come true, though in ways that would surely shock him. Today, the state can gather almost infinite amounts of data on anybody or everybody, can store the data so that the data is available forever, and can also search and analyze the data at will. Add to this a principle with the strange power to seduce security agencies: if some way of gathering data becomes possible, and thus *can* be done, then it should be done, and will be done. This principle, needless to say, stands in direct contradiction to the idea of limited government or, indeed, to the idea of the rule of law.

The point about technology is crucial. Governments have spied on each other for centuries. But technology makes the sheer scale of this activity vastly greater, and more powerful, than ever before. No matter how efficient or far-reaching were Hitler's Gestapo, the East German Stasi, and the Soviet secret police, there was only so much these horrific organizations could accomplish. The modern surveillance state has powers that older dictators only dreamt of. Democratic countries are committed, in general, to the idea of checks and balances. But checks and balances simply do not work when it comes to the surveillance state. There is, for one thing, little political will to keep the surveillance state within limits. And most people seem to accept, rather meekly, massive invasions of privacy in the name of security against terror and crime.

For one thing, most people shrug their shoulders and say, "I have nothing to hide" or "I don't care if the government wants to read my e-mails; let them. There's nothing there of the slightest interest to them." This is, however, not really a strong response. As Daniel J. Solove has argued, everybody does, in fact, have something to hide.[43] But even more to the point: "I have nothing to hide" ignores the concepts of privacy and personal dignity. Criminals and jihadists, of course, have something extremely serious to hide, something that they must hide at all costs. But the rest of us also have something to hide: our private lives and even our bodies. After all, we put on clothes to mask our nakedness every day. In many other respects, however, "hide" is the wrong word to use. I am not "hiding" my medical records, food habits, opinions on various subjects, financial status, or likes and dislikes; rather, I am keeping these things private (though never absolutely) because of the way I define who I am and how I want to live my life. I have nothing to hide, in a sense; but I still want to preserve my privacy. I don't want to be filmed and recorded. I don't want people poking around in my files or even looking through my trash. My anonymity in public spaces is also precious. "Privacy" is not just being left alone—that's the negative side of it. The positive side is a kind of social space in which people can construct and manage their personal lives, in which they can walk and talk and act freely, without the gimlet eye of the camera, or the heavy hand of the surveillance state, upon them.

Moreover, it is not the mere fact that the government is gathering data on you, me, and all of us; it is also the fact that this is done in secret, and for who knows what purpose, or for no purpose at all. Modern societies—not only authoritarian societies, but also those that claim to be democracies—are becoming more and more like the worlds of Kafka's novels, worlds in which people helplessly face labyrinths they cannot penetrate and mazes they cannot run—anonymous, faceless forces that frustrate them at every turn.

YOU HAVE NO PRIVACY

When Louis Daguerre created the camera, in the first part of the nineteenth century, he could not possibly foresee how far his new discovery would carry the world, or what wonderful and dreadful consequences the camera would ultimately produce. Early cameras were crude devices. They could not, for example, capture motion. Faster cameras, so-called candid cameras, became available later in the nineteenth century. It was then, for the first time, that your picture could be taken without your consent, and even without your knowledge. This made the camera a tool that could be used to invade personal privacy. Over the years, cameras grew nimbler, smaller, and more versatile; they could be hidden anywhere, they could be as tiny as a bee, and they could possess a sting of their own. Whatever its other uses, the modern camera is the indispensable tool of privacy invaders.

The government has all sorts and types of cameras at its disposal, along with other surveillance and data-gathering tools. But these tools can also be used by private citizens, and by businesses and institutions of all sorts. For $1,300, anybody can buy a little drone, the "Phantom 2 Vision Plus," fully equipped with a "camera attached to the bottom that can record high-resolution images and high-definition video."[44] Wedding videography is one popular use for this device. That is, in general, pretty innocuous; other uses may be less innocent. The technology is, no doubt, still in its infancy. And there are all sorts of ingenious ways of concealing little cameras, as we noted earlier. In 2016, this fact was alarming enough for the authorities in Germany to take legal action: manufacturers were no longer to put disguised "mini-cameras" on the market—including cameras concealed in smoke detectors, alarm clocks, and ballpoint pens.[45] Whether German official action can succeed in driving these devices off the market seems extremely dubious. Such devices, as we saw, are freely sold in the United States and no doubt in many other countries. They can surely be delivered to Berlin or Munich as well as to New York.

In the hands of malicious, irresponsible, or thoughtless people, even less sophisticated devices can be a real menace, a threat to personal privacy. One imagines that most people who buy cameras for home consumption simply want to protect their homes from burglars, or keep an eye on a sleeping baby. But, just as governments are able to "bug" suspects, private citizens can "bug" their neighbor's home or find some way to take secret photographs. We mentioned the sad case of Tyler Clementi in the last chapter, along with the noxious practice of "upskirting."

In London, one Andrew Meldrum, aged thirty, a kind of modern "peeping Tom," ended up in court in 2014. Meldrum helped women set up their computers, all the while secretly installing software that let him film these women in their bedrooms. His feeble excuse was that he merely intended to eavesdrop on these women, not to film them.[46] In fact, he had about eleven thousand images on his computer, including some images of women who were undressing, and in one case, images of a woman making love with her boyfriend.[47]

So far, one hopes, Meldrum and "upskirters" are fairly isolated individuals. Presumably, courts and local law enforcement agencies can handle these instances of men (it is almost always men) who invade the privacy of other people (usually women). Meldrum was lucky enough to escape with a suspended sentence, a ten-year stint on a sex offender list, and a hefty bill for costs.[48] Men with an itch to peek in on others—Peeping Toms—will probably always be with us. What they do may be illegal but it persists. In Georgia, for example, it is a crime to peep "through windows or doors . . . for the purpose of spying upon or invading the privacy of the persons spied upon."[49] In Alaska, "indecent viewing or photography" is a crime; you cannot take a picture of "the genitals, anus, or female breast of another" without consent.[50] In past times, voyeurs did not constitute a serious social problem. They had no technology to help them out—nothing to use but their naked eyes—and they had to create their own opportunities. Today, they have the benefit of technology. They have cameras and listening devices. They may even have "window-peeping drones" that can be used to make "voyeur videos."[51] We noted in an earlier chapter that there has even been a voyeur rabbi. Similarly, a restaurant executive, Kyle Muehlhauser, was "accused of secretly taping women in the bathroom of his company's restaurant."[52]

This executive used technology to spy on the bodies of his employees. This, one hopes, is a rare occurrence; but for bosses to invade the privacy of their workers for other purposes is not rare at all. Bosses have, apparently, broad powers to snoop and search their employees' offices and cubicles. Can they search their email? The law treats private letters as more or less sacred, but email seems to be different. It "can be intercepted relatively easily, . . . the data travels in packets through several intermediaries . . . [and it] can be retrieved from several destinations after it arrives," including "the employer's network computer, where it is often stored on backup tapes."[53] Potentially, employers can exercise far more control over the lives and affairs of their workers than they could in the past. A 2005 survey conducted by the American Management Association, in collaboration with another organization, found that 36 percent of companies "monitor workers on a keystroke-by-keystroke basis," 55 percent review email messages, and 76 percent monitor the websites employees visit.[54] A Spanish supermarket, suspecting (with good reason), that employees were stealing, installed cameras (some of them not visible) to monitor the work of the cashiers. The cameras showed five employees helping themselves to various items in the store—and helping customers do the same. The employees were fired but had the gall to sue in the Spanish courts for unfair dismissal. Ultimately, they lost in the ECHR in 2019, but they had won at various stages along the way, and even in the ECHR, a dissent criticized the idea of letting "individuals take justice into their own hands."[55] In the United States, which gives employers much more power over their workers, this would have been an easy case.

Private companies not only monitor their workers but have also gone in for mass gathering of information, and in a big way. In the old days, people went to the grocery store, bought tomatoes and canned soup and breakfast cereal, and paid cash for what they bought. Today, if you buy online—which is more and more common—you leave behind a digital trail. And even at the grocery store, people now usually pay with credit cards; thus they might leave behind data about what they buy and how often. Indeed, one grocery chain "archives every transaction of every customer." Students, too, "live in a world in which an increasing fraction of their lives is digitally surveilled." The quote is from a law school professor at the University of California–Los Angeles, who refused to let his classes be recorded. A "highly interactive classroom should be a space beyond the reach of the digital panopticon," he writes. "It should not be a space where every student utterance is archived on a college-run server, regardless of how supposedly secure that server might be." He is exceptional. The "default" arrangement is to record "all class sessions."[56] Of course, during the Covid-19 pandemic that began in 2020, recording classes became even more common—and was in general quite necessary. Whether this will change in the postpandemic world is unknown and unknowable.

Like UCLA, many companies and institutions hoover up data on customers, students, and visitors: "Amazon knows what you read; Netflix, your taste in movies. Search engines . . . retain your queries for months," and can figure out which sites you visit.[57] Every major online company gathers masses of data about their customers. They all have "privacy policies" that appear in small print on their websites, but does anybody read these privacy policies? And do they actually make any difference in practice?

One wonders: do people resent the data-gathering by Amazon and other big companies? The answer might depend on what Amazon does with the data. Most people, one supposes, do not want Amazon to turn data over to the government, for whatever purpose. Other uses of the data seem relatively harmless. A customer who logs onto Amazon might see an ad for a new book on gardening. If the customer is an avid gardener who regularly buys gardening books, the customer might find the suggestion extremely helpful and might even buy the book. Other customers, however, might not appreciate Amazon's practice; they might find it intrusive or even a little bit scary.

Millions and millions of people use Facebook and other forms of social media; they share information, some of it quite personal, with a whole host of friends. To a degree, they are giving up a part of their privacy rights. This is even more the case for the people who appear on "reality" TV—a form of entertainment that has mushroomed in recent years. Some people are willing or eager to wash their dirty linens in public; they voluntarily appear on *Judge Judy*, *Divorce Court*, or one of the many television quiz shows. They love to parade themselves before an enormous public audience. Only a few people actually succeed in getting on TV but millions more might be eager and willing to give up some anonymity in order to appear on TV, for whatever purpose. It is their only chance at getting their proverbial fifteen minutes of fame.

In the modern world, the price of fame and fortune is celebrity status. In chapter 9, we will discuss what "celebrity" means. Roughly, a celebrity is not just a famous person; a celebrity is a famous and *familiar* person. The celebrity is familiar above all because of TV; TV is a one-way mirror that beams the rich and famous right into our living rooms. Legally and socially, celebrities give up some of their privacy rights. The law about the privacy rights of "public figures" is complex, and differs somewhat from society to society. But the trend is strong: the public has a right to know about the lives and loves of public figures and, to this extent, these figures sacrifice their privacy. We deal with this issue in more detail in chapter 9. Celebrities are, in a way, only an extreme case of something more general. People in modern societies have lost a good deal of privacy, as we have seen—not only to surveillance cameras on the street, but to all the other devices, legal and nonlegal, which we have mentioned. People in general also feel a kind of right to invade other people's privacy. This is most obviously true with regard to celebrities and employees. But it is also true, to a degree, within the context of "friends" on social networks. Moreover, on the internet, we can easily discover how much a website thinks my cousin's house, at 250 Elm Street, in Plainville, is worth. The people who run the site search records of house sales in the neighborhood. They use that information to make shrewd guesses about the value of real estate all over the country. Records of real estate sales have perhaps always been "public," but that was only true in a technical sense. In the past, nobody could—or would—go to the trouble of hunting these figures down, certainly not en masse. Now, someone can, and does.

PRIVACY AND CULTURE

Issues of privacy, like so many other issues, vary from culture to culture. Each society has its own special definition of privacy, and its own way of protecting or invading it. In most countries, for example, there are national identity cards. In some countries, you are required to carry this card with you at all times; you may be obliged to produce it on request. In other countries, people have identity cards, but they are not forced to carry them. A few countries have no national identity card—Australia and Norway, for example. The United States is one of these countries; the very idea of a national identity card would surely be met with resistance. And yet, in the United States (and in other holdouts), there *are* identity cards, practically speaking. For example, the Social Security card and the Social Security number play an important role in the United States. Even more important is the driver's license, which, unlike the Social Security card, contains a photograph of the driver. The driver's license is so important that some states will even issue a non-driver's license, that is, an ID card resembling a driver's license, for people who, for one reason or another, do not or cannot have a driver's license. More and more, and for more and more purposes, a person must have some way to prove identity. "Identity theft" is a serious modern crime, but what is stolen is not the identity itself, but markers of identity, and those aspects of life that require some proof of identity.

Modern society is also a society awash with numbers and statistics. It is a society where things and people are counted, measured, and recorded. Prehistoric people might have had names, but to us, their names, faces, and general identities are completely lost. All we have to identify them are a few fossilized bones. Every advance in "civilization" has moved human beings another step further away from anonymity. Before the camera was invented, only the rich, the noble, and the famous left behind permanent records of what they actually looked like. Mass surveys of the population are specifically modern. Without a doubt, what we gain from birth certificates, death certificates, and the like far outweighs the loss of anonymity. Identity cards, driver's licenses, and the like are useful and valuable—and helpful in many regards. And millions of people now have faded photographs of their great-great grandparents. The faces of the dead are no longer lost forever.

The trend is clear and consistent. Nobody had an identity card in the middle ages; nobody was a statistic. Some people, and some societies, balk at the act of counting and measuring people. In the United States, the census is an old and established institution—census takers, in fact, began their work in 1790, and every tenth year since then has been a census year. There have been complaints and controversies on marginal issues—questions about the questions. In 2020, one issue was whether the undocumented could and should be counted. But on the whole, the census is an accepted aspect of American life and by law the census takers count absolutely everybody, or try to. The American census comes around as regularly and predictably as the seventeen-year locust, only seven years sooner. In the Federal Republic of Germany, on the other hand, the census became a divisive and difficult issue. In 1983, a movement arose to protest and boycott the plans of the federal government to conduct a national census. The German Constitutional Court indeed struck down some aspects of the proposed census. A new law was passed, and the government went through with its plan in 1987, but it was "dogged throughout by a boycott movement more widespread and well organized than the first."[58]

Societies differ, too, in their tolerance for surveillance. Japanese society, for example, is organized in a way that Americans, and perhaps also the Swiss and the Norwegians, would find intolerable—Japanese "door-to-door police family surveys" are "unlike anything seen in most western countries."[59] The Japanese accept this, as part of their normal life and part of their culture. Everywhere, life in small societies and towns is nosier and more intrusive than life in big cities. Clearly, scale, as well as culture, makes a big difference. But those differences may be diminishing. All over the world, we see definite signs of convergence—CCTV for example has spread to more and more places. This chapter has talked mostly about the American situation—its massive incursions on privacy in the name of the war against terror. The United States is big, rich, and technologically advanced. But so are many other countries. They have their own versions of this antiprivacy disease.

Here is the paradox: we live in an age in which privacy is both a legal and a social norm of enormous importance. People want, even demand, privacy. The law protects privacy, at least in theory. "Invasion of privacy" is a tort. Of course, not everybody means the same thing when they talk about privacy. But at a minimum, people do want some personal space, some zone of privacy that cannot be violated, either physically or metaphorically. There are, of course, people willing to give up their privacy to get something more precious—a seat in the United States Senate, a role in a movie, or a stint on reality TV. But perhaps even these people may have a tinge of regret, may feel they are giving something up, in exchange for something they want more. And for everyone, as we discussed in this chapter, the precious zone of privacy is more and more threatened by a giant technological juggernaut. In a real sense, we no longer *have* any privacy or, if we do, it is only because nobody bothers to invade it. But it could be invaded and, more and more, it *is* invaded.

The public, moreover, does not rise up in revolt against all aspects of the loss of privacy. On the whole, people accept a great deal of intrusion in the name of fighting crime, combating terrorism, and making everybody feel safe and secure. And because they feel they have nothing to hide, they are less worried than they ought to be about the danger that Big Brother will come after them.

And yet, as Jennifer Granick, among others, has pointed out, we all *do* have something to hide. All of us, with the possible exception of cloistered nuns, have done something wrong or criminal at some time in our lives, probably many times. Certainly all of us have broken traffic laws, but she mentions others: "marijuana use, computer misuse, petty theft, eavesdropping, obstruction of justice, [and] wire fraud," to name a few. And she asks us to consider "how very different your life could have been had you been caught and convicted for things you have done."[60]

The frightening truth is that modern technology *could* catch all of us. Cameras could record the license plates of every car that goes more than five miles over the speed limit—that would be bad enough. Modern technology could do more: it could peek through our clothing and look at our naked bodies—both figuratively and literally. It could record everything we do, it could turn all of our lives into reality TV. There is, in a way, a battle raging—perhaps we could call it a war—between two powerful social impulses. On one side, government and large institutions are armed with the latest technology; they can carry out massive invasions of our privacy. On the other side is the population itself, with its social demand for privacy rights. Its only weapons are the power of norms and the power of law. It is impossible to predict how the battle will play out in the future.

THE PUBLIC STRIKES BACK: THE RIGHT TO KNOW

One battle between the government and private citizens concerns what information the government can collect from and about them. Another is about when the government can keep its work private from private citizens. Privacy is, above all, a matter of relationships. If I have a right to keep something private, this means that you have no right to know it. A Peeping Tom has no right to see his neighbor's body; she has a right to keep him from seeing it. If my home is my castle, the government has to stay out unless it gets a warrant from a judge; to get this warrant, the government is supposed to have a good reason and follow legal rules. But if the government has a right to ask me questions for the census, and a judge has a right to demand that I testify at a trial, I have no right to refuse. Dozens of laws and rules can be analyzed in terms of who has the right to keep information private and who does not.

Moreover, results of the census are available to the public. The government cannot keep the figures secret. They have to be, as the expression goes, an open book. The issue, then, is not the right to keep matters private, but the right (under certain conditions) to pierce the privacy of others, that is, the right to know: specifically, the right to know what the government is up to.

As early as 1966, Congress passed the Freedom of Information Act (FOIA); it has since been amended many times. This Act, in theory, throws open to the public most records and proceedings of federal agencies. FOIA, however, has a long list of exceptions: for example, national defense secrets, personnel and medical files (releasing these would amount to an invasion of privacy), trade secrets, and certain records or information "compiled for law enforcement purposes." There is no question that FOIA has unlocked a lot of locked doors. Still, the exemptions are hugely important: "national security" is a very broad category, and government agencies are not the least bit bashful about invoking it. Many agencies are reluctant to comply with FOIA requests, and there are constant complaints that the agencies answer questions at an extremely glacial pace. Those who apply for information need, as one judge put it, "the patience of saints and the endurance of marathon runners." The judge was referring to the travails of Carl Oglesby, who, in the 1980s, tried to worm out of the government documents about Reinhard Gehlen, a Nazi general who ran West Germany's spy service, supposedly under American supervision. As of 2000, Oglesby had been fighting for the documents for fifteen years. He had gotten some but by no means all of what he wanted, and the process was like pulling teeth.[61]

Agencies basically do not want to release documents that would embarrass them or interfere with their work. It is "simply not in the perceived self-interest of a secretive agency . . . to release sensitive information," especially if the information might open the agency up to criticism. This quote is from an article whose subtitle tells it all: "How It Took Thirteen Years and Two Lawsuits to Get J. Edgar Hoover's Secret Supreme Court Sex Files."[62] Even when an agency grants an FOIA request, it may do so very, very slowly, indeed.

Of course, many government agencies are slowpokes; federal and state FOIA organizations are certainly not the only examples. Moreover, the arteries are clogged: there are thousands and thousands of requests. The total number of FOIA requests for the fiscal year 2017 was a staggering 818,271. The biggest chunk consisted of requests to the Department of Homeland Security: 366,036. But there were 82,088 to the Department of Justice and 55,198 to the Department of Defense. Agencies subject to FOIA requests are trying to reduce the backlog. The many exceptions to the general sunshine principle are one factor in delayed decisions. Of course, the exceptions to FOIA are not arbitrary and some of them are absolutely and unquestionably justified. The Atomic Energy Act (1954) forbids disseminating data on how to design or make an atom bomb.[63] This was before FOIA, but would clearly come within one of the exceptions. Nobody would argue that this rule is unreasonable or that it violates rights to freedom of speech. Other exceptions are more borderline and no doubt the agencies (and FOIA) give themselves the benefit of the doubt.

The states, too, have their versions of FOIA. New Jersey, for example, has an "Open Public Records Act." It begins with a broad statement of principle: for citizens of New Jersey, government records, in general, are supposed to be "readily accessible for inspection, copying, or examination"; all government records must be "subject to public access," unless the law exempts these records. On the other hand, "personal information" that is "entrusted" to the government is protected if disclosure would "violate the citizen's reasonable expectation of privacy."[64] And, of course, there is a long list of exceptions to the general principle. This includes various legislative records, "criminal investigatory records," and any photos that a medical examiner may have made of "the body, or any portion of the body" of a dead person. The Illinois FOIA announces a "fundamental philosophy" of "access" to the "official acts and policies of . . . public officials"; the agencies, however, are told to avoid "unwarranted invasion of personal privacy." This is defined to mean "information that is highly personal or objectionable to a reasonable person," and in which the "subject's right to privacy outweighs any legitimate public interest in obtaining the information." In Illinois, too, there is a long catalog of exemptions and exceptions, including such matters as "[n]ames and information of people who have applied for . . . Firearm Owner's Identification Cards" and "[r]ecordings made under the Law Enforcement Officer-Worn Body Camera Act, except to the extent authorized under that Act."[65]

Thus state and federal FOIA law do try to balance privacy—for the government and for individuals—against "sunshine" and transparency. Whether this balance is achieved, and how, is open to question. There are close cases; denied claims are adjudicated within the various FOIA agencies and some cases even end up in court. In *Department of Air Force v. Rose* (1976),[66] student editors of the *New York University Law Review*, who were researching "disciplinary systems and procedures" at the Air Force Academy, asked for "case summaries of honor and ethics hearings, with personal reference or other identifying information deleted." The Academy resisted, claiming the summaries included "personnel and medical files . . . the disclosure of which would constitute a clearly unwarranted invasion of personal privacy."[67] The Supreme Court was sympathetic to the claim for material—at least in part. The Court held that the lower courts should take a look at the materials, redact them if necessary, and decide what could and could not be released under FOIA.

FOIA and the state versions get a staggering amount of requests, as we saw, but from whom? Most of them apparently come from commercial companies that harvest information from the agencies and make a profit by reselling it to others. Forget the image of the investigative reporter digging for material for her story or the scholar looking for truth in the jungle of documents. These do exist, but much more typical is the work of FOI Services, Inc., a company that makes hundreds of requests to the Food and Drug Administration (FDA). The FDA's "FOIA records," the company claims, "usually aren't on the agency website—they're files from the desk drawers of reviewers, investigators, and other officials." FOI Services has "collected over 100,000 of these documents."[68] They are available to other companies—of course at a price. The FDA, in 2013, had 10,167 requests under FOIA. A full 75 percent of these were from "commercial requesters" who are "information resellers." FOI Services Inc. submitted 571 requests. It was only one of many of these "information resellers."[69]

Probably, all things considered, FOIA does more good than harm. We can even defend the "information resellers." Government produces millions of pages of stuff; consider, for example, the *Federal Register*, which runs to monstrous length every year. Agencies post proposed rules in the *Federal Register*. These proposed rules are open to the public, which gets a chance to comment on these rules; thus they can, hopefully, have their say, and have an effect on rule-making. Indeed, this sometimes happens. But the sheer bulk of the *Federal Register* is daunting: nobody can read tens of thousands of pages, nor would anybody want to. Still, lawyers for Walmart or lobbyists for the pharmaceutical industry, for example, can keep an eye on the *Federal Register* and pass on to clients any nuggets of information buried in those thousands of pages of text. Since lawyers and lobbyists are not charity cases, these lawyers and lobbyists act here as "information resellers," even though they are not technically selling anything. In the modern world of business, government, regulation, and rule-making, the work of the lobbyists, ferreting out government action, and the work of the resellers, passing on (for a price) what they've learned, are felt to be at least somewhat necessary and unavoidable.

That does not mean that the system works as it is supposed to. It most assuredly does not. A great deal of what the government does, even when it is supposed to be open to the public, is in fact private in any practical sense. You need some sort of middle-person or information broker, and that costs money. Also, a great deal of what the government does is private in a more literal sense: it does not leave a paper trail at all, or at least not one that is accessible under FOIA. This may or may not be a problem. Presidents, governors, members of Congress, agency and department heads need to be free to talk policy, to discuss matters in their offices without anybody listening in, or having the right to listen. The president has to receive intelligence briefings that are not for public consumption.

FOIA thus must balance open and closed doors. This is not the first time we have observed this kind of balancing act. The government is waging "war" on terror. This, like all wars, requires a lot of secrecy; the enemies must be kept from knowing about strategies and tactics. The war, to be sure, often encroaches on the privacy of the citizen. And, to be sure, it is not the first of these metaphorical "wars." There was, notably, the Cold War—which pitted the United States and its allies against the Soviet Union and its satellites. Under President Ronald Reagan, a "moderately open government" was turned into a "predominantly closed one," in order, supposedly, to "protect the American people from the great Red Menace."[70] There is also, of course, the war on crime—a war that has gone on for centuries and that will, of course, never end—and the current "war on terrorism," which is also unlikely to end, at least not in the foreseeable future. FOIA is supposed to be sensitive to the privacy rights of the individual, but, far more importantly, perhaps, are the limits on FOIA that are sensitive to the privacy of the government, and are designed to protect genuine government secrets.

FOIA and the state equivalents face all sorts of legal and technical issues. But the basic issue is a familiar one. In our times, some sort of notion of "privacy," some sort of protected zone around individuals, around their lives, their dreams and desires and opinions, their habits and their ways of coping—this zone is more important than ever, more precious to the average person. At the same time government—the state—has become a huge Leviathan, a giant machine, empowered by modern technology with weapons and devices that can pierce that zone, indeed, is capable of obliterating it. "Sunshine," the ideal that underlies FOIA, aims to put weapons in the hands of the citizens and to give them the right to know what the government is up to. How the plan works, and whether it works at all, is another question.

FOIA and the state versions are rights against the government—rights to transparency. But transparency is not simply a matter of getting access to reports and documents. There is also, in modern law, a right to know a great deal about the actual *people* who run the government, as we saw in an earlier chapter. You cannot make a formal request to the governor of Michigan or a senator from Texas asking them to explain their sex life or their financial history. That is way beyond the boundaries of FOIA. Nonetheless, these are questions the public does ask. And the media will be more than happy to try to answer these questions, along with many others of this type.

NOTES

1. *See* Mary Beth Sheridan, Doug Struck, and Marc Fisher, "Boston Marathon Bomb Blasts Kill at Least Three, Leave Scores Injured," *Washington Post*, April 15, 2013.

2. Brandon C. Welsh and David P. Farrington, *Making Public Places Safer: Surveillance and Crime Prevention* (Oxford, UK: Oxford University Press, 2009), 5. *See also* Michelle Lirtzman, "Surveillance Cameras Win Broad Support," *ABC News*, July 29, 2007.

3. *The Best Hidden Cameras in the Business*, BrickHouse Security.

4. *See Home Security & Video Surveillance*, The Home Depot.

5. *See* Lirtzman, *supra* note 2.

6. See David Murakami Wood, "The 'Surveillance Society': Questions of History, Place and Culture," *Eur. J. Criminology* 6 (2009): 179, 179–80.

7. U.S. Const. amend. IV.

8. 277 U.S. 438 (1928).

9. *Id.* at 456.

10. *Id.* at 464–65.

11. *Id.* at 475–76 (Brandeis, J., dissenting).

12. 47 U.S.C. § 605 (2018).

13. 316 U.S. 129 (1942).

14. 389 U.S. 347 (1967).

15. *Id.* at 351.

16. *Id.* at 361 (Harlan, J., concurring).

17. *Kyllo v. United States*, 533 U.S. 27 (2001).

18. *Id.* at 30–33.

19. *Florida v. Jardines*, 569 U.S. 1 (2013).

20. *See* Douglas M. Charles, *The FBI's Obscene File: J. Edgar Hoover and the Bureau's Crusade Against Smut* (Lawrence: University Press of Kansas, 2012).

21. 138 S. Ct. 2206 (2018).

22. *Id.* at 2217.

23. *Id.* at 2218.

24. *Id.*

25. *Id.* at 2220. *See generally* Paul Ohm, "The Many Revolutions of Carpenter," *Harv. J. L. & Tech.* 32 (2019): 357; Grace Manning, "Alexa: Can You Keep a Secret? The Third-Party Doctrine in the Age of the Smart Home," *Am. Crim. L. Rev. Online* 56 (2019): 25.

26. Press Release, NYPD, "New York City Police Department Releases Draft of Public Security Privacy Guidelines for Public Comment," Feb. 25, 2009.

27. "'Vidéoprotection' . . . or Big Brother?," *Connexion*, June 3, 2011, https://www.connexionfrance.com/Archive/Videoprotection-or-Big-Brother.

28. Hillary Mushkin, "Reconnaissance: Inside the Panopticon, A Low-Tech Visit to Mexico City's High-Tech Urban Surveillance Center," *Places Journal,* Feb. 2016, https://placesjournal.org/article/inside-mexico-citys-c4i4-surveillance-center/.

29. Dahleen Glanton, "In a City with Tens of Thousands of Surveillance Cameras, Who's Watching Whom?," *Chicago Tribune*, Feb. 26, 2019.

30. Omnibus Crime Control and Safe Streets Act of 1968, tit. III, § 2511(3), Pub. L. No. 90–351, 82 Stat. 197 (1968) (codified as amended at 42 U.S.C. § 3711 [2012]).

31. Jason Ross Arnold, *Secrecy in the Sunshine Era: The Promise and Failures of U.S. Open Government Laws* (Lawrence: University Press of Kansas, 2014), 367.

32. Laura Donohue, *The Future of Foreign Intelligence: Privacy and Surveillance in a Digital Age* (Oxford, UK: Oxford University Press, 2016), 18; *see also* Jennifer Stisa Granick, *American Spies: Modern Surveillance, Why You Should Care, and What to Do about It* (Cambridge, UK: Cambridge University Press, 2017).

33. Donohue, *supra* note 32, at 70.

34. Charlie Savage, *Power Wars: Inside Obama's Post-9/11 Presidency* (Boston: Little, Brown and Company, 2015), 580–81.

35. Granick, *supra* note 32, at 292.

36. *See, e.g.*, Glenn Greenwald, "NSA Collecting Phone Records of Millions of Verizon Customers Daily," *The Guardian*, June 6, 2013.

37. *Id.* at 368.

38. "Bundesnachrichtendienst: Geht richtig gut, In großem Ausmaß hat der BND befreundete Staaten ausspioniert," *Der Spiegel*, July 11, 2015.

39. This is a Grand Chamber decision, *Zakharov v. Russia*, App. No. 47143/06, Eur. Ct. H.R. (2015).

40. *Szabó and Vissy v. Hungary*, App. No. 37138/14, Eur. Ct. H.R. (2016).

41. *Id.* at ¶ 33.

42. *Id.* at ¶ 37.

43. Daniel J. Solove, *Nothing to Hide: The False Tradeoff Between Privacy and Security* (New Haven, CT: Yale University Press, 2011), 21–32. Solove further explains this idea throughout the remainder of the book.

44. "An Eye in the Sky, Accessible to the Hobbyist," *New York Times*, Sept. 11, 2014, at B6.

45. "Netzagentur geht gegen getarnte Spionagekameras vor," *Der Spiegel*, Apr. 25, 2016.

46. Hugo Gye, "Hi-Tech Peeping Tom 'Planted Spy Software on Women's Laptops to Film Them in Their Bedrooms through Webcams While They Got Changed,'" *Daily Mail*, Mar. 1, 2014.

47. Nicola Fitfield, "Cyber Stalker Bugged Women's Computers to Spy on Them in Their Bedrooms," *Telegraph*, May 30, 2014.

48. *Id.*

49. Ga. Code Ann. § 16–11–61(b) (West 2020).

50. Alaska Stat. Ann. § 11.61.123(a) (West 2020).

51. Ben Hooper, "Utah Police Seek Owner of Window-Peeping Drone Loaded with Voyeur Videos," *UPI,* Dec. 5, 2016, https://www.upi.com/Odd_News/2016/12/05/Utah-police-seek-owner-of-window-peeping-drone-loaded-with-voyeur-videos/9191480963549/. The drone "contained multiple videos of unsuspecting residents as seen through the windows in their bathrooms and bedrooms."

52. Alison Knezevich, "Technology Aids 'Peeping Toms,' Makes Trauma Worse for Victims," *Baltimore Sun*, Mar. 29, 2015.

53. Jeffrey Rosen, *The Unwanted Gaze: The Destruction of Privacy in America* (New York: Vintage Books, 2000), 70.

54. James Vlahos, "Surveillance Society: New High-Tech Cameras Are Watching You," *Popular Mechanics*, Sep. 30, 2009, http://www.popularmechanics.com/military/a2398/4236865/.

55. *Lopez Ribalda v. Spain* 1874/138567/13 (Eur. Ct. Hum. Rts. 2019)

56. John Villasenor, "Why I Won't Let My Classes Be Recorded," *The Chronicle of Higher Education*, Jan. 17, 2020, 66:17, A52.

57. *Id.*

58. Matthew G. Hannah, *Dark Territory in the Information Age: Learning from the West German Census Controversies of the 1980s* (Farnham, UK: Ashgate, 2010), 1.

59. Wood, *supra* note 6, at 187.

60. Granick, *supra* note 32, at 129.

61. Robb Mandelbaum, "The Paper Chase," *New York Times*, Dec. 3, 2000.

62. Alexander Charns and Paul M. Green, "Playing the Information Game: How It Took Thirteen Years and Two Lawsuits to Get J. Edgar Hoover's Secret Supreme Court Sex Files," in *A Culture of Secrecy: The Government Versus the People's Right to Know*, Athan G. Theoharis, ed. (Lawrence: University Press of Kansas, 1998), 97.

63. 42 U.S.C. § 2168 (2018).

64. N.J. Stat. Ann. § 47:1A-1 (West 2020).

65. 5 Ill. Comp. Stat. § 140/7.5 (2020).

66. 425 U.S. 352 (1976).

67. *Id.* at 357.

68. *See* FOI, http://www.foiservices.com.

69. The data here is from a comprehensive study by Margaret B. Kwoka. *See* Margaret B. Kwoka, "FOIA Inc.," *Duke L. J. 65 (2016): 1361, 1388; see also Gardiner Harris, "House to Weigh Overha*ul of Open Records Process," *New York Times*, Jan. 11, 2016, at A14.

70. Margaret A. Blanchard, *Revolutionary Sparks: Freedom of Expression in Modern America* (Oxford, UK: Oxford University Press, 1992), 442.

PART III

The Flight from Privacy

Chapter 9

Public and Private: Celebrities and the Rest of Us

Woody Allen's 2012 movie, *To Rome with Love*, told four separate stories connected only by the fact that they took place in Rome.[1] One story concerns an ordinary man: a Roman office worker named Pisanello who is married, middle class, and has two children. Suddenly, one day, as Pisanello leaves his house to go to work, hordes from the media descend on him, asking question after question, demanding to know everything about him, and eagerly reporting everything to the public. He has become, through some freak of happenstance, an instant celebrity. Every word he utters, every action he takes, and every aspect of his life is chronicled, repeated, and magnified. Everything about him becomes an object of fascination: whether, for example, he wears boxers or briefs. This earth-shattering fact is reported, sent out to the general public, and proclaimed (as it were) from the rooftops. Women throw themselves at him. Why is he such a celebrity, he asks at one point, only to get a cryptic answer: he is "famous for being famous." Once you become a celebrity, the rest follows: the obsessive invasion of privacy, and the public hunger for every tiny detail of your life. In the movie, Pisanello's celebrity vanishes as quickly and mysteriously as it came. In real life, however, this is not usually the case. Celebrity can dissipate, but it usually happens much more slowly.

This segment of *To Rome with Love* is, of course, a riff about the nature of celebrity culture. But Pisanello is an unusual sort of celebrity: he is famous, but for no obvious reason; he was not the heir to the Danish throne, nor did he win a gold medal in the Olympics or star in a hit movie. Woody Allen is satirizing modern celebrity culture. But a man like Pisanello can, in fact, become a celebrity by accident—by winning the lottery, for example, or by becoming the millionth person to shop at Macy's or by suffering from a rare disease or being the victim of some sensational crime or giving birth to conjoined twins or quintuplets. These accidental celebrities are the so-called involuntary public figures. How much privacy can and should such people have? The public zest to know and follow anything that it finds fascinating, and the right of the press and the media to give the public what it wants, can come in conflict with the privacy rights of public figures, and even more so with the privacy rights of "involuntary" public figures.

In real life, a great celebrity, William Jefferson Clinton, became engulfed in a sordid scandal while president of the United States. He had a sexual relationship with a young intern, Monica Lewinsky. Every last detail of this sleazy affair made front-page news. The president lied about his involvement and the scandal threatened his office. The opposition, the Republican Party, impeached him for his "high crimes and misdemeanors." He was charged with committing perjury. His presidency was saved, however, when the impeachment failed in the Senate; Clinton served out the rest of his term.

Of course, the lies that a sitting president tells are matters of legitimate public interest, and it would be hard to think of a figure more public than the president of the United States. The sexual life and the foibles of President Donald J. Trump have been meat and drink for the media. Trump survived not one but two impeachment trials. He was also accused of paying hush money to a porn star. Yet the Lewinsky affair and the scandals that swirled around President Trump do raise an obvious question: does the president have *any* privacy rights at all, and if the answer is yes, what are they? Is it relevant whether *he* wears boxers or briefs?[2]

ORDINARY PEOPLE

The distinction between ordinary people and public figures is quite crucial, both in terms of social norms and in terms of the law. Basically, ordinary people enjoy more privacy protection than public figures. This is largely because, to be honest, nobody cares much about ordinary people, outside of their family circle and their little knot of friends. The kind of underwear John and Mary Smith choose to wear is never going to make headlines; the mass media will never report on this earth-shattering fact. Their underwear is and will remain their private affair. And if somebody *does* step over the line and invade the privacy of John and Mary Smith in an egregious way—by recording their bedroom noises or filming their bedroom behavior, to take obvious examples—there is, indeed, some protection for them and other ordinary citizens. In California, for example, a plaintiff can sue for damages against anyone who "attempts to capture, in a manner that is offensive to a reasonable person," visual images of the plaintiff, or sound recordings, or the like, using any device, if the plaintiff was "engaging in a private, personal, or familial activity." These activities include "[i]ntimate details of the plaintiff's personal life" or "[i]nteraction with the plaintiff's family or significant others under circumstances in which the plaintiff has a reasonable expectation of privacy."[3]

The statute would clearly cover the hidden camera in the bedroom. Would it cover secret photos of a husband and wife eating dinner in the kitchen? That would presumably depend on whether it was "offensive to a reasonable person." Suppose a secret film showed us sitting at a table, eating an apple, a harmless activity. Still, if this event was recorded secretly in our home, people might be likely to object—if not to the subject matter then to the way the footage was obtained. It would certainly unsettle most people to realize that cameras were poking their mechanical eye into their daily life, no matter how humdrum the events that were recorded.

Note also that the California statute is completely general: it does not distinguish between ordinary people and public figures. But the statute would probably not apply to public figures—at least not in the same way as it applies to the rest of us; that is what the case law suggests. In a way, the California law, as it now exists, is a watered-down version of what was originally proposed. The original goal was to do something about the paparazzi, a group that has little or no interest in Tom, Dick, and Harry, not to mention Mary, Jane, and Joan.[4] Yet the statute does not refer to professional photographers; indeed, people who make a living taking pictures of celebrities may not, in fact, be covered, because "public figures" have so much less in the way of privacy rights than the ordinary Joe and Jane.

The New York statute is narrower but more explicit. It is directed at "unlawful surveillance," which is made a crime. The crime is to capture the image of "a person dressing or undressing or the sexual or other intimate parts" of a person without the person's knowledge or consent, if this is done for "amusement, entertainment, profit, sexual arousal or gratification," or to abuse or degrade a person. That familiar phrase, "reasonable expectation of privacy," appears in the statute. It applies to bedrooms, bathrooms, showers, changing rooms, homes, hotels, and motels.[5] Here, even more clearly than in the California law, the point is to protect sexual and bodily privacy. That, of course, is a major concern for most people—though not, to be sure, the only one. As we said, for many people, the idea of a surveillance society, a society in which cameras are everywhere, is profoundly unsettling. People accept these cameras, but selectively. Cameras at airports and courthouses are acceptable, but cameras regularly sweeping the street in front of your house or satellite photos of your backyard would seem invasive in an unjustified way.

PUBLIC FIGURES

The law of privacy, as we said, distinguishes between public figures and the rest of us. The law asks two connected, but quite separate, questions. First, exactly who counts as a public figure? And second, once somebody is defined as a public figure, how much privacy does that person enjoy? Or, more accurately, how *little* privacy does that person enjoy? This is why the line between the public figure and the rest of us is so important. Once you enter the emerald palace of the public figure, the law veers sharply in a different direction.

Public figures also have much less anonymity than the rest of us, that is, if their faces are familiar. A movie star cannot go to a restaurant and expect not to be noticed. Most people would recognize the president or the pope; whether they would recognize their Congressional representative is less certain but is possible. For many public figures, anonymity is a lost cause. But privacy is still very much an issue.

What constitutes a public figure? There are, of course, some obvious candidates. Clearly, the president of the United States, the queen of England, movie stars, and famous sports figures all qualify. So does the Dalai Lama, the pope, the president of Russia, and some business figures, especially the super-rich like Bill Gates and Warren Buffett. Television commentators and stars and game show hosts also qualify. There are people who are famous for shooting baskets in basketball, footballers, and famous artists like Andy Warhol. It is also perfectly clear which people are *not* public figures—almost all of us, as a matter of fact.

But the line between the two categories tends to blur in the middle. Is the governor of Wyoming a public figure? Probably yes, at least in Wyoming. And the mayor of Wichita, Kansas? Again, perhaps in Wichita. But then, is the chief of police of Wichita a public figure? The mayor of a small town in France? The dean of students at Oberlin College? A minor character actor in an occasional minor movie? A baseball player who has never made it to the major leagues? What is the "public" that makes a public figure public? How should we treat big frogs in little ponds? And, then again, what about people thrust suddenly into the limelight, sometimes for reasons out of their control? Is a woman who becomes Queen of Carnival at Mardi Gras a public figure? What about a man whose house was destroyed by an earthquake and who is interviewed on TV?

Generally speaking, all *celebrities* are public figures. We live in the age of the celebrity. There is a large and growing literature on the subject of the celebrity and celebrity culture. There is a clear distinction between simply being famous and becoming a celebrity. A celebrity is known not for accomplishment but for "visibility."[6] All celebrities, "to one degree or another," are people whose activities are "publicized."[7] In a famous passage, Daniel Boorstin defined the celebrity as someone "known for his well-knownness."[8] This was the situation that Woody Allen parodied in *To Rome with Love*.[9] The many definitions of celebrity, and the endless discussions of celebrities and celebrity society, are often, in their own way, quite helpful, as far as they go. But they often seem to miss a key point or mention it only in passing: a celebrity is more than famous. Fame is a necessary, but not sufficient, condition for celebrity. A celebrity is a famous and *familiar* figure.

Queen Victoria, for example, was certainly famous; her picture was on postage stamps and her face was on the coinage. She was both queen of England and empress of India. But she was not a celebrity in the modern sense. She had millions of subjects, but only a few of them had actually seen her, met her, or talked to her. Few people could recognize the sound of her voice. When her beloved husband, Prince Albert, died, she went into seclusion; for years, even though she was just as famous as ever, she was basically invisible to the public—she became a "sable-clad widow who shunned society."[10] George Washington was idolized, revered, and adored by his country, but again, how many people had actually heard the sound of his voice? Was he a good public speaker? What were his favorite foods? Did he own a dog? How many people actually knew him personally?

Victoria's descendant, Queen Elizabeth II, on the other hand, *is* a celebrity. She lives in a fishbowl to an extraordinary degree (or seems to). She is a constant presence in public and—more importantly—on television. We know, or think we know, everything about her: the way she walks and talks, the clothes she wears, her fondness for horse racing and dogs, even the travails of her children. There is, in short, an "illusion of intimacy."[11] Television "not only permitted such a feeling; it encouraged it, made it virtually inevitable."[12] The Queen, moreover, at one point deliberately cultivated familiarity: the royal family and palace officials were convinced they had to do this, to guarantee survival of the monarchy. When Princess Diana—a tremendous celebrity in her own right—died in a car accident, and the Queen failed for days to appear or to respond, the crown faced a major crisis of public relations. Unlike Queen Victoria, isolation was not an option for Queen Elizabeth.

The queen, of course, is a glittering personality, especially when she rides in a golden carriage or wears the paraphernalia of monarchy. But she is also a woman, a mother, and a lover of pets, an ordinary person as well as a queen. The "ordinariness" promotes, as Joshua Gamson wrote about entertainment stars, a great sense of "connection and intimacy between the famous and their admirers."[13] The celebrity, then, is both special and humdrum. The celebrity is familiar. And this familiarity is crucial to the status of a celebrity.

Of course, to be familiar means to be exposed. When the Dalai Lama lived in a palace in Tibet, screened from the outside world, his flock worshipped him, but he was also a mystery—august, distant, and hidden from view. Popes in the nineteenth century hardly ever left the Vatican. The emperor of Japan was a god, immured in his palace. Queen Victoria was, as we said, the "widow of Windsor." All this has changed dramatically in modern times. All of these figures—the Dalai Lama, the Pope, the Emperor of Japan—have become celebrities and feel, apparently, that they *must* become celebrities. But to become a celebrity, you have to step onto the public stage (or at least appear to). You have to let everybody see you, hear you; you must become knowable, familiar. Thus, a celebrity is, in a way, a person without privacy, or at least a person who *appears* to have no privacy. A celebrity is a person whose whole life seems to take place under the eye of the camera, like the main character in *The Truman Show*, which we discussed earlier, a person whose life, unknown to him was a show, an act, something broadcast to an audience, whose so-called friends and relatives were actually actors playing their parts.[14]

The celebrity culture did not evolve overnight. Gossip, scandals, scurrilous stories about political figures—these have a long and colorful history.[15] But actual *celebrity* status and celebrity culture is, we argue, a rather new and different social phenomenon. There was poisonous gossip in the court of Louis XIV, but this kind of gossip was confined to court circles in Versailles or among small groups of elites. In the nineteenth century, there were rumors that Thomas Jefferson had a sexual relationship with a slave woman (these rumors turned out to be true); later, rumors circulated that President Grover Cleveland had fathered a "love child" (also probably true). Rumors in the late nineteenth century spread rapidly; they radiated outward from a central core. That core was fed by the mass media of the time—the cheap and widely accessible newspapers. Indeed, the celebrity culture clearly coevolved with the mass media, on which it absolutely depends.

Then came radio. The award-winning movie *The King's Speech* (2010)[16] highlights the relationship between the future King George VI, who had a serious stammer, and an Australian speech therapist, Lionel Logue. The movie, as usual, takes liberties with the facts, but the King in fact did have a stammer and he did work with a speech therapist. The movie begins with the young prince stuttering his way through a speech in 1925 and ends with a big radio speech in 1939, after England had declared war on Germany—a speech given to an audience of millions.[17] Clearly, by 1939, it seemed terribly important for the King of England to reach the mass of his subjects, to speak directly to citizens on the street and in their homes, and to leave (so to speak) the confines of Buckingham Palace. Clearly, too, the audience expected to hear the King's own voice. Americans in the 1930s could listen to President Franklin Delano Roosevelt on the radio. Roosevelt's voice was famous: clear, melodious, effective. Millions of people heard Roosevelt's "fireside chats"; these talks had enormous political significance.[18]

Movie newsreels, and then television, above all, increased the visibility of celebrities—and of public figures in general. Now they became, as we said, *familiar* in a new and different way. Now it was not only their voices but also their faces, their bodies, and everything about them that people *experienced.* People looked at celebrities, as it were, through a one-way mirror. The country watched television and they learned—or rather thought they learned—everything about celebrities, their habits, their ways of life, their homes, their families, their foibles. Of course, we, the audience, were invisible to the celebrities. But they knew we were there. That surely affected their behavior. Meanwhile, the fact that we saw them, heard them, and read about them probably had a major effect on public attitudes: familiarity helped to create or strengthen the notion that the public had a *right* to know everything, even the most intimate details of the lives of public figures. They seemed transparent, and it was easy to imagine that they had a *duty* to seem transparent.

In American law, consequently, it is no surprise that the law has, for the most part, stripped privacy rights from public figures. Not all of their rights have been stripped, of course, but a substantial chunk of them. In American law, by and large, courts take the attitude that anything that interests the public is therefore in the public interest; thus, if the public wants to know something, it is something that they have a right to know. Add to this that, in American law, the definition of a "public figure" is extremely broad. In other societies, the situation is by no means so clear, as we shall see.

The famous case of *Sidis v. F-R Pub. Corp.* is a good illustration of what came to be the basic American attitude.[19] Indeed, Samantha Barbas claims that this case represented a kind of turning point—a "foundational moment" in the development of privacy law.[20] The plaintiff, William James Sidis, had been one of the most exceptional child prodigies in history. He graduated from Harvard at sixteen, spoke a number of languages, and was a genius at mathematics. But as an adult, Sidis flamed out. An article about him appeared in *The New Yorker* magazine in 1937 under the title "Where Are They Now? April Fool!" At that point, Sidis was thirty-nine years old. He lived alone in shabby digs in Boston. He was no whiz at anything; he worked at a dull clerical job. He was a neurotic recluse who collected streetcar transfers. The article dredged up these facts about Sidis's life; publication of the article upset him greatly, and he brought suit against the magazine, claiming invasion of privacy.[21]

Sidis, however, lost his case. Sidis was a public figure, and the public had a right to know what happened to him in his later life. His right to privacy had to bow before that right.[22] The Sidis case was, if not a turning point, at least an indication of the wave of the future. Ordinarily, to disclose private facts to the public might give rise to a lawsuit for invasion of privacy. But not, apparently, for anyone defined as a public figure.[23]

It is fair to ask, however, *why* the public had the right to know what happened to poor Sidis. And what kind of a "public figure" was he? He was at best a marginal and temporary one. A child prodigy is less newsworthy once the child becomes an adult. Obviously, the public had a certain amount of curiosity about Sidis, if they remembered him at all. Presumably his story sold magazines. But why is satisfying this interest of the public something that advances the public interest? How did this story—which clearly invaded Sidis's privacy—contribute to any sort of policy debate? Is it important to know that some child prodigies fizzle out? It is something of a stretch to claim some social value for the article.

In the 1970s, an article in *Sports Illustrated* dealt with the life of Mike Virgil, a well-known "body-surfer." Virgil, it seems, was a very strange person. He once extinguished a lighted cigarette in his mouth; he reportedly ate "spiders and other insects and things," but avoided red meat because it took up "too much energy."[24] Was this article an invasion of Virgil's privacy? The court felt otherwise. Body surfing was a "matter of legitimate public interest." These "personal facts" about Mike would help to explain to the readers why he indulged in an "extremely daring and dangerous style of body surfing."[25]

Thus, courts have not only chopped down the privacy rights of "public figures," they have also, and equally significantly, expanded the category itself. Sidis and Mike Virgil both turned out to be "public figures." *Sidis* also stands for the proposition that once you become a public figure, you are always a public figure.[26] Samuel Cohen was a professional boxer in the 1930s, known as "Canvasback Cohen."[27] In 1939, he gave up professional boxing. Ten years later, in 1949, Groucho Marx mentioned him on his program, *You Bet Your Life*; Marx said he "once managed a prize-fighter, Canvasback Cohen . . . he got knocked out."[28] Cohen brought a lawsuit for invasion of privacy. Like Sidis, he lost his case. A person who "by his accomplishments, fame or mode of life, or by adopting a profession or calling which gives the public a legitimate interest in his doings, affairs, or character [is a] public personage."[29] Cohen had voluntarily entered public life as a professional boxer, looking for "publicity and the adulation of the public." In so doing, he had "forfeited" his right of privacy "on matters pertaining to his professional activity."[30] He could not "at his will and whim draw himself like a snail into his shell."[31]

In the light of these cases, one is entitled to ask: do bona fide, full-blown public figures have *any* privacy rights? Is the public entitled to know about the president's sex life, what kind of underwear he wears, or whether he snores at night? It is hard to squeeze some sense of limits out of the current case law, on either prong of the issue: who counts as a public figure, and what privacy rights such figures have. Tommy Lee, a drummer in a rock-and-roll group, married Pamela Anderson, a television star. They took videotape pictures of themselves having sex. A contractor who was working in their Malibu home stole the pictures and peddled them to the highest bidder, which happened to be *Penthouse* magazine; the magazine, of course, was eager to publish the images. Lee and his wife brought a lawsuit, asking for $30,000,000 for this invasion of privacy. But a federal district court felt that the pictures were "newsworthy"; the sex life of this couple was a legitimate subject of public concern.[32]

As always, law here followed on the heels of social change. Samantha Barbas has seen what she considers a major change in society from the 1920s on—the rise of a culture of self-expression, in which the "tone of emotional life shifted from repression to release."[33] A "controlled public façade" was no longer important; people were encouraged to express themselves, to reveal their "inner self," to be "effusive and candid."[34] One can argue about the exact time and nature of this change in culture and whether the 1920s really represented a turning point. But it seems clear that what has been labeled expressive individualism seems to be a cultural feature of the times we live in. In this culture, true celebrities are not mysterious and distant figures but reflections of our own selves, people doing their own thing, but on a kind of public stage; they were free to shift themselves from "repression" to "release," but if "repression" implied privacy, then "release" meant, in a sense, that anything goes. For public figures at least, their right to express themselves implied a correlative right of the public to see them expressing themselves, in the open, and in almost every regard.

The "mass-circulation press" and the media in general both reflected and enhanced the slow, gradual rise of expressive individualism; they emphasized it, publicized it, and helped to disseminate it. Self-censorship was a dying practice. Newspapers and magazines felt free to fill themselves with gossip, celebrity tittle-tattle, self-help advice, and "human interest" stories.[35] This was a new form of journalism—a shift from the traditional function of reporting "practical important news," information about ships coming and going, and, to be sure, a great deal of political reporting, much of it hopelessly biased. But then, more and more, "news" came to include "interesting personal gossip," reports about lurid crimes, and whatever else might appeal to a mass audience. In the process, newspapers became "rich and powerful."[36] At this point, too, newspapers had the power and the ability "to make ordinary people visible," to transform them into "public figures."[37] For this, "they did not have to occupy a position of leadership or perform an extraordinary feat; all it took was for them to seem newsworthy."[38] And who was newsworthy? Besides the usual suspects, newsworthy individuals include victims of crime; people involved in scandals or litigation; people "who ran important political, economic, and civic organizations"; people "with expertise and inside dope on subjects reporters deemed interesting"; figures from the entertainment world; and even "obscure people whose travails . . . became the grist for colorful, often poignant human-interest stories."[39] Or, perhaps, plain people on the street, so long as they were stopped by a reporter and asked for their opinion on some subject. Newsworthy people might even include people who happened to live next door to the victim of some spectacular crime or whose home was destroyed in a flood or who won the lottery.

For genuine public figures, of course, publicity was often very welcome. Movie and television stars derived enormous benefit from the false familiarity that they got from the fan magazines, and, later, from television and YouTube and from the social media. Notices in gossip columns and stories in magazines were fodder for the careers of screen personalities; they spread publicity about these stars to a huge and hungry audience. This "news" included who they were dating, who they were marrying and divorcing, what they were "really" like.[40] For politicians, too, the publicity—the image—had enormous value; on the other hand, gaffes and mistakes could be dangerous or even fatal to a career. Publicity, however, matters much less for temporary or involuntary public figures. The queen of England, and royal families elsewhere in Europe, are keenly aware of how they can benefit from publicity—of the right kind, anyway. Queen Victoria, perhaps, had much less reason to worry about public opinion. The surviving monarchies of Europe are still in place precisely because the royals are no longer isolated in their palaces, surrounded by aristocrats and courtiers. They have all converted themselves into celebrities—"stars" of television and mass-market magazines. Nobody believes in the divine right of kings anymore, and nobody (or hardly anybody) in the developed world wants to give a king or queen true political power. What function, then, does Queen Elizabeth II serve? Why is she so popular? Her popularity depends on her behavior, of course, but beyond that, it depends on her celebrity status. She is a genuine "star." And this is something her public not only accepts but even cherishes.

But stardom has its costs and its pitfalls. In 2019, an interview by Prince Andrew, one of Queen Elizabeth's sons, was so disastrous that it cost him his position as a working member of the royal family.[41] Then Prince Harry, who had married a woman of color (and an American at that), split noisily with the royal family. He and his wife gave a TV interview with Oprah Winfrey and gained headlines in the popular press. Scandals cost the King of Spain his throne. Before the celebrity age, kings and princes could indulge themselves with mistresses, and misbehave in all sorts of ways, without any lasting damage to their position. No longer. The era of royal privacy is gone.

POISONED TONGUES: LIBEL LAW AND PRIVACY

The Supreme Court of the United States decided the celebrated case of *New York Times v. Sullivan* in 1964.[42] The plaintiff in this case, L. B. Sullivan, was a local official in Montgomery, Alabama. He brought a libel action against the *Times* and also against four black clergymen. His complaint was based on a full-page advertisement in the *Times* headed by these words, "Heed Their Rising Voices." The ad described the civil rights struggle in Montgomery and the tactics used by local officials to try to suppress the movement. It was signed by a long list of prominent people, including Eleanor Roosevelt; there was also a list of black clergymen. At the bottom was a kind of coupon that readers could fill out to make a contribution to the cause.[43]

No mention was made of Sullivan in the ad but he was in charge of the local police in Montgomery. Unfortunately, the *Times* had not checked the facts very carefully and a number of statements in the ad were just plain wrong. These were not particularly earth-shaking errors. The ad said that Martin Luther King had been arrested seven times; actually, he was arrested four times. Most of the mistakes, similarly, were not really substantial. The basic thrust of the ad was undoubtedly correct: civil rights workers and black leaders were targets of a "wave of terror" in Montgomery.

But the mistakes gave Sullivan his opening. The outcome of the libel trial was never in doubt. The all-white jury found for Sullivan and awarded him damages in the amount of $500,000; damages were also awarded against the black clergymen. The Alabama Supreme Court affirmed the work of the lower court. Sullivan had, on the surface at least, a good case. A jury had heard the evidence, had decided the statements were both untrue and libelous, and had awarded damages. All of this was normal jury work. But the case could have had disastrous results for the civil rights movement. It was not the only libel case pending against the *Times* and other news organizations. Indeed, the case was the "tip of the iceberg"; as a result of all the lawsuits, the *Times* stood to lose millions of dollars.[44] Damage awards could have crippled news organizations; at the very least, the awards would have made them super-cautious in criticizing the white South and in running ads for civil rights groups. The only hope lay in the Supreme Court; the *Times* and its lawyers had to convince that Court to craft a new, unprecedented doctrine of constitutional law, one that would rescue them, and end this type of lawsuit.

This is exactly what the Supreme Court did. Criticism of "official conduct," the Court held, was constitutionally protected against libel laws. Mistakes and errors were normal in vigorous debate and critique; officials simply had to swallow them or refute them as best they could. Only in cases of "actual malice" could the official win his case. That is, a libel action against a public official could be sustained only if an untrue statement had been made "with knowledge that it was false or with reckless disregard of whether it was false or not."[45] The decision was essentially unanimous, at least on the main issue in the case.

New York Times v. Sullivan came out of the civil rights movement. Segregationists in the South were doing everything they could to crush the movement with threats and violence—and then with lawsuits. Libel actions were a promising tactic. After the trial in this case, the assets of the four black clergymen were seized—Ralph Abernathy's car was taken, along with the bank accounts of the other defendants.[46] The Supreme Court—the same Court that had decided *Brown v. Board of Education*—was aware of what was at stake. The Court was not going to let libel suits crush the civil rights movement. This helps to explain why the Court felt obliged in this case to strike out boldly in a new direction.[47]

But it does not explain what happened afterward. For one thing, the doctrine spread to other countries; it might be more accurate to say that forces were at work that led to similar developments in other countries.[48] And in the United States, in later years, the *Times* doctrine burst out of its civil rights background, and the hatchling began to grow and grow. The doctrine applied to public officials; that much was clear. But what makes someone a public official? In a case from 1979, in Washington state, the plaintiff was "Administrator of the Cowlitz County Motor Pool." He was accused, in a newspaper, of illicitly installing "spark plugs, wires, oil, and an oil filter"—county property—in a car belonging to the sheriff's son. The court held that he was a "public official as a matter of law," and reversed a trial court award for libel.[49] Cases like this extended the concept of "public official" pretty far down the scale of government.

Even more significantly, in 1967, in *Curtis Publishing Co. v. Butts*,[50] the Supreme Court extended the doctrine to a broader category: "public figures." Butts was a football coach in Georgia. A magazine accused him of conspiring to "fix" a football game; he sued for libel. A private group of alumni paid his salary, rather than the state university. Technically, then, he was not a public official at all. But he was a "public figure," and this fact relaxed the rules about libel and slander. This was a major expansion of *Sullivan*. In some ways, the high-water mark was *Rosenbloom v. Metromedia, Inc.* (1971).[51] The plaintiff here was a distributor of nudist magazines. Justice Brennan, who wrote the main opinion for a badly fractured court, remarked that if "a matter is a subject of public or general interest, it cannot suddenly become less so merely because a private individual is involved."[52] This seemed to suggest that, in a libel case, so long as the subject was of "public interest," the *New York Times* rule, or something more or less based on it, would apply. This would have shut the door on many, perhaps most, libel actions.

But the Court never took up this somewhat radical suggestion and beat something of a strategic retreat, notably in *Gertz v. Robert Welch, Inc.*[53] The plaintiff in that case was a prominent Chicago attorney—but not (according to the court) a "public figure." Gertz won his case, and the Supreme Court rejected the "public interest" criterion. In *Time, Inc. v. Firestone* (1976), the plaintiff, Mary Alice Firestone, sued her wealthy husband for divorce; it was a long, bitter, and messy case.[54] The trial court in Palm Beach County, Florida, sided with the husband, who had counterclaimed. The wife's sex life, said the court, was a history of "bounding from one bedpartner to another with the erotic zest of a satyr," behavior that would make "Dr. Freud's hair curl."[55] When this was reprinted, Mary Alice Firestone sued for defamation. The Court refused to consider her a "public figure," even though the case was sensational, and even though "the marital difficulties of extremely wealthy individuals may be of interest to some portion of the reading public."[56] Which seems unquestionably true.

NOBODY KNOWS MY NAME

Most public figures have chosen this life or have chosen a path that would make them a public figure. If you decide to run for president or to rise in the Church hierarchy or to become a movie star or a hero of the sports world, you have to take the bitter with the sweet. You are exposed, in a celebrity society, to autograph hounds, to paparazzi, to the breathless reporting of the tabloids, and even to the stares and ogles of people who recognize you in public. You certainly have less anonymity than John or Jane Q. Public. For many celebrities, this is a small price to pay—or a big price, but a price worth paying. Many celebrities live and die on the basis of publicity. This is less true, we suppose, for the pope or the Dalai Lama than for the Kardashians, who have no visible talent *except* their celebrity, and who would fade into obscurity without a constant barrage of publicity.

But what about people who became famous without meaning to? These might include victims of a sensational crime, people who win the lottery, people who come down with some rare and dreaded disease, Or people, in general, who become tangled in some event that makes the headlines but who have certainly not asked to be in this position.

These people are "involuntary public figures." Another term found in the case law is "limited purpose public figures"[57]; they are "public figures" in one special regard, or in one particular way, but not in any others. Others have referred to them as "accidental celebrities"; that is, these are people who became "the focus of attention initially through no fault of their own, and through a process over which they can have very little control."[58] The line between the two categories is indistinct, or maybe "muddled" would be a better word.

In the case law, when an action is brought for invasion of privacy (or, as we will see, for libel), the defendant is usually from the media: a magazine, a television company, a newspaper. And the defense, almost invariably, includes a ringing and self-righteous appeal to the freedom of the press. A key case was *Time, Inc. v. Hill* (1967).[59] The Hill family's home had been invaded by three escaped prisoners who held the family hostage for almost an entire day, and then left in the family car. The family was not physically harmed—in fact, the convicts had been rather polite. It was, of course, an ordeal, and very frightening. What happened to the Hill family was headline news, but after a while, the story more or less died out, as stories do, and the Hills tried to get back to their normal lives.

Two years later, in 1954, Joseph Hayes published a thriller, *The Desperate Hours*, about a family held hostage by escaped convicts. Hayes drew on the experience of the Hill family, but embroidered it with a lot of juicy details, including some violence and even some hints of sexual tension. The book sold very well, and was turned into a play and a film. In 1955, *Life* ran a story about the play, and claimed, wrongly, that it was faithfully based on the experiences of the Hill family; the story in the magazine used their name and showed a picture of their house. This brought the whole trauma up again; the family was appalled and Elizabeth Hill, the wife and mother in the family, slipped into a deep depression. The family sued in the New York courts for invasion of privacy. A jury found for the Hills and awarded them significant amounts of money. Time, Inc., the publisher of *Life*, quite naturally appealed.

The case ultimately went all the way up to the United States Supreme Court. The justices found the case troubling, and they quarreled and bickered over it. An early draft, and an early straw vote, gave the nod to the Hill family; but in the end, after a certain amount of internal dissension, the court decided, six to three, against the plaintiffs. Freedom of the press got the upper hand. Justice Brennan wrote the majority opinion. You could not bring an invasion of privacy case against the media, even when the media got the facts wrong, as long as the subject was of public interest. This rule insulating the media was, like the *Sullivan* rule, applicable, except when the defendant deliberately lied or made its report "in reckless disregard of the truth."[60]

In 1980, Carlyne Campbell sued the publisher of *Brother to a Dragonfly*, a book written by her ex-brother-in-law, telling the story of his life. She claimed the book was libelous, and also that it invaded her privacy. Will D. Campbell, the author, was described by the court as a "contemporary religious and civil rights leader."[61] At the trial court level, Carlyne Campbell lost her case. The court saw nothing libelous about the book. The trial court also felt that a "public interest privilege" protected the publisher. On appeal, the

Fifth Circuit affirmed. Carlyne Campbell was probably not a public figure, but this did not help her here. The appellate court agreed that information on matters of public interest is "privileged." All that was needed was a "logical nexus" between what was printed and "the matter of legitimate public interest." In this case, the court felt that "private facts relating to her homelife and marriage with the author's brother" were germane enough to earn constitutional protection.[62]

What privacy rights do "involuntary public figures" have? The Hill family would certainly fall into this category. Carlyne Campbell, whose only claim to fame was that she married the brother of somebody who was arguably a public figure, might also qualify. A lot seems to turn on the subject matter, as far as courts are concerned. Is the issue one of "public interest" or not? And to what degree. Consider Merle Dameron, an air traffic controller at Dulles Airport in Washington, D.C. A magazine article had a sentence or two that implied that air controllers deserved at least "partial blame" for a 1974 crash in Virginia. Dameron was the sole air traffic controller on duty that day. Ninety-two people died in that crash. He claimed he was not to blame for the accident, that a court had completely "exonerated" him, and that the article brought him "into disrepute, and . . . caused him humiliation and mental anguish."[63] He sued for libel. The trial court granted summary judgment against him. In 1985, the D.C. Court of Appeals affirmed this judgment. Dameron, the court admitted, was an "ordinary citizen," who, before the crash, "was completely unknown to the public."[64] He was not and is not a "general-purpose public figure," but what happened raised him, "involuntarily, to the status of limited-purpose public figure."[65] And that was enough to cost him his lawsuit.[66]

This was, of course, a libel case. But notions of "involuntary public figures" or "limited-purpose public figures" are relevant to privacy cases. Libel cases are tough to win. The plaintiff has to show that the defendant lied, and that the lies were hurtful, economically and psychologically; then there is also the barrier of *New York Times v. Sullivan* and what came after. Plaintiffs are therefore tempted to throw in a claim of invasion of privacy.[67] Here, truth is irrelevant; the only issue is whether privacy was invaded in a way that deserved compensation. This is often a helpful argument. Still, there are formidable barriers, for example, the "privilege" that the press enjoys, and the menacing concept of the public figure, voluntary or not.

What about people thrust into the limelight because they suffered from the acts of criminals? Can states prohibit newspapers from publishing the names of rape victims and other survivors of horrendous crimes? Many states have banned the media from revealing names in the interests of privacy.[68] In Massachusetts, it is illegal to publish the name of an alleged victim. In Nevada, information in court or police records that identifies the victim of a sexual offense is confidential. The media can publish this information if a court decides the victim will not suffer harm, and the applicant shows good cause. In Nevada, too, a pseudonym can be used in place of a victim's real name.[69]

Of course, here "privacy" conflicts with the rights of the press and the media, and perhaps with the whole notion of freedom of speech and expression. In *Cox Broadcasting Corp v. Cohn*,[70] the family of a dead rape victim sued the media for printing the victim's name, which a Georgia statute prohibited. The Supreme Court denied the claim, but partly on the grounds that the victim's name was available through court documents, which were open to the public. In *Florida Star v. B.J.F.*,[71] a Florida statute made it unlawful to print the name of a rape victim "in any instrument of mass communication."[72] A reporter for the *Florida Star* found the victim's name in a police report, and it appeared in the newspaper, even though this was against the newspaper's policy. A jury awarded the victim damages, but the Supreme Court reversed; basically, a newspaper that "lawfully obtains truthful information" cannot be punished for publishing that information, except to "further a state interest of the highest order," which this was not.[73] Would the Court feel the same way about anonymous whistle-blowers? Or for people who have been given a new identity by the federal government, as part of the witness protection program?[74]

Courts find "limited purpose" figures and their lawsuits troubling. Consider the case of Oliver Sipple. Sipple was a former marine. He was also gay. In September 1975, the then-president, Gerald Ford, was visiting San Francisco. Sara Jane Moore tried to assassinate the president, but Sipple, who was in a crowd at Union Square, grabbed her arm as she was about to shoot at Ford, possibly saving the president's life. Stories about Sipple appeared in the local newspaper, the *San Francisco Chronicle*, and also elsewhere—the *Los Angeles Times* described him as a "husky ex-marine" and "a hero," but also a "prominent figure in the gay community."[75] The trouble was, Sipple had never come out to his family. He sued the two newspapers, and various others, on the grounds that they had published "private facts" that were "highly offensive" because of their effect on his family; they exposed him "to contempt and ridicule causing him great mental anguish, embarrassment and humiliation."[76]

Sipple did not, however, win. Two points were fatal to his claim. First, Sipple was not really in the closet, except to his family. He was, in fact, an active member of the gay community in San Francisco. Thus, said the court, his sexual orientation was already in the "public domain," and the newspaper articles simply gave this fact "further publicity." The second point was even more crucial: the stories about Sipple were "newsworthy." There was nothing "morbid and sensational" about the newspaper accounts. They were in fact "prompted by legitimate political considerations," that is, "to dispel the false public opinion that gays were timid, weak and unheroic figures."[77] Indeed, the *Los Angeles Times* made precisely this point: reports about Sipple "presented information contrary to the stereotype of homosexuals as lacking vigor."[78]

But didn't Sipple also have a point? He was a public figure, of course, but a temporary one, and basically an accidental one. He had compartmentalized his life—successfully, as it seems. Wasn't he entitled to hide his sex life from his family? Yes, he marched in parades. But does "privacy" mean absolute, total secrecy? And did the stories about him really advance a policy discussion? The court and the newspapers constructed an argument about heroic, manly gay people, and they made it sound plausible. But the argument would have been just as plausible if they hadn't printed Sipple's name. The logic of the case seems far-reaching. A person can construct an argument that is more or less plausible for *any* story in *any* newspaper, to the effect that the story deals with a policy issue of some sort and serves some sort of public purpose. If the public has a right to know about the funny eating habits of body surfers, it basically has a right to know absolutely anything about anybody—at least anybody that could conceivably be labeled a public figure, temporary or permanent, and anything that could conceivably be considered of public interest.

Take the question of whether David Beckham, the famous footballer (and all-around celebrity) was wrong to allow his four-year-old daughter to suck on a pacifier. Was this proper parental behavior? An English tabloid touched off debate on this earth-shaking subject in 2015 by showing a photograph of the child with a pacifier in her mouth. The tabloid criticized Beckham for letting this happen; apparently, some people think pacifiers can damage a child's teeth, and perhaps even its speech. The star responded vigorously in self-defense. All of this seemed important enough to warrant a detailed report in the *New York Times*.[79]

This incident is instructive in a number of ways. First, a newspaper assumed—correctly, no doubt—that its readers would be interested in this minor detail in the life of this celebrity. Did Beckham's daughter's pacifier have relevance to an issue of public concern? Arguably, it did: child-rearing practices are "newsworthy." It is assumed, of course, that the public has a *right* to this information—that they care enough about it, or are fascinated enough by it, to override any notion of Beckham's privacy rights. Beckham wrote in an Instagram post, "Why do people feel they have the right to criticize a parent about their own children without having any facts?" But clearly, "people" do feel they have this right. Celebrities, including Beckham, of course bring this on themselves with their hunger for publicity. Presumably, they would also like to see some limits. And perhaps there are limits—but not very many.

What applies to Beckham apparently applies also to anybody who, for whatever reason, comes to the attention of the media—and the public. Consider the case of Scott Thomas, of Jacksonville, Florida. In 2005, Scott suffered a terrible accident. According to his wife, Eliza, he tripped over a dog in their kitchen. Scott suffered massive brain damage and ended up in the hospital on life support, helpless and unconscious. His wife and mother quarreled bitterly; each wanted to be appointed his guardian. According to rumors, local law enforcement authorities had their doubts about the dog story. Local TV stations reported that Eliza wanted to transfer Scott to a hospice and remove his feeding tubes. Eliza, upset and angry, sued the media companies for libel and invasion of privacy.[80]

Before the accident, Eliza and Scott were nobodies. Now Eliza had become, in the opinion of the trial court, a "limited purpose public figure." Presumably, this would give her more protection than a celebrity would get. But it wasn't enough to win her case. The stories about Eliza were in the public interest. First of all, a law enforcement investigation is a subject people need to know about. Also, there is controversy and debate about when to keep comatose patients going, and when to pull the plug.[81] These are genuine arguments, and certainly plausible. But, like the argument about Sipple's heroism, they have a certain made-up flavor. Did the TV station really act out of a sincere desire to further a debate about life-support systems or to inform people about police investigations?

If not, then what *was* the motive of the media? Simply, the story was "news" and people found it genuinely interesting. People have always loved gossip. Almost everybody would relish knowing, for example, that their next-door neighbor was carrying on an affair with another neighbor. If the block they lived on had its own little newspaper, this tale of adultery would surely be headline news, but not because it contributed to some kind of public debate. You can certainly construct an argument: adultery is a social problem, family life is a pillar of society, and so on. But this would be, no doubt, after the fact. The real draw of the story is that it feeds people's hunger for gossip.

Television, and the media in general, are a huge presence in society. There are dozens and dozens of channels, and the web is, for all intents and purposes, infinite. Then there are the surviving newspapers, magazines, and other print media. The media have an insatiable appetite for material. They compete intensely, trying to capture some of the limited stock of public attention. Whatever captures the fancy of the public, or some part of it, is fair game for the media. In the process, the distinction between the public and the private gets blurred. There is news about the president of the United States, to be sure, and other public figures, but there is also news about the tragedies and triumphs of ordinary people—things that happen to them, or about them, or near them, but that are not part of their humdrum daily existence. In any case, you can, as we saw, always construct an argument that the stories in the media contribute to the debate about some genuine policy issue. This is not, of course, why the public is gawking and staring.

The question, then, is whether there are any limits at all. Is what the public *wants* to see and hear the same as what it has a *right* to see and hear? Is *everybody* whose name gets in the newspapers, or who is mentioned or shown on TV, a "limited purpose" public figure? Theoretically, no. On the other hand, the media do not mention people's names and write about them randomly. People appear in the paper because of some story, something that is presumably newsworthy, and thus, arguably, has some point, some connection with some issue of policy, or at least *something* that the public takes an interest in. And this means treating countless people as "limited purpose public figures"—dragging them out of anonymity into the bottomless pit of "newsworthiness." It means losing the right to sue for libel, or for invasion of privacy, or both, except in the most extreme situations.

The case law is not uniform, to be sure. Courts tended to see public concern or interest in almost everything in the 1960s and 1970s.[82] But, starting in the 1980s, the case law became somewhat confused and inconsistent.[83] The decisions seemed to backtrack to a degree. A lot seemed to depend on the exact situation, and the chords it struck in the minds and hearts of the judges. In *Brownie Miller v. National Broadcasting Company*, the plaintiff was the widow of a man who suffered a heart attack in October 1979.[84] The family called the Los Angeles fire department and the paramedics came out to try to save Mr. Miller's life. An NBC television crew also tagged along; the crew filmed the work of the paramedics and used the film on its nightly news hour. Miller died that night in Mount Sinai Hospital. NBC was working on a "mini-documentary" about the work of the paramedics. The trial court threw the case out, but the appellate court reversed. Not only was Mrs. Miller's home "invaded without her consent, but the last moments of her dying husband's life were filmed and broadcast to the world," showing "an alarming absence of sensitivity and civility." To be sure, "public education about paramedics" and about the "use of cardio-pulmonary resuscitation (CPR) as a life-saving technique" would qualify as "news."[85] And freedom of the press was certainly an important value, and an issue in this case. But there are rights besides the rights of the media and, in this case, the court felt those rights had to prevail.[86]

The Millers, of course, were just plain folks. The court reacted to their hour of grief, and perhaps also to the greed and callousness of the media. Yet courts, in general, do give freedom of the press the upper hand over the right of personal privacy. In many states, as previously mentioned, statutes insist on privacy for victims of sexual assault. We should also mention the so-called rape shield laws; these laws, which exist pretty much in every American state, protect the sexual privacy of rape victims. In a rape case, generally speaking, the defense cannot drag in evidence of the victim's past sexual behavior. There are, to be sure, fairly big holes in the law, but the basic goal is fairness to victims of sexual assault; another goal is to prevent the admission of painful and irrelevant matter into evidence. In essence, these are rules that protect the privacy and private lives of rape victims.

Law or no law, many newspapers and television stations have voluntarily adopted a policy of keeping these names private. Whether such policies are effective is another question. A study conducted in 2003 and 2004 examined newspaper articles about victimized children. The study found that in slightly more than half of the instances, the articles *did* reveal identifying information such as the name of the victim or the name of a school, street, or family member, although not always deliberately.[87] Newsworthiness often outweighs privacy considerations.

A California case, *Brown v. Kelly Broadcasting Co.* (1989), explored the limits of privilege and newsworthiness.[88] This was a defamation case, but the reasoning might well apply to privacy cases as well. The defendant was a television station in Sacramento. The plaintiff, Brown, was a licensed contractor. The station broadcast a program in which a homeowner complained about Brown's work; the homeowner claimed that Brown left him with "warped doors" and "peeling paint, cracking plaster, blistered wallpaper, shoddy work, inside and out."[89]

Technically, the main question had to do with a section of the California Civil Code, which, at the time, privileged communications in which speaker and recipient shared a common interest. The station claimed that "when the news media publish and broadcast matters of public interest they have a common interest with their audience."[90] Plaintiffs could recover only if they proved "malice" on the part of the station—a high bar.

The California court felt otherwise. Much of the opinion turned on a reading of the Civil Code, but the court also discussed the line of cases that followed *New York Times v. Sullivan*. This line, the court felt, did not support the station's argument. Besides, the claimed privilege was "so broad that it would apply to almost every defamatory communication."[91] The "practical result" would be that "nearly everything they publish and broadcast would be privileged" because the media publish and broadcast "only matters that the media believe are of public interest."[92]

It is hard to line the cases up and come out with some clear, consistent rule. What privacy right do you have, for example, if you are convicted of a crime? Some criminals, of course, are arguably "public figures": notorious gangsters and drug lords, for example, or men like the late Bernie Madoff, whose Ponzi scheme bilked people out of enormous sums of money. But not Arnold B. Huskey, an inmate in an Illinois prison. NBC, in making a film about conditions in the prison, took footage of Huskey, who was in the "'exercise cage' . . . wearing only gym shorts, leaving several distinctive tattoos exposed."[93] Huskey had not agreed to be filmed and he brought suit for an injunction against showing the footage. A federal district court held that Huskey had a case for invasion of privacy and denied a motion to dismiss. Husky was not a public figure and likely not even a "limited purpose public figure." NBC had never made a showing that filming Huskey was anything but "morbid and sensational" prying.[94] But what about one Steve Gates?[95] Gates served a sentence of three years; in 1992, he pleaded guilty as an accessory to a "murder for hire that occurred in 1988."[96] Hitmen had killed an automobile salesman in southern California. The story was that a "prominent automobile dealer" had masterminded the plot to keep the dead man from bringing a certain lawsuit. Gates was the mastermind's assistant manager.

The defendant in the case was a television production company; it broadcast an account of the crime in 1991—more than a dozen years later. Gates sued, both for defamation and invasion of privacy. He claimed, first of all, that the defendant got the facts wrong; he also claimed that he had served his time, had been leading a blameless life, and had a right, in effect, to sink into deep obscurity. The defamation claim came to nothing, since the plaintiff had trouble showing anything wrong with the station's facts, which were based on public records. The trial court thought there might be something to the privacy claim, but the California Supreme Court felt otherwise. The court cited *Cox Broadcasting Corporation v. Cohn*, which we mentioned earlier, where the name of a rape victim had been published. The *Gates* court also showed little or no sympathy for Gates's argument. There was no strong "state interest in protecting for rehabilitative purposes the long-term anonymity of former convicts."[97]

The *Gates* court did not discuss whether Gates was a public figure, either voluntary (he did plead guilty to a crime), involuntary, limited-purpose, or of any type. But that issue was more or less lurking behind the scene. Of course, not everybody, by any means, becomes an object of intense public interest by pleading guilty to a crime. But when you admit guilt and go off to prison, this casts a certain shadow over any claim to privacy, anonymity, and healthy obscurity. The right of the public to know, hear, and see is apt to take priority over this right—except, perhaps, when you are in the exercise cage and NBC comes along with its cameras.

In 2017, the US Court of Appeals for the District of Columbia further defined what it meant to be a "limited purpose public figure." In *Kahl v. Bureau of National Affairs, Inc.*,[98] the court wrestled with the question of whether Yorie Von Kahl, a man convicted of murdering two US marshals while attempting to evade arrest, was a public figure. Kahl brought a defamation suit against a legal publisher for erroneously attributing damaging statements to the sentencing judge instead of the prosecutor at his trial, and the case made its way up to the Court of Appeals. The court decided that Kahl was a "limited purpose public figure." "Public figures" are people "who have 'thrust themselves to the forefront of particular public controversies in order to influence the resolution of the issues involved.'"[99] In this case, Kahl "assumed a public role . . . when he used his access to the press to promote his cause."[100]

If we take the courts' views literally, then *anybody* who gets involved in a "public controversy" in some significant way becomes a "limited purpose public figure." *McKee v. Cosby* (2017) arose out of the tangled affairs of the comedian Bill Cosby, who was accused of sexual offenses and convicted of these crimes. Kathrine McKee was one of Cosby's victims, who went public with her accusations. Cosby's lawyer, Martin Singer, sent a letter to a newspaper claiming that her accusations were unfounded and denouncing her in ways that she considered defamatory. She lost her case; the court felt that she had thrust herself into an important controversy, had "deliberately come forward" with her accusations, and had become "as a matter of law" a "limited-purpose public figure." Her defamation claim could not meet the *Sullivan* standard. The Supreme Court denied certiorari in 2019 over a vigorous dissent from Justice Thomas, who attacked the *Sullivan* case and its progeny.[101] These were, of course, defamation cases, rather than privacy cases, and the shadow and substance of *Sullivan* hangs heavily over them (to Justice Thomas's annoyance). But by analogy, at least, the same considerations would apply to privacy cases. If you become entangled in a "public controversy," whether voluntarily or not, you have stepped into the world of the "limited purpose public figure," and at least some of your privacy rights fly out the window.

Judges are, after all, human beings, and they react to the facts of cases. The more outrageous and intrusive the behavior of the media, the more likely the case will go against them. *Conradt v. NBC Universal, Inc.* (2008) is a good example.[102] NBC cooperated with law enforcement to catch "sexual predators." They set up a sting operation to catch men who thought they were dealing online with young boys; Louis William Conradt—a prosecutor in Texas, no less—fell into their trap. With great hoopla, a SWAT team and NBC television crews swooped down on Conradt, who committed suicide. His sister, Patricia, sued NBC, alleging a great number of things, including invasion of privacy and reckless or purposeful infliction of emotional harm. Since Conradt was dead, his sister, the court said, was not entitled to bring a privacy claim for him; however, a reasonable jury, the court said, could find that NBC had "engaged in conduct so outrageous and extreme that no civilized society should tolerate it," that NBC pandered to "lurid curiosity" and had overstepped the bounds of decency.[103]

Diaz v. Oakland Tribune (1983) can be taken as a vivid illustration of some of the dilemmas and gray areas that bedevil privacy doctrine.[104] The plaintiff had been born Antonio Diaz in Puerto Rico. She underwent surgery and emerged as someone who, by "all outward appearances[,] . . . looked and behaved as a woman and was accepted by the public as a woman."[105] Diaz kept the surgery a secret except from family and close friends. In 1975, she enrolled in the College of Alameda; she was elected student body president in 1977–1978 and was also chosen as the student body representative to the Peralta Community College Board. While head of the student body, she became embroiled in a controversy—she accused the college administrators of misusing student funds. In 1978, the defendant, a newspaper, printed an article outing Diaz; the article stated that students "will be surprised to learn that student body president, Toni Diaz, is no lady, but is in fact a man. . . . I suspect his female classmates . . . may wish to make other showering arrangements."[106] Diaz claimed the story threw her into a depression; as a result, she suffered from insomnia, nightmares, and memory lapses. She sued for invasion of privacy.

She won her case before a jury, which found in a special verdict that her secret was "private and not public," was not "newsworthy," was "highly offensive to a reasonable person," and was disclosed with "reckless disregard" of the fact that it was offensive.[107] The jury awarded her compensatory and punitive damages. The newspaper appealed but the appellate court affirmed the decision in favor of Diaz.

Was Diaz a public figure? As student body president, she was, "for some purposes," a public figure, but not much of one: a big frog, but in an awfully small pond. Moreover, getting elected as the first woman student body president did not in itself open up her whole life to inspection. The story of her sex change had nothing to do with her fitness for office.[108] The story, in the court's opinion, was not "newsworthy." The court, quite clearly, was annoyed at the *tone* of the article in the newspaper. Its "attempt at humor at Diaz's expense remove[d] all pretense that the article was meant to educate the reading public."[109]

Clearly, this case came close to the line and could easily have gone the other way. Perhaps most other courts *would* have decided that this story—that the first woman to serve as student body president at a local college had been born a man—was newsworthy. Sex reassignment operations, in general, seem to intrigue the public; the rights of transgender individuals are hotly debated and are, today at least, a matter of intense public interest; they are also the subject of controversial legislation, especially on the point mentioned in the article: use of bathrooms and showers and whether women born as men should be able to compete in women's sports. Arguably, then, the story about

Diaz's sexual identification was "newsworthy," and it was something the public had a right to know; also, she was enough of a public figure to come under the *Sullivan* line of cases.

That was 1983; in 2021, perhaps the case might come out differently. What constitutes a "public figure," major or minor, and what constitutes a "newsworthy" story changes with the shifting winds of public opinion, public interest, and—not least of all—the thought processes and personal opinions of judges and juries. It might make a difference if the plaintiff seems to be a good guy, and the defendant a bad guy, or vice versa. A lot depends, too, on whether a court feels the public has a legitimate interest in whatever the topic may be.[110]

The cases are not easy to line up in a row. The question of "public interest" is crucial, and at times seems to swallow up everything else, but not always. The *Sullivan* rule does not apply to ordinary people, however; for these people, the usual rules of libel and slander apply, and privacy rights are also still relevant. As we have seen, the level of protection they receive may very well depend on how the plaintiff is classified.

Della-Donna v. Gore Newspapers, a Florida case decided in 1986, is a good illustration.[111] The plaintiff, Alphonse Della-Donna, complained that a newspaper, the *Fort Lauderdale News*, had libeled him. Della-Donna was a lawyer, trustee of a trust set up by a wealthy client. Nova University was a potential beneficiary of the trust. Della-Donna and Nova became embroiled in a dispute over the money, and this ended up in a tangled lawsuit. The newspaper ran seventy-eight articles about the trust and the lawsuit, and Della-Donna claimed that some of these articles had libeled him. The trial court threw the case out, and the appellate court affirmed. In the first place, this was a matter of "public interest or concern."[112] Nova University was important to the community, and the disagreement about Nova—who controlled it, how it was financed—had an "appreciable impact on the community."[113] This was also, judging by the newspaper stories, editorials, and letters to the editor, a genuine "public controversy."[114] Della-Donna "played a central role in the controversy" and, in the court's view, this indeed made him a "limited purpose public figure."[115]

ACROSS THE POND

It was reported on October 2, 2014, that the Duke and Duchess of Cambridge (better known as Prince William and Kate) had asked a photographer to stop "harassing" their baby, little Prince George. The photographer answered that he was taking pictures in a public park—pictures of Prince George and his nanny—and had a perfect right to do so. The royal family, on the other hand, muttered darkly about "stalking" and accused the photographer of "monitoring" the daily routines of the little prince. Prince William, according to the account, is concerned for his son; he wants the boy's life to be as "normal" as possible (which is not very likely). The royal family may have considered "legal action."[116] This was no idle threat. In 2017, topless photographs of the Duchess taken with a long-lens camera were published in a French magazine; a French court awarded damages and imposed fines. [117]

The feelings of the royal family are understandable, but in the background was a brutal fact: a rich market exists for photographs of celebrities, including celebrity babies. Angelina Jolie and Brad Pitt sold the right to pictures of their babies for a fortune. The photographer who took pictures of little Prince George smelled a market: a public hugely hungry for such pictures. If the little prince was in America, if the photographer was not actually trespassing and was violating no other laws, and if the little prince was a "public figure" (which he almost certainly was, from the day of his birth), the photographer could probably fend off any legal action. This would, apparently, be less true in the United Kingdom, or in the rest of Europe.[118]

Nonetheless, the United States is not the only celebrity-focused culture, and certainly not the only country facing issues of privacy. And the concept of a "public figure" is important elsewhere. Moreover, some legal systems have distinguished, as the United States has, between different types of public figure. In German law, for example, pure public figures are "Personen der Zeitgeschichte," literally, persons who are part of contemporary history. But then there are partial or "relative" public figures, and these are more or less the equivalent of the "limited purpose public figures" in American law.[119]

On the whole, courts in continental Europe seem more sensitive to rights of privacy than American courts—even for public figures. How much privacy do "public figures" enjoy in Europe and elsewhere? Each country will, of course, have its own way of answering this question. But generally speaking, doctrines that are dominant in the United States are less so in other countries.

The well-known German *Lebach* case (1973) grew out of a notorious crime and its aftermath.[120] A radical gang attacked an army base in the town of Lebach; four soldiers died. A minor figure in the conspiracy, driver of the getaway car, was convicted and sentenced to ten years in prison. Later, a public TV station in Germany planned a film about the crime. The plaintiff, who was about to be released from prison, objected to the use of his name and image. He claimed, like Gabrielle Melvin, the right to a fresh start in life. The film would violate this basic right; German law, he argued, guaranteed the sanctity of private life, and the right to develop one's own individuality. The TV station, quite naturally, objected; nothing in its film was inaccurate and the public had a right to know about this important crime and the significant issues it raised.

Yet the German Constitutional Court took the complaint quite seriously. The court balanced the plaintiff's rights and the rights of the TV station, and came down on the side of privacy and the plaintiff. The fact that ten years had gone by since the date of the crime was perhaps the crucial factor. The court protected the plaintiff's right to wipe out the past.[121] In the United States, as we saw, there is a tendency to hold that, once a public figure, always a public figure (Sidis, for example). The German court felt otherwise. Still, the matter was hardly cut and dried. By 2000, German courts had second thoughts, and a television producer gained the right to show the program on the air as part of a series on "Crimes That Made History."[122]

A later and more astonishing German case concerned one Armin Meiwes.[123] Meiwes, born in 1961, had committed a truly disgusting crime. He trolled the Internet searching for a victim, someone willing to indulge Meiwes's sexual fantasy: eating human flesh. But he didn't want just anybody's flesh: he wanted a "handsome" man "between 18 and 30 years old."[124] Believe it or not, he found what he was looking for: Bernd Brandes, an engineer from Berlin, was a bit older than desired, but otherwise crazy enough to volunteer to be Meiwes's victim. The two soulmates got together for their ghastly session. Meiwes mutilated Brandes and they both tried to eat some of his flesh; then Meiwes gave Brandes alcohol and painkillers, stabbed him to death, butchered the body, ate some, froze some, and made a video for his private edification.[125]

Later, Meiwes went back on the web to look for another victim. But this time, somebody went to the police and told them what Meiwes was up to. When the story broke, it was naturally headline news in the tabloids. Meiwes was tried and ultimately convicted of murder, despite some technical difficulties with doctrine. He appealed all the way up to the German Constitutional Court, but that Court upheld his conviction.[126]

What happened next would seem, to an American reader, quite extraordinary. A company produced a horror movie based on the Meiwes case. It was scheduled to be released in Germany in 2006. Meiwes had the gall to bring a lawsuit, arguing that the movie would violate his right of privacy, and should therefore be banned. The movie did not use Meiwes's name, but it followed the case quite closely. Probably no one would be fooled. A German court sided with Meiwes. Freedom of expression was important, of course, but the movie had no social value. It did not contribute to any serious discussion of policy. It was just a horror movie, mere entertainment for people who had a taste for that type of story.[127]

On appeal, at the level of the Bundesgerichtshof, however, this decision was overturned, and Meiwes lost his case.[128] The court pointed out that Meiwes himself had given out interviews—he was hardly a shrinking violet. He had no right to "demand that he be portrayed publicly only in the way he would wish to be portrayed."[129] Yet it is astonishing that his case had gotten this far and that it was taken seriously at all. In the United States, Meiwes would have been considered a public figure. End of discussion.

Human rights law in Europe is quite complicated. There are national courts, interpreting the constitutions of their particular states. There is the European Court of Justice, which interprets the law of the European Union. There is also the European Court of Human Rights (ECHR). Every European country, big and small, from Andorra to Russia, has signed on to the European Convention on Human Rights. The ECHR decides disputes arising under the Convention. Are the countries of Europe bound to follow the decisions of the ECHR? The short answer is: it depends. National courts and legislatures cannot simply ignore the decisions but whether countries must follow them, and to what extent, varies from country to country. If you ask a British or a German lawyer whether the courts of their country are obliged to obey or follow decisions of the ECHR, do not expect a short and simple answer.[130]

Nonetheless, one can talk about general tendencies and trends. The ECHR is both powerful and active, and its decisions have a strong influence on local policies. A much-discussed 2004 decision of the ECHR, *Von Hannover v. Germany*, turned on the privacy rights of public figures.[131] The plaintiff was Princess Caroline of Monaco, the oldest daughter of the Prince of Monaco, and a prime target of paparazzi. She brought a lawsuit in German courts, in which she tried to prevent publication of some photos taken by paparazzi. These were by no means sensational photos—they showed her riding a horse, canoeing with her daughter, shopping, playing tennis, sitting with a male friend in a restaurant, and, in one group of photos, dressed in a bathing suit at the Monte Carlo Beach Club, where she tripped and fell flat on her face.[132]

The Constitutional Court of Germany decided against the princess. For one thing, she was unquestionably a public figure. Outside of her home, she had only a limited right of privacy. She was fair game for photographers unless she was somewhere secluded.[133] The public, the Court felt, had a legitimate interest in knowing how the princess behaved, and where she did her behaving. The ECHR, however, disagreed. Photographers had violated her fundamental rights by intruding on her privacy. Moreover, the photos in question, according to the ECHR, had no real value in policy terms. They could not be "deemed to contribute to any debate of general interest to society."[134] Their only purpose was to "satisfy the curiosity of a particular readership."[135]

The ECHR followed up its decision a year later in a case involving a woman far less famous than the Princess—indeed, a woman who was not famous at all.[136] The plaintiff, Mrs. Sciacca, was a schoolteacher in Sicily. In 1998, a woman complained to authorities about "irregularities in the management of the school's affairs."[137] A criminal investigation followed, and Mrs. Sciacca was arrested. Two newspapers published articles about the investigation and published photographs of Mrs. Sciacca. She insisted that the information up to that point should have been kept secret and, in particular, that no photographs should have been released. The ECHR agreed. Article 8 of the European Convention begins with a ringing declaration: "Everyone has the right to respect for his private and family life, his home and his correspondence."[138] Mrs. Sciacca's rights under Article 8 had been breached.

Article 8 is vague, to say the least; it is a broad statement of principle, nothing more. Also, the state can supersede rights under Article 8, when this is "necessary" for "national security, public safety or . . . economic well-being"; "for the prevention of disorder or crime"; or to protect health, morals, or the "rights and freedoms of others."[139] The ECHR has, however, read Article 8 quite broadly, giving considerable privacy protection to European citizens, as these two cases illustrate. Under American law, at least arguably, Mrs. Sciacca would have been a limited purpose public figure; she was the defendant in a criminal investigation, which had political and social overtones. The photographs would surely have been privileged. And the Princess of Monaco would have had little or no chance in American courts.

One writer, somewhat overwrought perhaps, claimed that a "chasm as wide as the Atlantic" separates the United States from France on the matter of privacy law.[140] Apparently, French doctrine does not distinguish between public and private figures in the way that American law does. Both public and private figures have strong privacy rights. The key to French law is the concept of the public interest. Considerations of public interest—topics that are important to the state and to society—can and will trump privacy rights for public officials, but only if the information is germane to their public role. Hence, privacy doctrine protects them from people who want to know what kind of underwear they put on, or, for the most part, their sex lives. The cases are not exactly consistent; still, there is a strong case that French courts are more sensitive to privacy issues than their American counterparts.[141]

James Whitman, in a notable essay, argues that Europe and the United States embrace different and quite deep-seated "core sets" of cultural values. The core European value is "personal dignity, threatened primarily by the mass media." The core American value is freedom and personal liberty, which is "threatened primarily by the government."[142] The ECHR, in its interpretation of Article 8, leans toward strong protection for privacy and dignity; European doctrines sometimes do seem to clash with American doctrines.

Still, one can ask: is Whitman's thesis really right? It is an attractive idea, and there may be something to it, but the *actual* differences between the two realms of privacy law can easily be exaggerated. The ECHR held in favor of Princess Caroline but the German courts, after all, had denied her claim. On the other hand, in 2007, German courts ruled in favor of a woman ("Sonia F.") who was the girlfriend of Herbert Grönemeyer, a pop star in Germany.

A tabloid published pictures of her with her boyfriend in a café and strolling down the street. She won her case. Grönemeyer's wife had died and in his songs, he expressed sadness over his wife's death; fans were probably wondering what woman might replace her. But that issue, the court felt, did not justify publishing these photographs, which invaded Sonia's privacy.[143] Ray Madoff, in a book published in 2010, contrasted American and Italian law on an interesting issue: can privacy rights survive a person's death? An adolescent Italian boy killed himself, and a newspaper published pictures of his house, and the text of an essay he had written. His father demanded damages from the newspaper, and was successful. American law might well have decided differently.

Madoff also mentions a contrary instance. A sixteen-year-old killed himself. Photos, taken by the police showing the boy in his coffin, were displayed "at a public gathering." There were also statements that the boy had been involved in gang activities. The boy's mother sued for invasion of privacy and lost. Any rights he might have had died along with him.[144] Klaus Mann, the German novelist, in his book, *Mephisto*, wrote about a famous actor who sold his soul, so to speak, to the Nazis (hence the title of the book). This novel was based, in a fairly transparent way, on the career of Gustaf Gründgens, a famous German actor and director whose career continued during the Nazi period. After the actor's death, his adopted son brought a lawsuit to prevent the novel from being reissued. He won his case.[145]

An English decision in 2006 concerned the privacy rights of no less a public figure than the Prince of Wales.[146] The prince, when he went on overseas tours, was in the habit of keeping a handwritten journal in which he recorded his impressions of the trip. These were private; they circulated only among a few people in the prince's circle. A woman named Sarah Goodall, a member of the prince's staff, leaked the contents of one of these journals to the press. In doing this, she broke the conditions of her employment contract, which insisted on confidentiality. The prince had gone to Hong Kong at the time when the British were handing the colony over to the Chinese; the journal was full of frank comments on the event and the people involved. The prince won his case and the court enjoined further publication.

The English courts have never recognized the tort of invasion of privacy as such. But it is hard to read the cases without seeing something resembling the tort silently creeping into the law, sometimes disguised as a "breach of confidence." Moreover, the UK has signed the European Convention on Human Rights, has enacted a Human Rights Act, and is under a legal duty to conform its law, as much as possible, to the convention and to the decisions of the ECHR. The prince's case raised the issue of a (supposed) conflict between Article 8 and Article 10 of the European Convention on Human Rights.

Article 8 protects private life, and Article 10 protects freedom of expression and the press.[147]

Still, in the end, the prince won his case. To be sure, as heir to the throne, Prince Charles was very much a public figure. His opinions, which were often frank and rather political, were certainly something the public would be interested in. But the judge, Justice Blackburne, ruled in favor of the prince—and, indeed, on summary judgment. Prince Charles, he thought, had a reasonable expectation of privacy. Although the journals did not contain the "often salacious celebrity information that sometimes features in privacy claims" (paragraph 114), the journals were meant to be confidential. Any contribution of the Hong Kong journal to public debate, or to informing the electorate, was "at best minimal" (paragraph 132). The Prince was "as much entitled as any other person to enjoy confidentiality for his private thoughts"; these are an aspect of his "human autonomy and dignity" (paragraph 133). And in September 2012, the Queen of England's grandson Prince William and his wife, Kate, successfully blocked publication of photographs showing the couple sunbathing, taken with a long-distance zoom lens; Kate had been topless. The lawsuit was brought against a French magazine and decided by a French court.[148] Prince William had more luck than his brother, Prince Harry; nude pictures of Harry cavorting in Las Vegas were all over the web, and his body (the rear view, at any rate) was splashed all over *The Sun*, an English tabloid.[149]

In short, in England, and also in much of the continent, the public has a right to know a lot, but within definite limits. The English courts have, for example, issued injunctions that prevent newspapers from reporting on details of cases that, in the United States, would be classified as invasion of privacy cases. Other countries, too, have wrestled with the issue.[150] Outside the United States, in general, courts do not allow the media to publish or display photographs of celebrities and like without a valid reason. Mere curiosity about the lives of celebrities is not enough of a reason. European societies, to be sure, are celebrity societies; there is a hunger for details of the lives of the rich and famous. Obviously, there was a market for photos of Princess Caroline. But the ECHR, sounding a theme that resonated at some levels of the *Meiwes* litigation, felt that the mere fact that people *wanted* these photos was not enough. The same can be said about the photographs of Prince William, Prince Harry, and other "royals." An American court, most likely, would have allowed any such photos to be legally peddled to the media and from there to the general public.

A much-discussed English case in 2004 concerned Naomi Campbell, a world-famous model. *The Daily Mirror* published a story about Campbell with the headline: "Naomi: I Am a Drug Addict." She never actually said anything of the sort. The newspaper had discovered that she was attending sessions of Narcotics Anonymous; the story they concocted was thus essentially true (and Naomi Campbell had, in the past, lied in denying her drug problem). She brought a lawsuit against the *Mirror.* She did not claim that the facts were wrong; she wanted damages for breach of a duty of confidence. The case zig-zagged up the chain of courts in England, with various results; in the end, in a split decision, the House of Lords held in her favor.[151] Indeed, in the House of Lords, one of the judges spoke about an invasion of her right of privacy, even though there is, supposedly, no privacy tort in the UK. Again, there is no question that an American court would have sided with the newspaper. She was definitely a public figure and, in American eyes, the public had a right to know about her addiction. If what a body surfer ate was relevant to public debate, surely the private addiction of a famous model was legitimate grist for the media mill. Indeed, the House of Lords admitted as much, but still felt that the action of the *Mirror* crossed the invisible line that separated the right of the press from the privacy and confidence rights of Ms. Campbell.

Max Mosley had been the head of an auto-racing group, Formula One, which made him at least a minor public figure. He was, moreover, the son of Sir Oswald Mosley, who was, in his day, the most prominent and notorious leader of the British fascist movement. A British tabloid claimed that Mosley had indulged in a five-hour sadomasochistic romp with prostitutes in an apartment in Chelsea, London. Mosley sued for invasion of privacy and, in 2008, won a verdict of £60,000, which was enormous by British standards. The Mosley story, as one can imagine, sold scads of newspapers. The public was certainly fascinated.[152] But the court found "no public interest or other justification" for the antics of the tabloid, which had, for example, secretly recorded the goings-on.[153]

Perhaps this case too would have turned out differently in the United States. The court may have been influenced by the brazen behavior of the tabloid. There is a widespread feeling that the tabloid culture, in England and probably elsewhere, has simply gone too far. A big scandal in the early twenty-first century in England turned on the questionable tactics of the media empire of Rupert Murdoch. *The News of the World*, a Murdoch paper, had hacked the phones of famous people, including members of the royal family.[154] More shocking was the revelation that the paper had hacked the phone of relatives of Milly Dowler, a murder victim.[155] The scandal had major political and social consequences. Murdoch was forced to close down *The News of the World.* A number of executives of his companies had to resign; some of them were later arrested and charged with various offenses.[156]

The real villain in the Murdoch saga, aside from Murdoch himself, was the "anything goes" culture of the media, a kind of race to the bottom, feeding on the hunger of the public for "news" about celebrities. Ironically, a great media empire—an empire that thrived on scandal, especially sexual scandal—was itself humbled and wounded by scandal. Probably, invading the privacy of public figures, politicians, and royals disturbed people less than what was done to the privacy of the Dowler family.

Privacy law in Europe, and particularly in the United Kingdom, seems to be in flux. Still, case law at least suggests some difference between the way European courts deal with the privacy of public figures, and the way in which American courts deal with this issue. Whatever the reason, elites seem to enjoy more deference, at least marginally, in Europe compared with the United States. And this deference may go along with a *lack* of deference on the part of elites: a lingering suspicion of the masses and mass culture. In the European cases, judges, or at least some of them, seem appalled by mass culture, with its insatiable curiosity for celebrity gossip and its lack of respect for the private lives of the rich, the well-born, and the famous. But when all is said and done, these differences are at the margins.

And they may be transient. Europe certainly has all the trappings of a celebrity culture—the tabloids, the gossip magazines, the TV shows about the rich and famous. Tabloids in England have been as brash as any in the United States, and perhaps more so. They are willing to pay good money for pictures of little Prince George or of the babies of any celebrity, and for any information or pictures about any big, juicy scandal. *Bild*, a German tabloid with a huge audience, achieved a breakthrough of sorts in 1994 when it published a picture of Charles, Prince of Wales, taking a shower. This dubious scoop was featured on the front page, with a huge black headline that proclaimed (in German): "Charles Naked!" *Bild* was famous for its "page one girls": nude or seminude women displayed on the front page. It finally dropped this daily tidbit, after having shown five thousand of these "page one girls." Tabloids are, if anything, more raucous and shameless in Europe than in the United States. *Bild* was a prime German example, but vehicles in Spanish for celebrity gossip are flourishing. The pages of *Diez Minutos* and *¡Hola!* are full of "news" about media stars, sports figures, and European royalty. In Italy, you have *Cronaca Vera*. In France, there is *Oops!* In Mexico, *El Gráfico* also features naked or near-naked women, plus sensational crime news and gory pictures. The British tabloid *Closer* puts out a French edition, which is quite popular; this tabloid was able to "scoop" the journalistic world with vital news about the secret sex life of President Hollande of France. A Polish tabloid, *Fakt*, distinguished itself by publishing a picture of the naked body of a murder victim. Mark West's study of Japan details a vibrant and extremely popular market for scandal in that country, including magazines "best known for their illegal publication of surreptitiously taken photos of starlets, usually either nude in hot springs or in their high school uniforms on their way to school."[157]

It should come as no surprise that different societies, with different cultures, will have different legal attitudes toward alleged invasions of privacy or toward the gathering of data in general. Take the case of a national census. There are grumblings and mumblings even in the United States about the census but these seem to be confined to small groups and the occasional paranoid personality, or are focused on particular census questions. After all, there has been a census in the United States since the late eighteenth century; it is expected and accepted as part of our legal order. In Germany, however, a census law enacted in 1983 proved to be extremely controversial and made some members of the public nervous. The census law was challenged in court on the grounds that it violated some of the basic rights of the citizen. And, indeed, the German constitutional court held the law unconstitutional, at least in certain regards.[158] The court's opinion, if we look past its technical and legalistic aspects, reflected a genuine sense of social unease—a fear, no doubt fairly widespread, of the power of the state, and specifically, fear of the power of government to gather information, including extremely personal information, and to use it for whatever purpose the state decides to use it for. The German government could and did respond to the decision by crafting a new census law; this one passed legal muster. But the older decision is by no means obsolete. According to one account, the court invented a "new basic right of informational self-determination"—a right to have certain data protected, that is, kept private.[159] The new census was carried out in 1987.

Mark West, as we saw, noted the hunger for celebrity dirt in Japan. Yet, legally, West argues, the "conception of privacy is more European than American—and perhaps more 'European' than European."[160] West gives a number of examples: in 1995, the Osaka High Court found that a novel based "on the story of a boy who died in a juvenile mental institution" violated rights of privacy. Respectable newspapers "often obscure the details of accidents, crimes, and illnesses so that viewers cannot determine the identity of the victim."[161] An important case in 1964 concerned a novel called *After the Banquet*. It seemed to be based on the relationship of a political figure, Hachiro Arita, and his former wife, though the names were changed in the book. Both Arita and his ex-wife brought lawsuits; they won their case on the basis of a right of privacy (unknown in Japanese law up to that point). This right, said the Court, implied an "assurance that one's private life will not be unreasonably opened to the public."[162] According to West, courts since then have applied this doctrine in a number of cases. Note that Arita, in the United States, would unquestionably be considered a public figure and very likely he would have lost the case.

In Europe, there has been some attention to what one might call a "right to be forgotten." A Spanish citizen, Costeja Gonzalez, made a complaint against a Spanish newspaper, and against Google. His complaint was this:

if you googled his name, up came links to two pages of the newspaper, *La Vanguardia*, of January 19 and March 9, 1998; this was a story about "a real-estate auction connected with attachment proceedings for the recovery of social security debts."[163] Gonzalez wanted these matters removed; he argued that the "attachment proceedings concerning him had been fully resolved for a number of years," so that it was now "entirely irrelevant" to refer to them. The European Court of Justice, the highest court of the European Union, agreed with Gonzalez. The data was sensitive, it was sixteen years old, and there was no particular reason why the public should be interested in the data. Gonzalez's right of privacy thus prevailed.

Many people would agree with a decision of this kind. As one person put it, young people "do not want their drunken pictures to follow them for the next 30 years." There are things in people's lives that they would like to disappear forever. Others, however, express worries about letting people "rewrite history." You certainly cannot "rewrite history" in the United States if you are a registered sex offender: you stay on the list for life and, in many states, your name is available to anybody who wants to inquire.

Of course, history does get "rewritten," and legally so, in certain circumstances: when juvenile delinquency records are expunged, for example, and also when a transgender person gets a new birth certificate—under some state laws, this person has a right to ask for this document. But these are, perhaps, exceptional cases. It is a problem that "everything is now on our permanent records," as one expert put it; but he felt, at the same time, that the Gonzalez approach was a "bad solution" to the problem.[164] In October 2014, Google notified the *New York Times* that "links to five articles" were removed from some search results in Europe to comply with the new "right to be forgotten." Two of the articles were old wedding announcements. Another was a brief death notice from 2001. According to this account, since the ECJ decision, Google had received "roughly 140,000 privacy requests connected to more than 500,000 links." The company had approved about half of these.[165] As of this writing (December 2021) there is still heated discussion about expunction and deletion. This is an age in which the internet and social media are swamped with messages, some of them wrong; some of them the product of crooks, hackers, and scammers; some of them hateful; and some of them truly dangerous. Do the social media companies have a duty to monitor these messages? Do they have a duty to delete messages that are alleged to be lying and mendacious? Do they have a duty to expunge what users want to be wiped from the record?[166]

THE CULTURE OF PRIVACY IN A CELEBRITY AGE

Clearly, the law on the right of privacy, in this age of celebrity culture, is in flux—both as to public figures and for the rest of us. This reflects the fact that social norms and social expectations are also in flux.

Celebrity culture might possibly be more virulent in the United States than in other democratic societies. But this is far from obvious. As we pointed out, the celebrity culture seems pretty much universal, at least in developed societies. The European courts express noble sentiments on behalf of privacy and human dignity. But how influential are they? The adopted son of Gustaf Gründgens brought suit against the novel *Mephisto* and won, as we mentioned. But the novel was turned into a movie by a joint German-Austrian-Hungarian production company. The movie was called *Mephisto*, like the novel. It was extremely successful at the box office and it won an Academy Award for best foreign film in 1981.

Celebrity culture seems just as obvious in Germany and the United Kingdom as in the United States—perhaps even more so. Celebrities themselves may be just as eager in Europe as in America to *use* the media when it suits them, and to manipulate their own public image. Privacy can be dispensed with when the gains from coverage seem to outweigh the costs. The royal family of Great Britain, including the queen herself, have long since learned this lesson.

Prince William and his wife, Kate, filed a lawsuit and won their case. But this couple was hardly publicity shy. In September 2012, they were shown prominently on TV, smiling and gyrating, doing a native dance in Tuvalu along with the folks of that mighty nation. William and Kate knew what they were doing; they clearly wanted friendly, good publicity—images of a handsome young couple enjoying themselves while doing their political duty. The engagement and marriage of Prince Harry to Meghan Markle, who was American, divorced, and of mixed race, was big news from 2017 on. The royal family (and the couple) did not at first dislike the publicity. The wedding was a huge and magnificent event. Dissatisfaction set in for the couple only later. Members of the royal family, like other public figures, want to enjoy the fruits of celebrity culture, but they also, no doubt, would like to preserve at least a decent amount of privacy. Celebrities in general would like to choose when, where, and how to expose their lives to the public. Whether they can do that successfully is another question. When Prince William blocked offending photos in France, they had already appeared in print in Ireland and Italy, and on the internet.[167] Prince Harry and his wife were so perturbed by the fishbowl life of "royals" that they more or less quit royal life (or tried to), and eventually left England altogether. They now earn their own keep and play no formal role in the royal family. But surely they are able to earn their own keep only by using their celebrity status.

As we said, all developed societies are celebrity societies, with television, fan magazines, mass marketing, the internet, YouTube, and social media of all sorts. Tabloids, as we said, and paparazzi, are found in country after country. The *cultural* differences, if not the legal differences, are differences in degree and nothing more.

In short, mass culture on both sides of the Atlantic—and, for that matter, across the Pacific, not to mention Latin America and Africa—seems much of a muchness. Mass culture is, among other things, celebrity culture. Some "stars" are purely national; some are international. Local football players and television stars can be specific to, say, Argentina or Italy, but gossip and scandal also feed on international celebrities like the queen of England, notably, and her somewhat dysfunctional family, as well as the president of the United States, religious leaders, rock musicians, major movie stars, and TV personalities like the Kardashian sisters. The differences between, say, the United States and France in this regard may reside less in mass culture than in the culture of elites—which the law tends to reflect. The French edition of *Closer* had to pay good money for its story about the French president's mistress, on grounds of invasion of privacy. Such a lawsuit might come out differently in the United States, but the zest for gossip and scandal—and the temptation to cash in on it—seems pretty much the same in both countries.

And perhaps the desire for personal privacy is also not that different. It can be argued, as James Whitman does, that Americans value "liberty" above "dignity,"[168] but the two concepts overlap. Nobody wants people peeping into their bedrooms. They may not want people staring at them in public, either. Princess Caroline would probably have lost her case in American courts, at least in the federal courts. But would she have done better in California, under Civil Code §1708.8? This law makes a person liable for "constructive invasion of privacy" if he takes photos "in a manner that is offensive to a reasonable person," and if the photos show a person engaging in a "private, personal, or familial activity."[169] To be liable under this clause, you need not intrude physically on a person's property; it is sufficient to use a "device" (like a zoom lens, for example) that does the intruding for you. The remedy is a tort action for damages; if the "invasion of privacy was committed for a commercial purpose," the defendant is "subject to disgorgement" of any of his ill-gotten gains and is liable, as well, to a civil fine between $5,000 and $50,000.[170] The Code provision says nothing about the distinction between private and public figures. But it makes very little sense unless it applies to celebrities as well as to the people next door. Paparazzi have no interest in using a zoom lens to photograph Joe and Mary Jones having a barbecue in their backyard; nobody would buy those photographs. Photographs of a movie star would be worth money, however. To be sure, using a zoom lens to capture images of Joe and Mary Jones having passionate sex on their backyard lawn *might* bring in serious money, but any such photographs would run afoul of other California laws. The general point is that *legal* differences between European and American law, with regard to the invasion of privacy, may be real, but are probably marginal. The *cultural* differences may be vanishingly small.

In a sense, then, there are two distinct segments of society, both legally and socially. One small segment consists of celebrities, big and little, who, by virtue of their place in society, have lost some of their privacy rights, whether they want to or not. Also in this segment are the exhibitionists who go on reality TV, the contestants on *Judge Judy*, the participants in game shows, and all those who lust inordinately for their fifteen minutes of fame. A much larger segment of society is made up of ordinary people who treasure their own privacy and guard it as best as they can. But even these people are, on the whole, eager to invade (through the media) the privacy of others. In a sense, then, people in modern societies have a choice: they can be private, or they can give up their privacy. If they choose to enter the public sphere, the price of entry is the loss of much of their privacy. The difficult issue is what to do about the middle group: people who accidentally, incidentally, or involuntarily attract the attention of some or all of the public.

All of this, of course, has to do with invasion of privacy, or alleged invasion of privacy, occasionally by individuals but mostly by the mass media. Invasion of privacy by major institutions, other than the media—by businesses, universities, hospitals, and government at all levels—is another problem, and an extremely serious and intractable one, as we have discussed. One point should be stressed. The "reasonable expectation of privacy"—in short, the privacy that people want and value for themselves—varies from time to time, from place to place, from situation to situation, and from culture to culture. Most women would consider it a gross violation of privacy if somebody gaped at them in the street or stalked them in the aisles of a supermarket. Men and women would probably object to body scanning at the entrance to a movie theater or a grocery store. But they accept this scanning in airport security lines. They might resent a department store that demanded the right to look at purses and briefcases at the entrance and exit but they accept this at a courthouse.

Safety and security are general catch-all excuses for some invasions of privacy and they are, on the whole, widely accepted. Intrusions, however, are accepted partly because they are universal, and administered basically without discrimination.[171] There would be lawsuits and objections if airport security only patted down people with dark skin. On the other hand, some people, on grounds of modesty, perhaps for religious reasons, would object to a pat down altogether.[172] The airports are, one observes, scrupulous in having men pat down men and women pat down women.

Yale University at one point decided that all freshmen and sophomores had to live on campus. In 1997, a group of Orthodox Jewish students objected strenuously. They cited religious rules about modesty, sexual behavior, and the relationship between the sexes. The dormitories, they felt (probably correctly), were hotbeds of fraternization, drinking, and sexual activity.[173] Yet at one time, not that long ago, dorms were single-sex houses; men were strictly barred from entering the sacred portals of a women's dorm, and vice versa. When dorms went coed, many parents objected. These complaints gradually died down. They survive in conservative and religious colleges. A case in the ECHR arose when devout Muslim parents in Switzerland objected to mixed swimming classes in school for their daughters. The school was willing to have the girls wear bathing gear that covered them almost totally, but the parents were still upset—the girls would have to share a space with boys in bathing suits and this was something they did not want for their daughters.[174] We have dealt elsewhere with nudity: in many contexts the naked body *must* be kept private. In conservative circles, and some religious circles, the modesty rules go further than for the majority population. Different groups, in short, have different conceptions of privacy, mandatory and elective, and society must somehow decide which ones to accommodate.

NOTES

1. *To Rome with Love* (Medusa Film 2012).

2. There was also, of course, a massive invasion of the privacy rights of Monica Lewinsky, who began as an obscure White House intern and became one of the most famous (or notorious) women in the world. This was also true, for example, of "Stormy Daniels," the central figure in one of the juicier Trump scandals.

3. Cal. Civ. Code §§ 1708.8(b), (k) (West 2020). The plaintiff may recover "up to three times the amount of any general and special damages that are proximately caused by the violation of this section"; punitive damages are also available. And a violator is "also subject to a civil fine," from $5,000 to $50,000. Cal. Civ. Code § 1708.8(d) (West 2020).

4. On this point, see Erwin Chemerinsky, "Balancing the Rights of Privacy and the Press: A Reply to Professor Smolla," *Geo. Wash. L. Rev.* 67 (1999): 1152.

5. N.Y. Penal Law § 250.45 (McKinney 2020).

6. Lawrence M. Friedman, *The Horizontal Society* (New Haven, CT: Yale University Press, 1999).

7. Charles L. Ponce de Leon, *Self-Exposure: Human-Interest Journalism and the Emergence of Celebrity in America 1890–1940* (Chapel Hill: University of North Carolina Press, 2002), 10. There is a large literature on celebrities and the celebrity

culture. See, e.g., Leo Braudy, *The Frenzy of Renown: Fame and Its History* (New York: Vintage Books, 1986); Ellis Cashmore, *Celebrity Culture* (Milton Park, UK: Routledge, 2006); Lawrence M. Friedman, *The Republic of Choice: Law, Authority, and Culture* (Cambridge, MA: Harvard University Press, 1990), 112–30; Richard Schickel, *Intimate Strangers: The Culture of Celebrity* (London: International Publishing Corporation, 1986).

8. Daniel J. Boorstin, *The Image: A Guide to Pseudo-Events in America* (New York: Vintage Books, 1961), 57.

9. *To Rome with Love* (Medusa Film 2012).

10. A. N. Wilson, *Victoria: A Life* (New York: Penguin Books, 2014), 263.

11. Eric Burns, *Invasion of the Mind Snatchers: Television's Conquest of America in the Fifties* (Philadelphia, Temple University Press, 2010), 48.

12. *Id.* Burns contrasts the influence of television with that of the movies; when "the setting is as casual and emotionally manageable as our own living rooms," we can no longer regard the stars "with a distant veneration" and "with awe." *Id.*

13. Joshua Gamson, *Claims to Fame: Celebrity in Contemporary America* (Berkeley, University of California Press, 1994), 29.

14. *The Truman Show* (Scott Rudin Productions 1998)

15. *See* Gail Collins, *Scorpion Tongues: Gossip, Celebrity, and American Politics* (New York: HarperCollins, 1998).

16. *The King's Speech* (Weinstein Co. 2010).

17. *Id.*

18. Eileen Ambrose, "FDR's Fireside Chats Went a Long Way toward Calming Fears During Dire Times," *Baltimore Sun*, Oct. 19, 2008.

19. *Sidis v. F-R Pub. Corp.*, 113 F.2d 806 (2d Cir. 1940). The article in question was Jared L. Manley, "Where Are They Now? April Fool!," *New Yorker*, Aug. 14, 1937, at 22.

20. Samantha Barbas, "The *Sidis* Case and the Origins of Modern Privacy Law," *Colum. J. L. & Arts* 36 (2012): 21, 23.

21. *Sidis*, 113 F.2d at 807–808.

22. Sidis tried to appeal to the Supreme Court, but the Court denied certiorari. Barbas, *supra* note 20, at 57. He continued to struggle against the magazine, claiming that he had been libeled. In 1944, he settled for $600, and more or less claimed victory. *Id.* at 58. He died in the same year. *Id.* at 61.

In many ways, the *Sidis* case represents a turning point—a drastic reversal of the attitude shown in *Melvin v. Reid*, 297 P. 91 (Cal. Dist. Ct. App. 1931). Gabrielle Melvin had once been a genuine public figure, a defendant in a sensational murder trial; in 1931, she successfully sued a movie company that made a movie of her life and thus, she said, invaded her precious privacy. She was almost certainly lying but the court believed her, and even though she was in a way a public figure, the court sided with her. This was a pioneer case about the right of privacy in California.

23. On this point see Samantha Barbas, "The Death of the Public Disclosure Tort: A Historical Perspective," *Yale J. L. & Human.* 22 (2010): 171; Diane L. Zimmerman, "Requiem for a Heavyweight: A Farewell to Warren and Brandeis's Privacy Tort," *Cornell L. Rev.* 68 (1983): 291.

24. Curry Kirkpatrick, "The Closest Thing to Being Born," *Sports Illustrated*, Feb. 22, 1971, at 62.

25. *Virgil v. Sports Illustrated*, 424 F. Supp. 1286, 1289 (S.D. Cal. 1976). In *Virgil v. Time, Inc.*, 527 F.2d 1122 (9th Cir. 1975), the court sent the case back down to the trial court, which dismissed the lawsuit.

26. *See infra* notes 115–56 and accompanying text.

27. *Cohen v. Marx*, 211 P.2d 320, 321 (Cal. Dist. Ct. App. 1949).

28. *Id.*

29. *Id.*

30. *Id.*

31. *Id.*

32. *Lee v. Penthouse Int'l, Ltd.*, No. CV96–7069SVW, 1997 WL 33384309, at *5 (C.D. Cal. Mar. 19, 1997).

33. Barbas, *supra* note 20.

34. *Id.*

35. Helen MacGill Hughes, *News and the Human Interest Story* (Chicago: University of Chicago Press, 1940), 2.

36. *Id.*

37. Ponce de Leon, *supra* note 7, at 48.

38. *Id.*

39. *Id.*

40. *See* Barbas, *supra* note 20; *see also* Anthony Slide, *Inside the Hollywood Fan Magazine: A History of Star Makers, Fabricators, and Gossip Mongers* (Jackson: University Press of Mississippi, 2010).

41. *See* Mark Landler, "After Disastrous Epstein Interview, Prince Andrew Steps Down from Public Duties," *New York Times*, Nov. 20, 2019, at A8.

42. *New York Times Co. v. Sullivan*, 376 U.S. 254 (1964); for information on the background of the case and its meaning, *see* Kermit L. Hall and Melvin I. Urofsky, New York Times v. Sullivan: *Civil Rights, Libel Law, and the Free Press* (Lawrence: University Press of Kansas, 2011); Anthony Lewis, *Make No Law: The Sullivan Case and the First Amendment* (New York: Vintage Books, 1991).

43. The ad is reproduced in Hall and Urofsky, *supra* note 42, at 20.

44. *Id.* at 180. There were also five lawsuits against the Columbia Broadcasting Company, amounting to $1.7 million.

45. *Sullivan*, 376 U.S. at 297–98.

46. Hall and Urofsky, *supra* note 42, at 88.

47. Brennan's opinion does not explicitly refer to the civil rights background; Hugo Black's concurrence does, and he specifically mentions the many lawsuits pending against the *Times*, and against the Columbia Broadcasting System. See Anthony Lewis, *supra* note 42, at 151.

48. Andras Koltay, *Freedom of Speech: The Unreachable Mirage* (Budapest, Hungary: CompLex Publisher, 2013), 97–117. There was even a dim echo of the case in China. See Yi Zhao and Mark Richards, "The Diffusion of the Concept of Public Figure in China," *Law & Soc'y Rev.* 53 (2019): 1202.

49. *Clawson v. Longview Publishing Company*, 589 P.2d 1223, 1225 (Wash. 1979).

50. 388 U.S. 130 (1967).
51. 403 U.S. 29 (1971).
52. *Id.* at 43.
53. 418 U.S. 323 (1974).
54. 424 U.S. 448 (1976).
55. *Id.* at 450–51.
56. *Id.* at 454.
57. *See, e.g., Kassouf v. Cleveland Magazine City Magazines*, 755 N.E.2d 976, 982 (Ohio Ct. App. 2001).
58. Graeme Turner, *Understanding Celebrity* (London: SAGE Publications, 2004), 21.
59. 385 U.S. 374 (1967). For a full history and analysis of the case, *see Samantha Barbas, Newsworthy: The Supreme Court Battle over Privacy and Press Freedom* (Stanford, CA: Stanford Law Books, 2017).
60. *Hill*, 385 U.S. at 390. The case was sent back to New York, since the trial judge had not charged the jury that the Hills could only win if they showed knowledge or reckless disregard. On the role of Justice Brennan in this case and subsequent cases, *see* Lee Levine and Stephen Wermiel, *The Progeny: Justice William J. Brennan's Fight to Preserve the Legacy of* New York Times v. Sullivan (Chicago: American Bar Association, 2014).
61. *Campbell v. Seabury Press*, 614 F.2d 395, 396 (5th Cir. 1980).
62. *Id.* at 397.
63. *Dameron v. Washington Magazine, Inc.*, 779 F.2d 736, 738 (D.C. Cir. 1985).
64. *Id.* at 741.
65. *Id.*
66. For a criticism of the Dameron case, *see* David L. Wallis, "The Revival of Involuntary Limited-Purpose Public Figures—*Dameron v. Washington Magazine, Inc.*," *B.Y.U. L. Rev.* (1987): 313.
67. 376 U.S. 254 (1964).
68. See Deborah W. Denno, "Perspectives on Disclosing Rape Victims Names," *Fordham L. Rev.* 61 (1993): 1113.
69. *See* Mass. Gen. Laws Ann., ch. 265, § 24C (LexisNexis 2020); Nev. Rev. Stat. Ann. §§ 200.3771, 200.3772 (LexisNexis 2020). In Texas, a victim can choose a pseudonym, and all public records and press releases will use the pseudonym. Tex. Code Crim. Proc. Ann. art. 57.02 (West 2020).
70. 420 U.S. 469 (1975).
71. 491 U.S. 524 (1989).
72. Fla. Stat. § 794.03 (West 2020).
73. *Florida Star*, 491 U.S. at 524.
74. 18 U.S.C. § 3521. The Attorney General may "provide suitable documents to enable the person to establish a new identity" and may "refuse to discuss the identity or location of the person relocated or protected."
75. *Sipple v. Chronicle Publ'g Co.*, 201 Cal. Rptr. 665, 671 n.1 (Cal. Ct. App. 1984) (quoting news articles).
76. *Id.* at 667.

77. *Id.* at 670–71.
78. *Id.* at 671, n.2.
79. Christine Hauser, "Beckham Defends Daughter's Pacifier, Stirring Parenting Debate," *New York Times*, Aug. 11, 2015.
80. *Thomas v. Patton*, 939 So. 2d 139, 141–42 (Fla. Dist. Ct. App. 2006).
81. *Thomas v. Patton*, No. 162005CA003777, 2005 WL 3048033, at *2 (Fla. Cir. Ct. Oct. 21, 2005), aff'd, 939 So. 2d 139 (Fla. Dist. Ct. App. 2006). Ms. Thomas's case was doomed by virtue of other issues, some rather technical; here we are concerned only with the privacy point.
82. Note, for example, the previous mention of *Cox Broadcasting Corp. v. Cohn*, 420 U.S. 469 (1975).
83. *See* Peter Gielniak, "Tipping the Scales: Courts Struggle to Strike a Balance between the Public Disclosure of Private Facts Tort and the First Amendment," *Santa Clara L. Rev.* 39 (1999): 1217.
84. 232 Cal. Rptr. 668 (Cal. Ct. App. 1986).
85. *Id.* at 682–84.
86. Miller's daughter, who was not in the house at the time, also sued, mostly for the emotional distress she suffered after watching the broadcast. Her claim, however, was turned down by the court. *Id.* at 685, n.1.
87. Lisa M. Jones, David Finkelhor, and Jessica Beckwith, "Protecting Victims' Identities in Press Coverage of Child Victimization," *Journalism* 11 (2010): 347.
88. 771 P.2d 406 (Cal. 1989).
89. *Id.* at 409.
90. *Id.*
91. *Id.* at 413.
92. *Id.*
93. *Huskey v. Nat'l Broad. Co.*, 632 F. Supp. 1282, 1285 (N.D. Ill. 1986).
94. *Id.* at 1290.
95. *Gates v. Discovery Commc'ns, Inc.*, 101 P.3d 552 (2004).
96. *Id.* at 552.
97. *Gates*, 101 P.3d at 560.
98. 856 F.3d 106 (D.C. Cir. 2017).
99. *Id.* at 114 (quoting *Gertz v. Robert Welch, Inc.*, 418 U.S. 323, 345 [1974]).
100. *Id.* at 115.
101. *McKee v. Cosby*, 874 Fed. 3d 54 (2017); cert. den. 139 S. Ct. 675 (2019). Thomas called *Sullivan* and the Court's decisions "extending it" examples of "policy-driven decisions masquerading as constitutional law."
102. 536 F. Supp. 2d 380 (S.D.N.Y. 2008).
103. *Id.* at 383.
104. 139 Cal. App. 3d 118 (Cal. Ct. App. 1983).
105. *Id.* at 123.
106. *Id.* at 124.
107. *Id.* at 125.
108. Here, the court cited earlier cases in which the publication was presumably relevant: the fact that a union official had "six prior criminal convictions," for example.

109. *Diaz*, 139 Cal. App. 3d at 135.

110. See, for example, the discussion in Neil M. Richards, "The Limits of Tort Privacy," *J. Telecomm. & High Tech. L.* 9 (2011): 357.

111. 489 So. 2d 72 (Fla. Dist. Ct. App. 1986).

112. *Id.* at 76.

113. *Id.*

114. *Id.*

115. *Id.* at 77.

116. Peter Hunt, "Prince George 'Harassment' Warning to Photographer," *BBC News*, 2 Oct. 2014.

117. *Guardian*, Sept. 5, 2017. A lawyer for the magazine criticized the decision and its "Anglo-Saxon reasoning," and argued that the "public and private lives of the royal couple" are closely linked and that it was a matter of "public interest" to show that "future heirs to the throne have a solid relationship and are getting on well. It's all part of the royal business." *Id.*

118. *See* Scott J. Shackelford, "Fragile Merchandise: A Comparative Analysis of the Privacy Rights for Public Figures," *Am. Bus. L. J.* 49 (2012): 125.

119. *See generally* Judith Riede, *Die Person der Zeitgeschichte im Deutschen und Amerikanischen Bildnisschutz* (Hamburg: Kovač, 2000).

120. Entscheidungen des Bundesverfassungsgerichts [BVerfG] [Federal Constitutional Court] June 5, 1973, 35 Neue Juristische Wochenschrift [NJW] 202 (Ger.).

121. The German Constitutional Court felt that the goals of enlightening the public about criminal justice and arrangements for national security could be attained without identifying the plaintiff and directing attention to him personally. *Id.* at 242.

122. Entscheidungen des Bundesverfassungsgerichts [BVerfG] [Federal Constitutional Court] Nov. 25, 1999, 1 BvR 348/98 (Ger.).

123. Much of this is taken from Lawrence M. Friedman and Nina-Louisa Arold, "Cannibal Rights: A Note on the Modern Law of Privacy," *Nw. Interdisc. L. Rev.* 4 (2011): 235.

124. *Id.* at 235.

125. *Id.*

126. *Id.* at 235–36.

127. *Id.* at 237.

128. Bundesgerichtshof, May 26, 2009, VI ZR 191/08.

129. Lawrence M. Friedman, *The Human Rights Culture: A Study in History and Context* (New Orleans, LA: Quid Pro Books, 2011), 102.

130. See, for example, the discussion in Hans-Joachim Cremer, *Human Rights and the Protection of Privacy in Tort Law: A Comparison between English and German Law* (2011). Brexit (Great Britain's exit from the European Union) does not affect the issue, since Great Britain is still a party to the European Charter of Human Rights. Many people who voted to leave the Union are unaware of this; they confuse the ECJ with ECHR.

131. *Von Hannover v. Germany*, 40 Eur. Ct. H.R. 1 (2004); the case is also discussed in Cremer, *supra* note 130, at 42–93.

132. *Von Hannover*, 40 Eur. Ct. H.R. at 4.

133. *Id.* at 11. The court was willing to hold with the princess in one regard: photos of her dining in a restaurant were deemed to be secluded enough for her to have a right to privacy. *Id.* at 6.

134. *Id.* at 26.

135. *Id.*

136. *Sciacca v. Italy*, 2005-I Eur. Ct. H.R. 59 (2005).

137. *Id.* at 3.

138. European Convention for the Protection of Human Rights and Fundamental Freedoms, art. 8, *opened for signature* Nov. 4, 1950, Eur. TS No. 5, 213 UNTS 221.

139. The court felt it was not necessary to "determine whether the interference in question pursued a 'legitimate aim' or was 'necessary in a democratic society' to achieve that aim." *Sciacca*, 2005-I Eur. Ct. H.R. at 7.

140. Jeanne M. Hauch, "Protecting Private Facts in France: The Warren & Brandeis Tort Is Alive and Well and Flourishing in Paris," *Tulane L. Rev.* 68 (1994): 1219, 1221.

141. *Id.* at 1221–23.

142. James Q. Whitman, "The Two Western Cultures of Privacy: Dignity Versus Liberty," *Yale L. J.* 113 (2004): 1151.

143. Michael Hanfeld, "Privatsphäre vor Pressefreiheit: Der BGH sperrt im Fall Grönemeyer die Presse aus," *Frankfurter Allgemeine Feuilleton*, June 21, 2007, at 40.

144. Ray Madoff, *Immortality and the Law: The Rising Power of the American Dead* (New Haven, CT: Yale University Press, 2010), 126–27.

145. Bundesgerichtshof in Zivilsachen [BGHZ] [Federal Court of Justice] 50, 133 (Ger.).

146. HRH, *The Prince of Wales v. Associated Newspapers Ltd.* [2006] EWHC (Ch) 522 (Eng.).

147. English courts, as we suggested, are not absolutely bound by decisions of the ECHR But section 3 of the Human Rights Act of Great Britain (1998, ch. 42) requires the courts to interpret English legislation, if at all possible, in a way that accords with the European Convention.

148. Scott Sayare, "French Court Rules against Magazine on Royal Photos," *New York Times*, Sept. 19, 2012, at A6.

149. "Heir It Is! Pic of Naked Harry You've Already Seen on the Internet," *The Sun*, Aug. 24, 2012. Prince Harry's marriage, to an interracial American woman, created a sensation in the UK, and the incessant and often tasteless publicity so disturbed the couple that, at the beginning of 2020, they in effect "abdicated" their role in the royal family.

150. *See, e.g.*, *Hosking v Runting*, [2005] 1 NZLR 1 (SC), a New Zealand case that presented an interesting question. The suit was brought not by the celebrity but by his children. The plaintiffs were Ruby and Bella, the twin children of Hosking, a celebrity broadcaster—a man very much in "the public limelight." Hosking and his wife had twins; the "pregnancy involved IVF treatment." *Id.* at 9. The couple separated, and the issue in the case concerned photographs of the twins in a stroller, being pushed by their mother. The New Zealand court, after an exhaustive discussion of the law on the subject in Europe, England, the United States, and Australia, as well as its own

decisions, held for the defendant. Photographs of the twins, Ruby and Bella, would "not [publicize] any fact in respect of which there could be a reasonable expectation of privacy." *Id.* at 164. They were filmed, after all, on a public street.

151. "Naomi Campbell Wins Privacy Suit," *BBC News,* May 6, 2004.

152. "Mosley Wins Court Case over Orgy," *BBC News,* Jul. 24, 2008.

153. *Id.* Mosley also brought an action before the ECHR on a different point and lost. *Mosley v. United Kingdom*, App. No. 48009/08, [2012] Eur. Ct. H.R. 1 (2011). This did not nullify his victory in the English courts.

154. John F. Burns and Ravi Somaiya, "Panel in Hacking Case Finds Murdoch Unfit as News Titan," *New York Times*, May 2, 2012, at A1.

155. *Id.*

156. *Id.*

157. Mark D. West, *Secrets, Sex, and Spectacle: The Rules of Scandal in Japan and the United States* (Chicago: University of Chicago Press, 2006), 18.

158. Bundesverfassungsgericht [BVerfG] [Federal Constitutional Court] 65, 1 (Ger.) (1983).

159. Gerrit Hornung and Christoph Schnabel, "Data Protection in Germany I: The Population Census Decision and the Right to Informational Self-Determination," *Computer L. & Sec. Report* 25 (2009): 84, 85.

160. West, *supra* note 157, at 68.

161. *Id.* at 64, 67.

162. *Id.* at 63–64.

163. Case C-131/12 *Google Spain SL, Google Inc. v. Agencia Española de Protección de Datos, Mario Costeja González* [2014] ECJ.

164. David Streitfeld, "European Court Lets Users Erase Records on Web," *New York Times*, May 14, 2014, at A1.

165. Noam Cohen and Mark Scott, "*Times* Articles Removed from Google Results in Europe," *New York Times*, Oct. 4, 2014, at A3.

166. In 2021, the *Boston Globe* announced that people could request "updates" to coverage in the *Globe.* The basic idea was to allow subjects of certain stories—though not about major, serious crimes—to fill out a form, and get some sort of action that would prevent long-lasting harm from some story in the paper. The editor, Brian McGrory, said that, considering the nature of the criminal justice system, coverage of even minor crime "has had a disproportionate impact on people of color." See "Fresh Start: Revisiting the Past," *Boston Globe*, https://www.bostonglobe.com/2021/01/22/metro/globes-fresh-start-initiative-frequently-asked-questions.

167. Sayare, *supra* note 148.

168. *See* Whitman, *supra* note 142, at 143.

169. Cal. Civ. Code § 1708.8 (West 2020).

170. Under this code provision, too, anyone who, as part of the "first transaction following the taking or capture of the visual image," publishes it or broadcasts it "with actual knowledge" that it was done in violation of the code provision, is also in violation.

171. At American airports, people over seventy-five do not have to take off their shoes, as others do. Probably few people find this policy objectionable.

172. *See generally* Colleen Deal, "Faith or Flight: A Religious Dilemma," *J. Air L. & Commerce* 76 (2011): 525.

173. *See* Richard T. Ford, *Racial Culture: A Critique* (Princeton, NJ: Princeton University Press, 2005), 144–45.

174. *Osmanoğlu v. Switzerland*, App. No. 29086/12, 14 Eur. Ct. H.R. (2017).

Chapter 10

Privacy in the Modern Age

PRIVACY IN A TIME OF PANDEMIC

Early in 2020, the world woke up to a new reality: a dreaded viral disease, COVID-19. The virus sickened millions of people all over the world, and, by 2021 had killed more than half a million people in the United States alone.[1] Governments declared war on this invisible enemy: they fought it by shutting down the economy and locking people into their homes as much as possible. Millions of people lost jobs and businesses. Millions were under a kind of voluntary house arrest. As time went on, pressure to restart the economy, to "reopen," became too great to resist. Some countries stopped and started. In 2021, hope was on the horizon in the form of several effective vaccines. But as of this writing (December 2021), there was a long way to go. Some countries, including the United States and the United Kingdom, had vaccinated a substantial portion of their population. Others, particularly third-world countries, lagged far behind.

Wars tend to erode long-established rights. This was true of the so-called war on terror and it also became true of the war against the invisible viral enemy. Among these wounded rights were rights to personal privacy. Yet in a curious, even paradoxical way, this particular war *increased* actual privacy; indeed, government policies during the height of the pandemic insisted on what might be considered an extreme form of privacy: social distancing requirements. At the height of the pandemic, hugging, shaking hands, personal contacts of any kind outside of the household "bubble" were banned or at the very least frowned on; these expressions of affection could spread the infection from person to person. "Social distancing" meant that you could move about in society, if you could move about at all, as if surrounded by an invisible six-foot barrier or as if enclosed in a suit of armor made up of pure space.[2] This was a new form of mandatory privacy. It was seen as a way to save lives. And in this regard, it seemed at least moderately successful. When communities relaxed their demands and abandoned this enforced privacy, and people who were starved for fun and haircuts and restaurants and social contact rushed to beaches and shops and parks, the virus surged once more.

The virus loved big-city crowds. Rich people who had vacation homes could flee to these relatively safer places.[3] The *New York Times* published a tone-deaf article about the trials and tribulations of wealthy Manhattanites who had to convert vacation homes into their primary residences.[4] Others stayed put in their gated communities. Hence, during the pandemic, privacy and its values were one thing for the rich and something else for the poor. This kind of class distinction is not unusual in contemporary societies. For people in the slums, and, even more so, people in refugee camps, and for workers in meatpacking plants and slaughterhouses, social distancing was impossible. Many people during the pandemic learned to work from home. Doing your job through Zoom became a way of life. But millions of others, especially service workers, had no chance to do this; you cannot pick lettuce from home or cut hair or mop floors or care for the home-bound elderly.[5] As one scholar put it, "Self-isolation is an economic luxury."[6] Racial and ethnic minorities were disproportionately represented in the jobs and housing conditions where prevention of the disease was more challenging; as a consequence, the harm of COVID-19 fell disproportionately on those groups.[7] Essential workers were not the only ones stuck in dangerous places. People in jails and prisons were trapped in their cells[8] and the old and frail were trapped in nursing homes.[9] They died by the thousands. And those who stayed healthy in nursing homes survived by dint of total isolation: a privacy that meant loss of visitors, loss of family contacts, total loss of the outside world.[10] In 2021, widespread vaccination began to mitigate the situation, and to restore the lost sense of community.

In some regard, however, the pandemic strengthened the trend toward the erosion of privacy. The war on terror had prepared the way. People had come to accept higher and higher amounts of surveillance: cameras that followed them wherever they went and metal detectors in airports and at the entrance to government buildings, for example. Routinely, people's bodies were photographed. During the pandemic, taking temperatures became the new routine in some contexts.[11] The US Equal Opportunity Commission (EEOC) allowed employers to exclude workers with fever.[12] The governor of Ohio, Mike DeWine, at a press conference on March 18, 2020, asked employers in his state to follow the EEOC guidelines.[13] During the Trump and Biden administrations, there were guidelines (sometimes inconsistent) from the Centers for Disease Control and Prevention (CDC) and from other agencies of government. Generally, these guidelines were not enforceable, at least by the federal government. But there was plenty of private enforcement by institutions and by workplaces.

In an earlier chapter, we looked at various forms of "passing," including passing for healthy: whether and when does a person have a right to hide genetic and medical secrets or the right to keep genetic and medical information private? In some extreme cases—people who were HIV positive and sexually active—concealment of unhealthiness could constitute a crime. The issue of "passing for healthy" became deadly serious during the pandemic. People without obvious symptoms could still be carriers; some evidence suggested they might be even more contagious than those with obvious symptoms. The virus was, in effect, a kind of concealed weapon, an invisible threat to other people, hidden within the body. Some states and localities imposed fines on those who failed to adhere to isolation rules if they tested positive for the virus. A group of college roommates were slapped with $500 fines for hosting a party after testing positive; a couple in Kentucky was put under house arrest after refusing to sign a self-isolation order after they tested positive.[14]

To control the pandemic, social distancing, as we said, was useful. So was wearing some kind of mask or facial covering. Testing and contact tracing were even more important. Societies that tested and tested and tested, and who traced the contacts of people who failed the test or had symptoms, got a decent grip on the disease, Taiwan and South Korea, for example.[15] These societies were also serious about mask-wearing and social distancing. Other societies—notably the United States and Brazil—fell seriously short.[16]

In the United States, masks and testing became, in fact, politically controversial. President Trump insisted that testing was at best a "double-edged sword," because it would just give us "more cases."[17] Egregiously, he refused to wear a mask at all.[18] At a rally in Tulsa, Oklahoma, in June 2020, he appeared without a mask, before an audience of thousands, most of whom were also maskless.[19] A former presidential candidate, Herman Cain, attended this event without a mask; shortly thereafter, he tested positive for the virus and died.[20] In the summer of 2020, the disease surged in states that had loosened restrictions.[21] Medical experts insisted that masks were useful.[22] But to many people on the right, masks were an invasion of liberty and privacy.

Masks thus became politically charged. Conservative backers of Trump, among others, insisted on the right to go maskless. The bare face in public became a public statement. Critics attacked mask requirements or suggestions as "enforced cowardice." Wearing a mask "looks weak"; it was a sign of "political correctness." Some said it was not masculine to wear a mask.[23] The internet was full of viral videos of people throwing fits when asked to put on a mask before entering a store. Despite all the attention paid to the antimaskers, most people, of course, understood that masks were a simple, sensible protection against the virus—a protection for themselves and for others. A poll in June 2020 showed that 65 percent of respondents wore a mask most of the time in stores or other businesses, and another 15 percent did so some of the time.[24] And a majority of Americans agreed that masks should be required, at least in some contexts.[25] Although Texas governor Greg Abbott had resisted a mask requirement—and told cities they did not have the power to impose one even locally—he finally imposed one as cases, hospitalizations, and deaths surged to record levels.[26] President Trump donned a mask for a photo-op only after 130,000 Americans had died from the virus.[27] Still, widespread disobedience and carelessness led to an ever-increasing harvest of deaths. The Biden administration begged people to wear their masks. The mass vaccinations of 2021 made the issue if not moot at least somewhat less salient. In May 2021, the CDC issued a statement that, in effect, gave its approval to maskless behavior by those who were fully vaccinated. But the mask obligation remained for crowded indoor locations.

Masks make it difficult to recognize people; wearing a mask impedes data-gathering through "facial recognition technology." There had been, even before the pandemic, a movement to ban this technology. The movement continues—stimulated, perhaps, by the campaign against police brutality and racism, and for the "Black Lives Matter" movement. The Boston City Council passed an ordinance to ban this technology in city government.[28] Two liberal members of Congress from Massachusetts, in June 2020, introduced a bill in Congress that would require federal agencies to refrain from "using biometric technology, including facial recognition tools," on the grounds that these systems "disproportionately misidentify darker-skinned people." The technology was said to be "a grave threat to . . . privacy."[29] The bill failed to become law.

At this writing (December 2021), it looks possible that the virus will eventually be tamed. Vaccines have, in part, tamed the virus. But new variants continue to appear. Medical science may be developing tools to make it easier for society to live with the disease.[30] But whether things will go back to the way they were before the pandemic is an open question. We live in what Ulrich Beck has called a "risk society."[31] Beck wrote his book a generation ago in the shadow of the nuclear accident at Chernobyl. But the risk society is still with us, riskier than ever. Society indeed confronts huge human-made risks like climate change, and the threat of nuclear war still hangs over us. The pandemic is not human-made in the same sense as the nuclear threat or climate change, but it is global in nature, and it spreads and flourishes under the conditions of modernity. It is also powerful enough to bend the arc of history. Risks like the pandemic tend to swell the power of central governments, just as the threat of terrorism has done. Only central governments have the technological power, and the sheer institutional power, to cope with risks of this magnitude. This pandemic will end but there will be new pandemics in the future, beyond a doubt. Meanwhile, the risk society grows into the surveillance society, the society that can and does amass tons of personal data on its citizens. The implications for privacy and anonymity are profound. They will continue.

THE INTERNET

LaShawn Pettus-Brown had successfully eluded police across the country for over a year. He was wanted on wire fraud charges in connection with a failed business endeavor. Had he not made a key mistake—going on a date in the twenty-first century—he might have remained a fugitive. But the woman with whom he was scheduled to have dinner did what has become a normal part of dating today—she "Googled" him. She quickly learned that the FBI had issued a warrant for his arrest. Rather than showing up herself at Applebee's, she sent the FBI to the place she knew he would be.[32]

LaShawn's date was not the only one to use the internet to dig deeper into a potential partner. According to a Pew Research Center poll, 30 percent of people on the dating market have used social media to find out more information about a potential date—the percentage is even higher among younger daters.[33] A *New York Times* reader wrote to Randy Cohen, "The Ethicist," in 2002 to ask whether it was alright to "Google" a man after she came home from a date with him—and to lower her opinion of him once she learned that several medical malpractice suits had been filed against him. Cohen said that the inquiry was "social and benign" because it was casual and effortless. If, instead, she had spent hours at the courthouse reading legal records in search of the information, it might qualify as a mild kind of "stalking."[34] Cohen warned the reader that it was only because of the "novelty" of putting a date's name in a search engine that any ethical question was raised at all. He added that "[a]cceptable behavior is ratified by custom, and that takes time. As more and more people routinely Google their blind dates, nobody will feel uneasy doing so." Certainly, within a very short period, this became true. "Google" is a website, a search engine, a verb, and a way of life. It is a fount of information—information that never disappears, that can be retrieved with almost no effort and often by accident. And the "information" can be and often is wrong or misleading or spread by scam artists, angry people, and conspiracy theorists. Is there any way of controlling this information, any way to make sure it is benign and correct? In general, in the age of the internet, is there anything left of privacy? In many ways, the internet fundamentally challenges our notions of privacy.

Anonymity in the Digital Age

When the alt-right—a motley and menacing crew of white supremacists, neo-Nazis, Ku Klux Klan types, and anti-Semites—rallied in Charlottesville, Virginia, in 2017, many people were taken by surprise and horrified. Many of them had thought that a small, dying breed of elderly rednecks constituted the "alt-right" and the neo-Nazi fringe. That was clearly wrong, as later events were to show. But the alt-right, too, was in for a shock. The men chanting hateful slogans learned a lesson about modern society. They learned that it is hard, and maybe impossible, to stay anonymous in this day and age. They learned, too, that a person who is outed publicly as a neo-Nazi or white supremacist will sometimes pay a heavy price and suffer serious consequences. Similarly, when the far-right throng stormed the Capitol in Washington, D.C., on January 6, 2021, TV cameras followed them as they swarmed into the building shouting, menacing, and doing damage. Dozens of them were identified and arrested. For example, Eric C., forty-four, from Kentucky, was arrested on May 3, 2021; among other things, an anonymous tip showed screenshots from his Facebook page and from text messages. Security video inside the Capitol plus facial recognition software used on an Ohio driver's license photo earned an arrest for an Ohio man. A Pennsylvania man had texted photos from inside the Capitol. A New Yorker, Robert C., had bragged about his deeds on Bumble, a website.

A reader might question the use of the word "anonymous." How can marching in public and shouting a slogan, in full view of people—screaming, waving banners, and occupying the national Capitol—be "anonymous"? Of course, in a sense it is not anonymous at all. It is out in the open: but still, do you expect to be photographed or filmed marching in a parade or being part of a huge mass of people swarming inside a building? Do you expect your image to be captured and disseminated so that, in a sense, it can never be forgotten? The January rioters tended to brag about what they did and to post material on social media. Were they really unaware of the consequences?

The Charlottesville incident in 2017 was not quite so dramatic. But did the participants really expect that millions of people, far away from the parade, would see them and would know or find out their names and their personal details, and be able to recognize their faces? Yet this is what happened. A Twitter user writing under the handle @YesYoureRacist had been using his platform since 2012 to expose racism. After the Charlottesville event, @YesYoureRacist went into overdrive, posting pictures and asking followers to help identify the people who attended the rally. In the first of these requests posted at 11:43 a.m. on August 12, "If you recognize any of the Nazis marching in #Charlottesville, send me their names/profiles and I'll make them famous #GoodNightAltRight."[35]

In the age of social media, crowdsourcing works. Several individuals who appeared in news photos of the so-called Unite the Right rally were identified. Followers of the @YesYoureRacist account grew from sixty-five thousand before the rally to over three hundred thousand just a few days later. One of the identified marchers was fired from his job at a restaurant in Berkeley, California. Another left Boston University, where he was enrolled, because of the negative publicity. In 2021, similar actions were taken against the rioters of January 6, in some instances. One rioter wore his work ID badge during the riot; his employer, Navistar Direct Marketing, a Maryland company, promptly fired him. An adjunct professor at St. Vincent College in Latrobe, Pennsylvania, resigned, no doubt because of his actions; and Goosehead Insurance, in Westlake, Texas, fired Paul D., a lawyer.

Ironically, men and women who had gone to the rally or to the Capitol riot, people with deep and hateful prejudices against other groups, which they were proud to display, now complained that people who did not know them as individuals were judging them unfairly. A student at the University of Nevada whose image was captured in one of the most-shared photos from the Charlottesville rally, and who writes in his Twitter bio that he is a white nationalist, told CNN that he hoped "the people sharing the photo are willing to listen that I'm not the angry racist they see in that photo." Many of the rioters of January 6, 2021, considered themselves true patriots. They insisted what they were doing was right and proper. James L., of North Carolina, who was arrested in March 2021, claimed that he and his buddies were "stopping treason. Stealing elections is treason! We're not going to take it anymore."

The mass methods of finding and exposing the far-right elements in these incidents are hardly perfect. Mistakes are made. Some of the identifications can be wrong. @YesYoureRacist issued at least one correction. On another site, an assistant professor at the University of Arkansas was misidentified; he did resemble, more or less, one of the men carrying torches in Charlottesville but he was home in Arkansas at the time. There were death threats all around—for the men at the rally who were identified, as well as for the owner of @YesYoureRacist. The photos led one father to issue an open letter to his son, a white supremacist, explaining that the son was not welcome at family gatherings or in the family home unless he renounced his "hateful beliefs" and his conduct in support of those beliefs.[36] The outing process also revealed connections between the men at the rally and various conservative Republican politicians. As for the January 6 riot, it was plainly fomented by President Donald J. Trump; yet it was afterward defended by extremists on the right, including members of Congress.

Under Twitter's rules of service, users are permitted to "name and shame" anyone but they may not reveal private information (home address, phone number, social security number, etc.). And threats are not allowed. Punishing white supremacists for their hateful beliefs, so long as it is not done by the government, raises few if any legal issues. The rioters on January 6 plainly broke all sorts of laws. The white supremacists who paraded through Charlottesville perhaps did not.

A private employer in the United States is generally free to fire workers for any reason that is not prohibited by civil rights laws and white supremacists are not a protected class under those laws. Political affiliation is not protected against actions an employer might take. There are some states, to be sure, that do restrict the ability of employers to fire people because of their political affiliation or activities.[37] But the Charlottesville rally was probably not political, in any sense that would bring them under the protection of these statutes. A few states protect lawful off-duty conduct more broadly, and some such laws could be interpreted to protect against retaliation for attending an off-duty rally or protest. There has been talk in recent years about whether employers should or could legally make decisions about hiring and firing, based on what workers or applicants have done or said on social media. Some employers make workers or applicants turn over passwords to these accounts, so that the employer can monitor them and search their content. But people who support employees' rights, and who are also anxious to preserve employee privacy, are unlikely to favor giving bosses unlimited rights to monitor their workers' lives. The legal issues are, as yet, unresolved.

JOB HUNTING (AND JOB KEEPING) IN THE INFORMATION AGE

Talia Jane, a customer service representative from Yelp, turned to social media to complain that she couldn't afford to buy groceries or keep the heat on because she was so poorly paid; almost her entire salary went to pay rent. Her CEO acknowledged that San Francisco was an expensive place to live but, nonetheless, the company fired Talia for violating a clause in her employment contract.[38] It is a question whether contracts that forbid workers from disparaging their employers are illegal under the National Labor Relations Act. There is another, larger issue here. Talia could have groused about her job to a friend at lunch and nothing would have happened, even if the company overheard the conversation or if somebody had reported it. But the power of the internet amplified Talia's words a thousand times over. The internet gives every individual a kind of super megaphone. And the cyber megaphone is a double-edged sword. Thousands of people, maybe millions, could learn about Talia's problem and this might pressure the employer to react to her complaint. But employer rage, retaliation, and reaction were also likely.

Is it right for an employer to demand that its workers turn over social media passwords so that the employer can monitor whatever information and images they might post? Is it right to ask job applicants to do this as part of the screening process? These tactics are both common and controversial. This is so common, indeed, that states have begun to regulate access to workers' social media accounts.[39]

The explosive power of the media, and of the internet, magnifies the burdens and the benefits of common actions—in Talia's case, complaining about her salary. We have noted this explosive power before—in the case of the Korean dog-poop girl, for example, or the intrusive action of television crews filming a dying man. Should television be allowed in the courtroom? Since the nineteenth century at least, big trials, like Lizzie Borden's trial in the 1890s, have been media circuses. But television in the courtroom would turn a small circus into a gigantic circus, a mega-circus. The issue has been discussed and disputed for years. Cameras are barred from the federal system. Some states allow the practice. Its influence on juries, judges, witnesses, lawyers, and defendants is a matter of hot dispute. A trial is not "private," of course; in democratic societies, secret trials are forbidden. Yet the typical defendant enjoys a kind of privacy, in the sense that the larger world does not see or hear his ordeal. "Privacy" is not an all-or-nothing concept. It is a continuum. What the internet does, what social media do, what TV can do, amounts to enormous magnification, turning a small firecracker into a bursting atomic bomb.

Privacy, Group Affiliation, and the Horizontal Society

Social media and crowdsourcing are both examples of an important social trend toward what we might call the "horizontal society." Authority in traditional society was vertical: parents to children, teachers to students, and rulers to subjects. In a horizontal society, peers, friends, people on the same level, people who share your interests or your religion or politics, have gradually become bigger and more significant factors in the lives of ordinary people. Vertical authority is of course still strong but it has weakened substantially. The social media and, indeed, modern communications in general strengthen the horizontal society. They permit groups to form rapidly and noiselessly—groups made up of people who had been strangers before, but who have something in common, or who have a common goal or purpose or ideology. The internet makes it possible for people who collect antique teacups or who have a child with some rare disease—or for that matter, jihadists and potential bomb-throwers—to find their kindred souls. Social movements and social protests can be conjured up with warp speed. When President Trump, right after his inauguration, issued an immigration ban directed at a group of Muslim countries, protest groups sprang up overnight. Crowds of people got in touch with each other, made plans, and rushed to airports with banners and slogans. Lawyers materialized almost out of thin air. A mass movement appeared with incredible speed. The gangs of the alt-right in Charlottesville were recruited in a similar way, as were the crowds of counterprotesters in

Charlottesville and the mass of true believers who flocked to Washington, D.C., to take part in what became the riot on January 6, 2021.

In a free society, people have many choices about what to keep secret and what to reveal and to whom. This can be a personal, individual matter. Privacy is a social matter, as well as a legal one, as we have stressed throughout this book. Privacy is also a key area of choice. Some people would not tell anybody outside their family (or even inside it) how much money they make or what they are worth, even if you tortured them on the rack. Other people are proud to brag about their wealth. Most people hide their naked bodies from the world and reveal it only in darkened rooms or behind closed doors or in shower stalls. Members of a nudist colony have a very different take on nakedness. You can keep your thoughts and emotions strictly to yourself. Or you can write them down in a diary or, in some instances, publish your memoirs. You can plaster the most intimate facts about yourself on social media. You can go on Judge Judy's program or other "reality" programs and tell the whole world about your problems and your complaints. Or you can avoid all social networking and keep your actions, thoughts, and secrets close to your vest. What these choices are, who makes them, and with what consequences are important facts of social life

Anonymity in a World of Technology

On balance, most people value some sort of privacy quite highly. They also value a degree of anonymity. At home, we have a high degree of privacy. Home is the place where you can walk around in your underwear. Main Street is not that kind of place. On Main Street, you have much less privacy than at home. But you can and do have anonymity, a kind of privacy in the midst of strangers. In crowds, on busy streets, in the aisles of supermarkets, or strap-hanging on buses we are part of an anonymous mass. Everybody can see us, but we are still, in a sense, invisible. And most people like it that way.

Anonymity is a value that the legal system, for the most part, does not recognize explicitly. In *Talley v. California* (1960) the Supreme Court struck down a Los Angeles city ordinance that made it a crime to distribute any "hand-bill" without the names and addresses of the sponsors.[40] Justice Tom Clark wrote a vigorous dissent. The Constitution, he said, says nothing about "freedom of anonymous speech." The majority, on the other hand, had pointed out that "anonymous pamphlets . . . have played an important role in the progress of mankind" and that even the *Federalist Papers* were published under pseudonyms. Rules about the privacy of tax returns, medical records, and the like protect privacy, but they also, in a way, protect anonymity.

Most people take anonymity for granted. They feel they can live anonymously most of the time, even when they are "in public," walking down the street, sitting in a movie theater, or buying groceries. Nobody really sees them. But, as we have pointed out, this is no longer true today. We live in what is more and more a surveillance society. Millions of cameras are watching over us. Cameras on the street see us enter a bank or a courthouse or simply getting on or off a bus. At airports, we have to go through electronic security. Scanners record the stores we visit. On the whole, people do not seem to mind. They assume that nobody is actually watching these films and that no one will, except in the case of some crisis or crime. They also assume that the tapes get erased after some reasonable period of time. It is not clear that these assumptions are correct. And the fact that hidden machines record our preferences, the things we buy, and the things we do can also be rather unsettling. Amazon tells you what book they think you want to buy. If you buy flowers online, ads for florists will pop up on websites you visit from then on. When you pay for something with a credit card, that fact gets noted, stored, and is available for companies—and for the government?—to use.

THE RIGHT TO BE FORGOTTEN

We also noted before what we called the "right of evanescence"—the right to be forgotten, or if not completely forgotten, perhaps faded in memory, difficult to access. This is the right to have things, words, and actions expunged. The right, as it were, to have the tapes erased. At parades and rallies, you expect to merge into the crowd. A video camera, focused on the crowd, violates this expectation. It impairs anonymity but also evanescence. But evanescence is something most of us value. Up until now, most of what we say or do in our lives is soon gone with the wind. Memories fade. Images vanish. Our todays wipe out our yesterdays. Would we really like it if a giant camera recorded everything we did all day, every day, and if these images were kept forever, and if other people or businesses or the government could access these films and replay them whenever they liked? As Jeffrey Rosen has observed, "[A]s intimate information about our lives is increasingly recorded, archived, and made hard to delete, there is a growing danger that a part of our identity will be confused with the whole of our identity."[41]

The computer age and the internet are deadly threats to any right to be forgotten. Even email, we are told, is indestructible. People think the "delete" key wipes out messages. Apparently they are wrong. Our emails get stored somewhere, somehow, mysteriously, in some strange, magical cloud or storage bin in the sky. And they are stored there forever. And, what is worse, they are retrievable somehow, at least by people who know how to do such things.

Consider the plight of Maxwell Birnbaum, a college freshman on a road trip from Texas to Alabama.[42] He and his friends were riding in a van. They were pulled over, ostensibly for a faulty taillight; the driver allowed the police to search the vehicle. The police found six Ecstasy pills in Birnbaum's backpack and he was arrested. He entered a pretrial diversion program, common for first drug offenses and he was required to undergo counseling and drug testing, and to appear in court; if he successfully completed the program, he would get a clean record. Yet many years later, anyone who googled "Maxwell Birnbaum" would be rewarded right away with his mug shot posted on several for-profit sites. So much for a clean record. Birnbaum was haunted by these photos; any potential employer doing due diligence on a potential intern or employee could easily find this mug shot.

The sites generally offer to take down a mug shot in exchange for fees as high as several hundred dollars. Some will remove the photos for free upon proof that the charges were dropped or that the defendant was acquitted—but some will not. And even if they do remove the photos, that does not always repair the long-term damage to reputation. Lawsuits have been filed against several of the mugshot sites, alleging everything from extortion to violations of the right to control your own publicity.[43] A judge in Florida dismissed one such lawsuit. The court held that Justmugshots.com did not misappropriate the plaintiff's likeness; it did not use her picture to promote a product and did not engage in deceptive actions.[44] Shortly after the ruling was issued, the Florida legislature joined a growing list of states trying to rein in these sites.[45] More than a dozen states now impose at least some restrictions on commercial mug shot websites. A 2013 Utah law, for example, prohibits county sheriffs from sharing mug shots with anyone who will place it on a website that asks for payment to remove the mug shots.[46] But these restrictions are not without their critics, journalists among them. Booking photographs reflect the fact that persons were arrested. That remains true, even if they are later exonerated and the charges are dismissed. The fact of an arrest is no different from other kinds of information one might find through Google or other sites about a teacher, a mentor, a job-seeker, or a future dating partner. Moreover, the Supreme Court held in *Cox Broadcasting Corp. v. Cohn*, as we mentioned,[47] in a case that concerned a state law banning publication or broadcasting of the name of a rape victim, that crimes, arrests, and prosecutions are "without question events of legitimate concern to the public" and raise free speech concerns.[48] The information in that case was already available in a public record; free press issues outweighed privacy interests.

American law ignores, on the whole, the right to forget and to be forgotten, although not entirely, to be sure. Juvenile misconduct can be expunged from the records when the young person reaches the age of eighteen. Transgender people can, in some states, redo their birth certificates. European law has gone much further and has actually recognized a kind of right to be forgotten.[49] An important decision of the European Court of Justice in 2014, *Google Inc. v.*

Costeja, led the way. The plaintiff complained that if you Googled him, up popped new articles about some aspects of his financial history that, he said, hurt his reputation and were irrelevant because the matter had long since been resolved. The court agreed, citing Article 8 of the European Charter, which talks about a general right of privacy. Clearly, what was meant in the case was a right to be forgotten or, to be more specific, a right to erase the past. [50]

Whether the *Costeja* case actually accomplished this is another question. One might compare privacy to virginity: once gone, it is gone forever. You cannot get it back. Of course, the analogy is imperfect. Privacy cannot be totally restored, but you can move in that direction. Costeja could not entirely erase his past but he could prevent search engines from screaming it from the rooftops. In this way, Costeja could get at least part of his virginity back.

More and more, it is obvious that people do want a right to expunge, to delete, to make the system forget. And the law is responding—at least to a degree. Google must listen to these consumer demands. Moreover, under the California Consumer Privacy Act, a person has the "right to request that a business delete any personal information . . . collected" from that person.[51]

German law has been especially sympathetic to people who want to erase the past. Some cases have even taken seriously demands by criminals who, as the saying goes, have "paid their debt to society." They want to keep their names out of the public eye; the past, they say, is over and their crimes should be quietly forgotten if possible. A Bavarian actor, Walter Sedlmayr, was murdered in 1990. Two men were convicted of the crime, imprisoned, and then released on parole. In 2009, one of the men hired a law firm (with the wonderful name of Stopp and Stopp) to force Wikipedia to delete any mention of the man's name in their article about Sedlmayr, but this went too far for the German courts.

Perhaps the same result would be reached today. But the law in this area is evolving rapidly. In the wake of *Conseja*, there are procedures in Europe for getting Google and other search engines to do what the consumers demand. Article 17 of the General Data Protection Regulation of the European Union provides a "right of erasure"; this is a limited right, but it can apply when the personal data in question "are no longer necessary in relation to the purposes for which they were collected or otherwise processed." Thousands of people have already taken advantage of the Europe right to be partially forgotten. Pressure for this right seems likely to grow.

A CONCLUDING WORD

Privacy is a legal concept and it has legal ramifications, as we have spelled out in this book. But above all, it is a *social* concept; it reflects the norms that govern or prevail in society. And, of course, it is a reflection of the distribution of power in any given society. What Google thinks about privacy, or the United States government, weighs heavily on society.

Privacy, in human history, is a relatively recent concept. Nobody had much privacy in the middle ages. Even kings and queens lacked privacy: it was an age when aristocratic crowds might see a queen give birth, and the king received visitors while on the chamber pot. Technology and concepts of privacy grew up together—as both friends and enemies. For example, the late nineteenth-century invention of the candid camera made it possible, as we noted, to take someone's picture without that person's consent. This fact was mentioned in the famous, pioneering article in the *Harvard Law Review* on the right of privacy (1890).[52] Today, we have smartphones with cameras, selfies, and the internet as well as surveillance cameras and tools that can look through walls, smell through walls, and even see through walls. Dangers to privacy have multiplied enormously.

It is hard to feel much sympathy for those who go in for revenge porn or for the men who practice "upskirting." But revenge porn and "upskirting" are minor issues, compared with the threats and the possibilities from government, big business, and big institutions. In our times, privacy has become more precious than ever before, more valued, and more important for human personality. Choosing forms of privacy is important to human happiness and dignity. People want to do their own thing, go their own way, and, above all, choose how much privacy, anonymity, and evanescence they might want. Technology has enriched all our lives. But it also threatens privacy, anonymity, and evanescence. Just as there is a kind of arms race between antibiotics and superbugs, between pandemics and vaccines, there is another kind of arms race between the laws and norms that preserve privacy in the internet age and, on the other side, the instruments of surveillance, mass data collection, and the other tools for invading privacy. It is not possible to guess who is likely to win and who is likely to lose, and in what form.

NOTES

1. World Health Organization, *Coronavirus Disease (COVID-19) Pandemic*, Centers for Disease Control and Prevention, *Cases, Data, and Surveillance: Cases and Deaths in the U.S.*

2. Centers for Disease Control and Prevention, *Guidance Documents*, which recommends social distancing as a tool to curb the virus; Olivia B. Waxman, The Surprisingly Deep—And Often Troubling—History of 'Social Distancing,'" *Time Magazine*, which traces the phrase as far back as 1831 and noting that it was once used as a way to describe how comfortable one was interacting with individuals of another race.

3. *See* Tracey Tully and Stacey Stowe, "The Wealthy Flee Coronavirus. Vacation Towns Respond: Stay Away," *New York Times*, Jul. 16, 2020.

4. Julie Satow, "Turning a Second Home into a Primary Home," *New York Times,* July 24, 2020.

5. Centers for Disease Control and Prevention, *Increases in Health-Related Workplace Absenteeism among Workers in Essential Critical Infrastructure Occupations during the COVID-19 Pandemic—United States, March–April 2020* (National Center for Biotechnology Information, *The Plight of Essential Workers During the COVID-19 Pandemic*, U.S. National Library of Medicine National Institutes of Health; Johns Hopkins University of Medicine, *Racial Data Transparency*); Richard V. Reeves and Jonathan Rothwell, "Class and COVID: How the Less Affluent Face Double Risks," Brookings, March 27, 2020, which analyzes data in categories of infection risk factors such as rates of social distancing, ability to work from home, ability to stock up on necessities, and rates of underlying health problems and noting a link between higher risk factors and lower socio-economic status; *see also* Isabel V. Sawhill, *The Middle Class Faces Its Greatest Threat since the 1930s*, Brookings.

6. *See* Olga Khazan, "How the Coronavirus Could Create a New Working Class," *Atlantic*, Apr. 15, 2020 (quoting Justin Gest); *see also* Elise Gould and Heidi Shierholz, "Not Everybody Can Work from Home," *Econ. Pol'y Inst.*, Mar. 19, 2020 which provides data showing that Black and Hispanic workers are much less likely to be able to work from home.

7. CDC, "Health Equity Considerations & Racial & Ethnic Minority Groups," July 24, 2020); see also *Economic Pol'y Inst.*, "Black Workers Face Two of the Most Lethal Preexisting Conditions for Coronavirus—Racism and Economic Inequality," June 28, 2020; Sage J. Kim and Wendy Bostwick, "Social Vulnerability and Racial Inequality in COVID-19 Deaths in Chicago," *J. Health Educ. & Behav.* 47 (2020): 509.

8. *Equal Justice Initiative, Covid-19's Impact on People in Prison*; Matthew J. Akiyama et al., "Flattening the Curve for Incarcerated Populations—COVID-19 in Jails and Prisons," *New England Journal of Medicine* 382, no. 22 (2020): 2075–77.

9. Centers for Medicare and Medicaid Services, "COVID-19 Nursing Home Data," Data.CMS.Gov; Lindy Washburn, "Nursing Homes Have 1% of N.J.'s Population, but 40% of State's Coronavirus Deaths," Northjersey.com, which notes that "[c] ollectively, [nursing home] residents account for about 12% of the 78,500 people who have tested positive for coronavirus infection and 40% of the state's deaths due to complications of the virus."

10. Nirmita Panchal et al., "The Implications of COVID-19 for Mental Health and Substance Abuse," *Kaiser Family Foundation*, Feb. 10, 2021, which states that "nearly half (45%) of adults in the United States reported that their mental health has been negatively impacted due to worry and stress over the virus" in a recent

poll; Maria Cohut, "COVID-19: the Mental Health Impact on People of Color and Minority Groups," *Medical News Today*, May 18, 2020.

11. On the issue of temperature checks during the pandemic, see Jay Stanley, "Temperature Screening and Civil Liberties during an Epidemic," ACLU, May 19, 2020.

12. *See* "What You Should Know about COVID-19 and the ADA, the Rehabilitation Act, and Other EEO Laws," EEOC, updated June 17, 2020.

13. *See* Andrew J. Tobias, "Ohio Gov. Mike DeWine Asks Employers to Make Daily Temperature Checks of Workers," *Cleveland.com,* Mar. 18, 2020.

14. *See* Erin Corbett, "Thousands of College Students Tested Positive for COVID-19. Then They Threw a Party," *Refinery20.com*, Sept. 11, 2020; N'dea Yancey-Bragg et al., "A Kentucky Couple Refused to Sign a Self-Isolation Order, They Were Put on House Arrest," *USA Today*, July 20, 2020.

15. "Maps and Trends: Mortality Analyses," Johns Hopkins University of Medicine, Johns Hopkins University of Medicine Coronavirus Resource, which compares COVID-19 confirmed cases, mortality rates, case-fatality percentages, and deaths per 100,000 people across different countries; "Coronavirus Disease (COVID-19) Situation Report—175," World Health Organization, which compares coronavirus data from countries around the world.

16. *See, e.g.,* Brian Winter, "Copying the U.S. Is Leading Brazil to Disaster on COVID-19," *Washington Post*, May 28, 2020.

17. *See, e.g.,* Ted Johnson, "Donald Trump Refers to Coronavirus as 'Kung Flu,' Says Testing Is a 'Double Edged Sword,'" *deadline.com,* June 20, 2020.

18. Doina Chiacu, "'Wear a Mask!' Republicans Split with Trump as Virus Cases Surge," *Reuters*, June 29, 2020; Steve Karnowski and Kevin Freking, "Pence Comes Under Fire for Going Maskless at Mayo Clinic," *AP News*, April 28, 2020.

19. Lauren Egan, "Inside Trump's Tulsa Rally, No Distancing Despite Empty Seats, Few Masks and Plenty of Doubt about Coronavirus," *NBC News,* June 20, 2020; Tommy Beer, "Trump Rally 'More Than Likely' Led to Coronavirus Spike in Tulsa, Health Official Says," *Forbes*, July 8, 2020.

20. *See* Aimee Ortiz and Katharine Q. Seelye, "Herman Cain, Former C.E.O. and Presidential Candidate, Dies at 74," *New York Times*, Aug. 3, 2020, at A23.

21. "As States Reopen, Cases Surge in Places That Were Once Cold Spots," Kaiser Family Foundation, Kaiser Health News, June 9, 2020; Talal Ansari, "While Coronavirus Case Rate Slows in Some Areas, Others Accelerate," *Wall St. J.*, June 9, 2020; Dan Whitcomb, "University of Washington Forecasts 145,000 U.S. COVID-19 Deaths by August," *Reuters*, June 8, 2020.

22. *See, e.g.,* "Community Use of Cloth Masks to Control the Spread of SARS-CoV-2," CDC, Nov. 20, 2020.

23. *See* Peter Glick, "Masks and Emasculation: Why Some Men Refuse to Take Safety Precautions?" *Blog, Sci. Am.*, Apr. 30, 2020; Monica Hesse, "Making Men Feel Manly in Masks Is, Unfortunately, a Public-Health Challenge of Our Time," *Washington Post*, June 27, 2020; Jessica Valenti, "Toxic Masculinity Is Going to Get Us All Killed," Medium.com, May 7, 2020; Joanna L. Grossman and Linda C.

McClain, "'Might as Well Carry a Purse with That Mask, Joe': COVID-19, Toxic Masculinity, and the Sad State of National Politics," *Justia's Verdict*, Oct. 9, 2020.

24. Ruth Igielnik, "Most Americans Say They Regularly Wore a Mask in Stores in the Past Month; Fewer See Others Doing It," *Pew Research Ctr.*, June 23, 2020.

25. "Poll: Majority of Voters Support Mandatory Face Masks in Some Public Settings," thehill.com, May 22, 2020.

26. *See* Patrick Svitek, "Gov. Greg Abbott Orders Texans in Most Counties to Wear Masks in Public," *Texas Trib.*, July 2, 2020.

27. *See* Meghan Roos, "Veterans Group Condemns Trump after Mask 'Photo-Op' at Walter Reed Military Hospital," *Newsweek*, July 13, 2020.

28. *See* Sean Philip Cotter, "Boston City Council Votes to Ban Facial-Recognition Technology," *Boston Herald*, June 24, 2020.

29. *See* The Facial Recognition and Biometric Technology Moratorium Act of 2020, S. Bill 4084, 116th Cong., 2d Sess. (introduced June 26, 2020).

30. Current statistics are available through the *New York Times* Covid Vaccine Tracker, https://www.nytimes.com/interactive/2020/science/coronavirus-vaccine-tracker.html; Sara G. Miller, "Fauci on a COVID-19 Vaccine: 'We Will at Least Have an Answer' in Winter Whether It Works," *NBC News*, July 6, 2020.

31. Ulrich Beck, *World Risk Society* (Cambridge, UK: Polity, 1999); Darryl S. L. Jarvis, "Risk, Globalisation and the State: A Critical Appraisal of Ulrich Beck and the World Risk Society Thesis," *Global Society* 21 (2007): 23.

32. *See* Stepan Zeytunyan, Blog, "Googling for Potential Date Finds Fugitive," http://www.stepanzeytunyan.com/googling-potential-date-finds-fugitive. On the general subject of dating in the age of the internet, *see* Aziz Ansari and Erik Klineberg, *Modern Romance* (New York: Penguin Books, 2015).

33. *See* Maeve Duggan, "Is Social Media the New Wingman for Singles," *Pew Research Center*, Nov. 12, 2013.

34. Randy Cohen, "The Ethicist," *New York Times Magazine*, Dec. 15, 2002, at 55.

35. Twitter post, https://twitter.com/YesYoureRacist/status/896411734617075712?s=20.

36. Natalie Musumeci, "Family Disowns Racist Outed at Charlottesville Rally," *New York Post*, Aug. 14, 2017.

37. See Eugene Volokh, "Private Employees' Speech and Political Activity: Statutory Protection against Employer Retaliation," *Tex. Rev. L. & Pol.* 16 (2012): 295, which lists many of the states that do restrict employers' ability to fire employees for their political views.

38. *See* Madisyn McKee, "6 People Who Were Fired for Social Media Posts," Workopolis.com, Apr. 27, 2017.

39. *See generally* Alissa Del Riego, Patricia Sánchez Abril, and Avner Lavin, "Your Password or Your Paycheck?: A Job Applicant's Murky Right to Social Media Privacy," *J. Internet L.* 16 (2012): 1; Nicholas D. Beadle, "A Risk Not Worth the Reward: The Stored Communications Act and Employers' Collection of Employees' and Job Applicants Social Networking Passwords," *Am. U. Bus. L. Rev.* 1 (2011–2012): 397; Lisa M. Durham Taylor, "The Times They Are A-Changin': Shifting

Norms and Employee Privacy in the Technological Era," *Minn. J. L. Sci. & Tech.* 15 (2014): 949.

40. *Talley v. California*, 362 U.S. 60, 61–62, 66 (1960).

41. Jeffrey Rosen, *The Unwanted Gaze: The Destruction of Privacy in America* (New York: Vintage Books, 2001), 10.

42. *See* David Segal, "Mugged by a Mug Shot Online," *New York Times*, Oct. 5, 2013, at BU1; see also Allen Rostron, "The Mugshot Industry: Freedom of Speech, Rights of Publicity, and the Controversy Sparked by an Unusual New Type of Business," *Wash. U. L. Rev.* 90 (2013): 1321.

43. *See, e.g.*, Izzy Kapnick, "Lawsuits Seek to Bring Down Mugshot Profiteering," Courthousenews.com, Aug. 11, 2017.

44. *Bilotta v. Citizens Info. Associates, LLC*, 8:13-CV-2811-T-30TGW, 2014 WL 2050853 (M.D. Fla. May 19, 2014).

45. West's Florida Stat. Ann. § 901.43 (2020).

46. *See* West's Utah Code Ann. § 17–22–30 (2020). An up-to-date summary of relevant laws is available at http://www.ncsl.org/research/telecommunications-and-information-technology/mug-shots-and-booking-photo-websites.aspx.

47. *See* 420 U.S. 469 (1975).

48. *Id.* at 492. The Court gave the same First Amendment protection to a newspaper that published the name of a rape victim that was obtained from a publicly released police report. *Florida Star v. B.J.F.*, 491 U.S. 524 (1989).

49. *See generally* Jeffrey Rosen, "The Right to Be Forgotten," *Stan. L. Rev. Online* 64 (2012): 88; Michael J. Kelly and David Satola, "The Right to Be Forgotten," *U. Ill. L. Rev.* (2017): 1.

50. On the *Conseja* case, and the general right to be forgotten, see Ravi Antani, "The Resistance of Memory: Could the European Union's Right to be Forgotten Exist in the United States," *Berkeley Technology Law Journal* 30, no. 4 (2015): 1173; Jose Manuel Martinez and Juan Manuel Mecinas, "Old Wine in a New Bottle? Right of Publicity and Right to be Forgotten in the Internet Era," *J. Info. Pol'y* 8 (2018): 374.

51. Cal. Civ. Code § 1798 (a) (2020). There are exceptions; the company can refuse to comply, for example, to "protect against malicious, deceptive, fraudulent, or illegal activity; or prosecute those responsible for that activity."

52. *See* Samuel Warren and Louis Brandeis, "The Right to Privacy," *Harv. L. Rev.* 4 (1890): 193.

Selected Bibliography

Abagnale, Frank, and Stan Redding. *Catch Me if You Can: The True Story of a Real Fake*. London: Mainstream Digital, 2011.

Adler, Libby S. "A Short Essay on the Baring of Breasts." *Harvard Women's Law Journal* 23 (2000): 220–225.

Allen, Anita L. *Unpopular Privacy: What Must We Hide?* Oxford: Oxford University Press, 2011.

Arnold, Jason Ross. *Secrecy in the Sunshine Era: The Promise and Failures of US Governmental Laws*. Lawrence, KS: Kansas University Press, 2014.

Barbas, Samantha. *Newsworthy: The Supreme Court Battle over Privacy and Press Freedom*. Stanford, CA: Stanford Law Books, an imprint of Stanford University Press, 2017.

Barbas, Samantha. "The Death of the Public Disclosure Tort: A Historical Perspective." *Yale Journal of Law & the Humanities* 22 (2010): 171–215.

Beale, Sara Sun. "From the Many Faces of Overcriminalization: From Morals and Mattress Tags to Overfederalization." *American University Law Review* 54 (2005): 748–780.

Bentham, Jeremy. *Rationale of Judicial Evidence*. New York, NY: Garland, 1978.

Blanchard, Margaret Ann. *Revolutionary Sparks: Freedom of Expression in Modern America*. New York, NY: Oxford University Press, 1992.

Blasius, Mark, and Shane Phelan. *We Are Everywhere: A Historical Sourcebook of Gay and Lesbian Politics*. London: Routledge, 2009.

Boyle, Andrew. *The Climate of Treason*. Sevenoaks: Hodder and Stoughton, 1987.

Burnett, Betty. *The Trial of Julius and Ethel Rosenberg: A Primary Source Account*. New York: Rosen Pub. Group, 2004.

Burns, Eric. *Invasion of the Mind Snatchers: Television's Conquest of America in the Fifties*. Philadelphia, PA: Temple University Press, 2010.

Carr-Gomm, Philip. *A Brief History of Nakedness*. London: Reaktion Books, 2013.

Citron, Danielle Keats. *Hate Crimes in Cyberspace*. Cambridge, MA: Harvard University Press, 2016.

Citron, Danielle Keats. "Sexual Privacy." *The Yale Law Journal* (2019): 1874–1960.

Collins, Gail. *Scorpion Tongues: Gossip, Celebrity, and American Politics*. New York, NY: Harper Perennial, 1998.

Cramer, Renée Ann. *Pregnant with the Stars: Watching and Wanting the Celebrity Baby Bump*. Stanford, CA: Stanford Law Books, 2016.

Dennis, Donna. *Licentious Gotham: Erotic Publishing and Its Prosecution in Nineteenth-Century New York*. Cambridge, MA: Harvard University Press, 2009.

Donohue, Laura K. *The Future of Foreign Intelligence: Privacy and Surveillance in a Digital Age*. New York, NY: Oxford University Press, 2016.

Etzioni, Amitai. *The Limits of Privacy*. New York, NY: Basic Books, 2000.

Evans, Rob, and Paul Lewis. *Undercover: The True Story of Britain's Secret Police*. London: Guardian, 2014.

Ford, Richard T. *Racial Culture: A Critique*. Princeton, NJ: Princeton University Press, 2005.

Friedman, Lawrence M. *American Law in the 20th Century*. New Haven, CT: Yale University Press, 1992.

Friedman, Lawrence M. *Crime and Punishment in American History*. New York: Basic Books, 1993.

Friedman, Lawrence M. *Guarding Life's Dark Secrets: Legal and Social Controls over Reputation, Propriety, and Privacy*. Stanford, CA: Stanford University Press, 2007.

Friedman, Lawrence M. *The Horizontal Society*. New Haven, CT: Yale University Press, 2014.

Friedman, Lawrence M. "Limited Monarchy: The Rise and Fall of Student Rights," *School Days, Rule Days: The Legalization and Regulation of Education*, edited by David L. Kirp and Donald N. Jensen, 238–254. Stanford, CA: Institute for Research on Educational Finance and Governance, School of Education, Stanford University, 1982.

Friedman, Lawrence M. "Name Robbers: Privacy, Blackmail, and Assorted Matters in Legal History." *Hofstra Law Review* 30 (2002): 1093–1132.

Friedman, Lawrence M. *Private Lives: Families, Individuals, and the Law*. Cambridge, MA: Harvard University Press, 2005.

Friedman, Lawrence M. *The Republic of Choice: Law, Authority, and Culture*. Cambridge, MA: Harvard University Press, 1994.

Gamson, Joshua. *Claims to Fame: Celebrity in Contemporary America*. Berkeley, CA: University of California Press, 2007.

Givelber, Daniel J, William J. Bowers, and Carolyn L. Blitch. "Tarasoff, Myth and Reality: An Empirical Study of Private Law in Action," *Wisconsin Law Review* (1984): 443.

Goffman, Erving. *Relations in Public*. London: Penguin, 1971.

Goffman, Erving. *The Presentation of Self in Everyday Life*. Garden City, NY: Doubleday, 1959.

Gomez, Manuel A. "Order in the Desert: Law Abiding Behavior at Burning Man." *Journal of Dispute Resolution* 2013 (2013).

Gordon-Reed, Annette. *The Hemingses of Monticello: An American Family*. New York, NY: W.W. Norton & Co., 2009.

Greely, Henry T. "Genotype Discrimination: the Complex Case for Some Legislative Protection." *University of Pennsylvania Law Review* 5 (May 2001): 1483–1505.

Gross, Ariela Julie. *What Blood Won't Tell: A History of Race on Trial in America*. Cambridge, MA: Harvard University Press, 2010.

Grossman, Joanna L., and Lawrence M. Friedman. *Inside the Castle: Law and the Family in 20th Century America*. Princeton, NJ: Princeton University Press, 2011.

Guthrie, Chris, and Joanna Grossman. "Adoption in the Progressive Era: Preserving, Creating, and Re-Creating Families." *American Journal of Legal History*, 43 (1999): 235–253.

Hall, Kermit L., and Melvin I. Urofsky. *New York Times v. Sullivan: Civil Rights, Libel Law, and the Free Press*. Lawrence, KS: University Press of Kansas, 2011.

Hannah, Matthew G. *Dark Territory in the Information Age: Learning from the West German Census Controversies of the 1980s*. Burlington, VT: Ashgate, 2010.

Hasday, Jill Elaine. *Intimate Lies and the Law*. New York, NY: Oxford University Press, 2019.

Hazard, Geoffrey C. "An Historical Perspective on the Attorney-Client Privilege." *California Law Review* 66 (1978): 1061–1091.

Hughes, Geoffrey. *Political Correctness*. Maldon, MA: Wiley-Blackwell, 2010.

Jacobs, Jane. *The Death and Life of Great American Cities*. London: Jonathan Cape, 2020.

Johnson, David K. *The Lavender Scare: The Cold War Persecution of Gays and Lesbians in the Federal Government*. Chicago, IL: University of Chicago Press, 2006.

Kedrowski, Karen M., and Michael E. Lipscomb. *Breastfeeding Rights in the United States*. Westport, CT: Praeger Publishers, 2008.

Kendrick, Walter M. *The Secret Museum: Pornography in Modern Culture*. Berkeley, CA: University of California Press, 1996.

Koltay, András. *Freedom of Speech: The Unreachable Mirage*. Budapest: Complex Kiadó, 2013.

Lau, Estelle T. *Paper Families: Identity, Immigration Administration, and Chinese Exclusion*. Durham, NC: Duke University Press, 2006.

Lewis, Anthony. *Make No Law: the Sullivan Case and the First Amendment*. New York, NY: Vintage Books, 1992.

Longmore, Paul K., and Lauri Umansky. *The New Disability History: American Perspectives*. New York, NY: New York University Press, 2001.

Lucas, Edward. *Deception: The Untold Story of East-West Espionage Today*. New York, NY: Bloomsbury, 2013.

Malcomson, Scott L. *One Drop of Blood: The American Misadventure of Race*. New York, NY: Farrar, Straus and Giroux, 2001.

Middlebrook, Diane Wood. *Suits Me: The Double Life of Billy Tipton*. London: Virago, 1999.

Mottet, Lisa. "Modernizing State Vital Statistics Statutes and Policies to Ensure Accurate Gender Markers on Birth Certificates: A Good Government Approach to

Recognizing the Lives of Transgender People." *Michigan Journal of Gender and Law* 19 (2013): 373–451.
Murray, Melissa. "Strange Bedfellows: Criminal Law, Family Law, and the Legal Construction of Intimate Life." *Iowa Law Review* (2009): 1–65.
Pearsall, Ronald. *The Worm in the Bud*. Los Angeles, CA: Castle, 2008.
Pertman, Adam. *Adoption Nation: How Adoption Is Transforming America*. Collingdale, PA: Diane Publishing Co., 2000.
Ponce de Leon, Charles L. *Self-Exposure: Human-Interest Journalism and the Emergence of Celebrity in America*. Chapel Hill, NC: University of North Carolina Press, 2002.
Posner, Richard A., and Katharine B. Silbaugh. *A Guide to America's Sex Laws*. Chicago, IL: The University of Chicago Press, 1998.
Pound, Roscoe. "Interests of Personality." *Harvard Law Review* 28 (1915): 343–365.
Pratt, Ray. *Projecting Paranoia: Conspiratorial Visions in American Film*. Lawrence, KS: University Press of Kansas, 2001.
Ramsey, Carolyn B. "Domestic Violence and State Intervention in the American West and Australia, 1860–1930." *Indiana Law Journal* 86 (2011): 186–255.
Rosen, Jeffrey. *The Naked Crowd: Reclaiming Security and Freedom in an Anxious Age*. New York, NY: Random House, 2005.
Rosen, Jeffrey. *The Unwanted Gaze: The Destruction of Privacy in America*. New York, NY: Vintage Books, 2001.
Ross, Chad. *Naked Germany: Health, Race and the Nation*. Oxford: Berg, 2011.
Sandweiss, Martha A. *Passing Strange: A Gilded Age Tale of Love and Deception across the Color Line*. New York, NY: Penguin Books, 2010.
Savage, Charlie. *Power Wars: Inside Obama's Post-9/11 Presidency*. New York, NY: Little, Brown and Company, 2016.
Schickel, Richard. *Intimate Strangers: The Culture of Celebrity*. Chicago, IL: Ivan R. Dee, 1985.
Schweik, Susan M. *The Ugly Laws: Disability in Public*. New York, NY: New York University Press, 2010.
Shanley, Mary Lyndon. *Making Babies, Making Families: What Matters Most in an Age of Reproductive Technologies, Surrogacy, Adoption, and Same-Sex and Unwed Parents*. Boston, MA: Beacon Press, 2002.
Sharfstein, Daniel J. *The Invisible Line: Three American Families and the Secret Journey from Black to White*. New York, NY: Penguin Press, 2011.
Siegel, Reva B. "'The Rule of Love': Wife Beating as Prerogative and Privacy." *Yale Law Review* 105 (1996): 2118–2207.
Smith, David M. "A Theoretical and Legal Challenge to Homeless Criminalization as Public Policy." *Yale Law and Policy Review* 12 (1994): 487–517.
Solove, Daniel J. *The Digital Person: Technology and Privacy in the Information Age*. New York, NY: New York University Press, 2006.
Stafford, David A. T. "Spies and Gentlemen: The Birth of the British Spy Novel." *Victorian Studies* 24 (1981): 489–509.

Steinle, Pamela Hunt. *In Cold Fear: The Catcher in the Rye Censorship Controversies and Postwar American Character*. Columbus, OH: Ohio State University Press, 2002.

Stryker, Cole. *Hacking the Future: Privacy, Identity, and Anonymity on the Web*. New York, NY: Penguin Group USA, 2014.

Theoharis, Athan G. *A Culture of Secrecy: The Government Versus the People's Right to Know*. Lawrence, KS: University Press of Kansas, 1998.

Turner, Graeme. *Understanding Celebrity*. Los Angeles, CA: Sage Publications Ltd, 2004.

Warren, Samuel D., and Louis D. Brandeis. "The Right to Privacy." *Harvard Law Review* 4 (1890): 193.

Weiner, Tim, David Johnston, and Neil A. Lewis. *Betrayal: The Story of Aldrich Ames, an American Spy*. London: Richard Cohen, 1996.

Welsh, Brandon, and David P. Farrington. *Making Public Places Safer: Surveillance and Crime Prevention*. New York, NY: Oxford University Press, 2009.

Williams, Florence. *Breasts: A Natural and Unnatural History*. New York, NY: W.W. Norton, 2013.

Witt, John Fabian. *The Accidental Republic: Crippled Workingmen, Destitute Widows, and the Remaking of American Law*. Cambridge, MA: Harvard University Press, 2006.

Wood, David M. "The 'Surveillance Society': Questions of History, Place and Culture." *European Journal of Criminology* 6 (2009): 179–194.

Woodward, C. Vann. *The Strange Career of Jim Crow*. New York, NY: Oxford University Press, 2006.

Zimmerman, Diane L. "Requiem for a Heavyweight: A Farewell to Warren and Brandeis's Privacy Tort." *Cornell Law Review* 68 (1983): 292–367.

Index

About the Authors

Lawrence M. Friedman is the Marion Rice Kirwood Professor of Law at Stanford Law School. He is the author of more than forty books and is the most-cited legal historian in the United States. He lives in Palo Alto, California, with his wife.

Joanna L. Grossman is the Ellen K. Solender Endowed Chair in Women and Law at Southern Methodist University Dedman School of Law. She is the author of nine books, including *Nine to Five: How Gender, Sex, and Sexuality Continue to Define the American Workplace* (2016). With Lawrence Friedman, she wrote *Inside the Castle: Law and the Family in 20th Century America* (2011), which was awarded the David J. Langum Sr. Prize for Best Book in American Legal History. She lives in Dallas, Texas, with her husband and three sons.

www.ingramcontent.com/pod-product-compliance
Lightning Source LLC
Chambersburg PA
CBHW051254200926
51612CB00001B/47
* 9 7 8 1 5 3 8 1 6 2 2 9 3 *